VIOLENT DEMOCRACIES IN LATIN AMERICA

The Cultures and Practice of Violence Series

Series Editors:

Neil L. Whitehead, University of Wisconsin, Madison

Jo Ellen Fair, University of Wisconsin, Madison

Leigh Payne, University of Wisconsin, Madison

The study of violence has often focused on the political and economic conditions under which violence is generated, the suffering of victims, and the psychology of its interpersonal dynamics. Less familiar are the role of perpetrators, their motivations, and the social conditions under which they are able to operate. In the context of postcolonial state building and more latterly the collapse and implosion of society, community violence, state repression, and the phenomena of judicial inquiries in the aftermath of civil conflict, there is a need to better comprehend the role of those who actually do the work of violence—torturers, assassins, and terrorists—as much as the role of those who suffer its consequences. When atrocity and murder take place, they feed the world of the iconic imagination that transcends reality and its rational articulation; but in doing so imagination can bring further violent realities into being. This series encourages authors who build on traditional disciplines and break out of their constraints and boundaries, incorporating media and performance studies and literary and cultural studies as much as anthropology, sociology, and history.

VIOLENT DEMOCRACIES IN LATIN AMERICA

Edited by
Enrique Desmond Arias
and Daniel M. Goldstein

Duke University Press
Durham and London
2010

© 2010 Duke University Press
All rights reserved
Printed in the United States
of America on acid-free paper ∞
Designed by Amy Ruth Buchanan
Typeset in Minion by Keystone
Typesetting, Inc.
Library of Congress Cataloging-in-
Publication Data appear on the
last printed page of this book.

CONTENTS

ACKNOWLEDGMENTS

Any project such as this requires the support of a substantial number of individuals and institutions. The editors wish to thank all the contributors to this volume; they have been very patient with our editorial requests and conscientious in their writing and revisions. In this context it is important to single out Diane Davis and Robert Gay who have been involved with this project since its inception during a panel at the New England Council on Latin American Studies meeting in Boston in 2004. We also want to offer our thanks to Martha Huggins and Mark Ungar who provided helpful commentary on early drafts of the essays as discussants on panels at the 2006 Latin American Studies Association meeting in San Juan, Puerto Rico. Thanks also to Julia Paley, Paola Cesarini, and the Center for Latin American Studies at Rutgers University. Seminars at the Center for the Humanities and the Center for Place, Culture, and Politics at the Graduate Center of the City University of New York helped develop some of the ideas that have contributed to this volume. A fellowship from the American Council of Learned Societies provided support to Enrique Arias during the completion of the volume. The anonymous reviewers at Duke University Press provided insightful advice that greatly improved the final draft. Finally, we would like to thank Valerie Millholland, Miriam Angress, Tim Elfenbein, and Leigh Barnwell at Duke University Press; they have worked efficiently and effectively to bring this book to publication.

Violent Pluralism

Understanding the New Democracies of Latin America

ENRIQUE DESMOND ARIAS AND DANIEL M. GOLDSTEIN

Reactions to the 2005 election of Evo Morales as the president of Bolivia were in many ways indicative of the complex and often contradictory understandings of democracy extant in Latin America today. Many of Morales's supporters, in Bolivia and around the world, celebrated the election of Bolivia's "first indigenous president" as a triumph for the historically disenfranchised, as the undoing of five centuries of political marginalization and socioeconomic exclusion through the ballot box. In their often tearful inaugural addresses and in subsequent speeches, Morales and his vice president, Alvaro García Linera, spoke of the need to create a government that would work against corruption and the privileging of an elite few and toward a broader social inclusion for poor and indigenous Bolivians. Advocating for a "strong state" that would work to transform poverty, nationalize natural resources (specifically hydrocarbons), and combat transnational policies of neoliberal economics and the war on drugs, García Linera used the language of multicultural democracy to call for a state in which "different peoples, different languages, different colors are all valued equally, a *pollera* [dress typical of indigenous Bolivian women] is the same as a skirt, a poncho the same as a tie, lighter skin color the same as darker skin" (*Los Tiempos* 2006). The prevailing public sentiment, in the newspapers and on the streets of Bolivia's cities, was one of profound optimism, an almost unprecedented sense of confidence in the democratic process, and a cross-class and cross-party willingness to let the new MAS (Movement toward Socialism) government succeed in its stated goals of expanding the rights and benefits of democratic citizenship to all Bolivians.[1]

For other observers holding different conceptions of democracy, the election of Morales rather represented what one columnist called "the End of Bolivia." In a bulletin written for the Foreign Policy Research Institute, Michael Radu (2005), the co-chairman of the institute's Center on Terrorism, Counter-terrorism, and Homeland Security, reflected the opinion of many U.S. observers when he described Bolivia as "a black hole in the heart of South America." Radu considered Morales's and García Linera's calls for multicultural citizenship and the greater inclusion of indigenous peoples in the political and economic life of Bolivian society to be "racism," and he described the MAS 53.74 percent share of the electoral vote (compared with the 28.59 percent of the nearest rival) as only a "slight majority." Radu also blamed Morales personally for the social movements that drove from power the previous "democratically elected" president, Gonzalo Sánchez de Lozada, who fled Bolivia following the state's massacre of more than fifty people in the so-called Gas War of 2003. "So much for the Bolivians' thirst for democracy," he quipped. Radu concluded by calling for a strong U.S. policy response to Morales's "dubious election."

As the divergent reactions to this election indicate, the meaning of democracy in Latin America (and indeed, around the world) is today the subject of some contestation. In many ways the label *democracy* is itself of questionable merit in analyzing the quality of political democracy—including the existence of a rule of law, sociopolitical inclusion, and public fairness and transparency—in contemporary Latin American nations. Indeed, if one considers violence as a measure of democratic failure—with greater levels of violence indicating a breakdown of democratic institutions and values—then Latin American democracies could be considered profoundly *un*democratic. As recent research has shown, some nations that have been formally democratic for the past twenty or thirty years nevertheless oftentimes fall far short of the democratic ideal due to, among other things, high levels of state and interpersonal violence. The Gas War in Bolivia does not mark the only such instance. In São Paulo, for example, more people are killed by police every two years than the military dictatorship killed during its entire twenty-year reign.[2] Extrajudicial killings of criminal suspects (lynchings) are becoming endemic in nations like Mexico, Guatemala, and Bolivia (Daniel Goldstein 2003, 2005; Godoy 2005). Likewise, criminal, political, and domestic violence is widespread in such countries as Colombia, Ecuador, and Venezuela.[3] And, as is now apparent in Bolivia, violence between groups defined along lines of race, social class, region, and political affiliation remains a potent force in Latin American society, despite the existence of democratic elections and the expanding electoral participation of formerly excluded populations.

A focus on democratization, democratic consolidation, democratic institutions, and democratic behavior has driven scholarship by political scientists studying Latin America for the past twenty-five years. Despite more than a generation of internal and transnational efforts to change, improve, and westernize Latin American political systems, a consensus seems to have emerged among scholars that while democracy may exist in most of the region's republics, it is usually far from perfect. In the generation since the return of civilian governance, degrees of economic inequality have substantially increased, and large segments of national populations (especially poor and indigenous communities) have continued to suffer significantly from violence, including crime, police violence, domestic abuse, and human rights violations. As a result of this contradiction between the democratic ideal of peace and equality and the continued reality of insecurity and violence, a whole range of adjectives—including *imperfect, illiberal, incomplete, delegative,* and *disjunctive*—have been proposed to characterize the differences between democracy in Latin America and the supposedly more ideal forms extant in Western Europe and the United States (see Gledhill 2000). Similarly modified forms of citizenship (most influentially, Guillermo O'Donnell's "low intensity citizenship") have also been proffered in an effort to characterize what are increasingly seen as democracy's "failures" in Latin America (O'Donnell 2004:42). The extended debate that has cropped up around these taxonomic questions suggests that the democratization/consolidation paradigm that for so long has driven the study of politics in the region is not providing the necessary descriptive or analytical tools to conceptualize politics and society in Latin America today.

For anthropologists and some other social scientists concerned with similar issues in the region, the scholarly focus has not been on electoral patterns and the formal structures of democratic governance, but rather on the lived experience of ordinary citizens within these democratic or democratizing contexts. Concerned less with state typologies than with everyday realities, these scholars have nonetheless also adopted the adjectival approach to political analysis, deploying many of the same terms mentioned above or coining new ones to critique current political regimes and the inequitable social relations they have produced. Such critiques have largely focused on the deficiencies and inequities in the quality of citizenship and its attendant rights available to different categories of citizens in much of Latin America. For example, Teresa Caldeira and James Holston argue that in the absence of an effective rule of law that guarantees full and equal protections to all, formally democratic states are revealed to lack many of the fundamental qualities that are supposed to pertain to such states. In other words, though political democracies *senso stricto*, these societies in fact remain socially and economically undemocratic (i.e., "disjunctive"), with extreme levels of social and interpersonal violence being the clearest indicator of democracy's incompleteness (Caldeira and Holston 1999). As citizens are unable to secure justice through state institutions, they increasingly employ violence (e.g., vigilantism) as a means of creating their own extralegal forms of "security" (Goldstein 2004, 2005). The resulting inequality in access to citizens' rights reveals what Ana María Sanjuán calls "an institutional absurdity: democracies in which the majority of the population lacks citizenship" (Sanjuán 2002:89).

Despite these critiques, however, political scientists and anthropologists alike do not yet have an alternative framework within which to begin a new discussion of Latin American politics in the context of proliferating violence. The overwhelming number of adjectives (many of them grappling to express similar sentiments) deployed to conceptualize democracy and citizenship in contemporary Latin America suggests the need for a more synthetic framework, one that joins democratic state functioning more explicitly to the daily experience of citizens within these democracies. Starting from the pervasive social violence and apparent state breakdown that affects much of the hemisphere, in this introductory essay we will lay out the basis for an alternative conceptualization of politics in Latin America, one that recognizes the plural nature of its current governing regimes but, at the same time, does not confine discussions of violence to the failure of those regimes. Rather, we will focus on the multiple ways in which the politics of violence concretely affects lived political experience and is fundamentally inculcated in the production and maintenance of the "democratic transition," as well as in the operations of democratic states and civil societies in Latin America. We will argue that to understand politics in Latin America today, we need to understand how violence affects political practice and subjectivity, and how it remains an instrument for political rule and resistance in contemporary Latin American democracies. In other words, rather than understanding Latin America's endemic violence as simply a failure of democratic governance and institutions, we call attention to violence as an element integral to the configuration of those institutions, as a necessary component of their maintenance, and as an instrument for popular challenges to their legitimacy (Daniel Goldstein 2003).

In this sense Latin American democratic society can be conceptualized as "violently plural," with states, social elites, and subalterns employing violence in the quest to establish or contest regimes of citizenship, justice, rights, and a democratic social order. The idea of violent pluralism is not intended to suggest (as some interpretations of the pluralism concept imply) a kind of basic equivalency between types of violence in the region. Latin American democracies are not violently plural in the sense that these societies consist of a variety of groups maintaining equal access to power and equal use of violence to achieve or maintain it. Rather, what the notion of violent pluralism offers is a way to think about violence in Latin American society as not merely concentrated in the state or in "deviant" groups and individuals who contravene otherwise accepted norms of comportment in a consensual democratic society. Instead of viewing violence as indicative of democratic failure, we can, from a violently plural perspective, understand violence as critical to the foundation of Latin American democracies, the maintenance of democratic states, and the political behavior of democratic citizens. In contemporary Latin American society violence emerges as much more than a social aberration: violence is a mechanism for keeping in place the very institutions and policies that neoliberal democracies have fashioned over the past several decades, as well as an instrument for coping with the myriad problems that neoliberal democracies have generated. Of course, the recognition of these problems does imply a measure of failure or inadequacy on the part of the state in terms of its ability to address the needs of its citizens. But rather than seeing violence as an indicator of the distance a state has fallen from the (implicitly Western) democratic ideal, violent pluralism allows us to analyze the role that violence plays in preserving or challenging a particular form of lived democracy, understanding that reality in its own terms rather than as a measure of movement away from a base line that even occidental democracies would have a hard time living up to.

In offering this analysis, the editors of this volume (a political scientist and a political anthropologist) attempt to transcend the academic iron curtain typically dividing two disciplines that, at least in the Latin American context, could profit greatly from cross-disciplinary dialogue. Both anthropology and political science offer unique and important insights into political institutions and practices in contemporary society, yet each has its blind spots, areas of analysis that disciplinary commitments to particular methodological or theoretical approaches have historically obscured. In general terms, much of political science is typified by the top-down perspective that reveals the workings of states, institutions, and transnational processes at what may be called the macrolevel of analysis; anthropology, in contrast, typically works from the bottom up, with a concern for the everyday lived experience of ordinary people within the context of these larger states, institutions, and processes. Each of these approaches can offer valuable insights into the workings of politics in non-Western settings. But as this introduction hopefully demonstrates, these insights can be significantly strengthened by the kind of collaboration that we have undertaken here, one that joins the top-down and the bottom-up approaches to produce a more complete perspective than either one alone can provide.

Such collaboration is made all the more necessary by the subject matter we engage here. For violence is not merely an abstraction, the unpleasant working out of institutional failures and deficiencies. Nor is it only the reflexive actions of the oppressed, lashing out at one another or at the state in frustration and rage or in some romantically conceived "resistance." Violence, as we suggest here, is necessarily plural and dialectical—it stems from multiple sources, transforms all that it touches, and configures daily life and the workings of governance in various ways. Insight into these processes is the goal of the interdisciplinary analysis presented in this introduction and in the substantive essays that follow it.

Democracy in Action: A Brief Detour through Iraq

On 9 April 2003, the United States invaded Iraq. The invasion was justified, in part, to bring democracy to the Middle East, the region of the world arguably least affected by the "third wave" of democratization.[4] Before the U.S.-led war, Iraq in some ways resembled Latin America's political past: a throwback to a troubling time when political leaders wore olive drab uniforms and dictatorial regimes systematically jailed, tortured, and killed their political opponents. But the collapse of the Ba'athist regime, as is by now well-known, did not herald a smooth transition to democracy. After the fall of Baghdad, groups of adolescents and young men armed with light combat weapons arose to defend poor peripheral neighborhoods, crime began to grow dramatically, and occupying forces soon found themselves pinned down by an insurgency given to small-scale but widespread violence such as roadside bombings, suicide attacks, and kidnappings. Ironically, in its purported quest to establish democracy, the United States appeared to have succeeded in turning a brutal but stable dictatorship into a country mired in civil violence, a situation remarkably similar to that of other current trouble spots: Haiti, Afghanistan, Colombia, Pakistan, Sierra Leone.

All through this difficult period, as the Coalition Provisional Authority and the Iraqi Transitional Government worked to hold elections and build some form of pluralistic political institutions, the Bush administration and its allies employed the logic and language of scholarship on democratization, much of it produced by specialists on Latin America, to build support for their efforts in Iraq.[5] This unfolded in two principal ways. First, as Thomas Carothers has argued, the policy analysis of democratization explicitly asserts that political transition to more open government can occur under virtually any structural, historical, and social conditions, though actual consolidation may be greatly affected by social conditions (Carothers 2002:8).[6] Thus a country with a history of internal violence (e.g., Argentina or El Salvador), a country with no experience with democratic government (e.g., Russia), or a country with gross income inequalities (e.g., Brazil) could successfully transition to democracy if political conditions were skillfully managed by local political elites and outside powers and if those same groups could build the right types of democratic institutions (e.g., see O'Donnell and Schmitter 1986).[7] Second, many of the Bush administration's claims about the importance of establishing democratic institutions and holding elections reflected the belief by some working within the democratization framework that electoral processes can substantially resolve conflicts and alleviate internal tensions, and that countries transitioning out of authoritarian rule tend to move toward democracy (see Diamond 2005a:9–20; Carothers 2002:7–8).[8] This perception reflected Western commonsense notions, underscored by mainstream media interpretations, of democracy's inherently transformative power. As just one example, in 2004 the *New York Times* columnist David Brooks asserted explicitly that the civil war in El Salvador ended because (not when) both sides agreed to hold elections, leading him to declare the importance of holding elections in Iraq (Brooks 2004).[9]

The Iraq War points to a number of the limitations of the democratization paradigm as it is typically applied in Latin America. Despite this paradigm's potent legitimacy as an instrument for understanding and even facilitating the transition out of authoritarianism, it is not at all certain that this approach has provided scholars with the appropriate theoretical tools to explain how political systems operate in developing countries today. Viewed from the context of contemporary Latin America, where virtually every country is governed by a formally democratic regime but where social conflict, crime, and ongoing violence have become a way of life, the difficulties encountered in the Iraqi democratic transition hardly come as a surprise. Colombia, for example, despite having some of the region's longest-standing democratic institutions, is mired in a forty-year civil war. Peru also suffers from ongoing problems with insurgency and street crime despite the existence of formal democratic institutions and regular elections. Governments throughout Central America today face threats from *maras*, transnational youth gangs with roots in the deportation of young immigrants from the United States, whose existence has justified broad violations of the civil and human rights of poor young men in those countries (e.g., see AI 2003). Jamaica, Brazil, and Venezuela all suffer from astonishingly high levels of street crime. Bolivia, democratic for more than twenty years, has one of the world's highest rates of vigilante lynchings (Daniel Goldstein 2003). Despite the apparent success of democratic elections in that country, recent Bolivian history has been marked by state violence against coca growers, unionists, and political demonstrators, as well as by the more quotidian violence of police corruption and domestic abuse. Indeed, not long after the election of an indigenous, leftist government in 2005, Bolivia again experienced deadly clashes between police and public demonstrators. The transformation of private security firms (which have arisen in many countries to compensate for the inadequate administration of official policing) into mafias and paramilitaries is a phenomenon concerned observers are watching in countries throughout the region.

From one perspective, criticizing the U.S. government's apparent implementation of the democracy paradigm in Iraq may seem unfair to scholars of democratization. After all, this would not be the first case in which a government had optimistically interpreted academic work to justify its political efforts. The main reason why these criticisms have to be taken seriously, though, is that while scholarship on democratization is substantially more sophisticated than the claims made by the Bush administration, the structure of much of the existing literature, especially as it pertains to persistent criminal and civil violence, lends itself to misinterpretation. It is notable that in his January 2002 criticism of the "transitions paradigm," Carothers offered many of the arguments about democratic transitions that the Bush administration would eventually make in mid-2004 about the democratization process in Iraq.[10] Further, the noted democratization scholar Larry Diamond served as an advisor to the Coalition Provisional Authority in Baghdad. His analysis of the failure to build a stable democracy in the years after the U.S. invasion focuses principally on institutional failings on the part of the United States, such as not sending enough troops, a failure to build trust and legitimacy, improperly timing elections, and distributing funds around Iraq in unproductive ways. His work provides very limited discussion of the underlying social, political, and economic conditions that have given rise—not just in Iraq but in much of the developing world—to the types of guerillas, terrorists, and militias that today contribute to the violence and political instability in Iraq (Diamond 2005a:12–21). Diamond deals more extensively with the question of militias in *Squandered Victory*, a book-length discussion of his experiences in Iraq. While crime merits only three mentions in the book, he is aware of the threat militias could pose to democratic order; he calls for a heavier deployment of troops to crush militias at one point, and supports a demobilization effort at another. He does not seem to recognize that U.S. authorities would try to engage with militias to build something that could act like a democracy, but that may, ultimately, be very different (Diamond 2005b:225). The United States of course refused to act on his warnings and would, as with Anbar Awakening, engage with militias in efforts to control other violent actors and to establish order. What is most telling about Diamond's experience is how he interpreted events in a memo to his superiors on the threat militias posed to democracy: "The road to democracy in postconflict situations is littered with the corpses of transitions that failed because they could not establish this most basic condition of a viable state. . . . A common reason why is the presence of independent armed groups who refuse to play by the democratic rules of the game: who use force, fraud, thuggery, and intimidation to impose their will and corrupt power" (quoted in Diamond 2005b:226).

Latin America today, however, is littered with what appear to be viable states in various stages of democratic transition and consolidation that coexist and engage with subnational armed actors. It is not clear that states desire to control these actors. Indeed, as occurred with the United States in Iraq, governments in the developing world operate in a context where they often strengthen their political position by working *with* rather than *against* armed groups. Diamond sees the U.S. failure in Iraq as stemming principally from institutional and tactical errors, rather than recognizing the systemic processes—common to democratic transitions in Iraq and in other countries—in which order is constructed outside of, or with blatant disregard for, states and state power, and in the context of violence perpetuated by a variety of different actors. Democracy in Iraq may not have been "squandered" at all. Given the conditions of violence in much of the developing world, any nonauthoritarian system may have been heading in this direction.

An uncritical belief in the transformative power of democracy has limited policymakers' ability to forecast the violence inherent in democratic transitions. Similarly, the inability of democratization scholars to conceptualize adequately the complex and multistranded relationship between violence and politics has left these scholars unable to comment critically about problems that have arisen in the so-called democratic transition—in Iraq, Latin America, and elsewhere.[11] How can we conceptualize ongoing violence in these countries in a way that goes beyond simply blaming imperfect electoral processes and weak domestic institutions? In what follows we will argue that this involves necessarily moving beyond the constraints of democratization theory, which sees disorder principally as a failure of institutions resulting in a material loss of rights, to a conception of politics that looks to the complex ways in which order (and/or disorder) is created through the interactions of multiple violent actors, both within and without the state, a situation that characterizes many political regimes in the developing world today.

What's the Matter with Democratization?

Most scholars in what might be called the "democratization school" advance a minimal definition of democracy based on a conception (initially put forth by Robert Dahl) of polyarchy. According to this theory, democracy exists when formal institutions operate *and* when the basic civil, political, and legal rights necessary for the proper operation of those institutions are widely extended to the population (O'Donnell 1996:34–35). However, in its exclusive focus on elections, institutions, and rights, this formulation avoids the messy realities of actually existing political systems as they are found in Latin America (and elsewhere) today. Particularly problematic to these models is the existence of widespread violence, criminality, and insecurity in nations whose political systems might otherwise be characterized as democratic, if not polyarchic. Indeed, the obvious lack of basic public safety and a widespread distribution of rights, among many other problems, brings into question the possibility of establishing prototypical polyarchies in Latin America.[12]

This discrepancy between the ideal of polyarchy and the decidedly violent reality of political life on the ground in Latin America has led to unfavorable comparisons between the types of liberal or social democracy that exist in North America and Western Europe and those found in Latin America (Collier and Levitsky 1997; also see Diamond 1996:22; Schedler 1998:92–94; O'Donnell 2001:7–8; Armony and Schamis 2005). Political scientists' deployment of various negative modifiers to refer to Latin America's political regimes emerges as part of the effort to differentiate these "shallow" Southern democracies from the apparently "deeper," more successful Northern varieties. Such comparisons also imply a teleological or evolutionary trajectory, suggesting that, with external guidance and sufficient attention to improving the functioning of democratic institutions, progress can be made from the violent, "illiberal" democracies of "developing nations" toward the polyarchic ideal of the developed North.[13] This focus on institutions is part and parcel of the underlying assumption of the democratization school that democracy, given the right management and organizational structure, can evolve anywhere. As a result, writing on politics in Latin America in the major political science journals principally focuses on such issues as elections to fill presidencies and parliamentary bodies, the tensions within and among the varying levels of these institutions, the centralization or decentralization of political decision making, and the struggle among various levels of government and intergovernmental organizations (IGOs) about budgeting and policy.

Scholars' insistence on viewing contemporary politics through the lens of the democratic ideal, deviations from it, and efforts to improve existing political systems creates myopia in their perceptions of ongoing crime, violence, and rights violations among poor and marginal groups in Latin America. When these issues do come up, they are mentioned either in the context of ongoing or recently concluded civil wars or invoked as evidence demonstrating how failures of state institutions lead to violence.[14] Bloodshed and rights violations are high, it is claimed, because governments do not have enough money, because they are simply not able to manage the bureaucratic complexities in some police agencies to prevent excesses, or because interested politicians ensure that the state fails to have the capacity to maintain order in some areas (e.g., see Hinton 2006; O'Donnell 2004:42).[15] In this vein O'Donnell writes that "even in countries where aspirations for democracy have been satisfied by the inauguration of democratic regimes, the rule of law may be compromised. Indeed, most contemporary Latin American countries, like new democracies in other parts of the world, are cases where national-level democratic regimes coexist with undemocratic subnational regimes and severe gaps in the effectiveness of basic civil rights" (O'Donnell 2004:38). Along similar lines, the United Nations Development Programme's (UNDP) 2005 report on democracy in Latin America devotes only 8 of its 288 pages to issues relating to the widespread violence affecting the region, lodging its discussion of these issues firmly within the logic of state and democratic failure. The report reads:

> There is no doubt that since the end of military rule in the Southern Cone . . . and the resolution of the armed conflicts in Central America . . . progress has been made with respect to unjustified deprivation of freedom, torture and

political assassinations. Nevertheless, the progress achieved is not as great as could have been expected after the elimination of totalitarian regimes and the end of nearly all wars in the region. There is one substantial reservation: the vast majority of the violations are not the consequence of deliberate and planned action by the state, but, rather, of its inability (or sometimes un-willingness) to enforce the effective rule of law and to ensure that it enjoys a monopoly of force. . . . Another relevant issue concerns citizens' security and the State's ability to provide this public good. A serious defect is that, in many democracies in Latin America, the state does not ensure the physical security of wide sectors of the population. . . . This poses a challenge to our institu-tions, to the governments that are part of the system and to the future of democracy in Latin America." (UNDP 2005:112–13)

The rest of the report contains a little less than a page on illegal actors and the dangers they create for residents of the region's many republics.[16]

In other words, much of the writing on politics in Latin America today, while both sophisticated and insightful, is focused on how to get regimes that have formal but weak democratic institutions to become polyarchic. Though they do not say so overtly, all these texts implicitly advocate the "developed" democracies of Western Europe or North America as the target of this direc-tional improvement. In the process, it is assumed, such supposedly illiberal states may be able to drop the negative adjectives that often modify their democracies and citizenship will approach the high-intensity variety found in places like the United States.

In many ways, the limitations and problems with this approach are evi-dent.[17] As a reading of the UNDP report clearly suggests, simply labeling re-gimes "democratic" does not mean that they are normatively positive, inclu-sive, effective at guaranteeing rights, or able to accomplish the reforms many claim are necessary to achieve such conditions. Nor is there reason to believe, after twenty years of civil strife and growing criminal violence in much of the hemisphere, that Latin America's political regimes are on a path to polyarchy— a developmentalist fallacy based on the faulty assumption that the United States and other Western nations are, in fact, ideal-type polyarchies. Indeed, the political regimes that exist in Latin America, as elsewhere, may have sub-stantial difficulty achieving polyarchy. More important, they may also produce fairly static degrees of violence and rights abuse, and they may depend on a base level of violence to achieve collective political objectives. It is critical in this case to understand violence as more than merely the residue of democratic failure, the evident result of states failing to function as per the polyarchic prescription. Violence here emerges as a key element of Latin American democracy itself, as the basis on which it was founded and a critical component allowing its maintenance.

All this should not be taken to mean that we believe it impossible for these regimes to become polyarchies. Such a rigorous claim lies beyond the scope of the essays in this volume. The evidence we present here does, however, suggest that no simple path will lead to lower levels of violence in much of the region. Violence is implicated both in the institutional structure of the regimes and in the way these regimes are inserted into the international system. Violence stems from the structure and activities that support existing social relations and from the way state power is exercised. Changing this will require more than minor administrative fixes and reform programs and will, as shall be discussed in the conclusion to this volume, involve reorienting the relationship between Latin American polities and both the international system and internal practices of conflict in those countries.

Histories and Discourses of Democracy

Understanding the complex relationship between violence and democracy in Latin America also requires us to adopt a historical perspective, one that allows us to comprehend democracy emerging not out of some kind of inevitable evolution of "political man," but as the real product of a particular historical conjuncture unfolding in the context of actual Latin American society. Contemporary democracy in Latin America is deeply entwined with neoliberal capitalist relations of production, emerging out of a history of engagement in the region with global forces of imperialism, socialism, and the cold war.

Over the course of the nineteenth century Latin American states remained relatively weak, encountering limited interstate tensions. The resulting political systems in the region, as Miguel Angel Centeno has noted, developed militaries focused on dealing with internal dissent rather than on fighting international wars (Centeno 2002). Subnational political elites retained a substantial amount of power vis-à-vis central states. The reigning political system could be described as a form of exclusionary republicanism, in which a small portion of the population (generally property owners) retained the voting franchise and the remainder of the population (e.g., the small working class, women, Afro-Latinos, and indigenous people) remained largely excluded from political participation and court protections. In this environment empowered landowners retained a substantial number of legal rights and de facto power over much of the population, exercising control over politics and violence beyond the control of the national state.

These conditions began to change around the turn of the twentieth century as significant immigration from Europe and Asia, as well as a growing industrial sector, empowered segments of the urban working class, creating conditions for the emergence of political movements and parties demanding greater inclusion and collective rights. Over time most countries in the region, in the context of substantial political and social conflict, would extend some basic social guarantees to the working class. These rights were extended both under democratic regimes, as in Colombia during the Revolución en Marcha, and under more authoritarian regimes, as in Mexico under Lázaro Cárdenas and in Brazil during the Estado Novo. As Greg Grandin details, during the period immediately following the Second World War, most Latin American states had become democratic, adopting a model of what he terms "democratic socialism," which built on efforts at inclusion, invited the political participation of the working class, and advocated a developmentalist vision of the national economy that included notions of redistributing elements of national wealth from foreign ownership and some elements of the upper classes to parts of the working and middle classes (Grandin 2004). Despite the many deficiencies of these political systems, including a tendency toward repressive forms of state corporatism, at times allied with fascist ideologies, and the continued exclusion of large segments of the population, they offered a promise of empowerment to many groups long excluded from national political engagement, espousing a collectivist ideology that provided the intellectual basis of postwar democracy (Bethell and Roxborough 1993). With the emergence of the cold war in the late 1940s and early 1950s, these democracies over the next twenty years gradually gave way to military coups and dictatorships that (with the backing of the United States) cracked down on political dissent and implemented policies that regarded national development as inherently antagonistic to democratic governance. These states and their security forces relied on violence and new technologies of repression to combat the lingering influence of the postwar democratic period, crushing those elements seen as threatening to national development and stability (Grandin 2004).

The establishment of neoliberal economics in Latin America during the 1970s and especially the 1980s hinged directly on the introduction of a new model of democracy in the region, one based on an individualist concept of self and society. Rather than on a social welfare state that would provide for the needs of its citizens, neoliberal democracy would be based on a limited and circumscribed state whose principal task was to provide a stable and secure field for transnational investment and individual self-realization. This new kind of democracy, as Grandin argues, was constructed explicitly in opposition to the older midcentury model, made possible in the wake of cold war violence and terror, which had long targeted progressive social movements for elimination: "The threat of mid-century social movements was that they provided a venue in which self and solidarity could be imagined as existing in sustaining relation to one another through collective politics that looked toward the state to dispense justice. Latin American democracy as an ideal and a practice was always more participatory and egalitarian than it was procedural and individualistic. In many countries, Cold War terror changed that, imposing a more restrictive model, one that defined individualism as economic self-interest and advanced it through free market policies" (Grandin 2004:14). Such democratic conceptions as rights and citizenship were constructed along similar lines, ones grounded in a notion of the liberal citizen whose basic political identity derived from his or her individual nature and personal relationship to the national state, rather than from his or her membership in a particular group or class (as in, for example, more recent conceptions of indigenous rights) (Postero and Zamosc 2004).

Historic forms of political practice in the region were thus tempered by their being inculcated through a frame of neoliberal capitalism and economic globalization, whose emphasis on the individual nature of rights and belonging in some ways runs counter to the collectivist and participatory nature of democracy itself. From such a perspective, violence can only be understood as a failure, an obstacle to individual self-realization, rather than as a tool of the democratic state to break down opposition to its particular forms and manifestations, or as a collective behavior constituent of democracy's very fabric. Alternatively, though, democracy can be understood as a product of struggle, even of violent struggle, and conflict as a basic element of what democratic governance requires. As Geoff Eley puts it: "Let there be no mistake: democracy is not 'given' or 'granted.' It requires conflict, namely, courageous challenges to authority, risk-taking and reckless exemplary acts, ethical witnessing, violent confrontations, and general crises in which the given sociopolitical order breaks down. In Europe, democracy did not result from natural evolution or economic prosperity. It certainly did not emerge as an inevitable by-product of individualism or the market. It developed because masses of people organized collectively to demand it" (Eley 2002, qtd. in Grandin 2004:16).

Furthermore, as the many contradictions of contemporary global capitalism now make clear, neoliberal democracy is itself responsible for much of the social violence we see in countries throughout Latin America. Such violence is not the simple result of institutional failure but the logical outcome of neoliberal democracy's unfolding. As many studies have made clear, the trickle-down economic promises of neoliberal promoters have not been realized, instead leading to widening income inequalities and mounting poverty across the region. Such poverty, and the lack of employment and educational opportunities associated with it, are directly linked to the social violence we describe in this volume. Economic inequalities, along with a declining public confidence in the representative nature of many neoliberal states, have also been at the heart of the new social mobilizations emerging across the region in the early- to mid 2000s as popular groups and social movements have once again mobilized to contest the contradictions of neoliberal democracy. In their insistence on a more inclusive, even socialist democratic politics and economy, these groups sometimes employ violence, as does the state when it resists their calls for reform. The Gas War of 2003 in Bolivia offers a clear example: In the effort to enforce a neoliberal prescription for natural-resource exportation, soldiers defending the democratic state of Sánchez de Lozada fired on and killed more than fifty unarmed protesters, leading to the president's resignation and, ultimately, the ascendancy of leftist union leader Morales to the Bolivian presidency (Kohl and Farthing 2006). In other contexts the problems of insecurity unleashed by the policies and practices of neoliberal democracy have specifically created situations in which violence emerges as a logical response. The Bolivian state's compliance with the U.S. international war on drugs, for example, has generated circumstances of extreme precariousness for rural cultivators, who frequently experience the violence of police and security forces intent on prosecuting the drug war at the expense of poor farm families. Meanwhile, marginal urban communities lack police protection and so deploy vigilante violence as a technique of providing security and justice to their communities. Such violence, it must be observed, cannot be understood as relating to democratic failure but, perversely, to its success: lynch mobs, like private security firms operating in other contexts, are clear manifestations of the logic of neoliberal democracy, which urges self-help and individual responsibility to local communities confronting social welfare conditions in which the state does not consider itself obligated to intervene (Goldstein 2005).

As should be evident by now, violence in these countries is caused not only by a failure of institutions but also by patterns of international trade, transnational political and economic regimes, grave wealth inequality, and particular historical forms of social relations in specific countries, subnational regions, or cities. Violence, indeed, may be physical and structural.[18] As is well known, under neoliberal democracy many Latin American debtor states have been forced to comply with the structural adjustment dictates of transnational lending agencies, diminishing state investment in and the administration of national social and economic life, devolving responsibility for social reproduction to individuals, families, and local communities (Harvey 2005). In many parts of Latin America crime has risen, police corruption has mounted, and judicial services have been unable to provide security to the majority of the national population (Ungar 2002). Poverty, fragmented families, domestic abuse, fear, insecurity, and the instability of daily life for many Latin Americans form a part of life under the neoliberal democracies that have governed these societies over the past few decades: they are part of their structural logic rather than the result of their imperfections.

Violence has become so pervasive in much of Latin America in part due to the particular ways in which trade liberalization and neoliberal economic systems have interacted with the political environment of postauthoritarian Latin America. Growing pressure to lower trade barriers has led to an increase in drug and arms trafficking in the Americas (Andreas 1999:126–35). At the same time pressures for structural reform have led to cuts in state funding to both policing and social welfare programs (see Alcantara 2005:1661, 1668). Both of these trends have occurred in the context of improvements of military technology that have made it very easy to deliver relatively high-powered weapons into the hands of civilians.[19] The United States and other leading producers of firearms have been reluctant to adopt serious international controls on the trade in small arms. All this has resulted in the emergence of conditions in which violent nonstate actors have proliferated and states have faced serious challenges in controlling violent nonstate groups, or have demonstrated an unwillingness to try.

The critique of evolutionist democratization theory offered above is all the more important given that ethnographies of democracy and democratization point to profound and ongoing struggles within civil society, where the instantiation of democracy is contested and negotiated, and within the state itself, where the language of democracy may be used to paper over the reality of in-name-only democratic states (Nelson 1999). Research by anthropologists into what might be called "the discourse of democracy" includes the ways in which the language of and ideas about democracy circulate within society, mobilizing resistant political movements and justifying the maintenance of violent state regimes, demonstrating how democracy transcends state institutions and electoral processes. Thus Julia Paley urges anthropologists to consider "the strategic deployment of the term democracy, its power implications, competition over its meanings, its manifestations in institutions and social arrangements, and the way attendant discourses circulate within and among countries" (Paley 2002:475; see also Gutmann 2002; Ong 1999; Verdery 1996). Despite its potential for broadening scholarly considerations of the democratic, however, this anthropological work tends to be overlooked by those who understand politics as properly located only in the domain of political institutions.

Understanding democracy not merely as a set of institutional arrangements but as an ideological and discursive instrument in political struggle opens critical doors for the study of democratic society in Latin America. This is particularly the case for understanding violence in contemporary Latin American political regimes. Rather than viewing violence as simply an indicator of democracy's "failure" (as the democratization paradigm does), an anthropological perspective on democratic discourse reveals the ways in which democracy and violence are intimately entangled in both the establishment of democratic regimes and their ongoing maintenance. For example, in his study of the cultural politics of statecraft in Venezuela, Fernando Coronil has noted the shifts in the meaning of democracy in recent Venezuelan history. These include the use of the term by the political party Acción Democrática, which came to power in 1945 through a violent coup that toppled a constitutional government (Coronil 1997). In this case democracy was used to legitimate military rule and its accompanying authoritarian practices. In spite of Guatemala's transition from military to civilian rule, the repressive apparatus of the dictatorship continues to be manifest in the democratic state; as Jennifer Schirmer notes, "after decades of naked military rule, the Guatemalan military have crafted a unique Counterinsurgent Constitutional State in which State violence has been reincarnated as democracy" (Schirmer 1998:258; see also Warren 2000). Meanwhile, elsewhere in the region military regimes have actually come to power through democratic elections, thereby maintaining violent and oppressive practices within formal democracies, as Julie Taylor has observed in Argentina (Taylor 1993) and as the election of the former dictator Hugo Banzer in 1997 demonstrated for Bolivia (Sanabria 2000). Such examples indicate the complex relationship between democracy and violence in Latin America: as the violent legacies of authoritarian regimes have been reinscribed as democracies, their continued abuse is legitimated by democratic rhetoric. It also suggests, as Paley points out, that democracy cannot be considered a free-floating signifier detached from reality and infinitely malleable; rather, as the above examples demonstrate, the democratic discourse has important institutional referents through which it operates and exerts its force, a point that anthropologists of democracy and violence have frequently noted (Paley 2002:477; 2004).

An approach that focuses solely on formal measures of democracy, then, and which regards violence as a deviation from the ideal of polyarchy, is clearly inadequate to understand the intricate dialectic between state power and violence in Latin America, or the complex political, social, and economic circumstances that give rise to and maintain political and social violence for that matter (e.g., see Garro 1999). If, as we suggest, violence in Latin America today is an integral component of both the state-formation process and challenges to the state, then traditional approaches to both democracy and violence are limited in what they have to offer to our interpretations of local realities. Nor is it enough simply to require improvements in the quality of citizenship or an expansion of the rule of law, both worthy causes but nevertheless analytical dead ends, remaining as they do within the normative framework of democracy and its correlates. The question is not only how the legal system or police institutions operate or fail to operate but also how violence and contentious politics are foundational to the political systems of contemporary Latin America. This does not mean that understanding police, courts, or even elections and budgeting is unimportant. Rather, it means that these different institutional phenomena must be understood in a much broader political and social context, one that includes the operation, distribution, and structure of state and nonstate violence in the region. The regimes that exist in Latin America today may thus represent another type of political formation at variance from both democracy and authoritarianism, a type whose outlines the following section of this introduction explores.

Violent Pluralism: Toward an Alternative Paradigm

To understand the relationship between violence and democracy in Latin America today, we need to move away from the conceptual ground of democracy and democratization and the political projects associated with it. Ending authoritarianism was supposed to create a political outcome in which the means of violence wound up in the hands of a state apparatus controlled by "the people" that, by virtue of its popular nature, was unwilling to tolerate widespread violence against the population. What is significant about politics in the region today is not that democratic instead of authoritarian regimes control national governments (part, after all, of an alternating cycle whose recent history we have detailed above), but that the political regimes dominating much of the region appear to be unable to consolidate control over substate violence. These regimes coexist with organized, violent nonstate actors, and they stand side by side with multiple forms of substate order that exist separately from, but in constant interaction with, the state-sanctioned rule of law. Also significant is the changing nature of civil society in Latin America, which in many countries must be understood to include multiple violent actors. Rather than operating peacefully to expand and deepen the rights of democratic citizens, many organizations and groups that collectively constitute civil society in the region today operate violently, using violence and its threat as a basis for their own collective organizing. Contrary to expectations that civil society inevitably acts as a watchdog to prevent state abuses of citizens' rights, these civil society groups (which include vigilantes, paramilitaries, and other so-called justice-making entities, even local base communities) instead sometimes function to impose greater restrictions on rights (particularly the rights of criminals and the accused), often in the name of crime control and the maintenance of social order (Godoy 2005; Goldstein 2007).

If we look comparatively at Latin America we can thus observe an immense diversity of forms of violence. Colombia, for example, suffers from a forty-year-old guerilla war, paramilitary violence, and large-scale drug trafficking (Thoumi 2003; Crandal 2002). Brazil, a country with very different political and criminal dynamics, exhibits large-scale urban gang violence, police impunity, a growing problem with vigilantism and death squads in some cities, and rural land conflict in which wealthy landowners fend off landless workers through hired guns and private militias (see Arias 2006b; Leeds 1996; Gay 2005). Jamaica, on the other hand, faces gang conflict in cities and a growing problem of politically and criminally aligned private security firms (Sives 2002; Gunst 1998). Elsewhere in Latin America a myriad of other actors employ violence: these range from state actors such as the police and the military (who may or may not act in violation of the law, or who follow the orders of superior officers and elected leaders) to nonstate or civil-society actors including private security firms, lynch mobs, and death squads (whose members may double as police, soldiers, or firefighters at other times of day or during other periods of their careers) to groups institutionally further removed (though not always completely detached) from the state, such as drug traffickers and guerillas.

While none of these lists are exhaustive, they reveal something often ignored in scholars' focus on the operation and failure of democratic institutions: violence pervades much of Latin America, but the configuration and politics of that violence differ substantially from place to place. In the conditions that exist today in many of the Western Hemisphere's republics, multiple violent actors operate within the polity and maintain different and changing connections to state institutions and political leaders, whether those states are officially democratic, authoritarian, or otherwise. We can tentatively call these conditions of relationship violent pluralism. Understanding politics in Latin America now requires us to consider how dispersed, often amorphous, and seemingly apolitical violence is deployed and managed by various actors in the political system. The concept of violent pluralism as we describe it here has much in common with other theoretical approaches to violence emerging largely from anthropological analyses of these phenomena, including such concepts as Nancy Scheper-Hughes's and Philippe Bourgois's (2003) "continuum of violence," Paul Farmer's (2003) "structural violence," and René Girard's (1977) "cycles of violence." Violent pluralism goes beyond these to identify particular social locations within Latin American states and civil societies in which violence can be found, joining it specifically to democracy, from which we find it analytically inseparable.

Violent pluralism also helps us develop a fuller conception of what relationships civil society and violent actors maintain to one another and to different elements of the state, including politicians, police, bureaucrats, and the military. These connections can be obvious and apparent, such as when Brazilian police flaunt their relationships with death squads; or they may be more elusive, as when police take bribes from money launderers or politicians take campaign donations from drug traffickers. Sometimes powerful state actors will employ violence specialists to intimidate political or social opponents. In other cases, violence specialists from outside the state will work to buy off powerful elements of the political establishment. In yet other cases, such as in Colombia, military or police units may train and arm nonstate actors such as paramilitaries to support their political objectives. Finally, many of these nonstate groups have relationships with one another; they interact, build alliances, and engage in conflicts without direct reference to the state. As discussed above, some of these groups clearly fit into what has classically been identified as civil society, though they may operate violently and in opposition to the democratic or basic human rights of others in society.

Having identified the actors and relationships that operate in a violently plural society, we can begin to ask what effects these arrangements have on politics and social relations. Essential to this effort is developing an understanding of how violent actors and the relationships between them affect political practice at various levels of the polity. For example, the drug-gang domination of Rio's favelas has had a substantial effect on the practice of clientelism in those communities and on how the leaders of those communities relate to politicians (Arias 2006c). Domination by criminal gangs, as occurs in Rio, or by guerilla groups, as occurs in parts of Colombia and Peru, can lead to alternative forms of conflict resolution and modes of legal pluralism (Arias and Davis Rodrigues 2006). Alternatively, the ongoing presence of uncivil movements can have a corrosive effect on national-level politics, as Leigh Payne has argued occurs in Brazil, Argentina, and Nicaragua (Payne 2000). Funds delivered to politicians through criminals can have direct effects on the election of national political figures, as has occurred in Colombia (Bowden 2001: 30–40; Chepusiuk 2003:60). The growing power of criminal gangs can result in state reactions that lead to *mano dura* (iron fist) policies that circumscribe and transform political and civil rights, as has occurred in Honduras, where gang members recently were accused of engaging in terrorist activities. The control of violent nonstate actors by a political party can even result in riots and the collapse of a government (Auyero and Moran 2004).

Anthropological studies of the lived experience of poor and marginalized people in neoliberal democracies reveal the profound fear and all-encompassing sense of dread that surrounds daily life in such a context, and the ways in which this structural violence translates into more physical forms.[20] For example, Daniel Goldstein has explored the fear of crime and the mistrust of the democratic state that leads some urban Bolivians to turn to lynching as an instrument of crime control in their communities (Goldstein 2005; see also Goldstein 2004).[21] He argues that rather than some kind of primitive holdover from a violent past, vigilante lynching actually represents a fully modern response to insecurity, reflecting the very logic of neoliberal democracy that requires individual responsibility for self-preservation, without reliance on the state.[22] Similarly, in her studies of São Paulo, Caldeira has shown how violence, urban segregation, and the emergence of privatized security systems negatively impact the quality of life under Brazilian democracy (Caldeira 2000). Understanding these different types of outcomes and how persistent violent actors contribute to them is essential to interpreting how this violence brings into question existing social norms, contributes to the formation of the political order, and constructs political subjectivities.

These sets of questions about the relationships between violent actors and the democratic state, and about how these actors and relationships affect political practices and outcomes, offer very different insights than approaches that focus on the supposed failures of the rule of law. When scholars write about a rule of law, they imply a certain set of generally accepted international standards from which, for a variety of reasons, a given polity may deviate. From such a rule-of-law perspective the quotidian violence in Latin America represents negative deviations from an international, developmentalist standard. Rather than understanding the types of political formations that we confront in Latin America as somehow reflecting an absence or failure of a rule of law, we need instead to look at what orders are present in and produced by the (more or less) autonomous violent actors operating inside or outside a given political system.

The shape of citizenship and the role that it plays in Latin America's political systems has been a particularly powerful source of contention in debates about democratization between more institutionally oriented scholars arguing for a narrow, rights-based conception and others arguing for a broader vision of what citizenship entails. For this latter group citizenship rights include not just basic civil and political rights but also social rights and rights particular to group membership.[23] In recent years much research in political science has explored contestations over citizenship rights and efforts to expand and reconceptualize the notion of citizenship in Latin America. Yet these debates about citizenship are largely inscribed within a vision of the state and the individual involved in a mutual relationship of rights and responsibilities. Citizenship itself gains meaning from the idea that individuals can gain access to rights by acting within a rule of law guaranteed by a democratic state. However, if state power and the rule of law are openly contested, with powerful armed or otherwise violent groups establishing contingent legal and political orders interspersed and interacting with state-based systems, the notion of a general set of reciprocal rights and obligations distributed widely among the population becomes less meaningful. In the environment that exists in Latin America today, citizenship remains a useful way of conceptualizing a deficit of order and of discussing the failures of the state, but it provides a less useful heuristic for conceptualizing how Latin Americans, subject to the force of various different organized or spontaneous violent actors, conceive of their political subjectivity and their role in localized and more national visions of the polity.[24] Focusing on Latin American regimes' failures to protect rights provides a one-dimensional picture of the problem of violence and the treatment of the population. Rather, we suggest that the interaction of multiple violent actors has enabled the emergence of new forms of political order, constitutive of new modes of political subjectivity and contestation. How has political subjectivity been reconceptualized in light of regimes of violent pluralism, and how has this more broadly affected how individuals and groups attempt to protect and provide for themselves?

Answers to these questions become particularly evident in anthropological work recognizing that democratization does not occur solely within the institutions of the state but also within and among groups of people typically considered part of civil society. As discussed earlier in this introduction, the period of the democratic transition in Latin America has also been marked by the emergence in many countries of powerful, organized social movements aimed at exposing and transforming the social, political, and economic inequities inherent in neoliberal democracy, often employing the very language of democracy itself to underwrite and legitimize their interventions. In their struggles these social movements not only use but also strategically manipulate and rework the transnational language of democracy and human rights, adopting nonlocal concepts for their own ends (Paley 2002). Thus, for example, June Nash has written of the Zapatistas in Chiapas, Mexico, who have appropriated democracy to characterize their own consensus-building practices (Nash 2001; see also Nugent 1999). Similarly, Rob Albro (2006) and Nancy Postero (1999) have each described the role that concepts of democracy, citizenship, and rights have played in the rhetoric and political practice of Bolivian indigenous movements. Postero's work on Bolivian multiculturalism echoes that of Charles Hale (2002) and Kay Warren (2002) in Guatemala, who have analyzed the opportunities and the perils presenting themselves to cultural-rights movements that deploy the democratic language of multiculturalism in their own struggles. Such strategic self-positioning can cut both ways, allowing social movement actors to exploit emerging spaces of protest in the democratic context, while simultaneously enabling the state to contain their protests in the realm of what are deemed to be appropriate and acceptable forms of expression. Clearly violence is also part and parcel of the engagement between state and civil-society actors, as the recent histories of assassination, state repression, street clashes, and open warfare in Bolivia, Chiapas, and Guatemala (among others) have shown. This suggests that the struggle for equality and rights within democratic contexts may not be separable from the violent encounters such struggles entail.

Ethnographic studies such as these point to the many ways in which violence is deeply intertwined with democracy in Latin America, such that the two must be understood in tandem, rather than as two distinct points on a single evolutionary trajectory or as contradictory elements of an ongoing teleology. These studies also point to democracy's basic unevenness, the inequitable distribution of citizenship rights in Latin American countries, and the role that violence plays in implementing and challenging these inequities. In trying to understand the supposed failures of Latin American democracies, anthropological writing suggests, it is critical to look at democracy "from below" to understand the nature of people's demands, the violent conditions that they confront, and the sometimes violent responses they make to these conditions. Such a perspective may yield rather surprising insights. For ultimately, and perhaps ironically, what many social movements and individual social actors may be seeking is nothing short of the democratic ideal—full inclusion in national democratic society, with equal access to rights and justice for all citizens. In this sense, what they may be seeking is what Holston has identified as "substantive citizenship": not merely the voting rights that political democracy confers (and which the democratization paradigm takes as its baseline measurement) but the full range of social and economic rights that true polyarchy is said to guarantee (Holston 1999).

There are, of course, sites in the region in which police seem to function effectively, where crime is relatively under control even by Northern standards, and where a normal rule of law appears to operate. O'Donnell has called these places "blue areas," and he contrasts them with "green" and "brown areas" where there are progressively greater deficits in central order and in the effective national administration of justice (O'Donnell 1993). These areas, however, fit within the broader constraints of the concepts we develop in this volume. Some parts of Latin American polities do operate under conditions that some might consider similar to those believed to exist in Europe and North America (e.g., the South Zone of Rio de Janeiro, the northern part of Bogotá, and parts of Uptown Kingston). But even if this were not the case, the existence of these types of places would not be inconsistent with our argument here. Our notion of violent pluralism includes the idea that state security forces do operate and will operate as expected under some circumstances. This functioning constitutes, however, simply another element of violent pluralism. In some places the state does effectively maintain order, which is critical to the functioning of these political regimes. Emerald dealers, the owners of weapons factories, those shipping drugs, and even small gangs trying to get access to state patronage need certain parts of the political system to operate within a more formal rule of law to maintain working port facilities, have functioning financial systems to provide loans and guarantee deposits, and make sure a state budget is generated with access to international financing that can support different types of patronage. In other words, even when we see supposed blue areas of state functioning, they are deeply engaged with other parts of the polity and often operate in ways that support more unorthodox systems of order in some parts of cities and the countryside.

Similarly, spread across the region are a handful of states that experience comparatively lower levels of violence and that appear to experience, over national territory, a functioning system of sanctioned violence. These countries include Chile, Costa Rica, Cuba, Panama (outside of the Darien jungle where Colombian guerillas operate freely), and Uruguay. A discussion of these countries lies beyond the scope of this project, but we will note that the relatively lower levels of violence in these places, even those with advanced neoliberal reforms, stem from particular local characteristics that have to do with the social and institutional history of each and the particular ways in which these places are inserted into the international economy. Indeed, many of the factors that we note as contributing to violent pluralism in the cases discussed here operate in slightly different ways in these countries, leading to lower levels of violence and different political conditions. For example, Argentina experiences comparatively low violence by global standards but, as the essays by Javier Auyero and Ruth Stanley will demonstrate, these conditions of relatively low violence operate in the context of a form of violent pluralism.

The concept of violent pluralism thus inverts many of the assumptions of extant writing on politics in Latin America. We are not interested in whether or not there are deficits from a generally agreed upon standard of rights or political behavior. Moreover, we do not see ongoing violence in Latin America as a reflection of anarchy, state breakdown, or the failure of the rule of law. Rather, we are concerned with what particular forms of order are built up in polities in which multiple persistent violent actors operate. Who are these actors, how do they interact, and what types of orders do they build? How do these interactions create new forms of order such as networks of criminal governance or legal pluralism? By looking at the interactions of multiple violent actors and trying to understand what order they create, we provide a new mode for studying politics in the region. Similarly, we are not concerned with deficits of citizenship but, rather, with how citizenship and other forms of political subjectivity are built among different segments of the population under plurally violent conditions. Ultimately, these constitute much richer questions than those that can be asked under a paradigm that assumes certain fixed understandings about institutions, order, violence, and modes of political participation. Latin America does not live in a perpetual deficit of not being Europe or North America, and there is no indication that the particular patterns of political arrangement that exist in these countries are amenable to them becoming more like those Northern democracies. Indeed, pluralist political practice in Latin America, as we have suggested, may very well depend on a tolerance for privatized violence and ongoing abuses of large segments of the population. These are unique forms of political practice, order, and subjectivity that need to be studied on their own terms.

Violent Pluralism in Context

It is of course impossible to talk about politics in Latin America without talking about democracy. It has been the political project of the entire continent for the past generation: every country, even Cuba, has claimed it as its form of government, and it dominates academic and political discourse about the region. It is not our intention here to say either that democracy does not exist in Latin America or that we should not study democracy in Latin America. Rather, the purpose of this introduction has been to attempt to open a parenthesis in which students of politics can critically consider the state of the political regimes in Latin America without the weight of the democratization project hanging over the analysis. Within this parenthesis we can consider, counter to conventional political science, the actual condition of Latin America's political regimes amid and in concert with the various forms of political and social violence that characterize Latin American national societies. The questions and modes of analysis that we lay out in the previous sections of this introduction provide tools that can enable scholars to assess Latin American political society without assuming a priori the political project and the language of democracy and democratization.[25]

The essays that follow serve to deepen and extend the arguments laid out in this introduction. Drawing on detailed case studies from a variety of countries throughout the region (from the Andes and Brazil to Central America, the Southern Cone to the Hispanic Caribbean) and from a range of academic disciplines (including anthropology, history, political science, and sociology), they explore the multiple forms in which violence manifests itself as part and parcel of contemporary Latin American democracy. Some of the essays provide clear and compelling ethnographic and historical illustrations of the theoretical outlines of this introduction, while others expand on these outlines to contribute their own disciplinary or cross-disciplinary insights.[26]

Drawing on evidence from her research in Mexico, Diane Davis's contribution offers an important historical framing for the conceptual work provided by our introduction. As Davis points out, the initial enthusiasm with which politicians, citizens, and academic analysts of Latin America greeted the spread of political and economic liberalization throughout the region in the 1980s and 1990s has now been replaced by anxiety and fear as violence and insecurity continue to characterize postauthoritarian societies. "Forget big ideas about democracy and about how electoral rules of the game will lead to improvement in people's everyday lives"—as Davis observes, ordinary citizens today are much more concerned with creating security on their own terms, often bypassing the state and its democratic institutions and opting for more localized, violent measures of control that seem to promise more immediate returns. At the same time, organized groups of violent "mafias," often performing statelike functions, and often with the collaboration of police and military officials, have emerged as power brokers in or alongside of democratic states. Davis's essay provides the vital historical context within which these sundry forms of violent organization and practice can be understood in the realities of contemporary democracy. Why, Davis asks, has the transition to democracy not been accompanied by a transition away from the violent and coercive practices of the nondemocratic past? And how has this past laid the foundation for the kinds of violent democracies that we observe in Latin America today? The answers to these questions, according to Davis, lie in past decisions about economic development, state formation, and industrialization in the region, requiring us to place contemporary democracy within the context of this longer trajectory for it to be understood.

The historian Mary Roldán in her essay examines the intertwined relations between democracy and violence in Colombia, a formally democratic nation that nevertheless "has spent a not insignificant portion of the last four decades under states of siege or some form of political constraint." In concert with themes raised consistently throughout this volume, Roldán asks of Colombian democracy, "Is it possible that violence is both constitutive of and the product of fundamentally different understandings of what it means to practice democracy?" Her answer, of course, is "yes," a response she arrives at through a historical ethnography of a grassroots solidarity movement organized to seek nonviolent alternatives to armed conflict in the Antioquia region of Colombia. In contrast to Todd Landman's macropolitical perspective (see below), Roldán offers a microanalysis of the perils of practicing democracy in a context of violent pluralism, in which the constant threat or experience of violence jeopardizes local efforts to live peacefully and defend basic rights. Interestingly, though, as Roldán observes, violence in this case has not necessarily eroded local people's confidence in democracy or the democratic state; rather, violence here motivates previously unorganized citizens to join together to create democracy, even as this action brings local definitions of democracy into conflict with official state or transnational conceptions.

The contribution by the anthropologist María Clemencia Ramírez also offers a consideration of Colombia's violent democracy—an apt case for analyzing this apparent contradiction in terms, given Colombia's long-standing self-image as one of the oldest democracies in Latin America. In some violent democracies the ties between formal state institutions and violent entities are subtle and covert; in Colombia, as Ramírez clearly demonstrates, the relationships between official state and violent nonofficial, illegal groups are tightly woven and multiply configured. Especially in the so-called marginal regions of the country, an "alternative social order" has been established in which violent nonstate actors (i.e., guerillas and paramilitaries) have taken control of the regions, a control maintained through their various ties with local and state political officials. In this alternative order, antagonistic to but at the same time affiliated with the democratic state, security has emerged as the dominant paradigm of democratic rule, a paradigm whose hegemony is guaranteed by the forced participation of all citizens.

The essays by Javier Auyero and Ruth Stanley both examine violence and democracy in Buenos Aires. But whereas Stanley's work focuses on the experiences of violence's victims, Auyero, like Ramírez, is interested in its perpetrators, be they legal or illegal, official or unauthorized. Auyero focuses on what he terms "clandestine connections" between legal and illegal political actors, as well as on their critical role in the making of collective violence. Auyero's essay uses the case of the 2001 food riots in Argentina to examine the diverse ways in which covert and often unrecognized links between members of the polity—from politicians to activists to perpetrators of street violence—shape the emergence, manifestations, and diffusion of collective violence. Perhaps more significant is Auyero's recognition that political elites may oftentimes themselves perpetrate the violence: beyond simply tolerating the use of violence to achieve political ends, in Buenos Aires (as elsewhere) elites deploy violent tactics, or call on their allies to do so, in the pursuit of ostensibly democratic objectives. In a similar vein, Stanley's contribution engages the question of police impunity in Buenos Aires, focusing on the experience of the victims of illegal police violence and their efforts to organize and confront it. Stanley's analysis reveals the complexities and contradictions of a democratic system in which those authorized to use legal violence likewise function as illegal violent actors, calling into focus the potential consequences for democratic stability when state institutions are unable or unwilling to restrict the use of violence and coercive state power. These essays are particularly interesting in that they investigate the problem of violent pluralism in the context of what has been seen as a low-violence country until now. They show that while levels of violence may not be as high here, countries with relatively low levels of conflict can still experience many of the same political processes of violent pluralism as countries with higher rates of violence.

The essays by Lilean Bobea and Robert Gay also wrestle with the question of impunity and, like many others in this volume, respond to our call in this introduction for a scholarship that explores the connections between violent democratic states and the lived realities of citizens of those states. Bobea and Gay both highlight the connections between levels of abstraction often identified as the micro and the macro to understand daily life within broader forms of national and transnational organization and practice. Bobea's contribution, for example, begins with an ethnographic description of the experiences of poor residents of Santo Domingo and Santiago in the Dominican Republic, who live with criminal and state violence on a daily basis. She then moves to a macrolevel consideration of the state's Plan for Democratic Security, a proposal to "reorganize the public sector and rebuild society" in the fight against illegal violence. The extent to which security programs open the door to further violence, albeit of the democratic variety, is an important consideration here. Similarly, Gay examines local violence in Rio de Janeiro in the context of a transnational political economy of drug trafficking, demonstrating the extensive complicity of police and other authorities in the very violence and illegality they are supposed to combat. Both of these essays, like others in this volume (those by Auyero and Roldán come particularly to mind), also demonstrate the need for scholars engaged in the study of contemporary democracies to employ a variety of methods in their work. The macrohistorical and structural analyses of history, sociology, and political science combine usefully with the more ethnographic techniques of anthropology to provide these scholars access to sociopolitical realities at multiple levels of experience.

In many ways Latin America lies at the crossroads of the developed and developing worlds. While it has some things in common institutionally with the political and economic systems of Western Europe and North America, in terms of how political institutions function and how force is deployed in society Latin America has much more in common with Africa, the former Soviet Republics, and Central Asia. In his broadly synthetic contribution to this volume, Landman brings the perspective of comparative politics to his analysis of the conjuncture between violence and democracy in Latin America, and of its impact on human rights in the region. Systematizing what are often loosely deployed concepts, Landman offers a typology that distinguishes usefully between legal and illegal forms of violence and between state and nonstate or extrastate perpetrators of violent acts. Such typologizing, while foreign to anthropologists and other more typically qualitative analysts, serves to clarify exactly who are the violent actors in Latin American democracies, and how violence identified as legal or "legitimate" coexists with other forms that lie beyond the pale. Additionally, as Landman goes on to demonstrate, this classification enables us to identify rights-protective regimes, that is, "the degree to which states have the capacity to respect, protect, and fulfill rights obligations typically associated with democracy." This kind of analysis moves us beyond the tendency to pile ever more adjectives in front of democracy, instead facilitating an objective analysis of the extent to which any so-called democracy serves to guarantee the basic rights of its citizens. Landman's analysis provides a framework for interpreting the varieties of violent practice described in each of the preceding essays.

As many of the essays in this volume suggest, if we begin to reorient how we study politics in Latin America, we can also begin to think seriously about the scope and dimensions of reforms or more radical changes that are necessary to actually achieve something like polyarchy. By looking beyond political institutions and taking seriously the idea that some current political regimes in Latin America may not be able to move toward wide guarantees of basic rights, we can begin to think about what type of institutional and noninstitutional framework may lead to polyarchy. Do countries, for example, need a different orientation to international trade flows that contribute so much to the drugs and arms trades to create governments more capable of protecting their populations? Alternatively, as we begin to understand more about the relationships that governments maintain with other types of violent actors operating in a polity, we can develop an understanding about what types of networks of relations between the state and other violent actors succeed in transmitting basic protections to residents. Most important, if we do not critically assess the notion that the existing regimes can move in this direction we can never determine what type of extrainstitutional changes might be necessary to more effectively guarantee basic rights to Latin Americans. In the conclusion Enrique Arias ties together the various strands of argument in the volume through a discussion of the origins and operation of violent pluralism, and of solutions to the challenges it poses. The conclusion offers a discussion of future research needs on these issues in Latin America and the policy implications of the approach we offer. In the end the conclusion seeks not so much to close the volume as to open up space for an ongoing discussion of the issues discussed in the book.

This project does not pretend to offer a rigorous proof of violent pluralism as the exclusive model for understanding political systems in Latin America. Rather, by offering detailed examinations of the practice and politics of violence in a number of countries in the region, this volume offers a theoretical exploration of the challenges facing the region that should help open a conceptual space through which we can understand in a more nuanced and sophisticated way the challenges facing these polities and their inhabitants. By adopting a more critical approach toward our understanding of regime change and of efforts to build democracy, by moving beyond the democratization paradigm, we, as Latin Americanists and comparativists, can more effectively contribute to some of the larger policy debates that exist today. Since the second Clinton administration U.S. foreign policy has officially been driven by the "democratic peace" theory, which claims that the world will be a safer place for the United States if there are more democracies, since democracies do not go to war with each other.[27] To this end both the Clinton and the Bush administrations, in very different ways, officially worked to build democracy in far-flung parts of the world. The debacle of democracy building in Iraq and the resonance of that experience with ongoing problems of social violence in Latin America highlight an important contribution that Latin Americanists could have made to this debate. By taking seriously the idea of violent pluralism and by broadening our conception of how to study the elective regimes that predominate in Latin America, we can not only begin to contribute in a more critical way to the debate about democracy building but also identify factors that tend to lead to conditions of violent pluralism or, alternatively, to polyarchy.

Notes

1. This optimism and the political unanimity that seemed to accompany it turned out to be short-lived, as long-standing divisions in Bolivian society reasserted themselves over the next few years, leading to violent clashes between groups supporting the MAS government and those backing "traditional" parties from the lowland regions seeking more autonomy from the central state.
2. For statistics on murders in São Paulo, see Brinks 2003:6–7.
3. For statistics on violence in Latin America, see Hinton 2005:77.
4. On the third wave, see Huntington 1991.
5. Indeed, Larry Diamond, one of the leading scholars on democratization, served the U.S. government in Iraq in its efforts to build democratic government there and has written about the reasons behind that country's very rough transition process. See Diamond 2005a, 2005b.
6. On social conditions in the second phase of democratic transitions, see Przeworski et al. 1996:39–40.
7. On the hope for building democracy under difficult conditions, see O'Donnell 2002:8–9.
8. It should be noted, however, that recent studies of democratization have focused more substantially on the gray zone between authoritarianism and democracy; see Plattner 2005:5–6.
9. An expert on postconflict transitions debunked Brooks's analysis in a letter to the editor; see Whitfield 2004.
10. The controversial Carothers piece, published in the *Journal of Democracy*, was extensively criticized two issues later in the same journal by a host of practitioners and scholars.
11. The exception to this statement is Diamond, whose analysis of the failure to manage an effective transition in Iraq focuses principally on elections, institution building, developing a strong plan for the transition, and devolving decision-making power to local leaders quickly. See Diamond 2005a:13–21. Yet even these are stock answers that offer little in the way of a program for responding to armed insurgency or ongoing street violence, in Iraq or elsewhere.
12. This question has been addressed most notably by O'Donnell; see O'Donnell 2001.
13. Notably O'Donnell specifically eschews this, instead arguing that democratization itself is an unending process and that hence the democratization paradigm should remain the main theoretical basis for understanding democracy in Latin America. See O'Donnell 1999c. In its own way, this is also a teleological argument; it is just a teleology in which the telos has already arrived.
14. A comprehensive example of this approach can be found in United Nations Development Programme 2005.
15. On informal rules and police violence see Brinks 2003:6–7; and O'Donnell 1993; on policing and violence in Argentina and Brazil, see Hinton 2005, esp. 90.

16. An important variant on this approach focuses not on state failures but, rather, on how state institutions can be reformed to more adequately protect basic rights. For examples, see Zaverucha 1999; Correa Sutil 1999.
17. On the politics of the democratization project, see Paley 2001:5–7.
18. Structural violence refers to the ways in which a ruling regime or state structure systematically inhibits people from realizing their full potential through the institutionalization of such barriers to human achievement as poverty, sexism, or racism. For an application in anthropology, see Farmer 2003.
19. On the impact of light combat weapons on violence in Rio de Janeiro, see Dowdney 2008.
20. In other contexts, see Green 1999; Merry 1981; Rotker 2002b.
21. Interesting work from political science on this topic is being done by Godoy (2002).
22. A notable anthropological study of neoliberal democracy in Latin America is Paley 2001.
23. On this debate generally, see Jelin and Hershberg 1996:2; on a narrow political vision of rights, see O'Donnell and Schmitter 1986:7–8; for a good analysis of the interplay between civil, political, and social rights in the expansion of citizenship in postauthoritarian Latin America, see Jelin 1996; for a wider call for social and political citizenship, see UNDP 2005:27–28.
24. Although for some in Latin America, the idea of citizenship remains a potent tool for demanding expanded rights in the neoliberal era; see Postero 2007.
25. This is extremely important in light of recent work on "conditional authoritarianism" that looks at how otherwise repressive regimes employ electoral mechanisms to achieve political ends without extending broad rights to the population; see Levitsky and Way 2002.
26. A particular deficiency of the present volume is its lack of an essay that specifically addresses Central America. The editors recognize the limitations that this lacuna imposes on our analysis.
27. On the democratic peace, see Doyle 1986.

The Political and Economic Origins of Violence and Insecurity in Contemporary Latin America

Past Trajectories and Future Prospects

DIANE E. DAVIS

Not very long ago optimism flowered about prospects for democracy in Latin America. The spread of political and economic liberalization throughout the 1980s and 1990s produced a wave of hope, seen most visibly in countries like Mexico, Argentina, and Brazil. With their authoritarian past seemingly left behind and the advent of a reinvigorated competitive electoral system, citizens and newly elected officials faced their future with a sense of unlimited possibilities for positive change. But for many, dreams have steadily dimmed as problems of violence, crime, and insecurity emerged with a vengeance, having reached new heights by the mid- and late 1990s and continuing today (Bailey 2003; Frühling and Tulchin with Golding 2003). As Susana Rotker so astutely chronicled in *Citizens of Fear: Urban Violence in Latin America* (2002), the everyday Latin American experience is now haunted by the specters of fear, violence, crime, and police impunity, all of which permeate practically every aspect of daily life.

Elected governments seem hamstrung in their capacities to control these problems, let alone reverse them, in large part because those charged with keeping order and guaranteeing the rule of law on behalf of the state, the police and/or the military, are themselves frequently implicated in abusive practices or criminality (Hinton 2006; Leeds 1996). The result is growing cynicism, social fragmentation, and a renewed sense of hopelessness about the future and the potential of competitive political systems to deal with the deteriorating situation. The repercussions for democracy and citizenship are troubling.

Forget big ideas about democracy and about how the electoral rules of the game will lead to improvement in people's everyday lives. Forget aspirations that the embrace of liberalization will finally bring the resources and institutions to address problems of economic inequality and political polarization. Instead, growing numbers of citizens in Latin America are turning their attention away from formal politics and party-led solutions and looking for their own answers to the problems of insecurity in everyday life (Oxhorn and Ducatenzeiler 1998). The upside is that these efforts to reinvigorate civil society can at times lead to mass mobilizations against crime and insecurity. But there also is a downside. Hopelessness has become so extreme that some citizens are turning to violence themselves—whether in the form of vigilantism, seen as a last-gasp measure for achieving some sense of justice, or through the embrace of a life of crime, so as to be on the giving rather than on the receiving end of an unjust and unequal political economy—to recapture some control over their daily existence (Davis 2006c; Daniel Goldstein 2003; Moser 2004).

To be sure, violence and impunity are no strangers to the countries of Latin America, where an authoritarian past produced political torture, so-called disappearances, guerilla movements, and other forms of armed rebellion in prior epochs (Bodemaer, Kurtenbach, and Meschkat 2001; Huggins 1998). Yet contemporary problems of violence, daily conflict, and insecurity are much broader and perhaps more insidious and damaging to the quality of life than even the violent struggles over authoritarian rule in the past (Huggins, Haritos-Fatouros, and Zimbardo 2002). This is partly so because the violence in contemporary Latin America appears to be a more "garden-variety" type of insecurity that permeates the most routine of daily activities and is best seen in rising homicides, accelerating crime rates (despite a decline in reportage by victims), unprecedented levels of police corruption and impunity, and an inability to move around freely without fear of armed robbery, violent attack, or extortion (Davis and Alvarado 1999). It is these conditions that push citizens (and criminals) to take matters into their own hands, either through vigilante acts (Daniel Goldstein 2003) or, more commonly, by hiring private security guards, thereby fueling the environment of fear, exclusion, and insecurity (Smulowitz 2003).

One result is that in many parts of Latin America, mafias involved in various forms of illegal activities (ranging from drugs and guns to knockoff designer products and CDs) are calling the shots (Bailey and Godson 2001; Cross 1998). Well-organized cadres involved in illicit activities often take on the functionally equivalent role of miniature states by monopolizing the means of violence and providing protection in exchange for loyalty and territorial dominion (Lupsha 1996). More often than not, these illicit activities persist with the tacit support of the police and military, who often prioritize the protection of their own institutional sovereignty and/or involvement in these black-market activities, rather than the protection of citizens who suffer in the precarious environment of an elusive rule of law. With a wide range of institutions and actors involved in crime and brutality, and with many of the key protagonists both armed and dangerous, most governments, democratic or not, have failed to keep violence and insecurity at bay.

So what accounts for this distressing state of affairs? My aim in this essay is to answer this question with a focus on Latin America's developmental history and its current political and economic patterns. Three questions guide the narrative: (1) In what ways has the political, social, and economic history of Latin America laid the foundation for contemporary patterns of violence and insecurity, especially those involving the police and military? (2) Why has relatively successful political transition from authoritarian rule to democracy not produced a significant break from this coercive and violent past and a strengthening of the rule of law? And finally, (3) what can be done about this state of affairs in a democratic and increasingly global context in which the international scale of the problem fails to match the local or national scale of the available solutions? *bad questions*

I answer these questions with evidence primarily drawn from the Mexican case, although I proceed under the assumption that the general developmental challenges facing Mexico in the first half of the twentieth century resembled those faced by other large industrializers in Latin America. That is, despite the peculiarities of Mexican history, the story recounted here has been crafted to reflect larger dynamics relevant to many of the large countries on the South American continent.

The first half of this essay examines the history of political and economic development and how it set problems of violence in motion. It focuses on three distinct but interrelated processes: contested state formation, the institutionalization of an authoritarian political apparatus and its coercive arms, and industrialization-led urbanization. It argues that the combination of these three developments led to state-sponsored violence, reflected first in growing levels of police and military impunity and the rise of so-called political policing against enemies of the state, and later in a weakened rule of law. These outcomes generated an environment of violence and crime in which the police and military were routinely implicated, a state of affairs that helped institutionalize corruption within the police force, the military, and the entire administration of the justice system.

The second half of the essay examines recent trends of political and economic liberalization and their impact on politics and society in the current democratic period. It argues that the recent transformations have reinforced—rather than reversed—past patterns of impunity and violence in such a way as to limit the capacities of formally democratic mechanisms and civil society to counter the situation of growing insecurity. It focuses on new actors empowered by global trading patterns, on the challenges facing newly democratic party systems, and on nonstate developments within civil society, all of which have led to the growth of a large informal sector riddled with violence and illegality, a growing private security apparatus, and a delegitimized state. I argue that the combination of these changes has been more likely to limit, rather than facilitate, the democratic state's efforts to stem violence and a deteriorating rule of law.

Overall, my essay not only advances the claim that continuing violence in newly democratic Latin America is traceable to the path-dependent consequences of past political decisions about economic development, state formation, and industrialization; it also suggests that the current intensification of long-standing problems of violence owes as much to the wholehearted *embrace* of liberalization, both political and economic, as to the weight of history, however paradoxical this may appear at the outset. Specifically, in the context of a slow but steady democratic transition that does not necessarily make a clear break with the institutional structures and practices of the past, in which coercive elements implicated in authoritarian rule have remained in the picture, and in which new global patterns of trade support the informal and illegal economy as much as the formal, violence and the "unrule" of law have and will continue to persist.

Contested State Formation and the
Historical Roots of Violence and Impunity

For large portions of the nineteenth century and the early twentieth, most Latin American countries suffered through continuous conflicts over sovereignty, seen initially in struggles for independence from Spain (or Portugal), in civil wars and other similarly weighty regional conflicts, and, in a few cases, in revolution or other protracted battles leading to a major political rupture with a colonial or liberal past. Mexico is one of just a handful of Latin American countries falling into the revolutionary category. Even so, it shares a common profile with many of its Southern Cone counterparts: a history of center-region tensions over the mercantilist nature of the national economy and the efforts to centralize power; long-standing battles between agrarian and industrial elites about the nature of the state and the direction of the economy; pervasive social uprisings and rebellion on the part of the nation's most impoverished citizens, whose exclusion from the governing pact fueled their collective ire; and the emergence of a professional military linked to the power elite (regionally, nationally, or both). All these conflicts gave life to a single important fact about Mexico in particular, and about Latin America more generally: ongoing struggles over the nature, character, and direction of state power (Knight and Pansters 2005; Oszlak 1981).

While the roots of contestation over the state may be initially traced to the colonial period, struggles persisted beyond formal independence and marked the political and economic landscape of Latin America even in the twentieth century, producing a highly conflictive political environment in which an abusive state apparatus, untrammeled coercive power, and violence all flowered. In the case of Mexico, the 1910 revolution and its aftermath proved a key historical juncture, setting these dynamics in motion. In an effort to advance and protect the revolutionary cause, the state wielded considerable coercive power against real and potential enemies (Knight 1986). These practices, dating to the postrevolutionary era, ultimately helped institutionalize police corruption and the coercive power of an authoritarian state whose pervasive use of violence and disregard for the rule of law permeated civil society as well.

Complicating matters, during this early twentieth-century period, most Latin American states—whether newly formed in revolution, as in the case of Mexico, or those merely struggling to hold onto power—also faced the challenges of rapid economic expansion, or better said, of fostering industrialization. This meant that in addition to consolidating state power vis-à-vis political or ideological enemies, most Latin American states found it essential to manage if not control a nascent working class and/or organized agrarian elites, both of which were relatively well mobilized to act against the wishes of industrial capitalists (see French 1992). Having a strong military and police force was essential to undermining such opposition and to achieving larger industrial development aims. In this sense the economic development aims built on regime consolidation aims to reinforce the coercive power of the state.

Finally, and just as important for strengthening coercive aspects of the authoritarian state (while also institutionalizing corruption and impunity), the dual challenges of consolidating state power and expanding the economy frequently unfolded in the context of rapid urbanization, precisely because economies of scale and consumer markets concentrated most industrial development in a few cities, key among them capital cities that also served as seats of political power (see Davis 1998). In this environment police were as significant as the military in fulfilling the state's political, economic, and social aims, thereby extending the coercive arm of the state into the everyday life of large portions of the nation's citizens. This was so not only because large cities served as home to much of the industrial working class and to the owners of industrial establishments that the police sought to protect (Lear 2001). Police also became central actors because the rapidly urbanizing locales of Latin America required additional forms of control and regulation—relating to the production and consumption of new goods and services, the provision and management of transportation and traffic, the inspection of markets, and the monitoring of the urban unemployed and indigent, to name but a few—necessary to grease the wheels of commerce, keep the local economy growing, and guarantee social order in an environment in which rural migrants, informal-sector workers, and other new social actors appeared on the scene in droves (Bliss 2001; Piccato 2001; Meade 1997).

In this complicated environment of rapid urbanization, industrialization, and state formation, the power of the police expanded by leaps and bounds, often to the point of tension vis-à-vis the military. With the police becoming increasingly involved in everyday urban life, and the military struggling to keep its privileged position as the arm of the state used to root out enemies and defend the national interest, tensions emerged within these coercive arms of the state as well as between them and the citizenry. Both the military and the police—as individuals and institutionally—were given extraordinary leeway and operated with very little state-imposed discipline (Pereira 2005; Ungar 2002). This established the foundations for abuse of power on the part of the state's key coercive apparatuses, a legacy that persisted long beyond the successful achievement of the state's urban, political, and economic developmental goals. How this unfolded in early twentieth-century Latin America can be evidenced through a more focused discussion of the Mexican experience in the decades following the 1910 revolution.

The 1910 Mexican Revolution: Setting the Cycle of Impunity in Motion

From early on Mexico's police and military were drawn into ongoing tensions and political battles among and between revolutionaries, counterrevolutionaries, and, later, opposition groups that sought to reform or widen the revolutionary state's project. It is understandable that both forces were used to police counterrevolutionaries, tasks that were most intense from 1910–18 and focused in the capital, Mexico City. This was so not only because, in an unstable postrevolutionary environment, the newly founded Mexican state was not yet well institutionalized due to internal tensions in the revolutionary family and because the military was not united behind the revolutionary leadership (which itself was divided). The situation was also owing to the fact that the judiciary was dominated by political conservatives and others who remained sympathetic to the counterrevolutionary elite and had limited sympathy for the revolutionary project. Both conditions drove the revolutionary leadership to create new police institutions and powers that could be used to thwart the efforts of judges employing their power against revolutionary loyalists, as well as to keep the overwhelming power of the military at bay.[1]

In addition to founding a new "judicial" police that answered directly to the federal executive despite retaining local functions, the new political leadership (in a reform introduced by Venustiano Carranza and continued by Plutarco Elias Calles) also centralized control over preventative police, or "beat" cops, who prior to this reform worked mainly at the decentralized level of the municipalities (*municipios*), along with other actors more closely linked to citizens than the state, including justices of the peace (Piccato 2001). To establish authority over the city police, the revolutionary leadership not only created a new institution and chain of command intended to integrate all local police officers and justices of the peace into a single citywide police force answering to the federal executive. Political leaders also kept centralized control by linking this new citywide police directly to the military. This is evidenced by the use of military personnel in the upper ranks of the policing apparatus, as well as by the restructuring of police training and responsibilities so as to inculcate and build on military values and discipline.[2] These institutional transformations put a federally controlled, militarily linked policing apparatus onto Mexico City streets, where it maintained a visible presence in everyday urban life and was able to politically threaten (and economically extort) the most humble of citizens.

None of these changes occurred smoothly or without open conflict, however. The rank and file of the preventative police did not like the military involvement in their activities, especially in the early years of postrevolutionary consolidation when they still had pro-Diaz sympathizers or nonrevolutionary loyalists within their ranks. They also frequently found themselves competing with the judicial police for the power to investigate and arrest suspected criminals—for both political and rent-seeking purposes. More important, as the internal ideological contours of the revolutionary state shifted, so too did the loyalties of the police and the military. That is, even though in the initial stages Mexico City police may have joined with the revolutionary leadership in the goal of rooting out counterrevolutionaries, the following phases of political policing, in which the focus shifted to policing other revolutionaries and partisan political opponents, brought conflict and tension within and among the Mexico City police, the military, and the state. Over time these tensions further reinforced the violent and authoritarian character of the state, also leading to greater police impunity and a turn to violence to solve social and political problems. In Mexico much of this came to a head in the immediate postrevolutionary decade, and then again in the 1930s under the administration of Lázaro Cárdenas, when the democratic and class character of the state came under question.

As early as 1915 we see state efforts to use the Mexico City police to control political enemies not considered counterrevolutionaries through coercive actions against striking trolley workers and members of other transport unions. In part, the new revolutionary government was concerned to keep the urban economy functioning so as to facilitate urban and industrial development in the critical years after the revolution, when foreign capital had fled and the larger revolutionary project depended on jump-starting the economy. Like many elements in the labor movement with communist sympathies, both unions had actually been quite loyal to the revolutionary project, and many members had fought alongside the revolutionaries in the struggle against the Diaz dictatorship. But they did not necessarily support the factions in power, who were toeing a more conservative line, and thus the striking workers' disruption of the local economy was considered grounds for violent reprisal. The state repression of striking workers not only planted the institutional seeds of police complicity in rooting out ideological enemies, a tradition that would persist and become institutionalized over the years. It also gave police a key role in regulating transit—something that would later return to haunt the force as a whole, as the police control of traffic became a main source of bribery and corruption in the decades of the 1950s and 1960s.

Another round of intensive political policing occurred in the period 1925–28, this time directed against Labor Party members and other prodemocracy partisans in the Distrito Federal (DF) who opposed the authoritarian and centralizing tendencies of Calles's revolutionary leadership. In this particular conflict, a strong connection developed between the Mexico City police chief and Calles around the aims of monitoring political debate among Labor Party activists, dominating public information, and breaking up opposition rallies.[3] A third round of political policing took place in the early 1930s, just before Cárdenas's rise to power, when police again were used against laborers and communist-linked worker organizations, as well as against campesinos. The policing of political opponents was clearly not intended merely to silence an active civil society. It also found elective affinity with the political leadership's efforts to repress revolutionary rivals within the military and the state itself. All these forms of police practice trace their origins to the contested process of state formation and to the struggle to establish control and ideological contours—notably, in the Mexican case, the relative power and inclusion of laborers and peasants as opposed to industrial and agrarian elites.

In combination, these tensions pitted revolutionary against revolutionary, police against military, and president against mayor, depending on which coercive force was most loyally attached to which faction or level of government. In this environment, mistrust and violence became the modus operandi of political rule, and the institutions of policing became the battleground for power.

From Contested State Formation to Institutionalized
Police Corruption, 1920–40

Given the history of contestation over the direction of the revolutionary state, it did not take long before the police as an institution began to spiral out of control. This direction had become clear by the 1930s, at a time when the Mexican government hoped to turn its full attention to industrialization. More than two decades of political policing and complicity between revolutionary leaders and the police in the use of extralegal measures to achieve their ideological or state consolidation aims had created a corrupt police force increasingly hard to control.

The roots of institutionalized corruption probably trace to the period 1910–18 when the military, under Carranza, began usurping Mexico City policing functions to consolidate the revolutionary leadership's power over citizen militias and local municipalities who sought to maintain a decentralized system of policing. During this period police became directly involved in "garden-variety" corruption linked to urban regulation and servicing. This entailed taking bribes from *vendedores ambulantes* (street vendors) and *pulque* (fermented grain drink) sellers, or negotiating prices in return for ignoring labor law regulations, market permissions, transport violations, and the like. The pressure for so-called rent seeking among the police (i.e., corruption and bribery, or *la mordida*) came from a variety of sources. The police were poorly paid, in no small part because of the depressed economic environment in postrevolutionary Mexico City; getting a job was reward enough to keep salaries low. Yet even with low salaries, the police were required to pay for their own supplies and uniforms, an obligation that pushed them to find other sources for income. The lack of formal training in police work, and a limited commitment to the communities the officers were policing, also greased the wheels of bribery and impunity.

Some of the petty corruption unfolded among the rank and file, many of whom were ex-soldiers of humble means who got their jobs by petitioning to revolutionary leaders for police employment as payback for fighting with revolutionary cadres.[4] But corruption did not just occur in the rank and file. As early as 1918 we see high-level military officers requesting posting in the Mexico City police, precisely because of the money assumed to be circulating through this office via corrupt practices. The involvement of higher police officials in corruption helped regularize the practice throughout the entire system, in part because higher officials (police chiefs, military generals, and higher-positioned individuals) expected citizen payoffs to rank-and-file officers to be channeled upward. These practices helped establish a clear set of "prices" or rates for *mordidas* (two pesos for vending *pulque* on Sunday, etc.), which in turn helped normalize citizen expectations that such bribes were the officially sanctioned price for doing business.

Over time, even after the still fragile state leadership had effectively defeated its counterrevolutionary opponents, corrupt practices continued, and they soon became interlaced with the ascendance of political factions, further entrenching them, despite occasional efforts by the military leadership or governing officials to clean up the police force. This was reflected in the terms of office for police chiefs: Prior to 1921 almost all chiefs had left their positions after less than a year in office (Davis forthcoming). Starting in the mid-1920s, terms for police chiefs begin to extend, with some remaining at the helm for three to four years,[5] although the average tenure of Mexico City police chiefs remained erratic. Only around 1950 did police chiefs' terms begin to coincide with those of mayoral and/or presidential administrations. Paradoxically, however, the increased terms of individual police chiefs also allowed networks of corruption to deepen and flourish, not least because the long-standing complicity of the police made officeholding a lucrative business whose gains were seen as supporting national revolutionary projects as much as personal pocketbooks.

By the 1920s corruption had reached such heights that high-level police personnel were publicly known—and affirmed in internal secret police reports —to be involved in criminal activities, including an auto-theft gang known as the Banda de Automobile Gris that counted on Mexico City's police chief as a principal interlocutor.[6] Rogues like this did not last long in their posts, and most were recycled out of leadership positions because of undeniable corruption, the wrong political allegiances, or both. But they rarely disappeared entirely. Most just found other lucrative positions elsewhere in the administration—either in another police agency, in the military, and/or in other higher levels of the state (a favored posting was in customs, which had great rent-seeking potential). In fact, it is not farfetched to suggest that Latin America's later infamously high levels of corruption may have originated with corrupt administrators originally recycled out of police or military posts into other arms of the state.

From Police Corruption to Retrenched Authoritarianism, 1940–60

One of the great ironies of police corruption was that it accelerated in inverse relation to the revolutionary leadership's efforts to consolidate its political hold on the state. The dynamic reinforced the state's authoritarianism despite the government's efforts to strengthen the political system's democratic character during the 1940s and 1950s. In Mexico this shift corresponded with the administration of Cárdenas, the country's great populist leader and friend of the working class, who also wanted to spur on the economy through industrialization. Motivated in part by repressive police actions against peasants and laborers who struggled for a more inclusive and democratic state, as well as by the fact that police corruption ate into tourism revenues in ways that challenged his economic development aims,[7] Cárdenas came to office with a commitment to purify the police apparatus in the capital city. Doing so, however, required support from allies.

Perhaps the only force with the coercive capacity or political power to aid in this task was the military. And therein lay the conundrum. Indeed, Cárdenas's reliance on the military to deal with police corruption—even if done for progressive, populist purposes—only further institutionalized the state's authoritarian character, thereby undermining the larger democratic aims that had pushed Cárdenas to support police reforms in the first place. It also reintroduced a military mentality into the policing apparatus, something that had in the past, as described earlier, planted the seeds of police corruption to begin with. To his credit, Cárdenas did not turn to the military immediately, seeking instead other institutional reforms that might effect changes from within the police force. Yet his efforts to keep the coercive arms of the state "clean" and under his control failed.

The first of Cárdenas's reforms entailed an expansion of the city's police to include semiprivate security forces that had been operating parallel to the preventative police. This infusion of nonstate security forces into the public police ranks allowed Cárdenas to limit the relative institutional influence of the highly corrupted officer corps. At minimum, he hoped to offer the city's residents a renewed police force not tied into old networks of corruption and with a reputation of being responsive to the citizenry. Most important, by bringing private police into the city's public policing services Cárdenas strengthened his own ideological position within the conflictive revolutionary family at large. The new police officers, now called Policia Auxiliar (auxiliary police), were known to be extremely loyal to Cárdenas and his political ideals, and they were both organized and self-identified as part of his larger working-class movement.

The second major change was a reorganization of the police to reflect their class, employment, and/or state-worker status, putting them in sync with all others employed by the state. The roots of this shift traced to a piece of legislation from 1936 that divided state workers into two categories, *de base* and *de confianza*.[8] This legislation, also crafted by Cárdenas, helped reinforce the working-class consciousness of the new auxiliary police, bringing them in sync with other working-class forces who sought to limit the state's industrialization project. It meant that police could identify themselves as just another form of state worker. It proved a very popular move, and many officers requested full inclusion in the state-work legislation so as to benefit from job stability and access to social security.[9] However, both reforms met serious political opposition, primarily because they gave the new rank-and-file police powerful tools to expose the corrupt hiring and firing practices used by extant police cadres.

The higher-level officers had grown accustomed to a hierarchy of unquestioned authority that allowed them to extort lower rank officers for kickbacks and payoffs collected on duty. The state-worker legislation, however, allowed lower-rank officers to hold their superiors accountable, and they could refuse to be drawn into the circle of corruption and impunity. Further problems arose from the "effects" of this newly instated class consciousness. Organizational connections around state-worker identities between the rank-and-file police and the general working class made it impossible for the police leadership to continue its political policing of class enemies or to further use coercive force against rebellious citizens, especially those involved in the labor movement, who had long been on the receiving end of police brutality. Cárdenas's police reforms thus proved highly controversial. They created tensions within the police, especially between the new auxiliary and the old preventative police, and between some elements of the police and the military. And although Cárdenas himself held great prestige and considerable power in the military, as an organization it was also divided over the changes he initiated.[10] As a result, Cárdenas soon backed down on his plans to extend state-worker legislation to the police, despite their potential to move forward his agenda on both the class and police-corruption fronts.

The police did not, however, remain unchanged. To compensate for this failed reform and to repair the damage inflicted on police-military relations by the state-worker debate, in 1939 Cárdenas introduced a third and final police reform: its "militarization." Militarization meant organizationally subordinating the police to the military once again. In the words of then police chief José Manuel Nuñez Amaral, militarization was a means for "incorporat[ing] the administration of the police force within the army, so that it will become subject to military law and discipline."[11] Militarization undermined the radical aims of the state-worker legislation, because it endowed all police with the same juridical status as military personnel (who were neither allowed to strike nor to hold superiors accountable on employment decisions). It also helped assuage the fears of the conservative factions of the military, who worried about the inclusion of left-leaning cadres of private security forces in the police. Finally, militarization made it easier to control conflict between the preventative and auxiliary police forces, who were struggling over power, influence, and the control of corruption networks.

But the police's militarization most harmed the nation in the long term by establishing conditions in which *greater* corruption and more unconstrained political policing might flower and by increasing the military's control over politics and society. First, this reform, like the inclusion of semiprivate firms in the police, added a further layer of fragmentation to the personnel and institutions of policing, which were already divided between judicial and preventative police. The problem was not merely the proliferation of distinct coercive forces but the coexistence of different police who answered to different levels of government. Having so many police with the authority to coerce citizens upped the ante and widened the extent of corrupt practices, as each separate cadre of police used its distinct institutional vantage point to capture a piece of the rent-seeking pie. As citizens suffered the brunt of this structure, they pressured the state on reforms.[12] This in turn spurred the formation of new police forces who might act more efficiently or conscientiously, including the formation of a secret police corps to deal with internal corruption,[13] further fragmenting the police into new local and national agencies.[14]

Fragmentation made it difficult to coordinate police services, as the rank and file answered to their own subleadership, with each complementary force then communicating horizontally with the Mexico City police department. This arrangement also fueled the wheels of extortion and corruption both within these organizations and between them and the Mexico City police chief.[15] Further complicating matters, because of the history of adding new police services in response to shifting political dilemmas or requisites associated with revolutionary or state consolidation, police services had become organized around just about every functional basis *but* territory. This in turn reduced accountability between citizens and the police. And while much of this situation owed to the declining democratic potential of the political system at large, it also owed to the fragmented structure of policing, in which citizens had little possibility to hold individual police accountable. There was no single police authority to whom citizens could turn to make complaints about general servicing in the city. Likewise the leaders of police suboperations were kept partially protected from the formal channels of complaints managed by the Inspección General de Policía because of their semiautonomous status.

Still, perhaps the greatest obstacle to accountability was the militarization of the police. The decision to subordinate Mexico City police to the military meant that, institutionally speaking, the party was bypassed almost entirely, as was the Departamento del Distrito Federal, the Mexico City mayor, who could have served as a natural point person for citizens' complaints about police abuses. This did not initially constitute a major problem when the military had its own representative and organization within the Partido de la Revolución (PRM) linking its interests and actions to those of the party and the state. But after the successful campaign to demilitarize the Mexican state in the early- to mid 1940s, and following the creation of the Confederación Nacional de Organizaciones Populares (CNOP) in 1943, the military became completely isolated from the party's deliberations, at least as a formal body with sectoral representation. With the military controlling the police but absent from representative political institutions, citizens had almost nowhere to turn in terms of police accountability during the 1950s, 1960s, and 1970s.

The problem was not merely that citizens had no clear democratic or institutional mechanisms for complaining about police or military abuse and corruption. The militarization of the police also reinforced a centralizing tendency in the state, linking a unified military with the Mexico City police in ways that allowed for greater corruption and a more direct connection between local and national repression of the country's citizens. Combined with the fragmentation of policing and the overlaps of local and national coercive apparatuses, these legacies set the stage for the repressive political policing and abuses of power that materialized in the 1960s, leading to the 1968 student crisis, the emergence of an active and mobilized civil society in the 1970s and 1980s, and ultimately, struggles for the democratization of the Mexican political system in the 1990s.

Democratization: A Break with the Past or More of the Same?

So did the successful democratization of the political system put an end to the problems of police corruption, impunity, and violence? Sadly, the answer is no. By 1994, just when Mexico City residents obtained the right to democratically elect a mayor, the country found itself awash in robberies, kidnappings, car theft, extortion, and other forms of violent and nonviolent crime, including rape and homicide, much of it concentrated in the capital city (Davis and Alvarado 1999). Between 1995 and 1998 alone, the overall crime rate in Mexico City nearly tripled (Fundación Mexicana para la Salud 1997:16), and much of the violence was fueled by police participation in criminal gangs and military involvement in drug trafficking. Why?

The answer has a lot to do with how hard it has proven to change institutions and practices on the ground, given the weight of political history, despite the advent of formal democratization. For one, the long-standing nature and institutionalization of police corruption in Mexico, leading to the police's own proclivities to harass the state's political enemies and operate above the law, have made citizens understandably distrustful of police motives and of legal institutions, giving incentive to citizens to resolve violations of the law at the street level through coercive bribery rather than through juridical procedures guaranteed by the formal system of justice. These informal practices have not only kept a system of bribery and police corruption afloat but have also fueled judicial weakness and undermined the courts and the rule of law ("Recetan a policía del DF" 2003; Piccato 2004). Thus, even though a different party may now be in power, many citizens continue to rely on old practices.

Similarly, it is important to recognize that regime democratization—in Mexico and elsewhere—will not necessarily eliminate all prior institutions and practices, police-related or otherwise. Even after democratic transition, many late developers still face their neoliberal political and economic futures with the old coercive networks intact, especially in the rank and file of the police and the military. After years of working without effective institutional constraints— as part of a bargain with the elite to police the nation's political and economic enemies to guarantee state power and economic progress—the coercive arms of the late developmental state have become well-ensconced in a networked world of impunity, corruption, and crime. This is the institutional legacy bequeathed to many countries of Latin America, and democracy has done little to reverse it.

In the case of Mexico City, in particular, the democratization of governance constituted part of the problem of accelerating violence and insecurity, not the solution to it, for precisely these reasons. Indeed, without the Partido Revolu- cionario Institucional (PRI) at the helm in the capital, and with the party weakened by electoral defeat, the stability of the entire system of complicity between the police and the state was called into question. With the PRI unable to control the state and its budget, the police turned away from the same informal practices of patronage and rent seeking that in prior decades had kept them loyal to the state. Without guarantees from the state that the fruits of corruption and bribery would continue to cycle through the system, police turned toward citizens—and criminal gangs—for sources of income, contrib- uting to more impunity and violence, or failing to stop it. Democratization also meant that the PRI's control of the justice system faltered, further creating a void in the institutions and practices that upheld the rule of law. The rapidly deteriorating situation was not, however, solely the result of disruptions in old institutional networks of control and emergent weaknesses in the justice sys- tem. It was also the product of the creation of alternative practices, including a call by the city's last PRI-appointed mayor to "militarize" the city's police force, using the army to purge the corps of its most corrupt elements (López Montiel 2000).[16] Such measures only created new conflicts within and between the police and the military, which further fueled an environment of insecurity as these two forces struggled over dominion and the singular control of illegal networks that in the past they had shared. With competition between the military and the police for control over an expanding big-money network of drug- and gun-related criminal activities, violence and conflict accelerated. This situation, eerily if not ironically, replicated many of the problems of the postrevolutionary past.

This is not to say that democratically elected officials gave up. When democratic elections in Mexico City brought Cuauhtémoc Cárdenas (son of Lázaro Cárdenas) of the Partido de la Revolución Democrática (PRD) into the mayor's office in 1997, citizens were drunk with democracy's potential, and expectations about cleaning up the police force and reducing corruption rose dramatically. Cárdenas, like his father, was committed to democracy and reform to respond to the concerns of the country's most vulnerable populations. One of his first objectives was to mount a capable and trustworthy police force, purged of old and corrupted elements and replaced with those loyal to the PRD rather than to the PRI. Wisely, Cárdenas insisted that he would not bring in the military to reform the police, although some of his most loyal allies were in the military (owing to his father's legacy), and his first police chief was a retired military man. This generated considerable skepticism about the veracity of his claim, bursting the bubble of euphoria about real change in a newly democratic city. However, the subsequent appointments of the civilians Alejandro Gertz Manero (as DF police chief) and Samuel del Villar (as attorney general for the DF) soon reinforced his commitment to a new strategy of reform. Shortly thereafter, Cárdenas introduced new structures for hiring and formulated alternative mechanisms for oversight of the police. These changes included the introduction of lie-detector tests for new and returning police personnel, forced resignations among the judicial police (those empowered to bring criminals to court), and a new system of tracking preventative police (those entrusted with guaranteeing social order) by neighborhood. Yet, unfortunately, the reform's ineffectiveness became visible almost immediately, owing in no small part to the institutional legacies created by Cárdenas's father's reforms fifty years earlier.

First came opposition from leading police officials, one of whom went directly to the press to vigorously defend the "moral quality" of the city's police despite his surprising public acknowledgment of the "occasional" problem of "judicial police . . . linkages with mafia dedicated to the robbery and reselling of automobiles and auto parts" (see "Defienden calidad moral de jefes policiacos" 1999). Second, beat cops protested against the new government's anticorruption measures by withdrawing their services completely so as to actually facilitate criminal offenses. Crime rates immediately went through the roof as a direct product of police inaction—and perhaps even of concerted action, as some officers became blatantly involved in criminal acts as a form of retribution.[17]

This situation of open rebellion owed not merely to the unparalleled power of the police and of police institutions reinforced by strong connections to the military. It also occurred because the reform efforts did not touch the heart of the problem: the government's incapacity to legally indict criminal elements so as to get to the source of violent disorder and criminality. And this problem owed not just to the fact that most beat cops refused to cooperate with the state in investigating drug and other gang-related crime. It also owed to the fact that the strong-armed efforts to purify the judicial police had alienated key elements in that other stage of the administration of justice, the courts. In short, there was even less cooperation among different crime-fighting elements in the justice system after democratization than before. This problem was acknowledged publicly by then police chief Gertz Manero, who lamented a lack of institutional or legal "coordination which [could] link [crime] prevention with investigation" or "articulate civil, business, and penal codes" ("Aplica la SPP plan de emergencia," 1999).

But democratic transition also created a new environment in which political competition became so stark that congressional compromises on legislation or policies enabling police or military reform became well-nigh impossible. Mexico's democratization produced a country governed by a National Congress divided almost equally between the three parties vying for national power (PRI, PRD, PAN [Partido Acción Nacional]), with one or the other in power on the level of the city, the region, and the nation. The absence of successful reform, moreover, had its impact on civil society. With years passing and democratic governments failing to make headway on crime because of past legacies, civil society started to take matters into its own hands, although traditional recourses, like citizen protest, hardly mattered. In Mexico City a 2004 mobilization of two hundred thousand citizens marching in the name of public security brought almost no response from then mayor Andres Manuel López Obrador, for many of the political reasons noted earlier having to do with his key political bases. The mayor's failure to accommodate a highly mobilized citizenry further alienated them from the state, while also making them cynical about the possibility of true reform from above and diminishing their enthusiasm for standard routes of political claim-making.

To some extent, this was a vicious circle: without citizens organized and struggling for change, elected officials did not go the extra mile to root out police corruption, continuing instead to let themselves be hamstrung by their own party rivalries and the sheer magnitude of the organizational reform at hand. Yet in the absence of concrete gains in police reform or the fight against corruption, citizens became further alienated from the government, instead choosing alternative means—ranging from the privatization of policing to vigilantism—to address security problems. By 2002 the number of private security firms operating in Mexico City neared one thousand, and these companies together employed about 22,500 private security guards.[18]

Citizens cannot be faulted for turning to the private sector to solve problems that the newly democratic government proved incapable of tackling. Yet the decision to bypass public police in favor of one's own private security forces has a dark side, especially for democracy. Such actions not only let corrupt police off the hook by decreasing citizen pressure on the state; they also sometimes generate more violence and insecurity, all the while raising troubling questions about democracy, equality, and the rule of law more generally. Whenever a large number of individuals start bearing arms due to their employment in private security services, and citizens themselves start to carry guns for self-protection, violent "solutions" to questions of public insecurity become the norm, thereby fueling the vicious circle of violence.[19] The fact that private police forces frequently comprise ex-military or ex-police officers further helps account for some of the transference in impunity and the frequent human rights abuses within the ranks of the private police.[20] The recourse to lynching and the emergence of vigilante attitudes constitute the logical extension of a mentality to privatize security and the rule of law.

Of course not all citizens resort to such questionable tactics. Many grassroots groups take the problems of police corruption and public insecurity to heart, seeking alternative solutions and new community practices at the neighborhood level. In this sense, citizens are both building on and reinforcing the democratic practices and advances that have resulted from many years of struggle against authoritarianism. The Mexico City government has supported citizen security meetings at the level of the delegation, with the goal of bringing residents and police together in democratic dialogue about how to best guarantee public security. The results have been limited, however. Citizens do not speak frankly about police corruption and impunity in their neighborhood when those very same police are sitting across the table, armed with their notepads and badges (identifying citizens by face, street, etc.). Therefore, some degree of police reform must already be in place before grassroots citizen participation can make a serious difference.

The power to change endemic police corruption and a downward spiraling situation of insecurity rests partly in civil society's institutional capacity to transform the system of policing and the overall administration of justice. This requires, among other things, legislative and policy actions in which the state and political parties also emerge as key players. But again, the paradox of democracy looms large: these kinds of goals are difficult to realize in a virulently competitive democratic context in which the vying political parties are unwilling to cooperate with each other and in which citizens routinely bypass formal political routes for evoking change. In the meantime, as police remain relatively unaccountable, the sense of alienation, fear, and defenselessness becomes a modus operandi for daily life in places like Mexico City.

Will a Vibrant Democracy Matter in a Globalized World?

The final remaining question is whether a sufficiently strengthened democracy and relegitimized political system involving cooperation between civil society and the state could really make a difference in alleviating violence and insecurity. As in earlier historical periods, evidence from Mexico suggests that economic dynamics also pose obstacles, especially those that work at the level of the city and that build on trends toward globalization.

Two factors linked to prior economic development models are key: the extent of informality in the national economy and the extent of income and social polarization. And like the problems of corruption, impunity, and the unrule of law, both trace their roots to past patterns and historical trajectories of political and economic development.

In prior decades late developers trod a very rocky economic road in which formal employment in industry paled in comparison to informal employment in small-scale commerce and other petty services, with government employment generally taking up the slack. Such sectoral imbalances have long plagued Mexico, with the capital city an employment magnet for service workers in government and commerce. With the neoliberal turn advancing a downsized state, and with the desire for greater global competitiveness driving many countries to reduce traditional sources of manufacturing and agriculture, these sectoral imbalances have become more extreme. Growing income polarization and a failure to recover from more than a decade of recession have also meant that real wages have remained stagnant and under- and unemployment have been on the rise. These problems have proven particularly severe in Mexico City, a locale hit especially hard by the collapse of the import-substitution industrialization model.

The city's industrial sector has been mortally wounded by the opening of the economy and the relocation of Mexico City factories to the border areas closer to new markets favored by the government's export-led model. As a result, many previously employed in the city's industrial sector have looked elsewhere for income. Owing to Mexico's age structure, youth unemployment has been an especially big concern; it signals a demographic problem that has fueled the rise of youth gang activities and further contributed to criminality and public insecurity.

Similarly, the economic crisis and global pressures to liberalize the economy by cutting public expenditures and advocating the privatization of public services have contributed to the problem. In an economically squeezed environment, state downsizing has made it difficult for democratically elected authorities to raise public sector salaries, tempting police to further engage in crime. It is not uncommon to find police who act as frontmen for criminal gangs or who routinely extort criminals for kickbacks whether they do or do not arrest them.[21] Pressures for collusion with criminals accelerated in the 1990s, especially when the Drug Enforcement Agency of the United States achieved considerable success in cutting off direct supplies between Colombia and the United States, thereby inadvertently shifting much of the drug trade into Mexico (Andreas 1998). Slowly but surely drug money began to infiltrate a variety of agencies of the state and society, including the military and the police (Piñeyro 2004; Pimentel 2000; González Ruiz, López Portillo V., and Yáñez 1994; Kaplan 1991).[22]

However, the lure of employment in the illegal drug (and gun) trade is just as likely to entrap citizens as the police, owing to the sectoral changes associated with neoliberal economic restructuring. With fewer job prospects in manufacturing and many new employment opportunities beyond the educational reach of those laid off from factories, ever more Mexican citizens are being thrown into the informal sector. In the historic central district of Mexico City alone, the number of street vendors is estimated at fifty thousand, a number that has more than quadrupled since the pre-NAFTA date of 1991 (Baroni 2007:207). Such employment, which barely meets subsistence needs, is typically labeled "illegal" by the state, just as protectionist barriers drop, as fewer domestic goods for sale are produced, and as the globalization of the illicit goods trade picks up the slack. As a result, much informal employment is physically and sectorally situated in an illicit world of violence and impunity, not just because of the illegality of many of the goods traded but also because the big-money trade in guns, drugs, and other internationally sold contraband products generally necessitates its own armed forces for protection. The result is often the development of clandestine connections between local police, internationally linked mafias, and the informal sector, as well as the isolation of certain territorial areas as locations for these activities (Davis 2006c).

This illicit network of reciprocities, much of it unfolding on a global scale, and the territorial concentration of dangerous illegal activities in highly circumscribed neighborhoods of Mexico City that function as no-man's-lands outside state control, further drive the problems of impunity, insecurity, and violence. These dangerous areas often sit nestled against old central business districts where local chambers of commerce face a declining manufacturing base and are especially desperate to attract high-end corporate investors and financial services. This leads to a clash of forces and development models, and growing problems of insecurity, that can thwart the developmental aims both of would-be global cities and of a national investor class desperate for a new way of generating global capital and visibility. In Mexico these clashes have even spilled into the electoral arena, as pro-liberalizers on the national scale want to turn the capital city into a global mecca for foreign investors, while local authorities try to balance these concerns with those of the middle classes who fear declining security conditions and those of the urban poor (informally employed and otherwise) who are caught in between.

The Paradox of Democratization; or,
Full Circle from Cárdenas to Cárdenas

Many of the tensions over insecurity and the future of Mexico City first hit the public agenda in the mid-1990s, just when the city and the nation began fully embracing political and economic liberalization. In Mexico City most observers cite 1994 as the year in which criminality and public insecurity burst out of control. This was the year NAFTA changed several key aspects of the macroeconomy, directly hurting the more protected industries located in the capital. The 1990s also marked the decade in which the Mexico City government democratized with a series of constitutional changes introduced to empower a local consultative body with legislative power (the Asamblea Legislativa del Distrito Federal, ALDF), followed by a move to allow the direct election of the mayor for the first time since 1928.

So far, little progress has been made in balancing these tensions between democratization and insecurity. Many streets remain dangerous, and daily excursions from home to work can be unsafe, with murders and assassinations relatively unchecked and even the Mexico City police fearful of entering certain neighborhoods. A steady inflow of street vendors and other underemployed service workers fills most of the city's streets beyond capacity, reproducing the old-style informality and a mix of rich and poor more associated with past epochs and traditional third world cities than with a modern, globalizing metropolis. In other words, old problems of insecurity sit side by side with new urban megaprojects and other new urban infrastructural developments fomented by global capitalists intent on transforming the city into yet another world-recognized global city. We could identify these two distinct global networks as liberal and illiberal rather than legal and illegal, because the former are defined as legitimate in the eyes of economic liberalization proponents, primarily because they are constituted by a legally accountable network of corporate and property investors who operate in a global world of regulations, property rights, and formal contract law. The latter are defined as illiberal because they are considered illegitimate partakers of the global economy, given that they are constituted by networks of illicit (and often small-scale) investors whose global supply chain revolves around black-market, undercover, clandestine, or violence-prone activities in which the rule of law remains elusive.

Neither set of forces is peculiar to Mexico (see Wallace and Latcheva 2006). Both are present in cities and nations all over the developing world, which continues to be caught in the orbit of global trade and capital flows, licit and illicit. But they are now the key protagonists in Mexico City. It is further worth noting that these conflicts and struggles are usually as much about control over space as they are about the direction, or globalization, of the economy. To the extent that these struggles over space are linked to economic livelihoods and the potential for huge profits, the stakes are quite high. Yet precisely because the conflict involves illiberal forces who shun the rule of law, it can be quite violent and dangerous, and such battles are not easily remedied by urban politics, democratic or otherwise. For all these reasons Mexico and its capital city continue to be plagued by violence, and citizens face a downward spiral of insecurity, despite concerted efforts and high expectations. Since President Felipe Calderon took office in 2004, the number of annual murders linked to the drug trade has climbed with estimates suggesting a record six thousand persons killed in 2008 (Whitaker 2009:1). Violence has reached such heights that questions of whether Mexico is a "failed state" have emerged in policy circles, bringing diplomatic urgency to the problems of violence that now plague the country.

A study by the Cato Institute further affirms that "violence in Mexico, mostly related to the trade in illegal drugs, has risen sharply in recent years and shows signs of becoming even worse," in part because Calderon's deployment of the army has neither crippled the organized drug trade nor undermined the complicity of "local police forces, which are [suggested to be] thoroughly corrupted by drug money" (Carpenter 2009:1). Observers long known for their prudence in assessing Latin America's social and political condition have weighed in with equally somber tones. Larry Birns, director of the Council on Hemispheric Affairs, called the situation in Mexico "a sickening vertigo into chaos and plunder," while Peter Hakim, president of the Inter-American Dialogue, stated that "the entire population is very scared" (Brice 2009:1). While not all of this violence is concentrated in the capital, where the legacies of police corruption interacting with drug violence have their origins, Mexico City still hosts its share. In early May 2008, the residents of Mexico City awoke to the news that gunmen, acting on behalf of drug cartels, had assassinated Mexico's national chief of police outside his home in the city, the fourth such assassination in the course of a single week, an act that would later be attributed to infiltration of the police services by drug informants (Roig-Franzia 2008).

Conclusion

In light of these developments, it is hard to be optimistic about a way forward toward peace and security in the region, despite clear democratic gains in Mexico and elsewhere.[23] Given the political and economic legacy bequeathed by late industrialization, many Latin American cities and countries are in for a rough time. Democratic institutions and global market practices that seem to bring civic engagement and rising standards of living in the advanced capitalist world have not proven powerful or resilient enough to catapult Mexico and its Latin American neighbors out of the treacherous stranglehold of their developmental past. To do so would require a complete break with the global economic connections and local social or spatial practices that sustain violence. It would also entail a rethinking of prior assumptions about the scale of political and economic decision making, as well as about the importance of linking previously antagonistic actors in search of common solutions—whether they be civil society actors linked to the state or informal-sector advocates linked to high-end investors in services or real estate development.

To achieve any or all of these ends will take a new type of politics, one that may even jettison old democratic structures, practices, and discourses. At minimum, we must stop thinking that the mere existence of democracy will do much to reverse the violence spreading across the continent. Only then can citizens and politicians begin mobilizing to do something different.

Notes

Portions of the research for this essay were supported by grants from the John D. and Catherine T. MacArthur Foundation and the Carnegie Corporation of New York. I thank Arturo Alvarado, my fellow principal investigator on the first grant, for comments on the general ideas presented in this essay. All interpretations are mine.

1. This was best exemplified in the 1917 constitutional reform, crafted by Venustiano Carranza, that created two distinct police forces existing side by side: the judicial police (*policía judicial*) and the preventative police (*policía preventiva*). The purpose of this reform was to take the power of arrest out of the hands of beat cops, many of whom traced their positions and loyalties to the Porfiriato, and to give those police who were closer to the executive branch—that is, the judicial police—more powers of investigation.

2. A little discussed but well-documented fact is that almost all Mexico City police chiefs after 1915, with the exception of a handful over a span of almost sixty years, were high-level military generals rotating back and forth between the police and the military, some taking side trips to the congress or other major posts in the executive branch.

3. Pedro Almada sought and received funds from Calles to buy a key Mexico City daily for the purposes of generating pro-Calles political propaganda and keeping other political discourses out of the public sphere.

4. Many of these new rank-and-file police came from the provinces, and many from the north, because they fought with Carranza, Calles, or Alvaro Obregon. Thus they had little allegiance to the population they were policing, which translated into fewer social constraints on extortion. That large numbers of redeployed military veterans and other revolutionary loyalists joined the police just at the time when the postrevolutionary government began imposing a variety of urban reg ulations on the use of paper money, price gouging, and the like—to reverse some of the urban economic anarchy that had accompanied the revolution—further placed the police in a prime position for soliciting *mordidas*.

5. Before the 1940s the tenure of police chiefs tended to be erratic, shifting between relatively long terms in office (three to four years) to extraordinarily short stints (some lasting only a few weeks). Only around 1950 do police chief terms begin to coincide with mayoral and/or presidential administrations. This tells us something important about the volatility and institutional instability of police servicing, which was both the cause and the effect of infighting and political instability within the revolutionary state and its leadership and correlated with changing political conditions more generally.

6. Among the police chiefs involved in this gang was Valente Quintana, a former private detective who was appointed police chief in 1929 and who, perhaps because of his involvement with criminal gangs, was the first and last civilian police chief for decades. In addition to serving as a conduit to large sources of money that could potentially be redistributed among revolutionary leaders, he was known to have been involved in dirty tricks against revolutionary competitors.

7. Observers reported that the "inefficiency of the police in the capital [meant that] automobiles of tourists in front of the embassy (as well as cars belonging to members of the staff) have repeatedly been broken into," while reports of stolen items from foreign tourists were reaching new heights. See Archivo General de la Nación (AGN), Ramo Gobernación, 812.105/16, letter from Pierre de L. Boal, Chargé d'Affaires ad interim, to the Honorable Secretary of State, Washington, 17 October 1939. For more on the development of tourism as an industry, why Cárdenas supported it, and how he balanced the need to sell Mexican culture with his administration's nationalist ethos, see Berger 2006.

8. *Trabajadores de base* (base workers) were defined in terms of their location at the lower end of the pay, autonomy, and decision-making hierarchy. *Trabajadores de confianza* (workers of confidence) were better paid and made decisions on the job requiring greater skills and discretion. See Davis 2004:298.

9. AGN, Ramo Presidentes (Cárdenas); 544.211 (Empleados Públicos).

10. For more discussion of the class and military reactions to Cárdenas's efforts to restructure state-worker legislation, see Davis 2004: chap. 5.

11. AGN, Ramo Gobernación, 812.105/16, letter from Pierre de L. Boal, Chargé d'Affaires ad interim, to the Honorable Secretary of State, Washington, 17 October 1939.

12. Citizens were quite aware of the problem of growing corruption, as were party leaders and the president himself. As early as 1959 citizens began organizing themselves as advocates for police reform, writing letters to the authorities including the extensive documentation of police corruption and abuses of power. One of the most high-profile organizations of this sort was the Coalición Defensora de los Derechos Ciudadanos, located in the Colonia Moctezuma in the Distrito Federal, which started a massive campaign (1959–62) to inform the president and the local citizenry about the corruption, extortion, and sickness of the police at all levels. Yet their efforts hardly made a dent in the situation. After 1959 practically every

police chief who came to office identified himself as beginning a new (and "final") campaign for the "moralization" of the police. But over the years the conditions worsened, with corruption growing out of control and many of the same police chiefs who initiated moralization campaigns later identified as among the worst culprits. These citizens lamented that "little has been achieved [in combating police corruption] because the police, given their lack of culture and troubled background, continue believing that they have neither the authority nor capacity to guarantee citizens the tranquility one might expect from a conscientious and honorable police." See AGN, Galería de Presidentes (Adolfo López Mateos) vol. 652 exp. 542.1/104.

13. That is, the secret police (*policía secreta*) were initially formed in the 1920s to "police the police." The same logic manifested again in the 1930s, with the newly created Dirección de Investigación y Seguridad Política in the Distrito Federal, an organizational force for investigating corrupt police as much as political enemies. And finally, these same aims lay behind the creation of a new force of federal police in 1946, called the Dirección Federal de Seguridad (DFS), who worked directly for the president (thereby bypassing the corrupted Mexico City police department) and took over the job of investigating corrupt city police. With city and agency police so involved in corruption, the DFS soon became the principal arm of political policing for the entire party state, a function well represented by the role the DFS played years later in investigating and attacking student leaders and political dissidents during the 1968 uprisings. As such the formation of the secret police, and its fragmentation and expansion over time, strengthened the authoritarian ethos within the Mexican state apparatus.

14. In the late 1960s a leading Mexico City daily, *Excelsior*, contained an article that listed the following combination of local and federal police forces as active in the capital: "In actuality, in addition to the preventative and repressive police—both uniformed [i.e. beat cops] and judicial, respectively—'security' forces who work for the following local and federal agencies also exist and operate in the city: those employed by the ministries or agencies of federal security, the federal judiciary, narcotics, secret service, agricultural resources, military courts, civilian air forces, federal highways, forestry, internal revenue, migration, defense, railroads, the Bank of Mexico, industrial police, auxiliary police, banking police, etc. Without even including the range of private police." See Ravelo, 1968.

15. By the early 1960s the system of kickbacks was in full swing. Internal documents registered in the Ministry of National Defense indicate that going monthly payments from the Policia Bancaria Industrial (PBI) leadership to Mexico City's police chief were thought to be 75,000 pesos monthly, with the auxiliary police head receiving 125,000 pesos monthly in direct bribes, and the DF police chief taking 75,000 pesos from them as well. These monies came in addition to the 400,000 pesos extracted from the police lieutenants of each company under the police chief's jurisdiction and a reported payment of close to 500,000 pesos monthly

from the head of the army's Second, Ninth, and Twenty-Seventh Divisions. See the Secretaria de Defensa Nacional (SEDENA) Archives, personnel file on Gral. Luis Cueto Ramírez, expediente XI/III/1–543, letter to President Díaz Ordaz from Lázaro Cárdenas, 15 November 1968.

16. This response came partly in reaction to social movements clamoring for the revitalization of democratic structures and practices in the city, which hoped to see the fruits of their labor realized in legislation passed to fully democratize Mexico City governance starting in 1997. With crime rates skyrocketing after 1994, and with popular elections for a democratically elected mayor to be held in two years, it seemed evident to Villareal and the PRI leadership that the party that had the most to offer in crime fighting or guaranteeing public security might have the best shot at winning the city once democratic rights were established (González Ruiz 1998:90).

17. The level of calculated impunity in the first several weeks after the introduction of the reform was so extreme that Gertz Manero was compelled to publicly acknowledge that Mexico City's "40,000 member force [wa]s out of control" (Gregory 1999:4).

18. Data on private police drawn from interviews and documentation provided by the Secretaría de Seguridad Pública in Mexico City during summer 2002.

19. In 2002, when statistics were first compiled, Mexico City governing officials saw more than a fourfold rise (from five to twenty-two) in monthly complaints against private police between May and November of that year.

20. Statistics from the Registration Office suggested that one-third of the personnel (30 percent) in private security forces came from the military and police ranks. In personal interviews with several representatives from private security firms, the numbers were closer to 50 percent. Adriana Robles Zapata, Sociedad Mexicana de la Capacitación Profesional (SOMESCA), interview with the author, 21 November 2002.

21. Police often become involved in criminal operations because it will earn them much greater remuneration than their measly professional pay. This helps explain why foreign consultants uniformly suggest that raising police salaries constitutes an essential first step in professionalizing the police and gaining control of impunity. But such policies have not been seriously pursued, partly owing to the fact that macroeconomic policy constraints associated with the economic liberalization of the country have limited public-sector investment capacities.

22. While international drug trafficking and the sale of illegal drugs in Mexico has existed for decades, and some say since the 1940s (Sadler 2000), it had remained a relatively low-profile sector of the national economy until recently (Astorga 2000; Benítez Manaut 2000).

23. Although there are grounds for pessimism, I am not suggesting that scholars and policymakers have given up hope, or that there are no new ideas available that might lead to more optimism about the future. For a further discussion of possible policy options and new political strategies that seek to reverse conditions of urban violence, see Davis 2008, 2009.

End of Discussion

Violence, Participatory Democracy, and the Limits of Dissent in Colombia

MARY ROLDÁN

Enrique Arias and Daniel Goldstein suggest in the introduction to the current volume that the time may have come "to assess critically the usefulness of the concept of 'democracy' for understanding contemporary Latin American political society," given the emergence and proliferation of new forms of violence in a region in which democratic governments are at least a generation old. More provocatively, Arias and Goldstein suggest that violence may *not* be—as analysts have typically posited—"an indicator of democratic 'failure' " in the region, but rather an "integral part of contemporary Latin American democracies" and evidence of a "violent pluralism" emerging throughout the hemisphere.

Colombia offers perhaps the most extreme version of violent pluralism in Latin America—a many-decades-old democracy marked by selectively high levels of violence. Unlike many of its regional peers, Colombia has rarely hosted military dictatorships or authoritarian governments. It is characterized, on the one hand, by regularly elected civilian governments and one of the oldest and most stable two-party political systems in the Western Hemisphere.[1] On the other, however, it is also home to Latin America's oldest and largest leftist guerilla insurgency, most powerful paramilitary presence, and greatest production of illicit drugs (Palacios and Safford 2001). In recent years the escalation of violence and the proliferation of illicitly financed armed groups of the left, right, and the purely criminal prompted dire assessments of Colombia as a "failed" state or one on the verge of imminent collapse. Yet despite selective, intense intimidation, regular elections occurred without fail and new political movements such as the left-of-center Polo Democratico Alternativo (PDA) and the National Indigenous Alliance emerged, successfully capturing significant electoral support. Furthermore, previously ignored or politically marginalized groups (ethnic minorities, gays and lesbians, evangelical Christians) achieved important levels of visibility, office, and national political influence.[2]

If Colombian democracy has long coexisted with persistent violence, what distinguishes a new or emergent phenomenon of violent pluralism from what has existed before? This essay argues that in contemporary Colombia violent pluralism describes the growing resort to authoritarian and antidemocratic policies by the Colombian state in response to the proliferation of violence and to the emergence of grassroots demands from citizens most affected by violence for a greater participatory role in shaping the policies used to confront it.

Colombia's emergence as an epicenter of the global drug trade has fed the proliferation of criminal organizations and privately financed paramilitary groups and the expansion of already established guerilla groups, as well as the ability of these groups to undermine, co-opt, and manipulate politics and government in new and unprecedented ways. At the same time, citizens trapped in areas in which the proliferation of violent groups has combined to constrain even limited democratic participation have increasingly mobilized to demand the resolution of conflict through more inclusive and participatory understandings of democracy, rather than through an increased use of arms. The combined effect of the emergence of a discourse of terrorism and the conflation of counterdrug and counterinsurgency efforts into a single military objective, however, has enabled Colombian governments to dismiss grassroots demands for an expansion of democratic participation and to justify the restriction of civil liberties and dissent in a manner more typical of authoritarian regimes than of democracies.[3] Violent pluralism describes the situation that ensues when demands for democratic, nonviolent alternatives to conflict resolution that can bring into dialogue multiple, divergent voices are met with resistance by the state, while the civilians who embrace a nonviolent approach are treated as potential enemies threatening the integrity of Colombian democracy.

This essay grounds an examination of the workings of violent pluralism in contemporary Colombia in the trajectory and experience of a grassroots solidarity movement known as the Oriente No-Violence Movement. The No-Violence Movement emerged in response to a dramatic escalation of violence in the late 1990s in Oriente, a subregion comprised of twenty-three municipalities in the northwestern Colombian department, or state, of Antioquia. Known as "one of Colombia's richest regions" due to its central location, major roads, transportation facilities, and a concentration of water resources for hydroelectric power generation,[4] Oriente became the object of narcotics traffickers and of armed groups such as the ELN (National Liberation Army), the FARC (Revolutionary Armed Forces of Colombia), and right-wing paramilitary blocs, who established a presence in the region as early as the 1970s. Yet despite the proliferation of armed groups in the area and a long history of state indifference to local grievances and demands, Oriente was notable for its consistently higher-than-average voter turnouts and a vibrant and active civil society that stretched at least as far back as La Violencia, when the region's inhabitants first began to explore democratic forms of organization outside the clientelist party networks that have historically shaped individual political participation in Colombia.

Oriente's search for suprapartisan and socially just alternatives to community development were embodied in entities such as local *juntas de acción comunal* (communal action committees), civic action campaigns, ecclesial base communities, peasant producer cooperatives, and women's social networks from the 1960s through the 1990s. Participation in these social organizations was a direct response, first, to the overweening power of the state owned utility giant ISA (Interconexión S. A.) that determined the distribution and use of local resources and energy policy without taking into account local opinions or needs, and, second, to the government's limited ability to provide protection for local citizens' lives and livelihoods when special interests or armed violence threatened these.

By 1998, however, Oriente had emerged as one of the regions in Colombia most severely affected by massive internal displacement, massacres, electoral intimidation, and land mines. The twenty-three mayors of the municipalities that made up the administrative jurisdiction elicited and garnered broad support from members of local women's groups, Catholic Church dioceses, NGOs, peasant producer associations, and cooperatives for the creation of a solidarity movement to press for the right to explore the use of humanitarian accords to resolve what had devolved into a major humanitarian crisis. Support for the mayors' initiative crossed partisan, ideological, and class lines because the violence that had begun to affect Oriente's residents was qualitatively different from what they had lived with in previous decades. Despite the presence of armed groups since the 1960s and the many-decades-old conflict with ISA over land, energy prices, forcible flooding, and top-down development policies, most of Oriente's inhabitants had experienced violence only selectively and sporadically. This changed dramatically after 1997 when expanding armed groups—increasingly in competition with each other to control municipal revenues, territory, transportation routes, and the flow of illicit commodities across the region—spurred a dramatic escalation of violence that indiscriminately targeted entire villages and towns, barred the entry and exit of people, food, and assistance for weeks at a time, conducted indiscriminate massacres, and forcibly recruited child soldiers from local families.

Oriente represents a microcosm of the difficulties of forging democracy in Colombia in the midst of violence, the long-term efforts of local citizens to exercise their democratic rights and expand the definition of democracy in spite of it, and the ways in which a fragile coexistence between democracy and violence has given way to an unprecedented situation of violent pluralism in recent years, prompted by global and local changes in the sources and targets of violence. Oriente's No-Violence Movement also lays bare how the persistence of violence in contemporary democracies may not necessarily represent the "failure" of democracy, but rather the simultaneous presence of several incommensurate visions or understandings of democracy and democratic practice.

One vision in Colombia embodied in the attitude of the Colombian central state, its security forces, the dominant economic groups, and traditional party leaders appears to understand democracy quite narrowly as regular electoral contests mediated by participation in hierarchically organized, officially recognized political organizations such as parties. Some amount of fraud, corruption, and undue influence has historically enabled violence to coexist with and shape the contours of this more limited and clientelist form of democracy. Whether paramilitary or guerilla interests determine the distribution of public-sector jobs or the investment of locally generated revenues does not fundamentally alter or threaten this form of democracy in which power is exercised from top to bottom by political bosses and in which the ability of ordinary citizens to protest exclusionary arrangements remains limited.

A different vision, embodied in the 1991 Constitution and embraced by Oriente's No-Violence Movement, in contrast, understands democracy as participatory rather than limited or hierarchical. The No-Violence Movement was made possible in large part because Oriente, having existed in a situation of selective and sporadic violence for several decades with little support from the state, had forged "an important tradition of citizen participation . . . social organizations, public administration and local governments that [were] relatively well developed and trained in comparison with other [Colombian] territories" (Delegación de la Comisión Europea para Colombia y Ecuador 2004). Participatory democracy with its emphasis on transparency, consensus-based participation, and the decentralization of power is fundamentally at odds with the essence of exclusionary or clientelist democracy.

These contrasting visions of democratic practice have produced a lethal catch-22 in Colombia: a variety of democratic institutions (civic action committees, cooperatives, municipal action groups, peasant producer associations, etc.) have been promoted by sectors of the Colombian state and civil society as an antidote to violence since the period of extended civil war known as La Violencia (1948–58). Yet paradoxically, when citizens such as Oriente's use nonviolent democratic means to press for the redress of grievances or to demand from the government greater inclusion in decisions affecting local livelihoods and lives, their actions are interpreted as a challenge to the state and a threat to democracy.[5] Indeed, Oriente's insistence on including different political voices and all the armed actors in the resolution of conflict has been understood not as a defense of democracy against the threat of violence, but as a challenge to the existing balance of power and even, in the language of President Álvaro Uribe Vélez, as a "terrorist" act inimical to the survival of "formal" democracy.

Dismissed as the naive flunkies of armed interests, subversives in the making, and collaborators or "shields" for guerilla groups, citizens searching for inclusive, nonviolent solutions to conflict have emerged as targets twice over: of the armed groups whose tactics and ideology they repudiate, and of the state whose obligation it is to protect and further democratic deepening, but which intuits mobilizations from below as a threat to the supposedly democratic status quo. Violent pluralism has emerged as the state's default response.

Organizing for Life: The Genesis of a No-Violence Movement

In September 2001 Oriente's twenty-three mayors publicly announced their decision to organize a municipal solidarity coalition to protest the dramatic escalation of human rights violations due to armed groups operating in various Oriente towns. Although not all towns of Oriente were equally touched by the violence, mayors in unaffected towns joined in solidarity with their colleagues who were impeded in their work on a daily basis by armed pressure to draw the regional and central governments' attention to the broader reverberations of the region's humanitarian crisis. Although levels of violence varied dramatically in the region, no municipality remained entirely unaffected by the economic blockades and massacres taking place in towns such as San Carlos, Cocorná, or San Luis. As the number of internally displaced persons reached unprecedented proportions, towns bordering on the areas most directly affected experienced escalating demands for emergency food, shelter, and medical assistance by desperate survivors seeking succor and refuge.

In organizing the No-Violence Movement the Oriente mayors sought, in the long term, to replace an armed response to conflict with dialogue and negotiation. The mayors also pressed the state for the right of local authorities to engage in humanitarian rapprochements (*acercamientos*) with the various armed actors. The demand for a greater local role in the determination of matters of public order was legal and guaranteed in the 1991 Constitution as part of a broader project to strengthen local government and decentralize power in Colombia, but the Colombian state met the mayors' demand to exercise their authority on behalf of local constituents with resistance and suspicion. Beyond the immediate solution to the crisis created by unprecedented armed competition in their municipalities from 1997 to 2001, the Oriente mayors ultimately wanted to convert the entire subregion into a national peace laboratory underwritten by European Union (EU) economic and political support. A nationally recognized and internationally supported peace laboratory would be the only way to institutionalize the experiments in participatory democracy they had taken as their mandate on being elected to office in 1997.

The centerpiece of Oriente's experiment in participatory democracy was the *asamblea comunitaria* (community assembly), collective gatherings called by the mayor, civic leaders, or the parish priest in which townspeople and interested parties could give expression to their grievances or concerns and exchange ideas about the issues facing their municipalities and the best way to handle these.[6] As a former civic leader from the municipality of Nariño interviewed by the sociologist Ana Maria Jaramillo described it, "the *asamblea comunitaria* functions as a kind of public space where it is possible to give expression to and articulate the fears and uncertainties people feel, and where participants can come together to give their backing to the town's main authority, the mayor, and undertake actions that will demonstrate their strength as a community to the armed actors."[7]

Like local authorities and civilian populations in other strife-torn parts of Colombia, Oriente's mayors and townspeople were attempting to escape a critical dilemma: despite the popular direct election of mayors instituted in 1988, the decentralization of revenues and powers from the central to the local state government levels, and the Constitution of 1991's recognition of a greater arena of jurisdiction vested in local government bodies and authorities, the central government in practice had been wary of locally initiated efforts to deal with any aspect of Colombia's drawn-out conflict. Local attempts to establish dialogues or negotiate arrangements with armed groups for humanitarian purposes were frowned on by Bogotá as an unwarranted usurpation of executive prerogative or were taken as an indication of surreptitious collaboration with the guerillas or paramilitaries, even when the central government often proved powerless or unwilling to effectively impede repeated human rights violations or guarantee respect for local lives or the law.[8]

Local efforts at expanding the public sphere have a long history in Oriente, a region historically bound by strong familial, social, and religious networks with a tradition of mobilizing around common issues affecting the subregion. Oriente had been settled from the nineteenth century through the early twentieth by migrant families seeking employment on incipient estates and mining ventures who hoped to someday stake a homesteading claim to receive title for clearing and cultivating public lands. The vast majority of inhabitants were subsistence or small farmers who produced agricultural goods for local consumption and export to Medellín. Struggles over land tenure and the control of resources and jobs occurred throughout Oriente from the 1930s to the 1950s during the emergence of large-scale cattle ranching and the monopolization of woods and land by mining companies engaged in oil and gold extraction. The building of some of Colombia's largest hydroelectric dams in the late 1950s and 1960s and their effects on the landscape, on the survival of smallholder production and extraction, and on the physical integrity of particular towns also spurred conflicts over land use, energy access, and fair economic practices.

Vestiges of Conservative paramilitary forces armed and mobilized by local economic interest groups and selective sectors of the regional and local authorities, as well as remnants of Liberal guerillas who refused to accept an amnesty offered by the military government of General Gustavo Rojas Pinilla in 1953, remained intermittently active in eastern Antioquia during the 1950s.[9] What is notable about Oriente's experience during La Violencia, however, is the way in which local inhabitants gave voice to their analysis of what happened in their region and the role of the state in fomenting or failing to block the armed groups who acted with impunity to push people off land, extort, kill, and insinuate themselves into positions of local political influence. It is against this backdrop of a kind of collective local memory and *longue durée* that the discourse and ideals deployed by Oriente's current no-violence leaders must be read.

The towns of Oriente were among those that most severely felt the violence between 1948 and 1953. Although the state attributed the high rate of civilian casualties to the absence of a military presence in the area, local inhabitants saw as the problem not the absence of the armed forces but rather the latter's tendency to abuse their authority or to tolerate the violent actions of privately organized, right-wing armed groups known as *contrachusmas*. In the 1950s the state responded to these accusations by justifying the existence of right-wing armed groups in much the same terms as the later governor Álvaro Uribe Vélez would do in the 1990s, when regional officers and members of the state's armed forces were accused of tolerating or being complicit with human rights violations committed by privately financed rural self-defense units known as *Convivirs* and the AUC (Autodefensas Unidas de Colombia).[10] "They are not exactly *contrachusmas*," the governor would declare during La Violencia, "but men acting in defense of the interests they have created in that region."[11]

Eastern Antioquia's petitioners, however, refused to accept the government's characterization of the paramilitaries or their objectives as legitimate. They countered that the point of the *contrachusmas* was to push poor settlers such as themselves off the lands they had cleared for subsistence agriculture to convert these into cattle estates and to privatize control of natural resources such as the area's abundant woods and quarries. They rejected the suggestion that locals were somehow sympathetic to the itinerant Liberal guerilla bands that sporadically roamed their areas and exacted contributions of food and supplies simply because they shared the same territorial space. They also denied being "full of revolutionary ideas," as some officers of the state asserted to dismiss their complaints and justify policies to "cleanse" (*sanear*) the region of squatters and settlers (Roldán 2002:158). Oriente's petitioners justified their appeal to the state for the redress of their grievances by invoking a kind of contractual arrangement that governed the relations between citizens and the state. "Our lives are dominated by a lifetime of physical effort, exerted to forge wealth and [build] the homeland [*patria*] in inhospitable regions," they insisted. Oriente's inhabitants then went on to articulate what they believed were the mutual obligations that governed the relationship between citizens and the state: "After years of arduous effort bereft of the smallest comforts . . . and [considering] the payment of our taxes and obligatory contributions" it was the state's duty to "safeguard our lives and tranquility" (Roldán 2002:166). Decades later Oriente's inhabitants would once more reiterate their belief in the state and assert, "We [citizens] are the State. Because the State is everyone" (qtd. in Gutierrez 2004).

Oriente's petitioners were careful to represent themselves as law-abiding citizens, vested in a private-property regime, who recognized the right of the state to tax them and their own duty to contribute to the nation's economic development. But as several local landowners whose properties were besieged by guerilla attacks, yet who refused to hire paramilitaries on the governor's advice, reminded the state: "The monopoly of force is the sole prerogative of the authorities" (Roldán 2002:156). Inhabitants of eastern Antioquia also repeatedly pointed out to the regional authorities that when the state allowed privately armed groups to act in its name or usurp its authority, it compromised its legitimacy. When the regional state proceeded to do exactly this, the townspeople of municipalities such as San Carlos and San Luis responded by turning away from the clientelist politics they derisively referred to as *politiquería* and joined third party movements (such as the National Popular Alliance, ANAPO) in the 1960s and 1970s or redirected their energies into municipal committees dedicated to lobbying for and pursuing policies that would further nonpartisan, collective local interests.[12] Eastern women were particularly active in becoming important local civic leaders, participating in *juntas de acción comunal* and as *promotoras de salud* (local health promoters) in the adoption of long-distance radio education programs such as Radio Sutatenza and the ideals of Acción Cultural Popular (ACPO).[13] Civic movements organized to defend human rights and represent local concerns regarding the impact of large-scale development projects in the 1980s and 1990s built on these local attempts to foment the creation of a pool of local civic leaders and organizations and to repudiate the use of arms by private citizens as a valid means to resolve conflict or defend local property and life.

By the late 1990s, when violence had reached an unprecedented pitch in Oriente and mayors under threat of death sought support from their beleaguered constituents for a solidarity movement to advance the cause of nonviolence, Oriente's inhabitants could draw on over four decades of experience with participation in a wide variety of civic mobilizations and grassroots organizations. The citizens who answered the mayors' solidarity call did not necessarily belong to institutionalized or recognized formal groups like labor unions or NGOs, but they shared a common experience of severe violence and of lost faith in the use of arms to resolve Oriente's humanitarian crisis. Some had participated in ad hoc civic action campaigns to pressure the state energy company ISA/ISAGEN to lower energy rates for local residents who on average paid nearly double what other residents of Antioquia did for electricity, although they inhabited the region in which 30–35 percent of Colombia's electricity is generated. Some had taken part in civic action campaigns and in stoppages to protest the forcible flooding of towns for the building of hydroelectric dams in the 1970s and 1980s and had been radicalized by the murder of civic leaders and the loss of friends and neighbors to intimidation (Ruiz n.d.). Some were members of peasant producer cooperatives set up with the support of European Union Economic Cooperation agencies to promote nontraditional and sustainable crop development whose livelihoods had been destroyed by the armed takeover and forcible closure of community stores (*tiendas comunitarias*) during the economic blockades imposed by armed groups between 1997 and 2001. Some were rural teachers influenced by Paulo Freire's *Pedagogy of the Oppressed* or state and municipal employees who belonged to unions and had been harassed and intimidated by the armed forces and various armed groups (Hernando Martinez, former mayor of San Luis and cofounder of the No-Violence Movement, interview with the author, Medellín, August 2004). Many were women who had initiated their political journey by participating in ecclesial base communities or in NGOs dedicated to promoting nutrition and public health and to combating domestic violence and who after the loss of children and other family members to one or another armed group had become pacifist activists committed to pressuring the state for a negotiated rather than a militarized solution to conflict (Women's Association of Eastern Antioquia 2007:29–30).

Geography, Resources, and Violence

Oriente is a region of stark contrasts. In the towns nearest Medellín such as Marinilla, Rionegro, and Guarne, *minifundismo* (subsistence division of land) is the dominant form of land tenure. As one moves east toward the Magdalena River and southeast, however, the landscape and dominant forms of production and land tenure shift dramatically. In municipalities such as El Peñol, San Carlos, Granada, and Guatapé, watersheds with enormous potential for hydroelectric production on public lands controlled by the state vie with subsistence agriculture and wood extraction. In Cocorná, San Francisco, San Luis, and Puerto Triunfo, tropical forest coexists uneasily with extensive cattle ranching and mining (including oil production). Struggles over the shape of development (especially the right to own land and control resources) have for decades formed the backdrop for episodic conflict in the towns of Oriente.

In the 1960s and 1970s the guerilla groups FARC and ELN set up camps in selected parts of Oriente to target cattle ranchers, the energy company ISA, and oil producers along the Magdalena River for extortion and kidnapping, but the impact of the guerillas' presence on most civilians was selective and limited. Local inhabitants might be asked to provide guerillas with food or supplies, but civilian populations were not then subjected to the widespread forcible recruitment of child soldiers, massacres, or displacements that would become a hallmark of guerilla and paramilitary violence in the region by the late 1990s. Indeed, as a twenty-five-year veteran organizer of programs dealing with children's and women's issues in Oriente (1979–2004) summed up the relationship between peasants and guerillas when asked about the validity of official perceptions regarding local complicity: "They [the people of Oriente] had already lived through at least 15 years alongside the guerillas, and the peasant has within him a sense of hospitality. He is supremely hospitable; anyone who comes to his house receives food . . . the guerillas at that time took care of the peasants, helped the community, filled many vacuums left empty by the State. For example, whenever there were money problems, or problems between neighbors, the guerillas would intervene . . . and when it was planting season they would go and help with the planting. You might say that that's how a close and affectionate relationship was formed between the communities and the guerillas, a relationship that helped them a lot" (qtd. in Gutierrez 2004). Although "Guadalupe," the interviewee, acknowledged that proximity, isolation, and mutual assistance forged a relationship of coexistence and even affection between local inhabitants and guerillas, it is important to note that while the state may not have been present in the form of social services, investment, or as an arbiter of local conflicts, the armed forces, who also form part of the state, were never wholly absent from Oriente. Before the entry of a strong paramilitary presence in the late 1990s, local military or police commanders posted to the region knew of and tolerated the presence of the guerillas, making only sporadic efforts to root them out or monitor civilian–guerilla interaction. It was with the concerted arrival of the paramilitaries in 1998–99 that the conflict began to escalate.

The arrival of a paramilitary challenge to the status quo, and on its heels, the penetration into the interior of eastern Antioquia of the FARC from its traditional command posts along the Magdalena River, marked the turning point in Oriente's fortunes: "The paramilitaries start[ed] to look for the guerillas, and of course they start[ed] to kill townspeople who had been helping the guerillas. But all of them had helped, all of them, because they had lived so long with them" (qtd. in Gutierrez 2004). It was just this sense that "all of them" had lived side by side with the guerillas and had "helped them" that enabled paramilitaries and state security forces to consider Oriente's civilian population as enemies and to treat them as indistinguishable from the guerillas who operated in the zone, therefore rendering them legitimate military targets. The cycle of massacres, forcible displacement, and economic blockades through which competing armed groups sought to isolate and starve municipalities in Oriente into submission began to gain momentum in 1998.

The first full-fledged massacre in eastern Antioquia took place in San Carlos, a week before the town's traditional *fiestas del agua* (water celebrations). Shortly before the paramilitaries entered the town, the army, which was stationed in the town to protect the watershed and the local hydroelectric plant from possible guerilla sabotage, abruptly decamped. Paramilitaries killed thirteen people, among them several of San Carlos' civic movement leaders. Many of those who fled or were forced to leave the region by the paramilitaries relocated to shantytowns in Medellín (" 'Paras'-bandas, alianza mortal" 1998). By 2000 conditions in Oriente were such that in some places more than half the municipal population had fled as a result of unprecedented armed conflict primarily aimed at the civilian population. By the beginning of the twenty-first century the towns of Oriente had emerged as among those experiencing the highest national incidence of violence and displacement.[14] Regional statistics also indicated that Oriente had the highest rate of malnutrition in Antioquia (32 percent of children under seven), the greatest percentage of people under the poverty and extreme poverty lines (64.2 percent on average, with some municipalities reporting 90 percent and above), and an extraordinary number of antipersonnel land mines.[15]

The introduction and expansion of illicit poppy and coca cultivation and the forcible employment of local inhabitants in illicit production by armed groups had also risen dramatically by 2000.[16] The number and operation of illegal armed groups had grown to cover a greater proportion of Oriente's municipalities by 2000, as had the deployment of the Colombian armed forces. By 2004 six military battalions were present in Oriente and paramilitary operatives were present in all the urban centers of the region's twenty-three municipalities, as well as on the major roads in and out of the region. Guerillas of the FARC and ELN had expanded from localized strongholds along the Magdalena River and in towns where hydroelectric activities were greatest to establishing a presence in all of Oriente's rural areas (Grupo Oriente 2004). Between 1998 and 2002 massacres and blockades held hostage entire villages or settlements for weeks at a time.[17] After the FARC threatened to kill or not allow mayoral candidates in the mid-1990s, and local paramilitary units followed suit with death threats of their own, mayors of the towns under the greatest threat found themselves obliged to establish municipal governments in exile, running their localities via cell phone and Internet from undisclosed locations in the regional capital, Medellín (AI 2006).

By March of 2001 campesinos in Oriente described their situation as one of *encierro* (locked down or besieged). One Saturday afternoon the army came through the region conducting patrols through various villages near the dams, and as they walked along, the soldiers mentioned that the communal stores were going to disappear. The next day the paramilitaries installed a road block less than two hundred meters from the urban center of Granada, along the road that connects the town to outlying villages. The paramilitaries proceeded to take all the merchandise that transporters were bringing into town for the local stores and made one man get out of his vehicle, shooting him by the side of the road for all to see. From that day onward rural folk began to report the existence of an iron grip on all the campesinos' basic purchases (*mercado*). The *tiendas comunitarias* and the drugstores closed down. The paramilitaries justi-fied their actions by arguing that they were limiting the guerillas' access to goods and medicines, but local people held a different theory: they did not believe that the real object of the roadblock was their local production sold in *tiendas comunitarias* because the locally produced amount could not support "an army like that of the guerillas." Instead they believed that the paramilitaries had closed the Medellín-Bogotá road at night because it was the route the guerillas used to get all their food. The closing of the *tiendas comunitarias* was intended to force campesinos to shop in town centers and, once they had left the relative safety of their villages, to be targeted and shot (Zapata Yepes 2003).

Local inhabitants were also convinced that the army colluded with the paramilitaries because the latter set up their camp just meters from the army base and, with a list in hand, forced people out of their vehicles, many of whom "never got back in." During the first forty days of paramilitary control of the highway, forty-six people were killed. When men began to send children, the elderly, and women to shop to avoid forcible recruitment or death, the para-militaries threatened the women not to cover for the men "because according to them [the paramilitaries], if the men are afraid to leave their town, it must be because they're guilty of something [*porque la deben*]" (Zapata Yepes 2003).

Using Participatory Democracy to Confront Violence

It was in the context of an unprecedented rise in the level of violence that Oriente's mayors and their supporters worked to broaden awareness and sup-port for their no-violence approach among the regional, national, and interna-tional communities by holding a series of open or popular assemblies and by actively promoting the use of the Internet and the establishment of virtual communities that maintained links between displaced citizens and people who still resided in Oriente. One of the mayors' most novel projects was the creation of a user-friendly Web site called Oriente Virtual. Web site users could click on biographical sketches of leading international figures committed to nonviolence and on photo galleries accompanied by summaries of each of the twenty-three municipalities' geography, climate, and products. They could also access local press accounts of happenings in the area, information often not reported in the regional and national media, and read releases that laid out the movement's objectives while touting the area's magnificent natural resources and vibrant "human capital."[18]

The tone was deliberately hopeful and upbeat. The Web site, rural press and radio accounts, and the mayors' public pronouncements made frequent allusions to seemingly nonideological ends (so as to avoid being tainted by association with any of Colombia's warring groups). Local inhabitants were represented as "stewards of ecological biodiversity," promoters of "sustainable development," and advocates for a reconciliation of the market and "social equity."[19] Indeed, the language was a marvel of obliquity and diplomacy. It was hard to escape the sensation that within the shrinking confines of the politically permissible in Colombia, Oriente's No-Violence Movement felt compelled to *market* its way out of violence (Paley 2001).

Scholars of Latin American social movements have noted how local social actors often find themselves obliged to tailor their agendas to the interests and discourses vetted by international NGO and development communities to connect local communities to donors and interlocutors abroad (Escobar and Pedrosa 1996:15). Yet Oriente's approach in its Web site and public pronouncements was less a reflection of or adjustment to outside pressures than a tactically opportune appropriation of symbols and catchphrases (*sustainability, pluralism*) filtered, transformed, and reinterpreted through local experiences and needs.[20] The result is what the anthropologist Joanne Rappaport has aptly termed "interculturalism," that is, a strategy for indigenous intellectuals to absorb a variety of tools from dominant society and refine them for use in their own project of "pluralism in the political realm" (Rappaport 2005:5).

Oriente's No-Violence Movement, like Colombia's indigenous movement, emerged from and is a product of a decades-old (though not necessarily linear or homogeneous) history of accumulated experiences and experiments in which progressive Catholicism, leftist ideologies, organized labor, and developmentalist discourses have combined to influence the patterns and strategies of local civic engagement.[21] Indeed, despite temporal shifts in strategy and formulation, certain themes have remained constant in Oriente's history of mobilization, namely, the desire to call attention to unresolved structural issues that underlie local conflicts; insistence on the right of local inhabitants and civic leaders and authorities to express grievances and have a say in the determination of policies affecting local lives and livelihoods; demands that the state take local grievances seriously and that it make its presence effectively felt in the region as a source of protection, investment, and law.[22]

By adopting a no-violence approach Oriente's inhabitants attempted to claim a neutral space of interaction for the discussion of political and economic alternatives to conflict. "Enrique," a civic leader in "San Pablo," defined local efforts to construct a viable public sphere thus: "What we do in San Pablo is get together with representatives of everyone in the municipality, from the producer associations to the rank and file citizen on the street to defend a series of interests that are not so parochial or individual in focus, but rather issues and interests that touch all of us deeply" (qtd. in Gutierrez 2004). In this regard Oriente's No-Violence Movement resembles in its composition, objectives, and strategies those of other Colombian grassroots peace initiatives, where despite preexisting bonds based on shared ethnic, economic, or kinship relations, the representation of multiple voices and points of view, rather than narrowly defined interests, forms the basis of consensus-building efforts. At its most elemental this has meant a local substitution of a "search-for-humanity" approach for the "enemy-image" approach to conflict deployed by the central state, its security forces, and the armed left and right.

In his essay "Humanization of Extremists," the conflict analyst and mediator Juan Gutierrez, who has worked extensively in Oriente, defines the enemy-image approach as one that, among other things, "denies the humanity of the adversaries . . . if your enemies are devils, there is no common ground to be shared . . . human rights do not apply to them, whose life is perceived as their antithesis . . . to wait for legal procedure to produce evidence is a dangerous lack of responsibility. Association becomes complicity." The search-for-humanity approach, in contrast, takes the form of "the community leader behav[ing] respectfully and show[ing] appreciation for the armed actor's arguments and values . . . the leader then confronts the armed actor with the needs of the community and shows him the harm, destruction and pain that have resulted from the armed actor's violent behaviour . . . the leader constantly refers to the shared humanity of both the community and the armed actor and points out their joint undertakings and shared past . . . but refuses to show the slightest complicity with either the armed actor's destructive dynamics or with the armed actor himself" (Gutierrez 2004).[23] "The State's first offer," one civic activist in San Carlos noted, "was to encourage us to confront the armed actors with arms" (qtd. in Gutierrez 2004). But Oriente's civic leaders—the mayor, the priest, the other community leaders (heads of women's groups, cooperatives, etc.)—and ordinary citizens rejected the state's advice. Instead, townspeople authorized their civic leaders to approach the commanders of the different armed groups (including the state's security forces) to see if by appealing to them for suggestions on how to "bring in food, medicine, so innocent people wouldn't fall under fire, so that people wouldn't have to be displaced so much," the armed actors might cease to see the townspeople as "their enemies." Every proposal was subjected to endless hours of consensus-based deliberation, discussion, and refinement in local *asambleas comunitarias*. Only proposals perceived to reflect values that "were very much ours, very shared, very discussed, very concerted, where we felt united and could say [to the armed actors]: 'This is our proposal' " were endorsed (qtd. in Gutierrez 2004).

In the course of searching for ways to mitigate the combined effect of multipronged armed conflict in which the main casualties are civilians, Oriente's townspeople were implicitly spelling out what they considered the appropriate functions and obligations of the Colombian state and making clear how and in what ways the state has failed to live up to those ideals in the past. It is precisely in this back-and-forth exchange of expectations and definitions of state-citizen obligations and functions encoded in the language of alternative approaches to development and violence, and the state's response to these appeals, that the essential point of divergence between the Colombian state and citizens resident in areas of persistent violence lies, and where the contours of violent pluralism become fully apparent. Whereas Oriente's inhabitants work from the premise that the state's primary duty is to defend the interests and lives of its citizens and to include them in any decision-making process that directly affects their lives and livelihoods, different administrations and selective sectors of the state understand the call for an establishment of the state's presence and for the enforcement of its authority primarily, if not exclusively, in *coercive* rather than consensual terms.

Civic leaders' attempts to confront violence with the tools of nonviolent, participatory democracy, therefore, enjoyed no support from the state. Indeed, although "Enrique" noted that *acercamientos humanitarios* were adopted as the only possible way out of an emergency situation by Oriente towns as early as 1996, he also quickly added that Oriente took a risk in approaching the heads of armed groups because "from the President's office, from the [central] State, that was not allowed" (qtd. in Gutierrez 2004). Although local attempts to appeal to armed commanders were often rebuffed or met with disdain, *acerca-mientos humanitarios* in some instances did succeed in deflecting a possible tragedy. In San Carlos, for instance, the implementation of President Uribe's Democractic Security policy mandated that police set up permanent residence in the local police barracks. Yet police barracks were usually located in residential neighborhoods, putting the civilian population at risk in the case of a guerilla attack. Several neighbors approached the commander to ask if the police would "move over a little bit so as not to put us so strongly in the path of danger." Townspeople also appealed to the police's and military's sense of duty, pointing out, "look here, man, you're putting in danger the lives of our children and even the survival of the local infrastructure, the infrastructure you're supposedly encharged with defending." Townspeople felt that their use of democratic tools such as dialogue and negotiation ensured that the "the number of deaths went down, the approach worked" (qtd. in Gutierrez 2004).

In the end, however, as long as the commitment to nonviolent conflict resolution and participatory democratic practice is limited to the local or community level and, perhaps more significantly, not shared by the national government or even its international allies (as in the case of the United States in Colombia), violent pluralism is likely to characterize societies such as Colombia's for the foreseeable future, a future in which neither the state nor the limited "formal" democratic structure that has characterized it for several decades is likely to collapse, but in which the violence is also unlikely to disappear. Local civic leaders and inhabitants in Oriente are fully aware that the ability to create a more peaceful, democratically inclusive society

> is not in our hands . . . war isn't invented in a village or a town, ordinary people don't have the ability to buy themselves a rifle, people are given rifles, they're paid and given food [in exchange for taking up arms] but alone ordinary people don't have the power to make this war possible. This war is made possible, in my opinion, by some very powerful economic and political interests. It's daunting how many people are armed. Where does all the money come from? Where does the money come from to ensure all those people eat? And by armed I don't just mean the legal and illegal groups, but the Colombian military too because they're here in huge numbers. . . . Where do all those very powerful arms they carry come from? We [local, ordinary people] aren't [financially, logistically] sustaining this war. (qtd. in Gutierrez 2004)[24]

Conclusions

Violence in Colombia has tended to be cyclical, selective, and, with rare exceptions, also concentrated in areas with valuable resources but at a considerable distance from the urban centers of political or financial power where the majority of Colombia's population resides.[25] Consequently, the existence or threat of violence can very effectively be used to justify the expansion of executive powers, the restriction of civil rights, and the suppression or demonization of dissent, while appearing to do so in defense of democracy and political stability. Indeed, in cases (e.g., the demobilization of paramilitary groups) where nonstate actors perpetrate violence that benefits the state by targeting a common enemy (such as leftist guerillas or sectors of civil society who may oppose the unconditional implementation of state-endorsed neoliberal policies) while institutional actors erase any official "footprint" of such activities (e.g., the tacit toleration of paramilitary violence by the armed forces), violence may serve to shore up the power of the state even as it undermines the possibility of constructing a truly participatory or pluralistic democratic polity.

When a Latin American state such as Colombia under the Uribe administration coincides with the interests of a powerful regional influence such as the United States under George W. Bush, and becomes one of the northern state's few allies in the region and perhaps the only bulwark against the influence of Hugo Chávez in Venezuela, the chances that policies detrimental to participatory democracy, but endorsing the "right" side of the war on terror, will be condemned or used to isolate Colombia, despite its atrocious human rights record, are slim. Indeed, the so-called war on terror has given a new lease to antidemocratic policies that may increase the incidence of violence in Colombia, even as those policies shore up the executive power of the Colombian president at the expense of opposition parties such as the Polo Democratico Alternativo or citizens' civic mobilizations such as the Oriente No-Violence Movement.

Formal democracy in Colombia has a long history and, in all likelihood, a future as well, even in an environment characterized by persistent violence. The real question is whether the movement toward a more inclusive and expansive definition of democracy—one that can tolerate nonviolent dissent and even encourage local experiments in deliberative, consensus-based participatory democracy without labeling them as subversive—can survive or even counteract the region's emerging penchant for violent pluralism.

Notes

1. Harvey F. Kline considers holding regular elections a minimal standard for defining democracy. See Kline 1990.
2. For a concise synthesis of the arguments in favor of and against characterizing Colombia as a "failed" state, see Posada-Carbó 2004.
3. Policies endorsed under Plan Patriota and Uribe's Democratic Security measures include widespread surveillance; the establishment of an extensive system of paid civilian informants; demands of logistical assistance from civilians that blur the distinction between combatant and noncombatant status; and the like.
4. Oriente produces between 33 and 35 percent of all the electricity consumed in Colombia.
5. When Uribe publicly criticized and accused certain international NGOs of acting as "shields" or "fronts" for the armed left in a speech in September 2003, and then reiterated his comments before a meeting of the United Nations in October of that year, he put significant sectors of civil society and all those who received aid or support from such organizations at risk. More recently, the president's and vice president's unfounded terrorism- and guerilla-complicity accusations (later retracted) have endangered the lives of journalists and members of the opposition. See AI 2006.
6. The experience of the San Gil and Socorro municipalities of the department of Santander is similar to that of Oriente where priests and lay leaders promoted civic action and cooperative development initiatives—sometimes with the institutional support of the state—in an effort to coordinate alternative (nonarmed but reformist) community responses to the problems of political exclusion, poverty, and social inequality. See Bucheli 2006.
7. Interview with a civil leader from Nariño, qtd. in Jaramillo n. d. I thank Ana Maria for sharing her exhaustively researched analysis of the peace process in Oriente with me.
8. For a thoughtful analysis of the widespread and insidious nature of the deployment of accusations of collaboration by all armed groups in Colombia, see Fichtl 2004. The author also looks at how easily civilians may fall prey to such accusations.
9. For a more detailed analysis of the impact of La Violencia in eastern Antioquia and of the legacy of government public-order policies in the region, see Roldán 2002: 109–69, 281–98.
10. The AUC is an umbrella organization made up of right-wing, regional, illegal paramilitary groups, founded in 1997 to combat leftist guerilla groups. The last of the regional blocs affiliated with the AUC supposedly demobilized in 2006. However, death threats signed by the AUC continued to surface after 2006.
11. Secretaria de Gobierno de Antioguia 1953, v.3, 31 August 1953 letter from Guatapé (San Luis) to the governor concerning *contrachusma* occupation of land.
12. ANAPO was founded as a political movement around the former dictator-turned-

populist General Rojas Pinillas in the 1960s. The organization appealed to voters disgusted with the seemingly incestuous alternation of power and clientelist policies pursued by the Liberal and Conservative Parties during the National Front.

13. Acción Cultural Popular (ACPO) was initiated by the Catholic Church and later included extension agents and technical staff associated with private producer associations such as the Colombian Coffee Federation and vocational schools such as the SENA.

14. See Gutierrez 2004 for 1993 to 2005 displacement and population figures for Oriente's municipalities.

15. The Oriente municipalities of San Luis and San Carlos, along with the municipalities of Tibú and San Calixto in the department of Norte de Santander, hold the distinction of being the municipalities with both the highest rate of displacement (2002 figures) and the highest presence of minefields in Colombia (Consultoria para los Derechos Humanos y el Desplacamiento 2003).

16. These statistics are reproduced in Rivera 2005.

17. The year 1997 also marked the escalation and shift of violence against civilians in other parts of Colombia such as San José de Apartadó in Urabá and indigenous Nasa communities in the southern department of Cauca.

18. www.orientevirtual.org, accessed 7 March 2004. The original Oriente virtual Web site was shut down and the domain name sold. The new, far more market-oriented Web site uses the language of "corporate competiveness" and "technical excellence," replacing the older site's references to "sustainability" and "ecological stewardship."

19. www.orientevirtual.org, accessed 7 March 2004.

20. This view is confirmed by a recent published interview with Jaime Fajardo Landaeta, the Antioquia governor's assistant for the Plan Congruente de la Paz. When queried regarding the impact of European NGO support of the peace laboratories, he responded, "The peace laboratory is a process that didn't begin with the E.U.'s help. What it did [EU financing] was accelerate the process in new locations. It creates possibilities for channeling some resources to underwrite already existent productive projects" (Marin 2004).

21. For an excellent overview of the history of NGO influence, the factors shaping indigenous NGO development, and their influence in shaping community organizing in Latin America from the 1940s through the 1990s, see Meyer 1998.

22. Lack of space prevents me from elaborating on the nature of Oriente's history of civic mobilization or on the ways in which since the period of La Violencia the area's inhabitants have attempted to restrain the government's tendency to respond to conflicts in the region primarily with the use of force, including privatized forms of violence. For a more extended account see Roldán 2002, esp. chap. 3.

23. The stated objective of Democratic Security is "to recover territory from guerrilla control by strengthening the armed forces and increasing the number of military and police personnel to ensure their presence in all of Colombia" (AI 2006).

24. The sentiments expressed by "Enrique" regarding the national and international scope of the conflict in Colombia, and the limited power of local communities to do more than attempt to mediate a better rate of survival for the civilian population in their communities, were shared by the other interviewees.

25. One such exception was the explosion of largely urban-based violence directed against business rivals and particular sectors of the Colombian state by the Medellín cartel under Pablo Escobar in the late 1980s and early 1990s, which sought to force the government to abandon its extradition treaty with the United States.

Maintaining Democracy in Colombia through Political Exclusion, States of Exception, Counterinsurgency, and Dirty War

MARÍA CLEMENCIA RAMÍREZ

In February 2007, the Colombian president Álvaro Uribe declared in an interview with Caracol Radio that "under my [business suit] is the flesh and blood of a soldier and a policeman." This statement encapsulates the centrality of the security forces to the peculiarly Colombian form of political democracy: a façade of civilian government masks an increasingly militarized state, on which it depends for its continued existence.

Colombian political culture has been defined for decades by the coexistence of a stable and democratic institutional structure with an alarming level of political violence. Since maintaining order has marked a primary endeavor of Colombia's democratically elected civilian governments, the armed forces have become central participants in the state's institutional dynamics. Both Andrés Dávila Ladrón de Guevara (1998) and Mauricio García Villegas and Rodrigo Uprimny (2006) have called attention to the use of the "state of exception" as a government mechanism to legitimize military actions against civilians and thereby achieve long-term institutional stability. The state of exception is thus "[transformed from] a provisional and exceptional measure into a technique of government" (Agamben 2005:2) Between 1949 and 1991, when the current constitution was enacted, Colombia was under a state of siege for a cumulative total of thirty years (Agamben 2005:539). During those states of siege civilian government was subordinated to the armed forces, and the military grew increasingly autonomous as the guarantor of security, national defense, and domestic law and order. García Villegas (2000:17) refers to this process as "the military degradation of Colombian democracy" and contrasts Colombia with countries with openly military regimes: despite Colombia's formal democracy, social movements of the 1970s and 1980s were repressed through the use of states of exception, producing unintended consequences, including the strengthening of insurgent groups on the left and dirty-war activities on the right, leading to the emergence and subsequent consolidation of paramilitary forces. Illegal forms of political participation took the place of the social movements that struggled against the abuses of military regimes and for the restoration of democratic structures in other parts of Latin America.

Notwithstanding the above, Colombia's political self-image has been constructed around the idea of being one of Latin America's oldest and strongest democracies, a country that has not suffered long, open dictatorships.[1] It is often stated and has been the rule that Colombian voters never elect a former military officer as president. Nevertheless, the country's military institutions have played a central role in maintaining civilian governments in power. While Colombia was only briefly ruled in the 1950s by an open military dictatorship like those of the Southern Cone in the 1970s and 1980s, the contradiction between civilian democracy and military dictatorship in Colombia is more apparent than real. Militarism and clandestine repression constitute the hidden face of Colombia's formal democracy. In fact, international human rights monitors document that Colombia "presents the worst human rights and humanitarian crisis in the Western Hemisphere."[2] Colombia's democracy has also been characterized by the consolidation of a two-party regime in which the Liberal and Conservative Parties have long exercised a duopoly of power. The consolidation of this exclusive agreed upon duopoly was accomplished primarily through the use of violence, making violence integral to the configuration of Colombia's modern political culture. When the two-party hegemony was endangered by uncontrolled violence on a national scale in 1953, Colonel Gustavo Rojas Pinilla seized power. In 1957, however, Liberals and Conservatives signed an agreement establishing what they called the National Front, to last from 1958 to 1974, under the terms of which the two parties would alternate in power and divide political positions between them. This prevented the military dictatorship from consolidating itself.

Yet that the resulting political order was explicitly exclusive to all actors outside the duopoly, that it was established as a long-term structure, and that strict political exclusion was maintained by the state well after the official expiration of the National Front, combines to explain the emergence of political violence and illicit activities in marginal areas. I argue that political violence and illegality in the periphery is intrinsic to the maintenance of Colombia's model of democracy, characterized by a long-term exclusive duopoly of traditional political parties framed by a counterinsurgency metanarrative that legitimizes the dirty war carried out by the armed forces against political alternatives portrayed as leftists, at times with paramilitary proxies or in alliance with paramilitaries.

Colombian territory includes both central areas under state control and marginal areas in which the absence or weakness of the state and the presence of illicit crops and nonstate armed actors have become the norm. The central government represents these areas as prone to violence and illegality. Indeed, violence has become part of citizens' daily life there. This holds true in the western portion of Colombian Amazonia, which includes the departments of Putumayo, Caquetá, Guaviare, and southwestern Meta. Both the state and inhabitants of central Colombia have defined and constructed this area as excluded from the central order of things, a place "abandoned by the state" and "a forgotten region" outside the pole of "development" in the country's central region.[3] As a part of this region, the department of Putumayo shares a history of long-term colonization that began in the late nineteenth century and has continued ever since, mainly by inhabitants of the Andean highlands in response to social, political, and economic upheavals in their places of origin.[4] The nature of this colonization has evolved over time, seeking to incorporate frontier areas into the economic sphere of the centralized Colombian state to resolve structural problems of land tenure stemming from smallholdings insufficient to provide subsistence. It has also been fueled by violent confrontations in the country's center between the dominant Liberal and Conservative parties in their struggle to acquire and hold onto political power.

The conflation of marginality and illegality in Putumayo explains the expansion of coca cultivation and the ability of the FARC (Fuerzas Armadas Revolucionarias de Colombia, Revolutionary Armed Forces of Colombia) to regulate coca production, processing, and marketing in the department, from the time that the organization's so-called Thirty-Second Front arrived to stay in 1984 (Comisión de Superación de La Violencia 1992:102). It also explains why paramilitary forces managed to move into the area in 1997, challenging the guerillas' control of territory and coca revenues, thus intensifying the armed conflict in the region. Since then guerillas and paramilitaries have contended for control of territories, populations, and the trade in coca paste. Each in its own way and under its own premises, these nonstate actors have established relationships with the inhabitants and with local state officials, politicians, and military forces in the area. Thus has resulted in Putumayo, as in other marginal areas of Colombia, an alternative social order. I aim in this article to examine the way in which this alternative social order has been configured. I will do so in accordance with the guidelines proposed by Enrique Arias and Daniel Goldstein in the introduction to this book regarding the conceptualization of Latin American democracy as "violently plural." As Arias and Goldstein propose here, an account of violent pluralism requires an examination of the sources of this violence and the way in which particular configurations of violence affect politics and the way in which political practices, in turn, affect violence. On the other hand, it also demands scrutiny of the relationships "these violent actors maintain to one another and to different elements of the state, including politicians, police, bureaucrats, and the military."

To do this, I will first provide a brief review of the origin of nonstate armed actors in marginal areas and describe their interests and activities, which relate to their exclusion by the state and by the hegemonic political parties described above, as well as the militarism that has for practical purposes become state policy. In effect these represent aspects of the relationship between central Colombia and its marginal regions. Second, it is necessary to examine a third actor in the conflict in the regions: the armed forces and their relations with the central state and with nonstate armed groups. I analyze the emergence and consolidation of the counterinsurgency metanarrative that frames the military's approach to marginal, conflict-ridden areas. Paradoxically, so-called self-defense groups promoted by the armed forces as proxies to carry on the dirty war subsequently gained autonomy as a result of their connections to drug trafficking. They became a strong, self-motivated armed political group, the United Self-Defense Forces of Colombia (Autodefensas Unidas de Colombia, AUC), and as a result state forces have had to compete with both the FARC and the AUC for the control of peripheral regions. Third, I will analyze the superimposition of the global discourse of security over local relationships in conflictive areas. The escalating power of the AUC and the FARC poses a threat to traditional power groups, which to the latter means a threat to Colombia's putative democracy. As a result, in the name of "Democratic Security" and to gain control and assert state presence in marginal areas no longer useful as buffer zones, the central government requires the civilian population to take sides in the internal armed conflict, a practice that recalls the period of La Violencia, when Liberals and Conservatives promoted civil war in the name of defending the interests of their respective parties. Finally, I will examine the actions of the nonstate armed actors in the construction of local power arrangements in the marginal regions in which new social orders have been established. I argue that these arrangements respond to political exclusion and reflect the desire of the illegal actors to be included in the central political order of Colombia. It is necessary to clarify that I refer to Putumayo on several occasions only to exemplify the points of my general argument.

The Origins and Establishment of Nonstate Armed Actors in Putumayo and Other Marginal Areas

The origins of the FARC can be traced back to La Violencia.[5] The Conservatives held power during the 1940s, violently persecuting Liberal families. When Liberals tired of fleeing their homes, they formed armed self-defense groups. In 1949, in the Tolima region of central Colombia, the Communist Party also organized armed campesino self-defense groups that became mobile guerilla units to resist Conservative persecution. Liberal and Communist self-defense groups then joined forces under a newly formed Unified High Command in southern Tolima. Political and ideological conflicts led to a rupture, however, and open war between Liberals and Communists was acknowledged by the end of 1951. In August 1952 the Communist Party held its First National Guerilla Conference to unify various armed groups into a coherent campesino self-defense guerilla army (see Jairo González 1992). With the incipient consolidation of the guerilla movement, independent rural communities associated with campesino self-defense organizations gradually, but openly, took on the characteristics of a guerilla rear guard in the struggle against the oligarchy represented by the National Front. Although the National Front had opened a "democratic" space for the two traditional parties, it precluded alternative political expression, relied on a state of siege to maintain public order (Pizarro Leongómez 1992:159), and developed more sophisticated mechanisms of repression and terror (Chernick and Jimenez 1990:12).

Communist leaders wanted their party to be able to participate in government, but the Liberal and Conservative leadership neither supported nor recognized their repeated appeals. On the contrary, between 1962 and 1965 the government declared war on the so-called independent republics,[6] and dirty war became the daily reality in these regions. An offensive known as Operation Marquetalia was launched in 1964 against one of the communist strongholds, and the military seized the region.[7] In response the communists called the First Guerilla Conference of the Southern Front and announced the establishment of the FARC. Military attacks against the independent republics continued in

1965, including a military advance on Rio Chiquito (Department of Huila) and El Pato (Department of Caquetá), accelerating the transformation of the self-defense forces into guerilla units. At the subsequent Second Guerilla Conference in May 1966, Manuel Marulanda assumed command of the FARC, and its existence as a guerilla army was further institutionalized. Self-defense groups again became mobile guerilla units attempting to build a revolutionary army (Jairo González 1992:67). Guerilla fronts began to enter every region in the country as regional social movements with the political aim of transforming themselves into a nationwide armed revolutionary movement. Yet it is important to bear in mind that the FARC combatants were also campesinos, that they presented themselves as such, and that they were perceived as such by the rural population in the areas in which they engaged in revolutionary activities.

Paramilitary groups known as *autodefensas*, or self-defense groups, were initially promoted and supervised in the 1980s by the military (Kirk 2003:108–9) and financed mainly by drug traffickers and large landowners to fight the guerillas and protect contested areas from guerilla taxation. In 1981 the M-19 guerilla group kidnapped Marta Nieves Ochoa,[8] a sister of leading drug traffickers in Medellin, and Pablo Escobar of the Medellín cartel brought together two hundred traffickers from all over the country to form the organization MAS (Muerte a Secuestradores, Death to Kidnappers). Ostensibly MAS would free kidnapping victims and kill those guerillas directly or indirectly responsible for creating the scourge of kidnapping (Salazar 2001:82). At the same time that MAS was attacking guerillas and their putative collaborators, the army captain Oscar de Jesús Echandía Sánchez called on landowners, political leaders, and representatives of the Texas Petroleum Company in Puerto Boyacá to form a self-defense group to fight the FARC. It would be financed by landowners and businesspeople in the region. These self-defense groups constituted the beginnings of paramilitarism. They sought to maintain certain areas free of the guerillas and their illicit taxation or protection payments. Álvaro Camacho comments on "narcoterrorism" and its relationship to nascent paramilitarism: "That 'narcoterrorism' was also directed against the state should not obscure the increasing intensity of anticommunist and antiguerrilla violence. In fact, the latter mushroomed and took on a life of its own, independent of drug traffickers. Greater numbers of people became involved in it, and the most vulnerable population sectors were targeted. Campesinos and their representatives as well as leaders of urban and rural social movements were eliminated in campaigns of 'social cleansing.' This new wave of killings produced a panorama that in some ways harkened back to the dark days of the 1950s [the time of La Violencia]" (Camacho 2003).

Academics, NGOs, and popular leaders have considered these armed self-defense groups mechanisms of state terrorism, owing to their promotion by the state and by military officers (Medina Gallego and Téllez-Ardila 1994). In 1994, during the presidency of Ernesto Samper, the state in effect lent its support to paramilitary organization when it legalized groups known as Convivir through Decree 356, defining them as "special vigilance and private security services that function in high-risk areas to restore tranquility and ally themselves with military and police agencies." The decree also stated that through Convivir organizations "information networks shall be established to identify events that could disturb the peace" (Equipo de Alternativa 1997:9). The legalization of these organizations created a conduit for weapons to be legally purchased and channeled into other hands. After the inception of Convivir organizations, paramilitarism intensified and spread throughout the country. In a book that he wrote with the help of the journalist Glenda Martínez, the paramilitary leader Salvatore Mancuso gives a detailed history of how the existence of legal Convivir groups helped him consolidate his own organization (Corporación Arco Iris 2007:13). In November 1997 the Constitutional Court rejected a suit challenging the legality of the Convivir groups ("DAS y convivir harán inteligencia conjunta" 1997). That same year various paramilitary groups consolidated themselves into the AUC. While the separate components of the AUC had previously worked to defend a series of private interests from the incursions of the guerillas, with the formalization of the AUC as such, these illegal groups declared themselves participants in the overall antiguerilla struggle and assumed military functions normally reserved to the state. In the words of Carlos Castaño, "This represents a group of people who have not been protected by the state" (Aranguren Molina 2001: 200), legitimizing their assumption of state functions to provide "justice" in their territories of influence. This was the paramilitaries' way of declaring that they were "political subjects" who would thenceforth contest the FARC's control of territory. The summary document produced by the third national summit of the AUC in November 1996 stated the urgent need to regain control of certain areas that the guerillas had seized from them, among them Putumayo: "The Department of Putumayo is another priority. It is urgent to allocate men and resources to this mission. The insurgency has been able to create a parallel government there, something very dangerous for the nation" ("Golpes de pecho" 1998:30). They went on to declare members of the civilian population whom they considered "guerilla auxiliaries" "military targets." They began to contest, in particular, FARC's control of areas in which illegal crops were grown. These areas constituted strategic objectives as sources of financing for the intensifying armed confrontation and, accordingly, paramilitaries arrived in Putumayo, Meta, and Casanare in 1997.

The Armed Forces and the Promotion of the
Dirty War and Paramilitarism

The Colombian armed forces have preferred using illegal and clandestine dirty-war techniques, and strengthening paramilitary forces to maintain the social status quo, to instituting an open dictatorship. Permitting and promoting these activities makes the state guilty of state-promoted terrorism and culpable for the resulting violence. In this sense Colombia fits into the paradigm described in the introduction by Arias and Goldstein for various Latin American countries: violence originating both inside and outside the state has been used in Colombia to maintain the stability of political institutions. In the Colombian case the alleged purpose of this plurality of violence is to maintain its highly praised and long-lasting democracy.

By the end of the 1980s the dirty war had essentially taken the place of the states of exception imposed in preceding decades. The states of exception had served to provide the armed forces with the prerogatives of a military regime without being perceived as such by the population. In the words of García and Uprimny, "the culture of exception gave way to the culture of the dirty war" (Uprimny and García Villegas 2006:541) as a response to changes taking place in the 1980s with regard to legislative and political reforms that sought to promote respect for human rights and the current peace processes.[9] The dirty war has been characterized as "the illegal, violent, and parainstitutional repression of popular movements and various voices of political opposition and social protest through threats, disappearances, torture, selective killings, and massacres," and in Colombia it "has tended to impact above all the peasantry, and secondly the urban working class" (Uprimny and Vargas Camacho 1990:110, 116).

Many of the paramilitaries who used dirty-war tactics in antiguerilla activities had come from the ranks of the armed forces, and Human Rights Watch (HRW) has amply documented the close ties maintained between paramilitaries and nearly half of the Colombian army's eighteen brigades. These units operate in the zones corresponding to all five military divisions (HRW 2000). The military-paramilitary alliance and the strategic dependence of the armed forces on the paramilitaries was in evidence when the process of paramilitary demobilization began in 2004: certain military officers and other government officials stated on several occasions that "the dissolution of the paramilitaries could create strategic problems for the Armed Forces because they would not be able to maintain control of areas that the paramilitaries dominated at that time" (Wilson 2003). It should also be noted that the armed forces' long-standing determination to wage counterinsurgency war contrasts with their uncertain approach to the war on drugs.

History tells us that until the end of the 1980s the Colombian army did not participate in antinarcotics activities, despite repeated demands made on the Colombian government by the United States. Rather it was the antinarcotics police, established in 1981, that took on this responsibility for the national government.[10] This marked the beginning of the increasing militarization of the National Police in response to the distinct increase in drug trafficking. Tension between the armed forces and the police over their respective roles in the war on drugs would continue throughout the 1990s, but in the context of Plan Colombia beginning in 2000, their relationship would change as described below.[11]

Until Samper's 1994–98 presidency the police received most antidrug aid, to the extent that the police general Rosso José Serrano and colonel Leonardo Gallego of the antinarcotics police established direct lines of communication with members of Congress and others in the United States, over the head of the president. Although Lewis Tamb coined the term *narco-guerilla* and drug traffickers and guerillas began to be associated with each other by 1984, it was only in 1994 that the armed forces openly referred to the FARC as a "cartel" and turned their attention to policing matters in the interest of fighting drug trafficking, albeit always within the framework of counterinsurgency. Louis Alberto Villamarín, a major in the Colombian army, provides a very clear exposition of this point of view:

> The guerrilla–drug trafficker alliance was forged in the seventies to meet the reciprocal needs of the two parties. They both felt cornered by the security forces, and the subversives discovered in drug trafficking a . . . source of income. They agreed with the mafias to protect and defend the coca-growing areas, processing laboratories, and access roads, distracting military operations with the diversionary tactics of irregular war. For this they were remunerated by the drug traffickers with money, arms, and logistical support. But as one would expect, this just made Tirofijo [Manuel Marulanda]

and the other commanders in the secretariat want to form their own cartel that would generate them a very juicy income stream. The narco-subversive marriage was reconfigured, but the conception was the same. The FARC organized another drug-trafficking cartel, hiding behind the Leninist hypocrisy that "the end justifies the means." (Villamarín 1996:21–22)

The drug-related activities of guerilla groups in coca-producing areas led General Barry McCaffrey, the US Drug Czar, on a visit to Colombia in October 1997, to refer again to "narco-guerillas" and to advocate that restrictions on U.S. military aid to Colombia be reconsidered because guerilla groups were moving away from political struggle and becoming a threat to Colombian democracy. As a result the FARC was included on a State Department list of terrorist groups in October 1997, nearly four years before the AUC was added in September 2001. This suggests the tacit support of the paramilitaries by the state and the armed forces up to that time due to their shared anticommunist ideology. McCaffrey's statements convinced General Manuel José Bonnet that the United States now had a better understanding of the army and no longer considered its members "bad boys" (Evans 2002) for not participating fully in the war on drugs as the police had been doing. Bonnet reiterated the position of the armed forces that their priority should be counterinsurgency as opposed to the war on drugs. With the arrival of President Andrés Pastrana in 1998 and in the context of Plan Colombia, General Tapias, general commander of the Colombian armed forces, asked McCaffrey to redirect U.S. aid "not just to the police under the command of General Serrano, but also to the army, giving it a role as a counternarcotics force" ("El General del Plan Colombia" 2002:18). At that point, the military high command took the position that the guerillas were growing their own drug crops, and Tapias stated the following: "The guerillas will be economically powerful as long as they occupy drug-growing areas. If we are able to deprive them of that resource, we will then be facing guerillas who have to work very hard to support their fronts and their kidnap victims, and to prosecute open warfare to the extent that they have done up until now" ("De frente, mar . . ." 1999:32). In the view of the army, the increasing volume of coca in large part resulted from the protection that the guerillas provided to growers and from the operational challenges faced by the police in confronting them. None of these statements mention the paramilitaries, who were also involved in drug trafficking, as Carlos Castaño acknowledged in a 2001 interview with Mauricio Aranguren Molina: "There is no other option but to use the same method of financing as the guerrillas. . . . If we're going to combat narco-guerrillas then I agree that there should be narco–self-defense forces. . . . I understand that based on what I'm saying, if the war continues and intensifies, the United Self-Defense Forces of Colombia will end up [just as] involved in drug trafficking as the FARC is today" (Aranguren 2001:205–6).

Under the premises described above, the army formed its own antinarcotics battalion in April 1999, trained under the supervision of the U.S. Southern Command. By June of that year one company was already conducting operations, and the battalion was formally inaugurated in December 1999 at the Tres Esquinas base in Caquetá, with support from the Colombian air force and navy. New military structures were consolidated within the framework of Plan Colombia: the Armed Forces Joint Intelligence Center (Central de Inteligencia Conjunta de las Fuerzas Armadas, CIC) and the Task Force South (Fuerza de Tarea del Sur, FTS) (HRW 2001:90). According to Tapias, one of the principal tasks of the antinarcotics battalion was "not only to eliminate coca crops but to recover territory that has been in the hands of insurgent groups for years. . . . This will be key to beginning to win the war" ("De frente, mar . . ." 1999:34). In fact, this was the beginning of Plan Colombia's so-called Push to the South, the campaign against newly labeled narco-guerillas, with special emphases on Putumayo and Caquetá, the main coca-producing departments in 2000. The Twenty-Fourth Brigade, which operates in Putumayo and has proven ties to paramilitaries, lent logistical support to the first and second antinarcotics battalions. Due to the strategic situation, its support proved fundamental in Plan Colombia's military Push to the South (HRW 2001). As the war on drugs took on a counterinsurgent and counterterrorist focus, U.S. policy came to mesh with the internal security discourse of the Colombian armed forces with regard to the struggle against the insurgency, now redefined as narcoterrorist and narco-guerilla. Colombian officers found this version of the war on drugs much more appealing, and the armed conflict intensified during Plan Colombia. This perception of the problem by the Colombian armed forces, as a war on drugs inseparable from the counterinsurgency, has become its metanarrative and a long-term conceptual structure over the course of successive presidencies. It not only applies to the actions of the armed forces but also legitimizes the actions of the paramilitaries. It is among the factors, within the overall logic of counterinsurgency, that have impeded the implementation of policies for the eradication and substitution of drug crops in a process that would meet the needs of small growers. Instead, it has privileged repressive policies and the criminalization of coca growers not only as drug traffickers but as guerilla auxiliaries.

The Superimposition of the Global Discourse of Security over
Alternative Social and Political Orders in Conflictive Areas

Due to the presence of nonstate armed actors whose main income derives from the control and regulation of the market for illegal crops, it has been argued that the Colombian state has lost control of some parts of its territory or lost its monopoly on the legitimate use of force, suggesting its classification as a "failed state" and legitimizing the direct intervention of the United States in its internal affairs.[12] Commentators have suggested that the United States views Colombia primarily through a security lens, prioritizing relations with the armed forces and the police (Manwaring 2001:5). Moreover, the production of cocaine and heroin in Colombia is perceived by the U.S. government as a direct threat to the public health and national security of the United States (United States State Department 2001). The formulation of antinarcotics policy is influenced by national and international security concerns, but now it is all the actors involved in illegal drug activities, not just insurgents, that are seen as enemies and as a threat to stability. In the case of Colombia, the confluence of guerilla and drug-trafficking activities facilitates continued perceptions of communism as a threat, since in their Marxist rhetoric the guerillas still express the intention to take power. However, the freedom of autonomous action acquired by paramilitary groups, and their own connections to drug trafficking, also make them subject to pressure from the United States. On 24 September 2002 the United States announced its request for extradition of the paramilitary leaders Castaño and Mancuso. The then attorney general John Ashcroft stated that the United States would "pursue the terrorists that threaten U. S. security wherever they go in the world, and won't rest until we see them tried in their countries" ("El Llamado del Tío Sam" 2002:30). He also announced, as the result of a two-year investigation, three new sets of criminal proceedings against FARC commanders for conspiracy to produce and distribute illegal drugs with the knowledge that they would be sold in the United States. These proceedings would surely lead to requests for extradition.

Álvaro Uribe Vélez took office on 7 August 2002, after the attacks of 9/11 and after the United States declared a global war on terror. On 2 August, just one week before Uribe became president, the U.S. Congress provided for the transformation of the war on drugs in Colombia into a counterinsurgency war by lifting previous restrictions on the country's use of antinarcotics resources. These resources would now be available in a unified battle against drug trafficking and the organizations classified as terrorist. Uribe's Democratic Security policy was conceptualized under this tripartite discourse of counterterrorism-counternarcotics-counterinsurgency. Peace negotiations with the FARC had failed during the 1998–2002 Pastrana presidency, and Pastrana eliminated the *zona de despeje* on 20 February 2002,[13] helping to catapult the new counterterrorist discourse into a central position of government policy. In this environment, coca cultivation came to be viewed solely as a source of financing terrorism. Uribe prioritized counterinsurgency operations to break the link between drug trafficking and the guerillas and launched a campaign to "consolidate state control of territory through the presence of the military," equating military presence with the presence of the state. In a report on the first year of Uribe's government and of the National Development Plan to Provide Democratic Security, the National Planning Department stated that security forces expanded their presence by 120 municipalities, from 82 percent to 93 percent of the national territory. This data was provided as an indicator of territorial control and therefore effective national sovereignty (DNP 2003:1). As the International Crisis Group (ICG) points out, "the Uribe administration's unprecedented military effort has come at the cost of social investment, and even required that the budgets of many domestic programs be cut" (ICG 2005:24).

Because paramilitaries and guerillas control certain areas of the country, the government has considered residents of those areas "guerilla auxiliaries" in the past and "auxiliaries of terrorist groups" today, be those terrorist groups, guerillas, or paramilitaries. It has become customary to associate local government officials and residents of these marginal regions with nonstate armed actors, and when the central government talks about recovering sovereignty over these regions, it seeks to gain the confidence of the inhabitants so that they can work as informants to assist in the "conquest of the territory" by the military. Tapias, Bonnet's successor, recognized the situation of the civilian population trapped between different groups of nonstate armed actors: "In many parts of the country the people have only two alternatives: to go with the guerrillas or to go with the paramilitaries. And if they're not with one or the other, they definitely won't be able to survive" ("Estamos ganando" 2001:30). The fact that the civilian population is believed to always line up with one or another of the armed groups in the conflict, and the belief that it is impossible to pry them away, is sometimes used to justify the violation of their human rights by the army and especially to justify the demand that they perform military intelligence. Thus state forces play a role as one more armed group engaged in a competition with the FARC and the AUC for the control of territory and population. General Rosso José Serrano, commander of the Colombian national police, describes the expectation that residents will engage in intelligence activities. The Colombian National Police, he says, have pioneered "[a form of] intelligence that broke with the traditional paradigms. We don't believe in secrets, but in transparency, in openness. We believe in the intelligence of the community, an idea that may seem exotic to conventional police agents" (Serrano 1999:148).

This is the principle behind the formation of networks of paid informants as a central element of Uribe's Democratic Security policy, which states that "the citizenry will play a fundamental role in the collection of information" (DNP 2002:34). Reinserting the state into marginalized areas involves recruiting civilians as supporters of the military's presence and activities. Uribe's goal is "that the civilian population should define its position in support of our threatened democracy ("Los vecinos encubiertos" 2002). The Democratic Security policy has blurred the distinction between civilian and military engagement by the state and between the civilian population and combatants, violating a fundamental principle of international humanitarian law, above all when "the obligation to guarantee security is imposed upon the citizenry" (Comisión Colombiana de Juristas 2004:64). By August 2004 an estimated 2,500,000 people were registered as cooperators in intelligence gathering (Comisión Colombiana de Juristas 2004:65). Under the ideology of Democratic Security it is the responsibility of all citizens to confront the threat to democracy from armed groups, and any authoritarianism or violence perpetrated by the state against the civilian population is justified by the demand that all citizens declare themselves either for or against the government. Seen within the framework of neoliberal democracy as described in the introduction to this volume by Arias and Goldstein, citizens are expected to accept their responsibility to defend the state without any expectation that the state will assist them with their own needs. In this case the state seeks to reach a condition of "security" with the help of the citizenry under the understanding that Democratic Security is "democratic" in the sense that the population participates in reaching this goal. This conception of security stems directly from the principles of Colombian paramilitarism, as explicitly described by Castaño in a 22 March 2003 interview on the television news program *Lechuza*, referring to the political platform of the Uribe government: "The most important thing is that first with words and then with deeds the government convinces the population and the opinion leaders of each region that it can provide security and social investment but only when that local or regional society becomes one with the state, providing information, with security networks, with networks to directly help the state. If you read this government's defense and Democratic Security policies, the perfect self-defense force under the protection of Colombian law and international law is the society, the government, and the armed forces united as one. That's invincible. The state will only be able to defeat the guerrillas and offer security to the whole society if its power flows from society itself. Otherwise it's impossible."

In this interview Castaño made it clear that the demobilization the AUC was negotiating at the time with the Uribe government was more than justified in the favorable context of a security policy conforming to the positions of the self-defense forces. It is also perfectly clear from the content of the interview that the paramilitaries are "violent actors operating within a political system," to use the words of Arias and Goldstein. That is, the phenomenon of paramilitarism responds to a state policy that encourages civilians to participate in activities properly relegated to the military forces, much as during La Violencia. Involving civilians in the armed conflict is seen as a way to strengthen the presence of a state characterized as weak (see Kline 2003; Pizarro Leongómez 2004) or precarious (Pécaut 2001:33; González 1999:6) in marginal Colombian regions.

The 1991 Constitution sought to prevent the permanent imposition of states of siege, providing for a set of limitations on what was reformulated as the state of exception.[14] Even so, the various administrations since that time have tended to declare states of exception to maintain public order in peripheral regions with a weak state presence such as Putumayo, thus confirming the centrality in the political culture of these decrees as instruments of governance. This tendency produces a permanent tension between the Constitutional Court, charged with supervising compliance with the Constitution and promoting the rule of law, and successive governments that perceive this "legalism" as a limitation on their ability to guarantee public order. During the presidency of Samper, Decree 0717 of April 1996 established Special Public Order Zones, where fundamental rights were suspended subject to the declaration of a national state of internal disorder. These zones were designated at the request of regional military officers in coca-producing departments. In August 2001 Pastrana approved the National Defense and Security Law (Ley de Seguridad y Defensa Nacional) that authorized the minister of defense to determine what uses of force were legitimate in the maintenance of public order and that gave the armed forces new powers such those exercised by the judicial police. The president was also given the authority to declare what were called theaters of operation to delegate control of conflictive zones to the military commander in the area. In such cases the commanders' orders were to be applied immediately and would preferably override the authority of mayors and governors in the respective theater. In Putumayo a theater of operations was established in 2001, based on reports that "in Putumayo the situation is beyond the ability of mayors and governors to maintain public order" (Riveros Serrato 2001). It is important to mention that while the civilian central government has used the military to maintain its control, in the case of local government in marginal regions, the military is granted power to override civilian authorities, implicitly setting these areas apart as violent places, outside the law, with delegitimized local governments. On this basis the Uribe government convened its first Council of Ministers in August 2002 by declaring a state of internal disorder ("País en conmoción interior" 2002) and so-called zones of rehabilitation, in Sucre, Bolívar, and Arauca. These were areas with strong guerilla and paramilitary presences, but they are also areas of great geostrategic value. In these areas the military commander assumes operational control of all security forces and has the option to control the population's right to reside in any given area and the right to move freely, subject to punishment for violating orders. In November 2003 the Constitutional Court ruled again against preventive detention, against the armed forces carrying out the functions of judicial police, and against the military registration and restrictions on movement of those residing in zones of rehabilitation. The Constitutional Court continues to uphold the constitutional prohibition against the military carrying out functions of the judicial police as a violation of the principle of the separation of powers and in defense of civil rights.

Local Governments Caught between the Paramilitaries and the Guerillas

Both the guerillas and the paramilitaries have been more interested in influencing local governments than in confronting them. As they have consolidated their presence in given territories they have also sought to establish themselves as sources of local power. Thus it has been said that in marginal areas the state "no longer enjoys a unique position of authority; its position has been degraded to that of one more social actor that negotiates agreements with other social forces" (García Villegas and Uprimny 2006:558). The actions of nonstate actors in the construction of local power arrangements can be understood in the context of their origin as armed groups: the desire for inclusion in the central political order in Colombia.

In the AUC's foundational document the group defines itself as "an anti-insurgent political-military movement, exercising the legitimate right of self-defense that demands changes from the state but is not belligerent toward it" (Pizarro Leongómez 2004:122). The paramilitaries have sought territorial control, but above all they have sought to legitimize themselves as a political force and to enter into political negotiations with the state. With a peace agreement possible between the government of Pastrana and the FARC, certain local political forces decided to cooperate with the paramilitaries in establishing local governance. A fundamental consequence of this process has been "the dismemberment of the Liberal and Conservative parties and the rise of new groups that would have great impact on national politics,"[15] a phenomenon that played out in the elections of 2002, 2003, and 2006, finally calling hegemonic two-party politics into question (Corporación Arco Iris 2007:5).

For many years Putumayo has been a FARC stronghold, and the governor elected for 2005–8 represented hope for a possible political renovation. He had been a priest and had a history of working with peasant communities in the region. However, in August 2006 it was revealed that he had requested economic and political support for his campaign from the paramilitaries. This support translated into direct paramilitary influence over his new administration. Paramilitaries, for example, influenced the granting of a contract for the distribution of alcoholic beverages that established a percentage for the municipality in taxes from a business in which paramilitaries had a 30 percent share ("¿Quién manda aquí?" 2006:48–50). The armed actors have also been able to manipulate local public and private institutions to gain access to resources and, above all, to the distribution of social wealth (Ramírez Tobón 2005).

For its part, the FARC is ambivalent about its relationship with local state representatives. Before the intensification of the conflict due to the entry of paramilitaries into the region in 1997, the FARC supported decentralization and the strengthening of local power, based on the idea that "local government in the hands of the people is an alternative form of participation in civil society and an opportunity to denounce the reigning clientelism and corruption and works toward a solution to the people's most pressing problems" (FARC 1998). Thus the guerillas "supervised" the work of mayors in carrying out their duties and required them to justify their decisions to the FARC and to the population of their municipalities. This control by the FARC over local government has been seen as "compensatory for their political weakness at the national level" (Rangel 1998:34).

As a result of this approach, local government officials came to be associated with the guerillas. For example, a May 1997 article in the newsweekly *Semana* titled "The Guerrillas' Mayors" reproduced a document from military intelligence indicating direct links between 138 mayors and the insurgents, among them the mayors of Puerto Guzmán, Orito, Puerto Asís, Puerto Caicedo, and Puerto Leguízamo in Putumayo ("Los alcaldes de la guerrilla" 1997). Public prosecutors have subsequently interviewed these mayors several times, the latter having to request impartial investigations and providing evidence of their entrapment between opposing forces. In 1999 an adviser to the ministry of the interior stated that from the point of view of the government, the FARC had "control over governing authorities," that is, the mayors exercised authority but not control. He also stated that although the state was present through its official bodies (the public prosecutor, etc.), there was in fact a lack of state presence because "not everyone follows the same line; everything is mediated through and negotiated with other sources of power that are present there (interview by the author, Popayán, 28 July 1999).

In addition, because the FARC defines the paramilitary phenomenon as state sponsored, they consider mayors and governors in some sense responsible for it and have constantly threatened government officials in areas under their influence. Several mayors represented by the Colombian Federation of Mayors met with the FARC commander Marulanda in La Machaca in May 1997 and expressed their neutrality in the conflict, telling him that they were vulnerable to accusations from both the guerillas and the paramilitaries. Marulanda responded that "mayors cannot remain on the sidelines, because paramilitarism is a problem for the state. . . . Mayors cannot be neutral when faced with these murders and massacres. They should condemn and pursue these groups" ("Romería a la Machaca" 1999:72). On several occasions the FARC suspended peace talks with the Pastrana government, demanding action against paramilitarism, and one of the primary rallying cries of the 2000 armed strike in Putumayo was that the state "respond to our nonnegotiable demand to rein in the paramilitary groups that have sown terror here in the south" ("La batalla decisiva" 2000:56).

With the paramilitaries present in regions previously under guerilla control, the guerillas have had to strengthen themselves militarily to confront both them and the armed forces, which have intensified their actions under Plan Colombia and Plan Patriota (the Patriot Plan), a U.S.-supported military offensive involving nearly twenty thousand troops that was launched in May 2004 in the southern departments of Caquetá, Guaviare, and Meta. Uribe described its main objective as the defeat of the FARC by attacking its strongholds and capturing its leaders. Uribe's Plan Patriota stresses the need to "conquer" and seize control of territory from the guerillas. The population has resented this militarization of the region. Many inhabitants feel that none of the armed actors offers them security and that, on the contrary, they are involuntarily immersed in the escalating confrontations. Although these military confrontations continue, the different armed actors have also been able to carve out areas of control, providing some predictability to the situation. In Putumayo the paramilitaries control the town centers and the guerillas the more rural areas. However, since both guerillas and paramilitaries are involved in drug trafficking and are therefore targets of the U.S.-promoted war on drugs, they sometimes form provisional alliances to confront it ("El nuevo enemigo" 2004).

The political subjectivities constructed in these marginal regions stem from subjugation to whichever actor dominates the territory where one lives. The situation reflects a growing adaptability that has become a way of life. This is true not only for the population but also for the armed actors. Their behavior, too, changes after they have established themselves in an area and have become part of the order of things. The police inspector in the *corregimiento* of El Tigre in Putumayo described the results of this process in December 2003[16]:

> The security forces are not in control. There are other laws here that psychologically control the situation or do so by remote control. In any case, they say "do this" and it is done. Taxes are paid to the municipality and to the paramilitaries. The amount depends on the size of the business, but it's 10,000 pesos and up. Sometimes it's voluntary. They threw me out of town for protesting, for standing up to the paramilitaries, but now things have calmed down and you can talk to them. I'm friends with governors and other authorities, and I was concerned about the development of the town; they asked me to come back. There's been a huge change: We can talk to them [the paramilitaries], and propose things to them. People pay them because they carry out police functions. Two years ago it was the guerillas [who dominated the area]. Now there are fewer guerillas around here. Before there was a lot of social disorder, for example, the oil pipeline was blown up. The paramilitaries respect civil society. In the very beginning [when they arrived] they took censuses and the discipline was very harsh. Now people are used to them. (Interview with El Tigre police inspector in La Hormiga, January 2003)

The population reacts to the control of territory by the armed actors in the following ways: First, by submitting to the rules established by the controlling actor. This is stated in the testimony. Second, by declaring itself neutral in the conflict, as the mayors mentioned above did. In this sense they reject both the guerillas and the paramilitaries, and under some circumstances the armed forces as well. This is the case in the territories declared as Peace Communities.[17] And third, by seeking to establish direct relations with the central state, requesting its intermediation and its regional presence, but as a state that provides services and institutional space for citizen participation.[18]

In addition to limiting the use of states of exception, the Constitution of 1991 opened spaces for citizen participation in state decision making, implicitly assuming that the political and social exclusion of significant sectors of society helps explain the recourse to political violence. The FARC has a similar interpretation and calls on the population under its control to adhere to the principles it espouses regarding local participation: "Local power is the exercise of positive freedom, consecrated as participation in the 1991 Constitution. In other words, that the people participate, exercising power in the common interest, in the ideal of the general good, in the administration of the city, neighborhood, town, *vereda* [a politically undefined but coherent rural area], or *corregimiento*" (FARC 1998).

To the inhabitants of marginal regions this kind of social participation is not only a form of engaging with democracy but also a strategy to strengthen the social contract between the state and the citizenry and to promote independence from the armed actors. Thus, in the case of Putumayo, the population demands the presence of the "participatory" state not only to provide services and channel alternative community initiatives amid the violence but also to provide a platform of struggle against residents' stigmatization as violent people who act outside the law.[19] Political participation and citizen action constitute two forms of inclusion in the state and in the central order that it represents, an order that has long excluded broad sectors of society. This exclusion has been the central factor enabling nonstate armed actors to endure and to work in alliance with other forces to impose their political will.

Conclusions

The exclusion of other political forces by the Liberal and Conservative Parties has been a defining characteristic in the Colombian version of political democracy. For the two parties to maintain their power and hegemony, both state violence and violence carried out by nonstate armed actors have been legitimized, the latter with the acquiescence or collaboration of the armed forces and the civilian government. The effort to maintain Colombia's particular form of civilian democracy has thus gone hand in hand with forms of militarism as state policy, as evidenced by the tendency to declare frequent and long-lasting states of siege and states of exception, and above all by the promotion and/or tolerance of dirty-war practices in lieu of open military dictatorship.

The pursuit of forms of political inclusion is common to the political agendas of the guerillas, the paramilitaries, and the drug traffickers, each of whom has responded to social, political, and economic exclusion with its own form of exercising local power. Their alternative local social and political orders coexist with the central state. These alternative local orders highlight the contrast between the strong state presence in central areas and the state's and armed forces' metanarrative of reconquering marginal territories in which the influence of the central state is compromised by the presence of illegal crops and nonstate armed actors.

The alternative social orders include the supervision and vigilance of local elected officials by nonstate armed actors, deeply discrediting these officials in the eyes of the central state and opening them up to accusations of incompetence and corruption. The alternative orders additionally imply the acceptance of their authority by civilians inhabiting areas permanently controlled and supervised by nonstate armed actors, limiting their freedom.

At the same time, the connection of leftist guerillas to drug trafficking has been more stigmatized than that of paramilitaries, since the former have been present in the country since the 1950s and have long been the targets of counterinsurgency. The association of leftist guerillas with drug trafficking also represents a continuity with the anticommunist discourse of the cold war years, legitimizing the repressive antidrug policies of the state and above all of the armed forces. This discursive confluence was made even more evident after the events of 11 September 2001, when antidrug and antiterrorist struggles became conflated. These were the origins and underpinnings of Uribe's Democratic Security framework, which, on the one hand, reacts to the cultivation of illegal crops exclusively as a source of financing for armed groups and, on the other hand, stigmatizes the inhabitants of marginal areas as guerilla or paramilitary collaborators. They are furthermore portrayed as potential informants for the security forces, without regard for their well-being. The Democratic Security paradigm in contested areas and areas controlled by nonstate actors involves popular participation as intelligence auxiliaries of the security forces in lieu of integral social or political participation. Those civilians in conflicted areas who do not participate in this fashion run the risk of being singled out as collaborators of nonstate armed groups and considered "military targets." The Democratic Security framework abides no consideration of the structural causes that have led people in these marginal regions to grow coca. As a result, the pursuit of independence and autonomy from state and nonstate armed bodies has become a central survival strategy for the population.

The survival of the Colombian political system has been and remains contingent on state and nonstate armed actors that impose plural violences. Even though nonstate actors do not in practice seek to take power in the center, the activities of multiple armed actors in marginal areas have a transformative influence on Colombia's overall social and political order.

Notes

This article is part of an ongoing research project in the Department of Putumayo, Colombia, funded by the Colombian Institute of Anthropology and History and by Colciencias, the Colombian Institute for the Advancement of Development Science and Technology.

1. Colombia's only modern military dictatorship lasted four years under General Gustavo Rojas Pinilla, from 1953 to 1957. A military junta took power in August 1957 after a series of marches against the dictatorship and a plebiscite was held to restore civilian government.
2. Testimony of the Principal Specialist on Colombia of Human Rights Watch at a 24 April 2007 hearing at the United States House of Representatives. http://hrw.org.
3. For an extended analysis of the consequences of exclusion and the perception or assumption of this exclusion by the excluded themselves, see Ramírez 2001; a revised and updated English version is forthcoming.
4. The "colonization" of peripheral regions of Colombia by migrants from the center has taken place throughout the country's history, often in correlation with the boom-and-bust cycle of primary resources and often motivated by political violence and the increasingly concentrated ownership of land. Those who arrive as new inhabitants of peripheral areas are known as *colonos*.
5. The period known as La Violencia (1948–58) was characterized by widespread assassinations, torture, mutilation, kidnapping, dispossession, rape, and massive forced migration, all resulting from an unrestrained confrontation between the two traditional and hegemonic political parties, the Liberals and the Conservatives.
6. Once the military government of Rojas Pinilla was deposed, the armed communists reverted to campesino self-defense groups, mostly in six rural areas: Marquetalia (Department of Tolima), Riochiquito (Department of Huila), Pato (Department of Caquetá), Alto Sumapaz -Duda (Departments of Cundinamarca and Meta), Ariari, and Guayabero (both Department of Meta). The campesinos had

been excluded by the traditional party-based elites, expelled from their lands, and persecuted by the military because of their communist affiliation. They had also been forced to arm themselves to defend their lives and their families. Anticommunist forces referred to their communities as "independent republics," regarded as intolerable from the point of view of Colombian state sovereignty.

7. Operation Marquetalia was approved by the parliament in May 1964, and was signed by President Guillermo León Valencia, launching a military operation against the so-called independent republics of the communists. The institutionalized duopoly of power held by the two traditional parties during the National Front period characterized the operation as state military action representing elite social sectors. The objective was to enter the area held by the communist campesino self-defense groups and to destroy them. It was the cold war era, and the U.S. government had promoted the operation. This aggression became the foundational myth of the FARC.

8. This guerilla movement was established in 1974 and was constituted by members of a populist political party called the Alianza Nacional Popular (ANAPO), a majority of whom were intellectuals.

9. In 1985 a peace agreement was reached with the FARC. As a result, the guerilla movement founded a political party called the Patriotic Union (Union Patriótica, UP). The UP began to run candidates for political office, but by 1987 a murderous wave of persecution against them was unleashed nationwide. In 1990 and 1991, four guerilla groups demobilized: the M-19 (April 19 Movement, Movimiento 19 de Abril), Quintín Lame, the EPL (Popular Liberation Army, Ejército Popular de Liberación), and the PRT (Revolutionary Workers Party, Partido Revolucionario de los Trabajadores).

10. The Colombian police are a national body responsible to the ministry of defense, in effect an additional branch of the armed forces. The antinarcotics police are a body within the structures of the National Police.

11. Plan Colombia refers to the antidrug, counterinsurgency, and antiterrorist programs of the Pastrana and Uribe governments, and to the overall U.S. aid packages since 2000.

12. Colombia is listed in fourteenth place on the Failed States Index, after Ivory Coast, the Democratic Republic of Congo, Sudan, Iraq, Somalia, Sierra Leone, Chad, Yemen, Liberia, Haiti, Afghanistan, Rwanda, and North Korea (Foreign Policy and the Fund for Peace July-August 2005) (Comisión de Superación de La Violencia 1992:102).

13. In January 1999 a site for negotiations between the government and the FARC was established in southern Colombia. It comprised five municipalities: Mesetas, Vista Hermosa, Uribe, La Macarena in Meta, and San Vicente del Caguán in Caquetá. While negotiations were ongoing, the armed forces withdrew from this area, known as the *zona de despeje* (safe haven), but civilian government institutions continued to function.

14. According to Article 213 of the Constitution, a state of internal disorder (*estado de conmoción interior*) may last no longer than 270 days.

15. For a thorough analysis regarding the relationship established between regional political groups and the paramilitaries, see Corporación Arco Iris 2007.

16. A *corregimiento* is a small community organized within a larger municipality.

17. The Peace Communities are a form of organized nonviolent resistance in Colombia. They declare themselves neutral in the armed conflict and reject contact with any armed group, including state security forces. They also create mechanisms for nonviolent self-protection. These mechanisms do not include taking up arms to defend their territory and their families but rather strengthening community organization, creating nonviolent security procedures, generating sustainable agriculture projects, and developing political ties to the national and international communities. The first such Peace Community was established in March 1997 in San José de Apartadó, in northwestern Colombia.

18. For an extended analysis of the paradoxical perception of the state by the inhabitants of Putumayo, see Ramírez 2001.

19. For an extended analysis of the case of the coca growers' social movement in Putumayo, see Ramírez 2001.

Clandestine Connections
The Political and Relational Makings
of Collective Violence

JAVIER AUYERO

Luis D'Elia is the leader of the Federación de Tierra y Vivienda, a grassroots organization that, in 2000 and 2001, coordinated some of the largest and longest road blockades in protest against Fernando de la Rúa's administration. He lives in La Matanza, one of the most populated and poorest districts in metropolitan Buenos Aires, close to the crossroads of Crovara and Cristianía, a commercial area devastated during the food lootings of December 2001. In June 2005 I had an extensive conversation with him about these episodes. In a nutshell, this is what he had to say: Activists from the Peronist Party (the largest political party in Argentina) "did two sorts of things: some of them directed the looting. For lootings to occur there has to be a liberated territory. So, they moved the police away. And then they recruited people saying that they were going to loot. They did this from the Unidades Básicas [grassroots office of the Peronist Party]. The guys from the Unidades Básicas populated the area of Crovara and Cristianía with their own people, as if they had been recruited for such a day. They moved the police away; the police usually have their patrols stationed here. That day, the police disappeared. And, at a certain time, they hurled the people against the stores."

"We invite you to destroy the Kin supermarket this coming Wednesday at 11:30 a.m., the Valencia supermarket at 1:30 p.m., and the Chivo supermarket at 5 p.m." This and similar flyers circulated throughout poor neighborhoods in Moreno, a district located in the suburbs of Buenos Aires, inviting residents to join the crowds that looted several dozen supermarkets and grocery stores on 18 and 19 December 2001. Investigative journalists' reports agree that Peronist Party activists distributed the flyers. D'Elias's testimony and the flyers betray a connection that analysts of the recent wave of violent contention in Latin America have consistently overlooked: the obscure (and obscured) links that looters (and many other violent actors) maintain with power holders. Furthermore, the testimony and the flyers point to a dimension of collective violence to which scholars have only recently begun to give due attention: the role of political entrepreneurs in the promotion, inhibition, and/or channeling of physical damage to objects and persons. By dissecting the specific (and concealed) actions of political activists and the specific (and hidden) relations that they set in motion during the lootings of December 2001, this essay offers an in-depth examination of a concrete episode of disruptive collective violence, the 2001 food riots in Buenos Aires, and sheds light on the semisecret political interactions located at the root of mass insurgency. To foreshadow the argument: a close-up examination of the food lootings indicates a pattern in the distribution of violence (big-chain markets were protected by the police while small food stores suffered most of the damage). This pattern can be explained by the combined (though obscured) interactions between authorities, activists of the Peronist Party, and police forces. Activists and authorities (officials and police agents) created the opportunities for poor residents to loot: activists signaled the targets, and authorities validated their damage-making actions. Through a dissection of the Argentine food lootings, this essay demonstrates the central place of clandestine relationality in the genesis of collective violence.

Once we focus empirical attention on clandestine connections between perpetrators of violence, activists, and authorities, the analytical distinctions (among government agents, repressive forces, challengers, polity members, etc.) that the literature on collective action takes for granted collapse. During the December 2001 lootings repressive forces did not repress but, sometimes, looted, and looters were aided in their damaging actions by state actors. When confronted with such an empirical universe, most of the categories in which scholars of collective action routinely operate (categories very much informed by analyses carried out in the United States and Europe) prove misleading. While much of the literature agrees that the *interactions* between political elites, agents of social control, and protagonists of civil disorder matter, these categories remain discrete entities (for a paradigmatic example on U.S. riots, see Useem 1998). Most social-movement and collective-action scholarship maintains clear-cut boundaries between insurgents and authorities, dissidents or challengers and state actors—the "protest side" and the "repression side" (McPhail and McCarthy 2005:3; see Earl, Soule, and McCarthy 2003; Gamson 1990; but see Tilly 2003 for a notable exception). In point of fact, a recent illuminating collection devoted to studying the dynamic interactions between repression and mobilization (Davenport, Johnston, and Mueller 2005) remains silent about the possible participation of authorities (either elected officials or police agents) in the direct promotion of mobilization and/or the straightforward perpetration of collective violence. Rigorous empirical attention to clandestinity in the making (and demise) of collective violence seeks to address this silence in the literature.

In the introduction to this volume Enrique Arias and Daniel Goldstein assert that scholarship on Latin America needs to move toward an understanding of politics "that looks to the complex ways in which order (and/or disorder) is created through the interactions of multiple violent actors, *both within and without the state*" (my emphasis). We need, they rightly point out, to study the kinds of relationships violent actors "maintain to one another and to different elements of the state, including politicians, police, bureaucrats, and the military." In the relational spirit that Arias and Goldstein put forward, this article takes a close look at the dynamic and hidden interactions between a series of actors (inside and outside the polity) that were central in the making of the food riots. Scrutinizing these relationships not only allows us to better understand the dynamics of these particular lootings but also serves to integrate "extraordinary" collective violence into the study of "normal" politics— very much along the lines suggested by the editors of this book.

Riots in the Literature

Riots—both "race" and ethnic ones—have been widely researched in U.S. scholarship, mainly focusing on the 1968 wave following the assassination of Martin Luther King Jr. and on the 1992 episodes in Los Angeles following the acquittal in the Rodney King case (see, e.g., Stark et al. 1974; Baldassare 1994; for different comprehensive reviews, see McPhail and Wohlstein 1983; Useem 1998). Plenty of now classic studies on the individual attributes of participants in riots exist (Caplan 1970; Caplan and Paige 1968; Moinat et al. 1972), as do classic and contemporary studies on the demographic, economic, ethnic, and racial composition of rioting communities (Spilerman 1970; Lieberson and Silverman 1965; Wohlenberg 1982; Bergesen and Herman 1998). One of the strengths of this U.S.-based scholarship is its emphasis on the complex, diverse, interactive, and dynamic character of lootings. The current essay builds on two key insights from this body of literature:

1. *The relational underpinnings of lootings*: Contrary to common (mis)understandings, riots are carried out in small groups of people who are connected in some ways (through friendship, family, and/or community ties) and assemble, remain, and disperse together (Mc Phail and Wohlstein; Aveni 1977; Quarantelli and Dynes 1970). My essay shows that some of these connections clandestinely linked members of residents of poor barrios with members of a major political party. These connections gave form to the violence.

2. *The selectivity of looters' actions*: Far from constituting random collective actions, looters selectively target particular kinds of stores (based on the ethnicity of the store owner, the type of store, and/or other variables [Rosenfeld 1997; Tierney 1994]). My essay shows that those clandestine connections between party activists and residents-turned-looters directed the violence to small markets (unprotected by the police) and away from big-chain supermarkets (heavily guarded by state repressive forces).

Collective Violence and Clandestinity

Although far from constituting a clearly delimited area of inquiry, clandestine connections in politics have attracted some, still scattered, scholarly attention. In the introduction to this volume Arias and Goldstein review a series of studies that point to these sometimes "obvious and apparent" (but not for that reason well-researched), other times "more elusive" relationships at the basis of what they term "violent pluralism." Let me add a few other examples that connect well with the subject under investigation here.

Research on the origins and forms of communal violence in Southeast Asia highlights the usually hidden links between partisan politics and violence. Writing about the new migrants who live on the margins of modern cities and their role in communal riots in the region, Veena Das asserts that the "inhabitants of these slums and 'unauthorized colonies' . . . become a human resource for conducting the *underlife of political parties*. These are the people employed as strike-breakers; they make up crowds to demonstrate to the world the 'popularity' of a particular leader; and they form instruments for the management of political opponents. It is not surprising then that in the organization of riots they should play a pivotal role in the perpetration of violence" (Das 1990:12; my emphasis). Along these lines, Farida Shaheed's analysis of the Pathan-Mujahir conflicts in 1985–86 shows that the riots can be "traced directly to the actions of religious political parties" (1990:42). More recently Larissa MacFarquhar (2003) has charted the existing connections between the head of the Hindu-nationalist Shiv Sena party, Bal Thackeray, and anti-Muslim riots in contemporary India. Paul Brass's notion of "institutionalized riot systems" captures well these usually obscure connections: in these riot systems, Brass points out, "known actors specialize in the conversion of incidents between members of different communities into ethnic riots. The activities of these specialists [who operate under the loose control of party leaders] are usually required for a riot to spread from the initial incident of provocation" (Brass 1997:12). Sudhir Kakar's (1996) description of a *pehlwan* (wrestler/ enforcer who works for a political boss) further illustrates this point: the genesis of many episodes of collective violence is located in the area in which the actions of political entrepreneurs and those of specialists in violence (people who control the means of inflicting damage on persons and objects) secretly meet and mesh.

Linda Kirschke's (2000) work on transitions to multiparty politics in sub-Saharan Africa offers additional examples of the (usually masked) interweaving of party and state in the making of violence. Drawing on the cases of Cameroon, Kenya, and Rwanda in the 1990s, Kirschke shows that ruling elites, when threatened by local opposition and forced into reform by external actors (other powerful states or lending agencies), resort to "informal repression," that is, "covert violations sponsored by government authorities but carried out by third parties" (384). They do so, she argues, to frustrate democratic transitions.

That party leaders and/or state officials (bureaucrats and/or police agents) might be behind—rather than against—episodes of collective violence should hardly surprise students of Latin American politics. In a detailed study of La Violencia—as the wave of political violence that killed two hundred thousand people in Colombia in the 1940s and 1950s is known—the historian Mary Roldán has shown that in Antioquia "partisan conflict provided the initial catalyst to violence" (Roldán 2002:22). She asserts that state bureaucrats not only promoted the violence but that policemen and mayors also actively participated in partisan attacks. As she writes: "Violence in peripheral areas (of Antioquia) was largely the product of concerted and systematic harassment waged by selected regional authorities rather than the 'natural' outgrowth of partisan conflicts among local residents . . . the regional state and its forces were the primary instigators of violence on the periphery. . . . Governors and their administrative subordinates played an extraordinarily important role in the promotion of partisan violence in Antioquia between 1946 and 1949" (22). Political elites, she points out, did not simply tolerate or instigate the violence; they were its perpetrators. While party members organized attacks on places and peoples, police acted as partisan shock troops.[1] In a statement that will ring familiar to those studying political violence in other parts of the world, Roldán points out that "while many citizens attributed the escalation of violence to the absence of official forces, these forces were so often the perpetrators of violence between 1946 and 1949 that one wonders why anyone bothered to suggest that the presence of the authorities could have been of much help" (2002:82).[2]

In the contemporary Americas we have several ethnographic accounts of the working of clandestine connections in politics. Laurie Gunst's (1996) taxing exploration of Jamaican gangs illustrates the connections that so-called posses had with political parties during the 1980s, as well as the usually violent outcomes of these "mafia-style links" (83). The origins of Jamaican drug gangs in New York can be found, Gunst argues, in the posses that were, in fact, political groupings armed by party leaders linked to Edward Seaga or Michael Manley. Donna Goldstein's (2003) and Enrique Arias's (2006a, 2006b, 2006c, 2004) recent ethnographies of Rio de Janeiro's favelas provide further evidence of the collusion between state actors, political party members, and violent entrepreneurs (gang members associated with drug trafficking). Luis Astorga's (2005) detailed historical reconstruction of the mutual imbrication of the fields of illicit drug production and trafficking and of politics throughout twentieth-century Mexico provides another excellent example of concealed and illegal connections between actors inside and outside the political system, relations that should be seriously considered if we are to comprehend seemingly random upsurges of violence past or present.

What do all the above cases have in common? They all portray the activation of clandestine connections among political actors. These secret links prove crucial to understanding and explaining extraordinary collective violence. What role did these underhanded, concealed interactions play in the making of the 2001 food riots? What role, if any, do they play in the daily practice of democracy in contemporary Argentina? Let me focus on the first question and then offer a well-informed speculation on the second.

Methods

The data for this essay come from four different sources: newspaper accounts, journalistic reports, video archives, and qualitative fieldwork in two rioting communities. To reconstruct as thoroughly as possible what happened between 13 and 22 December 2001, I created a catalog of the events with information culled from several sources. I read four national newspapers (*Clarín*, *Crónica*, *La Nación*, and *Página 12*) for the days of the lootings (both the printed and online editions), for the month before, and for the year after the episodes. I also read ten local newspapers from the provinces where lootings occurred (*El Ciudadano*, *La Voz del Interior*, *La Mañana del Sur*, *Rio Negro*, *Cronica-Chubut*, *La Gaceta*, *El Litoral*, *El Liberal*, *Los Andes*, and *El Sol*) covering the months of December 2001 and January 2002, and the October, November, December 2001 and January 2002 issues of *Para Ud!*, a local newspaper printed in Moreno (Buenos Aires). For the purposes of data collection I considered a looting episode to be the activity of two or more persons either forcibly seizing objects in spite of restraint or resistance, or attempting to seize objects but meeting with effective restraint or resistance. In creating this catalog I relied mainly on hard news items (i.e., the who, what, when, and where of the episodes), which, as other researchers have pointed out, are generally more precise than so-called soft news (i.e., journalists' impressions and inferences) (see Earl et al. 2004:72). Journalistic accounts of the events were far from accurate and reliable, a limitation frequently pointed out by social movement scholars and one that constitutes a particularly serious problem in the case of episodic violent collective action (Myers and Schaefer Caniglia 2004; Earl et al. 2004; Koopmans and Rucht 1999, 2002; Myers 1997; Franzosi 1987). Despite its shortcomings, however, the catalog helped me create a model of the relationships among looting sites, the number of participants in the lootings, the presence or absence of the police, and party activists. The model created with the newspaper data tells the following story: the number of looters did not have an impact on police presence; police forces protected large markets rather than small ones; and party activists tended to be present at small market lootings when there were no police around (Auyero and Moran 2004).

The analysis that follows is also based on three reports about the lootings published by investigative journalists (Bonasso 2002; Camarasa with Veltri 2002; Young et al. 2002), as well as on the video archives of *Canal 11*, a major national TV channel, where I was able to watch the reports and the images (some of them never broadcast) produced at the time of the events. But the bulk of the account is based on fieldwork at two sites where the heaviest looting activity in Buenos Aires took place. Fieldwork comprised in-depth interviews and informal conversations with residents of the poor barrios Lomas Verde (in the district of Moreno) and BID (in the district of La Matanza). Both barrios are located roughly at the same distance (thirteen and fifteen blocks, respectively) from the two most damaged commercial strips during the lootings: El Cruce de Castelar in Moreno (hereafter El Cruce) and the crossroads of Crovara and Cristianía Streets in La Matanza (hereafter C&C). I chose both neighborhoods after a month of preliminary research that indicated that people from both enclaves had participated in the lootings. Two research assistants and I conducted sixty interviews with residents of both barrios. A third of these residents themselves looted, and two-thirds of them were able to provide detailed descriptions of what went on during the week under investigation, even if they had not taken part in the events. In both neighborhoods we asked similar questions of the residents. We asked them about their job situation during the month of December 2001 and about how they made ends meet during the month before the lootings. We also inquired about their daily routines during the day the lootings started, and about their neighbors' actions during the episodes. If they said they went to the looting sites, we asked them whether they went by themselves or with somebody else, about the goods they brought with them from the looting, and about the actions of the police. We then focused attention on the targets: how did they decide which store to enter? Were the store owners or managers there? How did the owners and/or managers react? We also reported what other people had told us about the lootings (i.e., that they had been organized, preplanned) and asked them about their opinions concerning that statement.

We also interviewed twenty store owners, managers, and employees at each site. Half of them worked in stores that were looted, and half of them worked at stores that were spared from the violence. We asked the same questions of them: What did they remember about those days? Were their stores looted or not? If their stores were ransacked we asked them to provide the most detailed descriptions possible of what they witnessed and how they felt at the time. If their stores were spared we asked them to describe their actions and thoughts during that week. We then also asked them whether or not they knew the looters; whether the looters were customers or not; whether they saw the looters after the violence ended; and whether or not there were activists among the looters.

After a brief description of the geographic distribution of the 2001 lootings and their diversity, this essay examines the unfolding of violence in two poor communities of Moreno and La Matanza. I describes the workings of two mechanisms, usually present in other types of collective action (Tarrow 2005; Tilly 2003; Mc Adam, Tarrow, and Tilly 2001), that were crucial in the creation of opportunities to loot: (1) the signaling (i.e. information sharing) spirals carried out by party activists (in seeming coordination with the police); and (2) the implicit certification of looting by state authorities (officials and police agents). Analytically the account that follows disaggregates the episodes into two dimensions—the production of opportunities to loot and the taking advantage of those opportunities—and focuses most of the attention on the former.

Argentine Lootings

During the week of 13–22 December 2001 grocery stores and supermarkets were looted in eleven of the twenty-four Argentine states. By the week's end, eighteen people (all of them under thirty-five years old) had been killed either by the police or by store owners. Hundreds more had been seriously injured, and thousands were arrested. The states of Santa Fe, Entre Ríos, and Mendoza and the districts of Avellaneda and Quilmes in the state of Buenos Aires were the first to experience the uprisings, with hundreds of persons blockading roads, publicly demanding food, and eventually looting stores and markets. Yet the violence soon extended unevenly to the south, center, and north of the country, reaching the highly populated and urbanized state of Córdoba and spreading rapidly through Buenos Aires. Record levels of unemployment and poverty and massive cutbacks in already meager welfare programs were at the root of these episodes.

Lootings varied in terms of their location, number of participants, type of store attacked, and the presence of police and party activists among the crowds. One-third of the 289 episodes reported in newspapers—a combination of lootings and attempted lootings repressed by the police and/or store owners—occurred in Buenos Aires (96), the most populated province, mainly in the Conurbano (the metropolitan area surrounding the federal capital). Another 20 percent occurred in Santa Fe (61), the third-most-populated province. Around 10 percent each occurred in the two southern states of Neuquén (29) and Rio Negro (27), and the northern state of Tucumán (27). The remaining 49 episodes were scattered over seven other provinces. The number of actors involved also varied. There were thousands of participants in Concordia (Entre

Ríos), Banda del Rio Salí (Tucumán), and Centenario (Neuquén) and dozens in many smaller episodes in Rosario (Santa Fe), Guaymallén (Mendoza), and Paraná (Entre Rios). Of the episodes with participant-count information, the modal category of estimated participants ranged between one hundred and four hundred (close to 70 percent of the total number of lootings).

The crowds attacked different types of targets as well. Nearly 60 percent of the episodes reported by newspapers took place in small, local markets and grocery stores. Police presence was reported in 106 of the 289 episodes (37 percent), sometimes outnumbered by the looters, sometimes not, sometimes deterring the crowds with rubber bullets and tear gas (and in a few reported cases with real bullets), other times dissuading potential looters simply by their presence (more details on the police presence and actions later). The number of arrests also varied widely from province to province, from dozens in Entre Ríos to about two hundred in Rosario and close to six hundred in Tucumán.[3] Successful lootings and those effectively stopped by restraint were evenly distributed when the targets were big, chain-owned supermarkets. When incidents occurred in small, local markets and grocery stores, successful lootings outnumbered rebuffed attempts by nearly three to one. Based on a statistical analysis of newspaper reports, it can be asserted that the odds of police presence at a looting site were 268 percent higher when the site was a large chain supermarket (Auyero and Moran 2004).

Detailed newspaper reports exist for fewer than half of the recorded 289 episodes. Newspapers and investigative journalists' accounts provide some sort of detailed descriptions of the composition and actions of the looting crowds in about 130 episodes. In half of these reports reporters noted the presence of Peronist Party activists among the crowds, particularly at the two sites of the heaviest looting activity (La Matanza and Moreno) and in the lootings that occurred in small stores with little police presence. Small-store lootings thus had a lower likelihood of police presence *and* a higher visibility of party activists.

Secondary reports and our own interviews indicated that the looting "crowd" was composed of small *groups* that would arrive *together* at the looting site. This confirms arguments made about the existing linkages among participants in joint action, destructive or otherwise. As Adrian Aveni (1977) would say, looters were a "not-so-lonely crowd" (see also McPhail and Wohlstein 1983). Recent research on contentious politics (McAdam, Tarrow, and Tilly 2001; Diani and McAdam 2003) and on collective violence (Tilly 2003) highlights precisely this aspect of collective-action episodes: "In practice," writes Charles Tilly (2003:32), "constituents' units of claim-making actors often consist not of living, breathing whole individuals but of groups, organizations, bundles of social relations, and social sites such as occupations and neighborhoods." Most scholarship on collective action highlights the existence of *horizontal ties* between insurgents—so much so that formal or informal relations among individuals work as a sort of precondition for their joining in social-movement activity (see, e.g., McAdam 1988). *Vertical connections* between insurgents and authorities, however, have received much less attention. Some of the looting crowds (mainly those in episodes that took place in small markets) were also connected in this second sense of the term. Investigative journalists' reports and our own interviews (with participants and bystanders) point to relationships among the actions of looters, the presence of party activists, and police inaction. To figure out exactly how these two types of connections matter in the making of collective violence, we need to look more microscopically at specific incidents.

The Cases: Lootings under the Microscope

Moreno is a district located in the western part of the Conurbano Bonaerense, thirty-seven kilometers from the city of Buenos Aires. Close to a third of its 380,000 inhabitants have "unsatisfied basic needs" (Alsina and Catenazzi 2002). La Matanza is a district that borders the federal capital on the southwest; half of its 1,255,288 inhabitants live under the poverty line (for a description, see Cerrutti and Grimson 2004). La Matanza is the most populated district in the Conurbano, with 106 shantytowns (Torresi 2005). Both La Matanza and Moreno share the plight that has affected the whole region since the early 1990s: skyrocketing poverty due to hyperunemployment. In May 1997, 24.8 percent of households in the Buenos Aires metropolitan area (and 32.7 percent of the population) were living below the poverty line. By May 2003 these figures had almost doubled: 50.5 percent of the households (and 61.3 percent of the population) were experiencing this kind of poverty (INDEC-EPH 2003).

The end of 2001 found the inhabitants of Moreno and La Matanza, like those of many other poor areas throughout the country, struggling to make ends meet with record levels of unemployment and shrinking state assistance. Food assistance and other welfare programs (most notably, unemployment subsidies) had been steadily declining with the deepening of the economic recession of 2001.

Karina, a resident of one of the most destitute enclaves in Moreno, remembers that at the time she had an unemployment subsidy (then known as Plan

Trabajar) but that the monthly payments were delayed (something quite common in the district and in Buenos Aires): "They were supposed to be paying by the end of the month [November] and they didn't. They would set a date, then another one. Christmas was right around the corner and . . . well, then the lootings happened." Payments for the unemployment subsidies were not only delayed but dwindling (relief was cut by 20 percent in many districts).

Lootings in El Cruce began late on 18 December, but the heaviest looting activity (in which the most people participated and the most stores were affected) took place on the afternoon of 19 December. That day witnessed most of the destruction in La Matanza, too. But days before, neighbors, looters, and shopkeepers knew "something was coming." Sandra, who stayed home in Lomas Verde during the episodes, told us that a week or so in advance a neighbor told her about the impending lootings. Mono, a looter, told us: "I was in school, and my classmates and friends were talking about the lootings like two weeks before it all began." "In Moreno," Mónica Gomez told the journalist Laura Vales (*Página12web*, 20 December 2001), "we knew that the lootings were going to happen for at least about a month, but nobody did anything. They gave us [unemployment] subsidies, and then they cut them. They gave us bags of food, but they suddenly stopped giving them. Nobody can take that." Rumors were running rampant among shopkeepers in El Cruce and in C&C. As two of them told us, "There was a lot of gossip saying that the sackings were about to start"; "a week or so before, other shopkeepers and customers were spreading rumors that there was a group of people who were going to create disturbances."

Signaling

My field notes of 17 July 2004 read as follows:

> Delia lives with her brother and her three kids in Lomas Verde (Moreno). She's been involved in politics for twenty years, always as a member of the Peronist Party. She heads a small cooperative that is building housing units with funds provided by the local state. She distributes resources (food, medicine, clothing) among poor residents. She obtains these resources through her connections in the municipal building ("I have a phone number I can call in case I need something"). During electoral times, she brings her followers to Peronist rallies and hands out ballots for the Peronist Party ("among my people"). Asked about the December lootings, she smiles and replies: "What do you want to know? What did we take?" Sensing that she is

sort of defending herself, I react with, "No, no . . . I'd like to know how it was? How did you find out?" Her response encapsulates one crucial dynamic of the looting: "We [the members of the party] knew about the lootings beforehand. Around 1 a.m. [the lootings began by noon] we knew that there was going to be a looting. We were told about them by the municipal authorities, and we passed the information along [among the members of the party]." She recounts that she went back and forth along the fifteen-block stretch between her home and El Cruce (the area in which most stores were located) six times. I then ask her about police presence in the area.

Where were the rumors coming from? Dozens of interviews with residents, looters, the looted, grassroots leaders, and activists from the Peronist Party point to the latter as their source. Delia told us so. Pascual, a store owner in c&c, put it this way: "We knew a lot of political activists . . . they came to the store when they did fundraising. . . . They brought us news [about the lootings]."

Before and during the lootings, Peronist activists communicated the location of targets, the presence or absence of police, and thus the feasibility of risky practices. Signaling, a crucial mechanism in the generation of collective action (McAdam, Tarrow, and Tilly 2001), was at work.[4] Friends and neighbors, in cooperation with political activists, indicated to each other when lootings were about to start and where it was safe to loot. Signaling basically comprised protection from potential repressive action (as many residents told us, "I didn't go through that street because neighbors told me the cops were there"); and logistics (participants told us some places were spared because they had heavy or electrified gates or private security).

The reporting of Young et al. (2002) provides a description of the signaling activities that took place. In December 2001 Josefa was living in a small shack located in a poor neighborhood of Moreno. On the eighteenth of the month she received a small flyer inviting her to "bust" a group of markets. The next day she showed up on time in front of Kin, and soon two hundred people were gathered in front of this small market clamoring for food. She recalls seeing a police car leaving the scene and a man who worked at the local municipality talking on his cellular phone. Soon a truck loaded with a *grupo de pesados* (group of thugs), known in the neighborhood as Los Gurkas, arrived at the scene. "They broke the doors and called us in," Josefa remembers. "A few days later, I met one of them, and he told me that people from the Peronist Party paid 100 pesos for the job." Far from Josefa, in another poor enclave in Buenos Aires, residents of the barrio Baires (located in the municipality of Tigre) seemed to have received similar news about an imminent looting through their children: "When my son arrived home from school, he told me that a man from the local Unidad Básica came to inform the teachers about the sites of the lootings. The teacher told my son that she was going to go. And we went to see if we could get something."

The looting crowd did not form at the site but was connected beforehand. Looters went to the looting scene with trusted others, mostly family members. As Diana told us: "Yes, I went to El Cruce, but I was scared . . . I went with my brother. In El Cruce I saw a lot of people I knew, classmates, friends." Claudia was watching TV that day and at first could not believe what she saw: lootings were taking place a couple of blocks from her home in Lomas Verde, at a place where she did most of her shopping on a daily basis: "My aunt and my daughter wanted to go. My daughter wanted to know what a looting was all about. We went to El Cruce, but we didn't bring shopping bags with us. I hadn't gone before because my husband would have gotten very angry at me, but then I went anyway. We took this street because there were no cops, and it was calmer there. . . . We got to this supermarket, but . . . I don't [remember taking] stuff from inside the store. . . . I only took the stuff that other people would throw on the street." Given the goods that Claudia brought home, it is hard to believe that she was not inside a store. She listed: soft drinks, ice cream, olives, sugar, yerba maté, frankfurters, and noodles. Then she added: "Before arriving home, I found a bag with school stuff for the kids." In a process known as relational diffusion (Tarrow 2005; McAdam and Rucht 1993), the signaling (secretly activated by party activists) traversed through these bundles of proximate social relations and connected looters with (unprotected) targets.

Certification

Looters realized early on that authorities (local state officials and police forces) condoned, sometimes even instigated, their damaging actions. Once they became aware of this, looters used supermarket carts to make not one but several trips to El Cruce and c&c. If we look at this process in depth we see another mechanism at work: certification.[5]

Antonio, a looter in Moreno, told us: "We went to Caburé [a supermarket located five blocks from his home]. The owner was there, but then the cops advised him to leave. That's when we got in, and we took the stuff. Even the cops put stuff in the police car." A neighbor, who witnessed looting scenes from her house, said: "When they were sacking the butcher shop [across the street], the cops would calm people down and then put all the meat inside their patrol car!" "What can I tell you about the police?" asks Claudia, who participated in the lootings. "They were the ones who took most of the stuff, the best things. They would get you and grab your bags. The computer they now have is from the lootings."

In contrast to newspaper accounts indicating otherwise, police forces were not absent when lootings took place in small markets. The police were present in El Cruce and in C&C: sometimes police agents collaborated with the ransacking crowd; at other times they simply witnessed the looting from a distance. Almost every shopkeeper at both sites mentioned the passive police presence: "There were cops . . . but they had orders not to do anything" (Antonio, El Cruce); "cops were patrolling the area with two old patrol cars . . . they didn't do anything" (Daniel, El Cruce); "the police were right by our side, with their weapons. I told them: 'Brother, guard my store. What are you here for?' And his reply was: 'I can't, I can't, I can't. If I do something, I'll lose my job' " (Pablo, C&C).

The police were, in part, following orders. The then secretary of security ordered them not to act if they lacked antimutiny equipment. As he put it in an interview with me in July 2005: The state police had few "antimutiny elements . . . but I decided to use only those. I gave explicit orders: Those who lacked antimutiny equipment should leave the scene, should go home and stay with their families. My orders were clear: The police should move out, should kill nobody. That's when I said: 'I would rather lament the loss of a can of tomatoes than the loss of a life.' " (This statement was broadcast on radio and published in the 20 December edition of *Clarín*.)

But the police were not simply following orders. They were also acting on their own: my own evidence shows that they protected certain small markets in exchange for material goods (TV sets, other valuables, or money) and that they took part in certain lootings. The following detour should help the reader understand police actions. Their participation in the looting and the exchange of special protection for money shows clear continuities with their routine (and many times illegal) operations.

It is generally agreed that the police of the province of Buenos Aires have been involved in gambling, prostitution, drug dealing, kidnappings, and car theft for the past two decades (Rother 2003; Isla and Miguez 2003; Binder 2004; Klipphan 2004). A former undersecretary of security in the state of Buenos Aires and a highly perceptive analyst of the state police's (mis)behavior asserts that there is a "perverse relationship between politics, crime and police action" (Sain 2004:87).

During the early 1990s, Marcelo Sain (2002:85) asserts, the government of Buenos Aires made an explicit agreement with the state police: to attain "respectable levels of public safety" the government provided the police with numerous material and financial resources and a significant degree of freedom of action (i.e., unaccountability). The state government also assured the police that it would not intervene in the illegal self-financing activities that the force had long developed. This "circuit of illegal self-financing," as Sain calls it (2002:86), is the product of the participation of key members of the police hierarchy in an "extended network of criminal activities that revolved around illegal gambling, prostitution, drug and arms trafficking, and robberies" (Sain 2002:86). In 1998 the minister of justice and security of Buenos Aires, León Arslanián, admitted that reform attempts had been unsuccessful in dismantling the "clandestine collection [*recaudación clandestina*] that feeds the police system with resources that come from criminal activities" (Sain 2002:115).

Illegal and clandestine practices are thus institutionalized in the police force (Isla and Miguez 2003). In her perceptive and detailed ethnographic account of shantytown life in Quilmes (Buenos Aires), the anthropologist Nathalie Puex looks at this very same phenomenon from the bottom up, examining shanty dwellers' perceptions of the connection between criminal and police activities, as well as the actual linkages between shanty youngsters and authorities: "For many shantytown residents (*villeros*) the cop is another thief (*chorro*), much like a politician. The police officer does not represent the law because he himself takes part in criminal activity. [This participation creates an] image of the police as both a repressive force and a provider of jobs. Most of the young delinquents in the shantytown 'work' for the police; in other words, they are part of an illicit organization directed by policemen who offer work to these shanty youngsters. Many of these youngsters obtain their income through participating in this organization" (Puex 2003:66).

Besides the existing connections between the crime and law-enforcement worlds, there is also an area, as analysts point out, in which both worlds intersect and interact with party politics. Part of the funds the Buenos Aires police collect from their illegal activities goes to finance the force itself; another part, observers affirm, helps to sustain the machine of the largest political party in the country, the Peronist Party. As Sain (2004:22) remarks: "The world of politics, the security system—mainly the police—and crime constitute three intimately linked instances." Or, as a former justice minister told the *New York Times*: "There are politicians who are thieves and finance their campaigns with money from police corruption" (Rother 2003). It is no wonder that state initiatives to reform the Buenos Aires police (which took place in the mid- to late 1990s) met with stubborn resistance from "Peronist local politicians, mayors and brokers [*punteros*], as well as those belonging to the Radical Party" (Sain 2002:90). These groups "had a well-oiled relationship with the police machine," whose illegally obtained resources went, in part, to finance party activities (Sain 2002:90). Police forces are hardly the only ones participating in illegal actions: "important sectors of political parties, state bureaucracies, including the judicial branch, are involved in extended systems of corruption" (Isla and Miguez 2003:318). Noting the extent to which security forces are involved in crime, Alejandro Isla and Daniel Miguez (2003:323) assert that police forces "function as a mafia organization (especially in Buenos Aires) that itself produces criminal violence."

· · · · ·

Shopkeepers (and even some of the looters themselves) have little doubt about the political underpinnings of the lootings. Almost every shopkeeper we interviewed in Moreno located the origins of the lootings in a rally organized by the mayor, Mariano West. On 19 December Mayor West, himself a strongman in the Peronist Party, declared an economic emergency in his district and organized a rally to demand a change in economic policy. Together with party members, local officials, and union leaders, the mayor led thousands of citizens from the main municipal building through the streets of Moreno, until national police stopped the rally at the border of the federal capital. Significantly, the rally passed through El Cruce before it dissolved. According to most of our interviewees, the heavy looting began on the margins of this procession. As a bystander recollects: "And the worst thing I remember is the caravan. It was organized by the mayor. He was at the head of it in a station wagon, and, following him, there were three blocks of people, cars, trucks, everything . . . and behind that . . . they were all looting. He instigated them to loot. All of the looters came with the mayor, breaking everything up, looting."

Almost every storekeeper points to the rally as the moment at which the heavy looting began. They see the fact that the violence got underway at the margins of a rally organized by the mayor as the best proof of the political (i.e., organized, preplanned) character of the lootings. As Mirta, a shopkeeper, describes it: "Everybody around here was saying that it was all organized. I don't know anything about politics, but people were saying that the mayor prepared everything. . . . There was a caravan, and he brought all the people here."

While the caravan signaled authorities' certification of looters' violent actions, it was hardly the only signal that participants received. Looters and witnesses saw (and clearly remember) political authorities (the mayor, but also councilmen and other officials) at the looting scene; they also saw the police passively witnessing the ransacking. To them this was a clear indication that the authorities did not condemn their actions. Furthermore, since *trusted* sources spread the news about imminent lootings (sources connected with municipal authorities like political activists), looters at both sites believed their actions to enjoy some legitimacy. Certification by public authorities, a key causal mechanism in the generation of violence (Tilly 2003; McAdam, Tarrow, and Tilly 2001), was at work in situ as the lootings proceeded.

Clandestinity Matters

There is little doubt that Peronist activists were indeed involved in the looting episodes that took place both in El Cruce and in C&C. Investigative journalists reporting from Moreno and La Matanza stated this, and my own research has also found evidence of their presence. But how exactly were activists involved? Although some Peronists might have promoted the lootings by recruiting followers, their main activity (at least the one for which I have the best evidence) seems to have been spreading news of the upcoming looting opportunity, as Delia matter-of-factly told me. Peronist activists did not take their followers to the stores, nor could they control their actions. Yet they did do something crucial: they passed the word about the location of the looting—simply by spreading rumors that lootings were "coming" at the crossroads of Crovara and Cristianía in La Matanza and in El Cruce in Moreno, places populated not by large chain supermarkets but by small retail stores. These were "safe places" to loot—police would not be present and, if present, would not act. How did activists and people in general know about police future (in)activity? In part they assumed it because news about upcoming lootings was coming from above, from well-connected state actors. In part they also experienced it on site when they saw that the police were, in the words of one activist-turned-looter, "worse than us, they were the ones who took most of the things . . . and when we were inside El Chivo [a devastated supermarket in El Cruce], they even told us where to escape so that we wouldn't get in trouble."

As mentioned earlier, rumors proved crucial at the onset of the lootings. They misinformed residents of food distributions by certain supermarkets and, in doing so, created the conditions for collective violence. Rumors also multiplied at the end of the looting cycle (20–21 December); yet then they had the opposite effect—they prevented further looting. Press reports and our interviews indicate that uncertainty about what was going to happen next and anxiety about further violence became widespread among residents of low-income neighborhoods and shopkeepers.

At the time of the episodes the Canadian anthropologist Lindsay DuBois was living in Billinghurst, a working-class neighborhood in the district of San Martin, also the site of heavy looting activity. She writes:

> The night of the 19th–20th, I awoke to the sound of firecrackers and barking dogs. When I looked out the window, I saw fires burning in the intersections at both ends of our block. Daniel, my husband, went out to investigate, and returned looking for wood scraps and other fuel for the fires. When I asked what was happening, he told me neighbors had been warned that hordes of people were coming to invade our houses, and that the large firecrackers were being set off to wake up everyone so that they would be on the alert. In response to my disbelief, Daniel's rushed answer was he had to seem to support neighbors who set themselves up for an all-night vigil tending the fires. Those of us inside did not get much more sleep. A brief tour of the neighborhood in the morning showed signs that similar fires had been set at virtually every intersection in the neighborhood. The bonfires and vigils continued for two more nights. (DuBois 2002:4)

Bonfires and barricades in poor and low-income neighborhoods, set up by residents to defend their few possessions from the presumed attacks of angry looters rampaging nearby, were widely reported in the press. Always a good source of police information and a widely read newspaper among low-income groups, *Crónica* on 21 December 2001 reported that "early this morning fear was widespread among residents of the Conurbano. They armed themselves and set up guards because they were afraid their homes would be sacked. . . . Afflicted residents from diverse localities, using sticks, cudgels, knives, firelocks, and guns, firmly gripped by men and their sons, mounted guard since dawn in front of their homes because of the 'imminent attack' of 'hordes' of looters who were coming from the 'shantytowns.'" In the many conversations we had with residents of Lomas Verde and BID, they all remember how "chilling" and "frightening" that night was, with the impending invasion from other poor barrios: Andrea said, "We closed everything because news went around that they were going to loot the private houses, that they were going to break into them. . . . The same people who looted the grocery stores were coming from everywhere. . . . They were coming to loot. Many people went around the neighborhood in trucks, telling people to close their doors, to put locks everywhere." And Leonor: "Around 4 a.m., everybody said that they were coming from other barrios. And so we started to secure our home. We started to block the alleyways, with sticks and with whatever we had at hand. Every neighbor did that. Those who had weapons carried them. Me and my husband did not have a gun; my husband stayed outside with a big stick. We didn't sleep that night."

The attacks never materialized. Juan José Alvarez, then secretary of security of Buenos Aires, informed the public at a press conference on 22 December that "police precincts received close to five thousand calls concerning possible lootings in private homes, but in every case they were false alarms." Reporters from *Crónica* said that, having checked with several police precincts of Buenos Aires, they did not have information about lootings in private homes.

Where were these rumors coming from? Based on her conversations with her neighbors in Billinghurst, DuBois (2002) attributes this rumor-mongering to the police and speculates about its impact. The rumors of "invading hordes" had, she asserts, a demobilizing effect: they encouraged people to stay at home to defend their barrios, thus preventing further looting. Her view dovetails with the diagnosis made by the most detailed journalistic report on the lootings (Young et al. 2002). Describing the actions of the Buenos Aires police, reporters from *Clarín*, the main Argentine newspaper, assert that the police:

> broke out of its passivity with one precise objective: to impose fear, sometimes wearing uniforms, other times in plainclothes. The technique was simple and effective. Policemen went to a barrio and told neighbors that people from a nearby barrio were coming to rob. They advised neighbors to arm themselves, to stay awake, to tend fires and barricades on the corners, and to lock themselves at home. . . . In Lomas they told residents that invaders were coming from Camino Negro. In Avellaneda, cops in uniform announced that thieves were coming from Villa Tranquila. . . . In La Matanza, policemen were spreading the news about an invasion of Villegas by residents of El Tambo. . . . Such a level of coordination . . . could only be explained by a decisive action of the leadership of the police department. (Young et al. 2002:2)

While rumors spread quickly both at the beginning and at the end of the looting week, the outcome of these various rumors differed quite markedly. Rumors (spread by activists) fostered lootings but also contributed (those spread by the police) to their demise. If DuBois and investigative journalists are correct (and based on interviews with officials and other journalists, I find their accounts highly plausible), we can thus conclude that members of the Peronist Party and the Buenos Aires police (at the time controlled by Peronist officials) were at both ends of the collective violence that traumatized Buenos Aires in December: they secretly created the opportunities to loot and furtively closed those same down again.

It is not far-fetched to assert that sectors of the Peronist Party promoted the violence: Peronist activists were highly visible in places of significant looting and in those that were highly consequential in terms of the political impact of the lootings (i.e. metropolitan Buenos Aires); and Peronist government officials in the state of Buenos Aires prevented the police from acting once the lootings broke out. To what end? While the reasons remain a matter of hotly contested debate, many of my interviewees, including grassroots leaders, believe that the Peronist Party was instigating a civilian coup d'état. Members of the Peronist Party deny this. Yet indisputably Peronists, in fomenting violence, displayed what Frances Piven and Richard Cloward (1979:26) have termed the "power of disruption"—a way of doing politics by noninstitutional (and violent) means.

The food riots occurred alongside thousands of people blockading roads and bridges throughout the country and banging pots and pans in the main plaza of Buenos Aires (episodes known as *cacerolazos*). Less than a month after these events, the Peronist Party was back in power.

On Collective Violence and Democracy

This article unearthed, in as detailed a form as the available evidence allows, the concealed dynamic interactions among looters, political activists, and police forces that shaped the incidence and form of collective violence. It also highlighted the presence of two main mechanisms crucial to the creation (and closing) of opportunities to loot: signaling and certification.

The December 2001 lootings in Argentina can (and should) serve to open a broader inquiry into the clandestine relational underpinnings of collective violence and, more specifically, into the role of third parties (in our case, party activists and police agents) who, as the American Sociological Association's report on the social causes of violence asserts (Levine and Rosich n.d.:70), "are often involved or present during violent encounters; yet, our knowledge of their role is very limited" (see also Tilly 2003).

What does this article's in-depth look at one episode of collective violence teach us about other similar cases? In other words, what are the analytical implications of this study? Let me tackle this question by presenting a (limited) sample of other food lootings in Latin America and by proposing a way of examining them based on knowledge garnered from the Argentine case.

Food lootings took place in almost every Latin American country during the past decade. In the context of subsistence crises brought by natural disasters (droughts, flooding, or earthquakes), in that of suddenly imposed grievances due to politicoeconomic crises, or in the margins of collective protests against neoliberal policies, hundreds and sometimes thousands of desperate people have attacked food markets and looted merchandise. The 1989 *caracazo* or *sacudón* in Venezuela is probably one of the best-known cases of massive looting (López Maya 1999). In December 1999 the state of Vargas, in Venezuela, also experienced food lootings following floods that left thousands deprived of the basic means of subsistence (*El Universal*, 18 December 1999). In April 2002, during the attempted coup against President Hugo Chávez, Venezuela was also the site of numerous lootings in mainly low-income *barriadas*.

Brazil and Venezuela are hardly alone in witnessing their citizens forcibly seizing food from markets. After the January 1999 earthquake in central-west Colombia left approximately one thousand dead, hundreds of distressed inhabitants of the city of Armenia invaded and sacked local food stores. Peru also saw its share of lootings: in June 2002 food lootings took place in the context of protests against the privatization of state-owned electrical companies in Arequipa. In May 2003 the roadblocks manned in protest against President Alejandro Toledo's economic policies created food shortages on the northern coast. Desperate residents of Barranca and Huarney looted local markets, mainly for food. Food looting also occurred during the protests against the Bolivian president Gonzalo Sánchez de Lozada in both La Paz and El Alto in February 2003 (lootings that involved attacks on the Coca-Cola company and on Lyonnaise des Eaux, the French company that has provided water to La Paz since 1997). Finally, Uruguay also saw its citizens plunder food stores. Following one of the worst economic crises in years, at least sixteen stores were ransacked by dozens of residents of low-income barrios in Montevideo in 2002 (*Clarín*, 2 August 2002).

Conclusion

What light does my analysis of the lootings of 2001 shed on these other cases? Analysts interested in riotous Latin America during the past two decades would certainly benefit from looking at key background conditions and the way in which they articulate with local conditions (Walton and Ragin 1990; Walton and Seddon 1994). Likewise, for analysts interested in collective violence, there are two lessons to be learned: first, we need to place cases of episodic collective violence under the microscope and investigate multiple primary and secondary sources to systematically examine the relational underpinnings and the mechanisms (and their sequence) at work. Second, and most important, we should carefully scrutinize the (possible) connections between perpetrators of damage and the authorities and/or established political actors.

What are the larger implications of this study? In other words, besides the case of the food lootings, what can students interested in the "complex relationship between democracy and violence in Latin America" (Arias and Goldstein this volume) learn from the above analysis? Let me conclude with a well-informed speculation regarding the place of violence in everyday politics.

The interactions among local leaders, looters, and police dramatized during the 2001 episodes are, in fact, the infrastructure, the foundation, of all kinds of politics. They are not a remnant of the past, they are not alien or primitive. On the contrary, they form a constitutive part of democratic Argentina. A grassroots leader I interviewed during the course of my fieldwork put it this way: "When officials and politicians talk about governability . . . what do you think they are talking about? Do you think they refer to their ability to pass a law in Congress? To have one or two more party members in the House? No. No way. Listen carefully. They are talking about the capacity to generate a big mess [*un gran quilombo*] in the Conurbano. That's what they mean when they say governability." The threat of collective violence (in this leader's words, "the capacity to generate a big mess in the Conurbano") is part and parcel of existing politics in contemporary Argentina. The episodes described above are hardly part of the dim past; they are very present in politicians' and officials' ways of doing and thinking about politics (the interest and vehemence with which public officials talked to me about the 2001 lootings lend evidence of this). What local political actors and police are (secretly) capable of doing (and not doing) is vivid in everybody's mind. The grassroots leader quoted is implicitly referring to the power of disruption held by the actors capable of tapping into the clandestine connections "within and without" the political system.

With the shrinking of the state that has characterized the past three neoliberal decades, the lack of accountability of repressive forces (Isla and Miguez 2003; Sain 2002), the sustained strength of clientelist networks, and the consolidation of urban marginality (Auyero 2000), these clandestine connections become increasingly relevant in everyday politics. Those who have the capacity to activate them will be able to use the threat of violence and, eventually, to dislocate institutional life. Although difficult to quantify, the amount of leverage, of political power, that these actors gain by being (cap)able of using what Piven and Cloward term the "threat of disruption" (1979:35) is immense.

In other words, those who can set in motion these connections will be capable of creating civil disturbance *and* of keeping it at bay. If this speculation based in an in-depth look at the lootings is correct, the power of disruption wielded by groups within established political parties and within the repressive forces is something to be seriously reckoned with. Relationships between state and society in present-day Argentina should take these actors and their power of disruption into account.

Students of Latin American politics should start paying sustained empirical attention to *clandestinity* in the analysis of routine and contentious politics. We need, in the words of the grassroots leader quoted above, to learn how to "listen [and to look] carefully." The kind of politics most analysts see and discuss, the "respectable" politics, the "civilized" kind, the sort that takes place in Congress and in the Government Palace and that enjoys media attention, depends to a great extent on clandestine, illicit relationships. We, students of politics, should take them seriously, making them the empirical focus of sustained research efforts. In her critique of the overly institutional trend in democratic consolidation studies, Deborah Yashar (1999:102; my emphasis) calls for "more conceptually and analytically nuanced studies of democratic politics," that is, of "institutional reforms, political norms, and *practices*." If we are going to pay rigorous scholarly attention to the ways in which "democracy is practiced" (Yashar 1999:97), and if we are to "reorient how we study politics in Latin America" (Arias and Goldstein this volume), clandestine connections between established political actors and perpetrators of violence should be excluded from neither serious theoretical nor empirical consideration. Visible state-society relations are undoubtedly important to the quality of democracy in posttransition Latin America (Friedman and Hochstetler 2002), as are hidden and clandestine links between different political actors.

Notes

Funding for this project was provided by a Harry Frank Guggenheim Fellowship. Parts of this essay were adapted from Auyero 2007.

1. For further evidence on the Colombian case, see also Braun 1980, which studies the violence during the 1948 Bogotazo, the massive riots that followed the assassination of liberal leader Jorge Eliécer Gaitán.

2. A similar point regarding the participation of party and state officials in the perpetration of violence was also made by Steffen Schmidt (1974). In his study of the clientelist bases of political violence in Colombia, he wrote: "Colombia's political violence . . . is in great part due to the existence of widespread, competitive, aggressive, patron-client based politics" (Schmidt 1974:109). On the connections between patronage networks and interpersonal violence, see Villarreal 2002. The author makes a strong argument about the relationships between increased electoral competition, weakening patronage networks, and the (subsequent) increase in violent crime (homicide) during the transition to democracy in Mexico.

3. Interestingly, in the provinces in which data is available, the overwhelming majority of those arrested had no penal records—confirming what classic studies on rioting (Moinat et al. 1972; Caplan 1970; Caplan and Paige 1968) assert: looters are not the tiny criminal minority in poverty enclaves.

4. Signaling refers to a set of events whereby participants in a risky situation "often scan each other for signs of readiness to incur costs without defecting, modulating their behavior according to estimates of the likelihood that others will flee" (McAdam, Tarrow, and Tilly 2001:20).

5. Certification refers to "the validation of actors, their performances, and their claims by external authorities" (McAdam, Tarrow, and Tilly 2001:106).

"Living in a Jungle"

State Violence and Perceptions of Democracy in Buenos Aires

RUTH STANLEY

Systematic abuses of human rights and the weak hold of the rule of law are widely recognized as characteristic of many new democracies—and of numerous older ones. Such abuses reflect not only the inability or unwillingness of state institutions to enforce the law but also the persistence of systematic abuse on the part of the state's apparatus of coercion. Following the return to democracy, the police, rather than the military, in the normal course of events hold primary responsibility for exercising the state's monopoly of the legitimate use of physical force vis-à-vis its citizenry. Hence we should focus our attention on the police, rather than the military, if we wish to grasp patterns of violence. Yet reviewing the vast body of literature devoted to processes of democratization in Latin America, Eastern Europe, and elsewhere, one is struck by comparatively little attention paid to the role and function of the police forces, questions of continuity and discontinuity in policing practices, reform projects concerning the institutions of policing, and related topics.[1]

This initial gap in the research agenda has to some extent been overcome in recent years, not least because the phenomenon of police violence in Latin America is so widespread as to have thrust itself onto the originally narrower agenda of democratization research. In particular, the growing body of literature on the so-called unrule of law (Méndez, O'Donnell, and Pinheiro 1999; Pinheiro 1997; O'Donnell 1993) and the quality of democracy (O'Donnell, Vargas Cullell, and Iazzetta 2004) has paid increasing attention to the subject. Research on the role of informal institutions and the rule of law (Brinks 2008,

2006; Van Cott 2006) has also contributed to the debate. Whereas the polyarchy paradigm focused on the electoral process, the literature on the rule of law and the quality of citizenship considerably widens this focus by looking at the workings of a broader range of institutions including, crucially, the judiciary. It thus takes into its purview phenomena of violence that democratization studies based on the concept of polyarchy leave untouched. This second research agenda has been questioned in turn, however, for its tendency to posit phenomena of violence simply as deficits of democracy while failing to engage with the meaning of such phenomena and the ways in which they affect lived political experience (Arias 2006a; Arias and Goldstein this volume). This critique argues that research needs to look more closely at the "brown areas" of ineffective statehood identified by Guillermo O'Donnell (1993) to grasp the precise configurations of the relationships between state and nonstate actors including criminal networks, and to understand how these impact people's lives.

The present essay focuses on the experiences of those who are the object of illegal state violence in metropolitan Buenos Aires, an underresearched topic (but see Pita 2004, 2005). These experiences are important because they can shed light on the patterns of violence and on the perpetrators' motives, on the response of the state to illegal violence, on forms of resistance to such violence, and on citizens' perceptions of the quality of the democracy under which they live—in short, on the particular characteristics of violent democracy as it affects those under its sway. Yet these voices are seldom heard. The victims—generally among the poorest sectors of society—are not easily accessible. Indeed, they often remain almost invisible: violence outside the law is so ubiquitous that it usually goes unreported and is frequently accepted by its victims as a fact of life, as a part of the way things are. Even in cases of murder the victim's family often refrains from taking action for fear of intimidation, due to a fatalistic acceptance of violent practices, or simply because family members do not know how to set about a quest for justice and reparation. Research on the experiences of the victims of illegal state violence is only possible where they render themselves visible through protest and organization.

I draw the evidence in this essay from interviews with people who have lost family members in acts of violence perpetrated by the state security apparatus in the city and province of Buenos Aires.[2] What distinguishes the metropolitan area of Buenos Aires from other regions and states in which illegal violence is still more pervasive is, first, a vigorous human rights movement that has for many years monitored the behavior of the police and other internal security forces. Second, many of the victims have formed autonomous organizations to protest against such violence, seek justice, and provide each other with advice and support. This makes their experiences accessible in a way not the case in other major cities.[3] I made initial contact with many of the people interviewed through CORREPI (Coordinadora contra la Represión Policial e Institucional), an organization that describes itself as antirepressive and that defends the rights of victims of state violence.[4] Given the networks among victims' families, interviewees were able to facilitate further contacts, including with some families who had no connection with CORREPI.[5] I conducted most of the interviews in the interviewees' homes, although one took place in the offices of CORREPI, two were conducted in a community center used for meetings of the local organization of family members against police violence, and three took place in cafés. Altogether I carried out eighteen semistructured interviews lasting between two and four hours between August 2003 and November 2005 in the city of Buenos Aires and its environs.

This article presents the testimony of those interviewed. It first reviews accounts of the act of violence and the institutional response to it, focusing here on the reactions of the state security institutions and the judicial system. It then looks at the role of the public sphere, in particular that of the media. The final section offers some conclusions on the meaning ascribed by victims' families to their pursuit of justice, as well as their perceptions of democracy in the light of the experience of state violence. Throughout this article the focus lies on the subjective understanding of these events to those caught up in them. Thus I make no attempt to "validate" these experiences through triangulation with other sources. A comparison with ethnographic research into the phenomenon of police violence in the metropolitan area of Buenos Aires, however, does suggest that the experiences narrated here are typical (see CELS and HRW 1998).

Illegal State Violence and the Institutional Response

The first thing to note is the great variety of situations in which lethal violence occurred. Twenty-three-year-old Rodolfo was beaten so severely by prison guards that he fell into a coma and died in hospital three days later (1992). Blanca (thirty-six) was shot accidentally by a private security agent who turned out to be a member of the coastguard, the Prefectura Naval, pursuing thieves who had robbed the supermarket in which he was working, illegally, as a security guard (1999). Sixteen-year-old Ricardo was shot dead, supposedly while attempting to rob a policeman on a bus (2000). Marcelo, also sixteen, was shot dead in 2002; according to the police, he fired on them while escaping from the scene of a robbery on his bicycle. Hugo, a twenty-five-year-old, was killed by a retired policeman in 2003, apparently because he had refused to commit armed robbery on behalf of the police. Maxi was killed in 2003 at the age of sixteen when police started shooting at a group of youths vandalizing an abandoned car. Fifteen-year-old Héctor was shot dead in 2001, allegedly in the course of an armed robbery. Mariano was twenty-three when he was taken hostage by a bank robber fleeing from the police; both he and the assailant, Darío, were shot dead by the police. Rodrigo was twenty-seven and driving to his girlfriend's house in his father's car when police shot him, allegedly in the course of an armed confrontation (2003). Thirty-one-year-old Jorge was detained by police in December 2002, ostensibly so that they could check his criminal record; in fact the police used his detention to blackmail his mother, threatening that they would invent a charge against him unless she paid 2,000 pesos to secure his release. He was so badly beaten while in police detention that he died in hospital some two weeks later. Ezequiel was killed in 2003 under peculiar circumstances: police with whom he was on friendly terms fetched him from his home so that he could be present at a police operation, in the course of which he was shot dead, aged nineteen. Cristián, also nineteen years old, was tricked by accomplices of the police into threatening a shop assistant with a weapon; on leaving the premises the police shot him dead, claiming that he had carried out an armed robbery (2002). Cristián's case was one of a whole series of supposed crimes set up by the police to enhance their image (Stanley 2005; PNG 2003).

If the circumstances vary, some common elements nevertheless obtain. First, almost all the victims are young men, indeed, boys. Second, almost all the victims are poor people, many inhabiting precarious settlements. In this respect the sample accurately reflects the data gathered by human rights organizations such as CELS (Centro de Estudios Legales y Sociales) and CORREPI.[6] Third, it is striking how readily firearms are used, frequently with lethal intent but at the very least with a remarkable disregard for the safety of bystanders. That the police use firearms as a weapon of first rather than last resort, in contravention of local laws and international norms, in itself speaks volumes about the culture of impunity for illegal acts of violence that is created and reinforced not only by the institutions of public security but also by the judicial system in Argentina. Finally, in all these cases, the illegal use of lethal force represented only the start of a tortuous and often humiliating process for the victim's family. It is not the experience of unlawful killing at the hands of agents of the state that most undermines citizenship, but rather the response of other state agencies to such acts, which leave the victims feeling absolutely defenseless. Blanca's sister expressed this sentiment by describing Blanca's shooting as the moment "when our suffering began."

The great variety in the situations in which these victims met their death at the hands of the police (and in one case, of prison guards) suggests that it would be difficult to explain illegal police violence in terms of a single motive or underlying cause. In some cases extortion is the motive: victims are tortured to extract a payment to avoid trumped-up criminal charges against them, or they are shot dead as punishment for refusing to commit robbery on behalf of the police. In some cases the police set up their victims to present themselves as an effective crime-fighting force. Police involvement in organized crime, specifically in areas such as drug trafficking and car theft, is a further source of violence. (In one of the interviews, the family was convinced that the victim's death arose from a botched attempt at car theft.) Despite the differences in these individual cases, what emerges as a general picture is a profile of the police (and of other agents of state violence) making use of the material and symbolic resources they enjoy as the ostensible upholders of the state's monopoly of legitimate violence to pursue different ends that range from personal gain through involvement in criminal activities to enhancing the prestige of the police force by means of spectacular "successes." One noteworthy aspect is the habitual presentation of these cases as "armed confrontations," an allegation that serves to justify police violence; to lend substance to such accounts, the police routinely plant weapons on their victims after these have been killed (CELS and HRW 1998).[7] Individuals from deprived areas are thus routinely cast as actors in various dramas staged by the police and enforced through the illegal use of state power. The activities of the police reflect the institution's involvement in a complex series of illegal activities that leave little time and resources for bona fide policing; police "effectiveness" is sporadically demonstrated by violent confrontations, and often the choice of victim appears quite arbitrary. So the emerging picture is not one of an underequipped police force struggling to combat rising crime, but one of public resources directed toward nonpublic ends, frequently in collusion with criminal gangs and in a way that is criminal in itself. In this context individuals from poor areas are not citizens but become resources employed by the police in pursuit of diverse goals.

The testimony of Mariano's parents, Jorge and Raquel Witis, offers a graphic description not only of the police's use of indiscriminate and totally disproportionate force but also of the subsequent misrepresentation of events and of the use of threats and intimidation intended to make the victim's family desist from their investigation into the case. Mariano was an atypical victim of police violence in that his family is solidly middle class; his parents are professionals and own their own house in the prosperous neighborhood of San Isidro. The couple disposes of financial, educational, and social resources not typically available in cases of this kind. As mentioned above, their son was caught up inadvertently in an attempted bank robbery when he was taken hostage by Darío Riquelme. The police shot both Mariano and Darío dead, both in the back, a fact that disproves the police version of an armed confrontation between criminals and the police. A firearm was ultimately placed by the dead body of Darío to lend credence to this false account. The police also at first asserted that Mariano was an accomplice and had been carrying a weapon. Assertions of this kind cannot be understood as genuine mistakes; they fit the pattern of police routinely claiming that a murdered citizen was a criminal—and by implication deserving his or her fate. Mariano's parents begin by claiming that the responsibility for Mariano's death lay squarely with the police:

> Who is responsible for this death? It was the police, who did not comply with the procedures established in the Security Law of the Province of Buenos Aires. When the car [in which Darío and Mariano were traveling] came to a halt—that was when the policeman fired the shots. And they speak of an armed confrontation when the victims died from gunshots in the back!
>
> We were involved from the day after, trying to push this thing forward. And the very same day we received a threat, a telephone call. A woman's voice said: "Stop screwing around with the media, because the same thing could happen again." Darío's mother suffered intimidation too. They tried to frame one of her children, Darío's brother; they tried to frame him as a bank robber. They said to him: "You're Riquelme's brother." We gave her support. In those days she was working very long hours, and she didn't plan to undertake anything because she felt guilty. But even if Darío had gone out to rob, the police reaction was totally excessive. In this country the death penalty doesn't exist, but de facto it does: in the minds of the police it exists.
>
> The boy [Darío] had had problems before that. She [Darío's mother] asked for help from the courts, she asked them to provide a psychologist. But the judge never gave her an appointment. The state was absent. And afterward she was paralyzed; she felt unable to demand anything because she felt that in part the punishment was just. But it was excessive; we cannot accept it.

When this happened to Mariano, many people contacted us. Raquel is a primary school teacher, we've lived here for many years, and the children go to school in the neighborhood, so a great many people contacted us. And many of them told us anecdotes about police corruption or even police criminality. But very few cases had ever been brought to the attention of the authorities. So they were purely anecdotal. No-one claimed their rights. And that's because the system itself discourages people. If a bicycle is stolen, knowing the problems you're going to have, knowing that no-one will take it seriously, people don't register the theft. And at the police station they'll say to you: "But why bother to register the crime; why take the trouble, since we'll never find the bicycle anyway?"

Some elements of the police behavior recounted by Mariano's parents are typical. The warning to "stop screwing around" is one issued, verbally or by means of threatening gestures, to all families who refuse simply to accept the police version of events. While the family members are not easily cowed into abandoning their quest for justice, in many cases witnesses are intimidated into withdrawing their evidence. The family of Hugo, who was apparently shot dead because he refused to commit robbery on behalf of the police, found its efforts to establish the facts hampered by neighbors' and victims' fear of police intimidation:

His [Hugo's] friends, now they don't want to say anything. They're afraid they'll be called to give evidence. They're being threatened too. The police came through the streets the next day; they stopped in front of the houses and threatened them. The whole thing was done very openly. The neighbors heard the police saying: "Keep your mouth shut or the same thing will happen to you." The kid told the whole story, the kid who was with him when they killed him.[8] The kid's parents offered to collaborate with us. But when it came to giving evidence, they said no, the kid hadn't seen anything. It was the father who gave evidence, but he denied everything. Probably the police will have threatened them too. This is really slowing everything down; if the kid's parents had helped us, everything would be much further along. The neighbors don't want to give evidence. It's like they don't want to get involved, because they're afraid, because of the threats. They prefer to keep silent, not say anything.

The effectiveness of this method of imposing silence is particularly evident in a case in which witnesses protested quite spontaneously against the police but were later cowed into submission: "The neighborhood marched on the commissariat. They wanted to set it on fire. But later no-one gave a statement to the legal authorities. This is something that causes you double pain, it's very bitter."

Threats against other children in the family are a potent weapon that the police do not hesitate to employ. Blanca's sister, Esther, recounted how she was finally intimidated into ceasing to organize protest marches calling for a proper inquiry into the circumstances of Blanca's death:

I've had phone calls. It's me they call because I was the one who led the marches. Sometimes they threaten me directly, saying I should stop screwing around. Or they call to let me know there's going to be a march of family members in such-and-such a place and that I should come. It's to get me in some place where they can intimidate me. But I always called other family members to check if there really was a march or not. Then they make signs. When I'm at work, on the street corner [Esther is a newspaper vendor], one will pass by in a car, or on foot, and he'll do this [makes the gesture of cutting her throat] or this [extends the index and middle fingers of her right hand to form the shape of a pistol]. Recently we haven't done any more marches. Someone had come up to me and said:" I know you've got little boys who go to school. I could kill them just like that." I think he was a policeman.

Teresa, Héctor's mother, tells a story of persistent police harassment against her family following the police shooting of her son:

At three o'clock in the afternoon, three patrol cars arrived at the street corner where there were maybe ten kids. They beat up Roberto [her son] in the street, he was the only one. Then they took him to the police station, they thought he's an adult. I arrived with his identity card, I said he's still a minor, and why did they arrest him?

"Because he made fun of the police."

"What did he do?"

"He laughed."

"Are we supposed to bow our heads when we see you?"

"It would be better if you did."

This was said to me by a subcommissioner. When I was leaving with my son he said: "Take care of your son because he goes out in the evenings." And then, yes, I was afraid. These are hidden warnings. This was fifteen days after the death of Héctor. My nephew, my sister's son, the police took him as a witness to a robbery. He'd seen what had happened but he didn't want to be a witness. In the end they charged him with being an accomplice to the robbery although he had nothing to do with it. The police realized that he was Héctor's cousin. The person who'd been robbed, he said, "No, he had nothing to do with it," but they kept him in detention anyway. He was detained for seven months in the police station. . . . My other nephew, Jorge, they pressured him as well. The police said he should stop the marches, him and my sister, if they didn't want to end up being thrown into the Riachuelo.[9] We stopped doing the marches for a long time. . . . Then we decided to start again, otherwise it all ends in nothing, just like always; we still haven't had justice.

There was a witness. . . . The witness heard how Héctor begged the policeman not to kill him. Héctor was 150 cm tall, the policeman over 190 cm. There are two bullets that entered his body lower down and went upwards. The first entered his heart, that's the one that killed him. The witness saw how he [the policeman] takes hold of my son like this [Teresa takes hold of the collar of Luis, a neighbor, and imitates dragging him up by the scruff of his neck], he pulls him up and puts the pistol here [demonstrates putting a pistol into the boy's ribs, pointing upward], and the last one in his head, when he was already on the ground. . . . Now he [the witness] doesn't want to give evidence. His mother said to me that she too has a son, and that my son is already dead, but hers is still alive, and no [i.e., her son would not give evidence]. And I understand her too. And he went to another country for a long time, to Paraguay, for about nine months. He's Argentinean but his family comes from Paraguay. He changed his evidence and then he went. And I wasn't able to talk to him ever again. I want him to help me, but I understand that his mother is protecting the life of her son. I went from door to door, asking. There were many witnesses, but no-one wants to give evidence.

Graciela's son was killed under obscure circumstances. According to the police version, Marcelo indulged in a gun battle with the police while simultaneously riding his bicycle away from the small shop he had allegedly just robbed of a few pesos. Friends who had been with him until shortly before his death were too afraid to tell Graciela even privately what had really happened, much less give formal evidence:

Marcelito, he was a friend from the neighborhood, he was fifteen at the time. He sent me a message to say they hadn't committed a robbery. He sent someone to tell me that, because he was being held in a detention center for minors. He sent someone to say he was going to help me. The killing took place on March 4 and Marcelito was released from detention on March 28. He came round to our place; it happened it was my daughter's birthday. He said he'd come again and we'd talk. The days passed and he didn't come. One day he came with another lad and told me everything the other way around. He said there *had* been a robbery. The whole time he was talking, he didn't look me in the face once. One day he was with Elisa [Graciela's daughter] and a patrol car goes by.

Elisa continues: "Marcelito had his hand on my shoulder, like this. When the patrol car came by, his hand started to tremble so hard, it made my shoulder shake. He just looked at the ground, he was so frightened. He told me that when the police arrested him, they said to him: "You'd better watch out or we'll blow your head off." And they said: "Keep quiet or we'll kill you." In all the cases covered in my sample police issue threats of retaliation, either against the families of those who had been killed or against witnesses to the events.

Another element typical of these cases is the practice of planting incriminating evidence on the victim to lend credence to the police version of events. Such evidence usually consists of a firearm intended to prove that the death occurred in the course of a gun battle or, in official parlance, an "armed confrontation" with the police: "He [Hugo, the victim] had gone out around nine at night to buy cigarettes. They killed him two blocks from home. The police version was that Hugo was about to commit an assault on this man, that's to say, on the policeman who killed him. According to the police, my brother took out a gun and the policeman killed him in self-defense. Then they put a weapon beside his body. The neighbors were livid when they saw the police planting the weapon. So then the police took it away again, because the neighbors protested. The neighbors told us what they saw. . . . There was no trace of gunpowder on [Hugo's] hand—in other words, he didn't shoot. . . . They'd made him kneel down. That means it wasn't an armed confrontation. It was an execution."

In the case of Héctor the coverup was intended to present him both as a violent criminal and as a glue sniffer: "One of the witnesses is a teacher. She didn't see [Héctor's killing], she came out of her house afterward, after she heard the gunshots. . . . She saw that my son was bleeding and that his body was there, but there wasn't a weapon there. He begged [the policeman] not to kill him. She saw how the policeman planted a gun on him and a tin of Poxirán."[10]

Fear of police reprisals makes for a powerful weapon. It frequently guarantees no overt challenge to the police version of events on the part of eyewitnesses who have seen the police manipulating the crime scene: "A neighbor who lives close to where they killed Marcelo, heard him [Marcelo] saying to the police, please, don't shoot. This man was watching what was happening from the window of his house. He told the police not to kill him [Marcelo], because he wasn't doing anything. The police said to him: "You shut your mouth and get inside." I doubt whether the people who saw everything that happened will give evidence. They only live four or five blocks from the police station, so it's very unlikely. But they saw the police planting stuff on him. They saw them planting coins."[11]

Police attempt to enhance the plausibility of their version of events not only by planting evidence that supports the official story but also by making untrue assertions. As we have seen, in Mariano's case the police claimed he was an armed accomplice of the young man who had committed the robbery, although in fact he had been taken hostage. In the case of Ricardo, shot on a bus, the homicidal policeman offered various accounts, none of them convincing:

> When the policeman first made a statement, he said that he encountered my lad on the street and that he [the boy] fired. But in his second statement, the one he made before the state prosecutor, and the statement only counts as evidence if it's made to the state prosecutor—in other words, the first statement, the one he gave in the police commissariat, it doesn't count—he said my lad was one of the thieves who was about to rob him. But they never found anything that had been stolen and they never found a weapon. There's the evidence of the bus driver, he knew nothing of a gun battle. . . . Two passengers said there was a shootout. They're friends of the police. All the other passengers saw no such thing. But they did hear the policeman shouting: "I'm a policeman, stop the bus, they're robbing me!" And two shots. The policeman admits to having fired two shots. Before that, the boy had supposedly fired eight times. But none of the passengers saw or heard this.

Given that this case happened to include a busload of passengers as witnesses, one might imagine that it would be quite straightforward to establish the facts. Yet the judicial proceedings have not advanced and the case has been archived. Sometimes the official version is quite simply ludicrous. Rodrigo was shot dead by police when he was driving his father's car, recently purchased, to his girlfriend's house. The police of the province of Buenos Aires are known to be involved in car thefts and the illegal trading of stolen spare parts, and it may be that the police intended to steal the vehicle. As usual in such cases, they claimed that Rodrigo fired on them. The driver of the police car was required to give a statement on the events in which he had participated: "When they called A.N. to give his statement, they asked him, 'What did you see?' And he said that when he was driving the patrol car over the bridge he shut his eyes because he suffered from vertigo, and that he'd never mentioned this weakness before because he was afraid of losing his job. He said that he did hear two shots being fired, but even then he didn't open his eyes, although there's a curve in the bridge and he was driving at around seventy to eighty kilometers per hour." Again, one is left with the impression that the police need a coverup story (or, as in this case, a version that allows an individual officer to neither confirm nor deny) but are not unduly concerned to make it watertight or even minimally credible—they can usually rely on a sympathetic hearing. Even where the police version is not given credence, incriminated police officers rarely are investigated for giving false evidence.

If illegal killings lead to further illicit acts such as those described above, they also follow in the wake of, and in many cases derive from, other illegal practices. Hugo was apparently executed because he refused to commit robbery on commission.

[He] spent three months in prison. When he was murdered, that was a year after he got out of prison. He'd been in for attempted robbery. Prison was terrible. They put everyone together: murderers, rapists—it was horrible. . . . The police made him an offer. A policeman even put a gun in his hand so that he would go out to commit robbery. They told him the place they wanted him to rob. Most of what gets stolen, the police always take it. . . . There's someone who knows about all this, but he doesn't want to talk about it because he's been threatened by the police. It's a lad who was with my son when the policeman made him this offer. He even knows the name of this policeman, but only his nickname. They call him "The Dog". . . . It's because Hugo refused that they made trouble for him. He had to cover his back. He tried not to be out on the street; he went to work and came home and that was it. But we didn't know about this at the time. . . . He was threatened. They [the police] had said to a neighbor, "Tell your friend that we're going to get him." That was two months before his death.

Jorge had also served a prison term for attempted robbery. He was arrested with the aim of extorting money from his family.

The police officer Gómez called me; he demanded 2,000 pesos to get [Jorge] out of there. I said: "But I haven't even got 200 pesos—how am I going to pay 2,000?" He said to me: "If you don't pay, we'll charge him with aggravated robbery, attempted robbery, and a few more things besides." Because [the police] want the money. When I told him I didn't have 2000, he answered me: "OK, I'll give you two hours, if you don't get that money, we'll see what happens." . . . When they use blackmail, they share it out among all of them. So that's why, when I told Gómez I didn't have 2,000 pesos, he said: "But I've got to give some to the chief and some to the cops who arrested [Jorge], so it's got to be 2000." . . . Jorge had been in prison. He got out when he'd served his sentence. It was for attempted robbery. He was in for about a year. After that, if someone works for the police, everything is OK, but if not. . . . If you've got a criminal record, the police never let you alone.

Borrowing money from friends and neighbors, Jorge's mother, Ramona, scraped together 2,000 pesos over two days and was able to get her son out of detention. But he had been so badly tortured that he died in hospital some weeks later: "They tortured him, they beat him on the testicles, they broke his ribs. In the commissariat they did the dry submarine on him.[12] That's something they always do." Both Hugo and Jorge had been identified as easy targets because they had already served prison sentences, both for attempted robbery. The police knew that this would make it difficult for them to disprove police allegations against them, making them particularly vulnerable. Cristián was one of over a hundred victims of police actions designed to present the police in a favorable light that involved the intentional framing of innocent victims (his case is discussed in further detail below). Thus these cases depend on and form part of wider patterns of illegality within the police force (Oliveira and Tiscornia 1998).

The practice of illegal killings also depends crucially on the culture of impunity, and this in turn relies on the complicity of the judicial system, which is perceived as being both partisan and incompetent:

And in the judicial system, too, there are employees who discourage you. In Mariano's case, there was a witness who wanted to make a declaration in the prosecutor's office. The prosecutor's secretary took his personal details, but he refused to hear his testimony, saying that the policeman was already pretty much incriminated, that it wasn't necessary; it was like insisting on something that was already more than sufficiently established. But the state prosecutor's office has the obligation to take witness statements from anyone who wants to make such a statement. In this case the witness insisted; he went to see the state prosecutor himself, and the prosecutor did hear his evidence. The witness was a former policeman, a *pentito* policeman, one could say.[13] But many witnesses don't have the courage to insist. It's asking a lot that witnesses give their evidence, considering the treatment they get. . . . People simply don't use the judicial system. . . . They treat you as though you were the criminal. The victims get turned into the guilty party. The prosecutor told us he didn't believe us. Of course, for them I was the mother of a criminal. They said to me: "We have videos showing your son with weapons." The videos don't exist, obviously. It was just to put pressure on us.

The judicial system presents itself as the shield of the police. It will slow down any initiative it sees as going against the police. Investigations are minimal. . . . Apart from the question of ideology, there's the matter of the budget; the judicial system lacks resources and the people there have a managerial attitude: they invest the resources where they can get an immediate result.

The Law on Security is very clear as to when a policeman may use a firearm. But here the police go out on the streets and start firing on the public highway as though they were at a shooting range. In the case of Levikas, for example: that happened on a boulevard in the middle of a working day.[14] The police fired seventy-three times. And the judges said that the use of force was proportionate! This wasn't a comment they made to journalists, it was part of the judgment. The police force shouldn't permit such behavior, but in the final instance it's the judicial system that should punish it. And that wasn't even a case of a robbery, but only of suspected robbery. And the judges call that a proportionate use of force! . . . If the judicial system doesn't fulfill its role in cases of police abuse, whom can the citizen turn to? He is totally unprotected.

Others expressed a similar lack of confidence in the judicial system. One interviewee described state prosecutors as "accomplices" of the police who "didn't want to investigate anything"; they were "useless." Another offered this perception of the prosecutor's role: "The prosecutor, rather than investigating the police, he's on the side of the police. He coaches the policeman on how to give his testimony, tells him what he should say. If the policeman is going to say, 'I killed him, it was an error, I made a mistake,' the prosecutor will tell him he mustn't say this. . . . Here, the prosecutors depend on the political authorities.

The prosecutor has told me to my face that he's never going to accuse any of his personnel—that means the police."

In the case of Maxi, killed in a situation in which police were firing indiscriminately, the family was determined to have it established in court that the boy had been hit by a bullet fired from a police weapon and not, as the police alleged, by a shot fired by the criminal they were supposedly attempting to apprehend: "The judge alleged that the facts weren't as we said. The judge who was dealing with the case sits down every Sunday to a barbecue with the police. This is the lack of protection we're faced with. There was absolutely no effort to clarify what had happened; the judge simply accepted the police version."

Héctor's mother had a similarly discouraging experience when she attempted to place charges against the police for the unlawful killing of her son: "The state prosecutor said that I'm crazy. He told the lawyer that I was crazy, that I needed to see a psychologist. He didn't believe anything I said, and he refused to hear my testimony. . . . The prosecutors don't investigate anything; they just use the police version."

Making progress in judicial investigations of unlawful state killings is thus extremely difficult. From the perspective of the victims' families, little or no help could be expected from the state agencies formally charged with investigating crime: state prosecutors view themselves as being "on the same side" as the police or accept the police version of events to spare themselves the trouble of an independent investigation. Understaffing encourages this attitude. Those of low socioeconomic status, especially inhabitants of so-called *villas de emergencia* (precarious housing settlements that usually lack the most basic infrastructure) feel that the judicial system is heavily prejudiced against them: "If a kid is killed in the *villa* neither the prosecutor nor the investigating magistrate will come. They say that they're afraid to. They can't be bothered. And anyway, if someone dies in the *villa*, they always say that he was a criminal."

Apart from the partisan attitude of judicial authorities who perceive themselves as the shield of the police, the law's delay constitutes a further factor that leads many families to abandon their struggle for justice: "There are family members who give up the struggle because of the threats. But many also give up because the legal system is so slow. The judicial process is so long, and the families get tired. There are cases that have been going on longer than my son's—the case of Walter Bulacio was in 1991 and still no-one has been imprisoned.[15] The families get tired and give up the fight."

Some families see the inordinate delays they face as deliberately contrived: "In the criminal law system, you have to wait so long! Not because that's the way it is, but because they do it that way to benefit themselves, to cover things up. You feel so powerless." Intimidated by the police and frustrated by the judicial system, some family members appeal to the national or provincial government. None of them felt that their demands were adequately treated by their elected representatives:

> I had a meeting with Ruckauf [then governor of the province of Buenos Aires]. And he told me he couldn't do anything because the judiciary is a different branch of government. But he's the same one who said, "For every criminal killed by the police, I'll give the police a reward." The government thinks we'll stay humble, that we'll say, "Yes, sir."
>
> We went to speak with the deputy minister of the interior, Nilda Garré. This was during the government of [Fernando] de la Rúa; Federico Storani was minister of the interior and she was deputy minister. She gave credence to our version. But she told us how her hands were tied. She said that it was a really big problem, this thing with the police, that it was a very difficult problem, and that she couldn't do much. If the deputy minister of the interior says that, what can we expect of common citizens?

Blanca's family was visited by the local mayor, who strongly advised them to abandon their public demonstrations: "The mayor of Almirante Brown [a locality in the province of Buenos Aires], he came to visit us at home. Nowadays, he's a senator. It's J.V., he's a Peronist. And he too demanded that we put a stop to the marches; he said we weren't going to achieve anything. And he said that even though we're well known [to him], we've worked for him in the political arena. We're all Peronists! But that did us no good whatsoever. That's why we feel this awful pain, this frustration. . . . The mayor was on friendly terms with the police; he was a lawyer before."

Ambiguities of the Public Sphere: Policing and the Media

Argentina's return to democracy in 1983 opened up a public sphere of debate and contestation, with public security policy and police reform gradually becoming central issues on the political agenda. At the same time the problem of crime and insecurity has become increasingly highlighted. The conflict between what Claudio Fuentes (2005) has termed the rights coalition and the order coalition—those who press for the enforcement of guaranteed human and civil rights and those who emphasize the law-and-order motif—is played out in this arena, with civic associations of varying hues, the media, and—in keeping with a long-standing Argentine tradition—the street being loci of debate, argument, and protest.

Engaging with the public sphere is seen by some activists as a necessary response to the lethargic and partisan judicial system: "The officeholders, above all in the police, but in the judiciary as well, they have access to a lot of things. They can make your life difficult or create different types of obstacles. So to compensate for that, one has to go public." Protest marches and demonstrations serve not only to keep individual cases in the public eye and to emphasize the habitual nature of police brutality; they also constitute a means of stressing the discourse of universal rights: "We organize marches, that's already become a tradition. . . . We've done camp-ins to demonstrate to society that we're fighting for justice and to show what's happening. To show that everyone has a right to life. That's why, when I talk about the case of my son, I don't say: 'He wasn't a thief.' That's something I'll prove when it comes to court. But even if he had gone out to commit a theft, they had no right to kill him. This is our message."

Some activists recognize that their rights discourse conflicts with a widely held view that criminals deserve what they get. Delia's son was beaten to death by prison guards when he was serving a term of six months for having failed to comply with the terms of his parole: "There are many people who believe if someone is a criminal, it's better that he's dead. Yes, my son committed robbery. I never denied that. If I had denied it, that would have been like justifying what happens." This discourse of rights for all, including those who have committed a crime, is a central message of public actions: "The struggle of family members is about showing that their son, even if he was committing a robbery, has a right to life. That's why CORREPI says: 'We don't defend the criminal, we defend life.' . . . Many families say, 'My child was innocent.' But there are others who say he committed theft, he was a drug addict. And we say: Even if that was so, they had no right to kill him." Although public demonstrations and protest marches organized by the families tend not to be very large, they are clearly a thorn in the side of the police. Many of the veiled or explicit threats the police issue are intended to put a stop to precisely this kind of activity. It is the constant public reminders of police brutality, rather than the judicial process, that the police seem to fear.

Some activists see the mainstream media as part of the problem, since they foment a perception of insecurity that results in tolerance for police violence: "Support for a tough law-and-order policy, yes, there is support; the media play a part there. A dead policeman is good for sales, insecurity is good for sales. The kid that they kill in the *villa*, he's not good for sales—unless they say that he was an armed robber. As to the reaction of society: I blame the media. Who owns them? We don't get a hearing; we're excluded from the communication market. Only a very few cases make it onto the TV screen or into the newspapers. We have to work against that with our protests on the street."

But this criticism is tempered by the recognition that the media can also offer a forum for family members to present their case: "We try to be present in the media. They sometimes send a reporter; often it doesn't get in the papers, because it doesn't sell. But when it does get in, however short the report is, we've won something. The alternative media give us a chance to be heard. And within the commercial media, there are journalists who listen to you and who carry out investigations. But there's a lot of indifference too."

To a large extent the critique of the media expressed by victims' families manifests a disappointment that the media have failed to act as watchdogs and as defenders of citizens' interests. In particular, media coverage of police violence is seen as being governed by considerations of what "sells," and what sells is in turn seen to reflect popular prejudice; thus a report on a young person killed by police in a precarious housing settlement is only "good for sales" if the story is framed in terms that confirm preexisting assumptions among readers and viewers.

If the rights coalition seeks to make its views heard in the media, the same is obviously true of the order coalition: right-wing think tanks and social movements with a repressive agenda have had a major impact on debates around public security, voicing demands for greater police powers, harsher sentencing practices, and "zero-tolerance" policies. The discourse of *mano dura* (iron fist) and the discursive criminalization of the poor reflected the fragmentation of Argentine society in the 1990s, with the wealthy increasingly escaping to privately guarded gated communities and shantytowns being discursively constructed as areas of violence and criminality, outside of and threatening to society. The police themselves have proved to be virtuoso manipulators of the media, framing innocent victims with crimes never perpetrated to present themselves as an efficient crime-fighting force. Cristián's mother recounted how he had fallen victim to this practice. Cristián, without formal employment, tried to earn a little money by washing the windscreens of cars while they were caught at a red traffic light. While engaged in this occupation alongside some friends, Cristián was approached by a man who offered him and another young man a few hours' work. It supposedly consisted in loading a truck, and the pay seemed better than the uncertain income to be gained by cleaning windscreens; often Christián earned barely enough to cover his bus fare. So he and his friend Daniel gladly accepted the offer, made to them by a man who identified himself only by his nickname, "the Pole." Having reached an agreement, the Pole promised to return two hours later to drive the two young men to the place where they were to carry out their work. Cristián never returned home. His mother, Raquel, learned of his death the next day from a newspaper report according to which he had been shot dead by police after committing armed robbery.

This practice of framing victims represents a public-relations strategy on the part of numerous police serving in the Federal Police of Argentina, which as of 2009 polices the capital city.[16] Analyses of these cases have shown that the police mainly intended not to secure a conviction (many of the victims were mentally unfit to stand trial and the evidence was often unconvincing) but to generate media reports showing the force in a favorable light, highlighting in particular the officers' capacity to respond in an effective and timely manner to a dangerous crime (Stanley 2005; PNG 2003; Rafecas 2002). The strategy appears to have been used most widely in the 1990s, a period during which the police faced a barrage of criticism from human rights groups and victims organizations. Their presentation of their crime-fighting abilities as a media performance can be seen as an attempt to combat their image as a violent, corrupt, and inefficient crime-fighting organization. Paradoxically this mise-en-scène therefore only makes sense in the context of a democratic system that guarantees a public space for debate and criticism.

If the media constituted an essential element in the police public-relations strategy, it was also media attention to the investigation into these cases that enabled Raquel to understand what had actually happened and to appreciate that her case was one of many: "There's a [TV] program called *Punto Doc*. They get complaints and investigate them. It was July 28 or 29, it was after Cristián's death, and it was about the investigation into the cases invented by the Federal Police. I saw Rafecas in the program,[17] he was explaining how it works, how there's one who is the decoy and talks to the boys and gets them to go somewhere else with him, how they set it up. And my daughter turned round and looked at me and she said: That's what they did with Cristián! I wrote everything down, they put everything on the screen, the telephone numbers, the address, everything. And I went to see him [Rafecas]. He helped me a lot."

Media coverage of protests against police brutality, even if slight, has helped communication among victims, generating a consciousness that their cases form part of a pattern and, in some instances, helping them connect with groups engaged in the same struggle. In general the media were acknowledged as important to the families' campaigns to secure justice, although many interviewees felt that the police version of events was much more readily believed than their own, and indeed that it was extremely difficult for them to get their views aired in mainstream media.

Conclusion: Making Sense of Violent Pluralism

In their introduction to this volume, Enrique Arias and Daniel Goldstein ask for closer attention to be paid to the nature of people's demands in the context of violent pluralism. This essay attempts to contribute to this incipient debate by focusing on the experiences of a specific group of actors organizing against illegal state violence in metropolitan Buenos Aires. What understanding of police violence is conveyed in these interviews with victims' families, and what meaning do activists ascribe to their struggle against illegal police killings? What are their perceptions of democracy in the light of such experiences? How do they view state institutions that permit the de jure enforcers of the state's monopoly of legitimate violence to abuse this authoritative power with impunity, converting the legitimate use of force into a de facto source of illegitimate violence?

Not surprisingly, these experiences shattered the victims' confidence in central institutions of the state. A few interviewees stated that they had already been aware of the frequent use of illegal violence by the police and referred to their experience as political activists in opposition to the military regime and its reliance on violent repression by means of the state security institutions. Others found the experience utterly unexpected: "When our children were small, we always taught them: if you have a problem, if you need help, find a policeman, he'll help you. So it was like two blows to the face. At first I was stupefied. The police are supposed to protect us, not to assault us. We didn't have a negative attitude toward the police. For us the policeman was someone deserving of great respect. But not any longer. We know how it is now, how they operate. And the neighbors too—it's opened their eyes."

Interviewees frequently made reference to the fact that the police operated as de facto lawmakers, imposing the death penalty at their own discretion: "In this country, the death penalty doesn't exist, but de facto it does: in the minds of the police it exists." One interviewee pointed out that in carrying out summary executions with impunity, the police—agents of the state—were not only acting in contravention of domestic law but also effectively violating Argentina's international human rights obligations: "There are cases of lads who died with fifteen bullets in the body. So was it necessary to execute them? The death penalty doesn't exist here because of the Pact of San José, but for the police it does exist. They are the executioners, they are judge and executioner."

Arbitrary police violence is compounded by the inadequate response of the judicial system. Many family members at first felt confident that the judicial authorities would take appropriate action against the perpetrators and ensure justice. Yet such an outcome remains the exception. Far more typical are accounts of indifference or hostility, of police coverups in which state prosecutors and judges connive, of a judiciary at times quite explicitly partisan in its support of the police even in the face of egregious violations of civil rights. If the initial homicide represents a tragedy, it is this lack of an adequate response by the state to acts of unlawful killing perpetrated by the state's own agents that makes the experience so traumatic and further undermines confidence in state institutions. The perception of a generalized failure of state institutions to protect basic rights profoundly affects perceptions of democracy; one interviewee whose brother had been shot dead by the police described the experience as "living in a jungle": "If we had a real democracy, this kid who has committed a robbery would have to be tried in court, he'd have to go to prison and pay for what he did. But not like it is now, where the kid is a pariah. In theory we've got a democracy. But in everyday life, we're living in a jungle. If the people who are supposed to protect us kill us—what can we expect from the rest?"

Despite certain commonalities in the victims' perceptions of state violence, some significant differences also exist. Many family members see their efforts in terms of prevention—if trigger-happy police officers are convicted and removed from the police force (or at the least, if the police realize that their illegal actions will not pass unchallenged), other lives may be spared: "What I want is for this miserable person to be off the streets for good. Because what he did to my son he could do to anyone else. I keep going by trying to fight so that they shall have to pay for what they did. It's going to take years. And even if they don't go to prison, perhaps they won't do the same thing again to other boys. Perhaps this can save other boys. They [the police] think these are street kids and that no-one cares about them. They think no-one is going to be bothered, whatever they do to them. It can't be this way, they can't just do as they like." These activists see themselves as fighting to establish the principle that the agents of state violence are not above the law, and to the extent that the denial of impunity in every individual case is seen as helping to undermine a general culture of impunity, each case has a larger significance: "Sometimes I ask myself, "Why am I doing all this?" It's not as though he [the speaker's son] were in prison, it's not as though we were fighting to have him released from jail. Sometimes I feel so disheartened. Then I say to myself, "No, I shall go on!" They're going to pay for this. I want to see them in prison, not just suspended from duty. I want to see them in prison just like any other murderer. They [the police] killed him deliberately. I don't know if he planned to commit a robbery. I don't know if there was a robbery. But even if there was, they had no right to execute him. Detain him, handcuff him, take him to the police station—yes. But they had no right to kill him."

One mother stated: "They're murderers and they shouldn't be allowed to hide behind a uniform." Blanca's sister said: "There must be justice, no matter who is the guilty party." Establishing accountability is seen as essential to the defense of basic rights. Effective horizontal accountability is called for: "There should be changes in the professional training of the police. It's a question of political will. And it's about the role of the three branches of government within the system of representative democracy. Nowadays, the judiciary answers to whatever politicians are in power. It's a vicious circle. . . . But if each of the three branches of government, if each of them would start to play the part assigned to them. . . ." For some the fight against impunity for illegal police violence is a singular endeavor that can only be achieved by a single-minded concentration on this one issue; such activists rather resent what they see as attempts to draw them into broader struggles for social justice. They react skeptically to such proposals, seeing them as a distraction from the issue at hand, and they reject the view that their struggle forms part of a broader one:

> We don't identify with CORREPI. With the other families, we do. It [CORREPI] wasn't what we expected, we expected something more combative, more stuff about what we needed to do. It was like they held us back a bit. CORREPI fights, yes, but we didn't have the same view. When we started organizing the protest marches, we said we didn't want any political slogans of any kind. Yes, we wanted support from everyone. But we don't see our struggle as part of the struggle of the landless people, of the unemployed. We weren't in agreement with that. We said: This is a case of a trigger-happy killing [*gatillo fácil*], and that's what it's about. We have to fight for just this one thing.
>
> You can't jumble a whole lot of different things together. It was difficult to talk about this. Because they [CORREPI] have this ideology that all these groups should join together. That's partly because they give each other

mutual support. The others join a march of CORREPI, so the people from CORREPI, they go to the marches of the landless or the *piqueteros* (pickets). You end up rushing from one thing to the other. And the thing is, you're trying to fight for something specific, so you're not doing this the way you should be. Even so, we do need CORREPI. It's good that CORREPI is there.

The perceptions of victims' families thus reflect the inadequacy of horizontal accountability (O'Donnell 1999c), the abuse of basic human and civil rights, and the "unrule of law" (Méndez, O'Donnell, and Pinheiro 1999). The experience of illegal violence without redress illustrates O'Donnell's observation that while "the more properly political, democratic freedoms are effective . . . [the more] basic liberal freedoms are denied or recurrently trampled" (O'Donnell 1996:186). The perception that a democracy without the rule of law and the defense of essential civil and human rights is "phony" or merely "theoretical" indicates that effective limits on the state's coercive powers are intuitively felt to be an essential element of any democracy worth the name.

Other activists, however, were profoundly skeptical about the prospects for change, seeing arbitrary police killings as simply the most drastic expression of an inherently exclusionary and violent system. In this view, illegal killings reflect not simply the evident deficiencies of state institutions but also basic structures of inequality and the values of a society that discriminates against the poor and marginalized, above all the shantytown dwellers (*villeros*): "Society discriminates against the poor and the police feed on that. If I demand that they send a police patrol to protect the *villa*, they won't do that. They'll send it to patrol around the outside of the villa, to keep the *villeros* in. They think that everyone who lives in the *villa* is a lowlife [*chorro*], or if they're well dressed, they say that they're thieves [*ladrones*]. And they shoot them in the back. These kids have no chance of escaping, not to study and not to work either. They're never going to give the poor what they should give them." Family members of those killed by the police are fighting the common prejudice that sees the poor, especially those that inhabit shantytowns, as dangerous criminals by definition. One mother expressed it by saying: "Let's put it like this: there are no blue-eyed blonds in the prisons."

Shantytown dwellers are acutely aware that their social and economic status makes them easy targets for the police, who "feed on" pervasive discrimination. Activists see the poor and marginal as expendable in the eyes of society; their integration is neither desired nor possible in the context of the neoliberal economic model relentlessly pursued during the 1990s and not significantly modified since then. Consequently one interviewee dismissed the policies of the former president Néstor Kirchner as "cheap populism" and claimed that they did not differ substantially from those of the preceding governments of Carlos Menem, de la Rúa, and Eduardo Duhalde, despite Kirchner's presentation of his policies as a break with the past. In this perception, inclusion of the poor, either as economic actors or as genuine citizens, remains an illusion. Social control of those thus marginalized has nothing to do with integration into society; rather, it is simply a matter of naked physical repression against the poor who are stigmatized as outsiders and enemies: "The only control the state exercises is through repression—that's to say, by means of the police, the *gendarmería* and the *prefectura*."[18] In this perception, democracy is "phony" in two related senses: it is based on profound economic and social inequality, and it has failed to end the repressive practices of the military dictatorship: "The way the police act, it's a continuation of the military regime. There's more liberty. There are no political prisoners. But this is a phony democracy. A lot of things have changed. But a lot of things haven't changed. The police still use torture; there are still the same forms of repression. The same things happen. . . . For me, democracy would be social justice. In my view, things go on the same as under the military regime."

This speaker sees the structural violence of exclusion and inequality as an integral element of Argentina's "phony democracy"; police violence reflects and reinforces these underlying inequalities. Making common cause with other emancipatory social movements on this view is not a matter of "jumbling a whole lot of different things," as another family member expressed it, but a logical and necessary step. Moral panics about rising crime rates and the discursive construction of shantytown dwellers as the criminal others bolster demands for *mano dura* and deflect attention from illegal police violence; indeed, they feed such violence by calling for an expansion of police powers and by reinforcing the perception of *villeros* as a separate and dangerous species. Against a view that tends to see police violence as the actions of a few "bad apples," many activists perceive such practices as functional to a regime of exclusion built on structural violence. In the context of growing socioeconomic inequality throughout the 1990s and the incapacity of the labor market to integrate widening sectors of the population into the economy, the state's coercive apparatus and the use of arbitrary violence against marginalized sectors of the population reinforce these processes of exclusion and give rise to a new form of authoritarianism that coexists with formally democratic institutions. Broadly speaking, then, the meaning that family members ascribe to protest and organization differs depending on their assessment of the prospects for change. While some see their struggle as instrumental and aim to enforce respect for the rule of law, those who consider the system inherently violent view their protest as having a more purely expressive function: it serves to draw attention to structural and individual violence, without giving much real hope that these practices can be overcome.

What light do these cases shed on the phenomenon of violent pluralism? Two elements stand out as being of particular salience to the concept of violent pluralism expounded in the introduction to this volume. First, the cases discussed here themselves bear testimony to the pervasiveness of violent pluralism and to the multiple motives for illegal police violence. Such violence, as the cases show, is prompted by diverse ends, from corruption and police involvement in common criminality to improving the image of the police—it can, in other words, be motivated by the intention to generate material or symbolic resources. In pursuing these goals the police forces enjoy distinct advantages over the civilians they police, being endowed in their turn with both material and symbolic resources. Their access to weaponry, vehicles, and information, and their right, as public law-enforcement officers, to take actions that private citizens may not, represent the material advantages they enjoy. Yet arguably far more important is their symbolic advantage—the residual authority accorded to them as the ostensible upholders of law and order *within a democratic system*, which confers a prima facie credibility on their actions. As the testimony of family members shows, the police can generally (though not always) count on this credibility bonus and therefore on the connivance of those state institutions formally charged with overseeing the legality of state actions. Thus the police will construct their violent acts in such a way as to make them appear legitimate, but they know that they need not go to any great lengths to make this construction watertight, since they can usually rely on the judiciary to accept their version.[19] Paradoxically, therefore, illegal violence is legitimized by the very agencies charged with controlling the legality of state actions. Thus violence of this kind is fomented by the willingness of a range of other actors to give it effective support. Seen in this light, police homicides point to a tolerance for illegal violence that extends far beyond the police themselves into other state agencies.

A second important conclusion from these cases links up with the previous observation. Although it is undeniably the case that the security forces in Argentina have a long and inglorious tradition of using arbitrary violence—including torture, assassination, and enforced disappearances—it would be a mistake to see the present-day phenomenon of police violence as merely a remnant of authoritarian rule. Rather, the persistence and ubiquity of arbitrary police violence can only be properly understood in the context of pluralism and contestation. As discussed above, many of these cases, notably the Federal Police's strategy of inventing crimes and framing innocent victims, respond precisely to a perceived need to influence public opinion in favor of the police, and this specific type of manipulation only makes sense in a plural setting in which public opinion and media coverage are not subject to censorship. More generally, the police enjoy a significant degree of popular and elite support for their *mano dura* approach, particularly when it is explicitly directed against marginalized sectors of the population. These attitudes translate into electoral victories for self-proclaimed torturers such as the former police officer Luis Patti (see CELS 1999), as well as into majority support for putting bullets (*meter bala*) into supposed criminals (see Brinks 2008:119). As the interview material has shown, many victims' families identify media and popular support for illegal police violence as a factor of central importance in fomenting such violence, as well as in making it virtually impossible for them to obtain any kind of redress. Viewed in this context of explicit demands for draconian police action against perceived criminals, police homicides appear less as an aberration within the democratic system than as one of its components, with clear popular support.

Notes

Some of the research on which this article is based was carried out in the context of a project on the governance of public security in Argentina and Mexico funded by the German Research Association (SFB 700). I gratefully acknowledge this support, as well as the helpful comments of the anonymous reviewers and the editors of this volume.

1. For critical comments on this blind spot in democratization research, see Pereira 2000:228–29 and Sain 2002:11–12.
2. Most of the victims were killed by the police. One was so badly beaten in prison that he died shortly afterward; one—the only woman among the victims—was shot by a member of the coastguard working illegally as a private security guard.
3. For example, in Rio de Janeiro, 1,195 civilians were killed by the police in 2003, while in the same year forty-five police were killed. The imbalance challenges the official version that civilians killed by the police died in armed confrontations between the police and drug dealers. Not until 2004 did victims' families begin to organize the still embryonic Rede de Comunidades e Movimentos contra a Vio-

lencia (Rio de Janeiro) to combat such violence. This network has pointed out that the majority of the victims remain anonymous and forgotten (Rede de Comunidades e Movimentos contra a Violencia press release, October 2005).

4. Thanks to CORREPI for assistance and especially to Pedro, an activist and himself the father of a child killed by the police, who not only put me in touch with a number of other families but also accompanied me to some interviews that would probably have been impossible to conduct without his help. My biggest debt of gratitude is, of course, to all those who agreed to be interviewed and whose experiences are presented in this article. For information on CORREPI's activities, see http://www.correpi.lahaine.org.

5. There is a wide spectrum of victims' and human rights organizations active in this field with differing ideological positions.

6. The CELS regularly reports on police violence, legislation pertaining to police powers, police reform, and relevant legal decisions in its yearly report on human rights in Argentina (most recently CELS 2008), besides devoting specific publications to analyses of aspects of policing in Argentina (see, e.g., CELS and HRW 1998). CORREPI maintains an archive of cases of extralegal killings by the security forces, available online (CORREPI 2007).

7. Interviews with members of the judiciary confirmed a widespread willingness on the part of judges and prosecutors to condone police killings so long as these were declared by the police to have occurred in a "shootout" with violent criminals. One federal judge spoke of a "symbiosis" between police and the judiciary.

8. According to what this young man told Hugo's family, Hugo was forced to kneel down and was then shot twice—as his mother said, he was executed. The family identified the perpetrator as a retired policeman notorious for his role in the apparatus of repression during the previous dictatorship (1976–83).

9. Other cases of police violence prove that this is not an idle threat. In a widely publicized case that occurred in September 2002, members of the Federal Police arrested three adolescent boys and forced them at gunpoint to jump into the putrid waters of the river Riachuelo. One of the youths, Ezequiel Demonty, was drowned. The media attention surrounding this case prompted people from Ezequiel's neighborhood—a *villa*—to wonder whether his family had some special importance, since, as they stated, what the police had done to Ezequiel and his two friends was a commonplace occurrence. They found the scandal surrounding the occurrence mystifying. See *Página 12*, 24 September 2002.

10. Poxirán is the trade name of a powerful adhesive favored by glue sniffers.

11. In this case the victim had supposedly just robbed a shopkeeper of around 50 pesos

12. The dry submarine consists in putting the victim's head inside a plastic bag until he or she is almost at the point of suffocation, as contrasted with the wet submarine—holding the victim's head under water until he or she is almost at the point of drowning.

13. The term *pentito* (literally, repentant) is used in Italy to describe former mafia collaborators who provide information and evidence leading to criminal convictions of leading *mafiosi*.

14. Adrián Levikas, like Mariano Witis, was taken hostage and shot dead by the police along with his captor.

15. Walter Bulacio was illegally detained by the police in 1991 along with a number of other young people. He was so badly mistreated that he died a few days later. His case became a cause célèbre of the human rights movement and a rallying point for the opposition to police violence. It came before the Inter-American Court of Human Rights, which, in 2003, determined that the Republic of Argentina should punish those responsible for causing Walter's death, should reform police powers of arrest and detention to bring them into line with international norms (specifically, those established in the American Convention of Human Rights), and should pay compensation to Walter's family. For a detailed analysis of this case, see Tiscornia 2008.

16. Historically, the city of Buenos Aires was constituted as a federal district with virtually no self-government. The constitutional reform of 1994 gave the city autonomous status and theoretically opened the way for the creation of a city police force, but for a long time there were no serious moves in this direction as the city and national governments could not agree on how to fund a new force. Only in 2008 did the conservative government of the city start its own Metropolitan Police, but it is still of only marginal significance. This force is intended to eventually take over the policing duties now carried out by the Federal Police.

17. Daniel Rafecas, then a state prosecutor, was the prime mover behind and then a member of the official committee of investigation that documented these cases.

18. The *gendarmería* and the *prefectura* are border police responsible for land borders and maritime and navigable borders, respectively. Increasingly since the 1990s they have been employed to assist the regular police forces in general policing activities.

19. The tendency of the judiciary to give ready credence to the police version of events, especially if an armed confrontation is alleged, was graphically expressed by a senior judge who stated in an interview (Buenos Aires, September 2007): "When I was an investigative magistrate I had to deal with two or three cases of armed confrontations with the police; one would tend to view them [police actions] favorably and not unfavorably. This is the tendency. Unless you come up against a judge who clearly has a position that is . . . antipolice or suspicious of the police. . . . If its an armed confrontation with the police, where there is little room for decision in the instant when the [police officer] is fighting to defend his life against that of the other, etc., etc., I, at any rate, was pretty careful with that. . . . No, no, when I say 'careful,' you could say, 'Ah, I see, he favored the police.' And indeed, you can look at it like that."

Organized Violence, Disorganized State

LILIAN BOBEA

For decades transitions to democracy and incipient institutionalization through-out the Caribbean have coincided with an ongoing rise in social, political, and criminal violence, as well as with a reshaping of local and transnational crime patterns.[1] Many countries in the region are experiencing a sharp increase in violence, changes in patterns and structures of crime, and the addition of new sectors as victims and perpetrators. More and more often street crime and domestic violence are systemically complemented by organized violence—not only that of criminal gangs but also that exercised by actors linked to the state through the extrajudicial executions of suspected criminals and the abuse of human rights. Private criminality and violence promoted by segments of the state are perversely linked, since the complicity of public officials with organized crime means that some bureaucratic elites provide security to gangs involved in drug trafficking and other lucrative illegal activities.[2]

This essay addresses the question of citizen insecurity and the organized violence that shapes it in the Dominican Republic. My objective is to explore state and criminal violence at the level of national policymaking and at the microlevel, in underprivileged urban areas where the state has long failed to provide services and where police have traditionally limited their so-called community relations to uniformed violence. The essay draws on a series of in-depth studies that I carried out in thirty-six lower-income neighborhoods located mostly in the northern part of the metropolitan area of the capital city, Santo Domingo, in 2005 and 2006, using focus groups, interviews, and sur veys.[3] The first section of the essay explores how Dominicans living in the poorest urban areas of Santo Domingo and Santiago experience violence and insecurity in their daily lives. I document how these impoverished Dominicans perceive and experience crime and violence and the different ways in which they themselves reproduce it in their neighborhoods, how they interact both as victims and perpetrators of violence and how those relationships define Dominican society, institutions, and government. The essay then moves to the macrolevel to analyze the impact of the government's most recent proposal for public policy and institutional reform, the Plan for Democratic Security, introduced by Leonel Fernández Reyna in 2005. The plan began with the studies mentioned above as an attempt to understand the complex social realities from which criminal violence emerges so as to reorganize the public sector and rebuild society. By connecting public policy to street-level reality, this essay answers the call of the editors of the current volume to seek a "more synthetic framework, one that joins democratic state functioning more explicitly to the daily experience of citizens" in the region's democracies.

The Dominican Case in Regional Perspective

The growing criminality and related violence in the Dominican Republic makes the country part of a broad regional trend. The Caribbean has progressively become a center of organized crime,[4] which connects resources, actors, and institutions in what a United Nations official for the region has described as a transition from "illicit business" to "illicit (political) power" (Sandro Calvani, qtd. in Farah 1996).

One factor that fosters organized crime is the illicit drug trade, which by 2001 represented as much as 3.1 percent of the Caribbean gross domestic product (GDP) and generates an estimated income of US$3.3 billion (United Nations Office on Drugs and Crime 2003:6). The invasion of the formal economy by an illicit economy organized around the production, distribution, and transport of drugs cuts across the most dynamic sectors: free trade zones, hotels, construction, casinos, and the leisure industry. As Anthony Bryan has pointed out, transnational criminal networks are better articulated and more efficient and competitive than are most legal businesses in the era of globalization. Moreover, they are a direct product of the globalization process, the communications and technology revolution that make them more interactive and interrelated (Bryan 2000). The same phenomenon occurs at the local level, where transnational drug networks outperform community organizations and government agencies.

That these illicit networks are well organized does not, however, mean that they eschew violence. Peter Phillips, Jamaica's minister of national security, estimates that 60 percent of the murders that occur on the island are drug related (see Patterson 2007). In general terms, as Jorge Rodríguez Beruff and Gerardo Cordero (2005) have pointed out, drug-related violence and corruption have proliferated in the region, making problems that stem from drug consumption and trafficking the primary concern for the people of the Caribbean (Rodríguez Beruff and Cordero 2005).[5] In the case of the Dominican Republic, for example, drug trafficking has become one of the main causes of violence and insecurity, particularly in middle- and lower-class urban neighborhoods, where distribution and consumption activities concentrate (Rubio 2006:54). Although drug-related criminal activity dates back to the 1980s, it became worse in the early 1990s when the country, which until then had been a conduit for cocaine, heroin, and marijuana, established itself as a major retail drug market. The commercialization and distribution of drugs in the Dominican Republic has continued to grow in recent years.[6] This resulted in connections among local networks of distribution, sale, and consumption, networks in which important sectors of the country's economic, political, and institutional elites are represented.[7] This change affected specific segments of the population, especially young people from socially and economically excluded urban areas who were recruited to establish and defend their turf and the structures of illicit distribution. It has also had an impact on state institutions, as demonstrated by frequent purges of corrupt elements from the public security forces.[8]

In the same vein, among the more prominent variables contributing to the new violence in the region is the illegal weapons trade. Throughout the region "guns and the illegal trade in drugs have formed a symbiotic relationship" (Women's Institute for Alternative Development 2005:5). Furthermore, the use of firearms has escalated during the past decade. According to a report issued by the Women's Institute for Alternative Development (2005:10), the percentage of homicides by firearms in Trinidad and Tobago increased from 63.5 percent in 1995 to 72.5 percent in 2005. The same holds true for Jamaica, where the number of murders committed with illegal guns rose from 56 percent in 1993 to 68 percent in 1996. More recently, the Caribbean Crime Task Force reported that 68 percent of robberies committed in Jamaica in 2000 involved firearms. In Trinidad, 50 percent of deaths were caused by firearms (CARICOM Regional Task Force 2002:15). In the case of Haiti, Robert Muggah estimated in 2005 that there were some 210,000 small arms in the country, most of them illegal (Muggah 2005:xxiv). As is well known, one of the major challenges facing the post-Aristide governments is disarming gangs and informal guerilla groups (Bordenave and Davis 2004). The possession and use of firearms by gangs residing in the capital's most crowded neighborhoods and linked to street-level drug trafficking is one of the main sources of insecurity that residents cite.

A direct link exists between street crime and illicit transnational activities. These activities take place within Caribbean states, but they are essentially intermestic,[9] taking advantage of the political fragmentation and vulnerabilities of a region constituted by microstates. The vast sums of money and illegal merchandise moving through the region have had the effect of dramatically corroding governments and the private sector, giving rise to a deep-seated permissiveness among both politicians and ordinary people concerning corruption. The lucratively violent and structurally criminogenic nature of these societies undermines democracy,[10] since both criminals and security forces establish themselves outside of the citizens' control, obliterating mechanisms of social control, transparency, and direct or indirect governance.[11]

In many countries of the region crime has become a factor in the reorganization of social space, a regulator of the processes of accumulation, and a link between public and private spheres (Harriott 2000).[12] This condition has generated gray areas in which the state has progressively lost its monopoly of legitimate violence (Koonings and Kruijt 2004), as well as the control of its own security apparatuses and agencies (Moser and McIlwine 2004; Zaluar 2004).

Unsurprisingly given the overlap of criminal organization and state power, the responses to criminal violence at the national level have proven inconsistent and insufficient in addressing the problems. This incapacity results from several factors: (1) the lack of a real understanding of the social dynamics that create violent actors; (2) the social construction of violence in Dominican society; (3) the complex interaction among victims and perpetrators; (4) the instrumental use of illicit gains to achieve political ends (Nordstrom and Robben 1995; Klein, Day, and Harriott 2004); (5) the absence of comprehensive and consistent public policies for crime prevention; (6) directives for the police and armed forces to repress the public rather than prevent crime; and (7) authoritarian traditions that have impeded popular participation in the search for solutions.

Furthermore, many Caribbean governments have continued to rely on fundamentally punitive measures to control crime even in recent decades. This approach has also frequently encouraged actors linked to the state to use coercive practices that serve their own interests (Koonings and Kruijt 2004). Afraid of succumbing to the new violence and sheltered by widespread demands for tighter security, many liberal governments appeal to the populism of fear (Chevigny 2003) to sustain policies of order and control.

The disparity between organized violence and the erratic responses to it thus promotes growing tension between national security and human security. The dilemma originates in the extreme weakness of states and their attendant inability to implement institutional reforms that guarantee citizens the social and security services they require.[13] In the face of this absence, the abrupt emergence of crime cultivates insecurity and fear, triggering apprehension in broad sectors of the citizenry, who expect drastic measures from the government, usually ones based in the use of excessive force as a shortcut to deal with the limitations or absence of more rational crime prevention that actually protects constitutional guarantees.[14]

In the broadest sense, the struggle between organized crime and disorganized states is the current incarnation of a long contest between the private and state sectors in Latin America and the Caribbean. Ultimately, the fight between criminals and governments constitutes a dynamic in which the state attempts to reinvent itself to defeat stronger private-sector forces that boast better technology, human resources, and infrastructure, particularly in the realm of security. Organized crime as a system penetrates government agencies, recruiting followers inside the bureaucracy and undermining policy initiatives. This appropriation of the political and normative functions of supplying services and control presents a challenge to the state, particularly to the aspirations of democratization.

The Dominican Republic: Failed State or Challenged Democracy?

Clearly the reality of democracy in the Dominican Republic is at odds with idealized, paradigmatic versions of democratization. The debate about "states in democratic transition" versus "failed states" is usually the domain of academic experts, but in mid-2005 the issue became front-page news in the Dominican Republic.

That summer the U.S. journal *Foreign Policy* published a list of "failed states" based on a study by the nonprofit Fund for Peace and included the Dominican Republic among them, triggering a heated debate in the Caribbean nation (*Foreign Policy* 2005:59; *Clave Digital* 8 September 2005; Díaz 2005). The editor-in-chief of *Foreign Policy*, Moisés Naim, noted in an interview that he considered failed states to be those "where governments have lost the capacity to govern" (Ortega 2005). The Dominican ambassador to the United Nations swiftly replied that for decades the republic "has not experienced a coup d'état, nor a civil war, nor a guerrilla movement nor a breakdown of the political system." On the contrary, Dominican officials noted, "power has been transferred peacefully between the country's three leading political parties, in a fundamentally democratic context" (Espinal 2005). The Dominican president Fernández felt obliged to add that, given the efforts of his own government to combat corruption, the goal of his administration was "to fortify the democratic state that we have today—with weaknesses, but which does exist" ("Leonel Fernández denuncia plan" 2005).

The debate turned on *Foreign Policy*'s assumption that democracy constitutes an ideal type against which particular cases can be measured and found lacking. Underlying this idealized perspective is the view that violence, authoritarianism, disorder, and corruption are atavistic traits that wither away as states modernize. Many contributors to the current volume instead hold the view that violence and other supposed atavisms define modern democratic states in Latin America and other less developed regions. From whichever perspective the issue is theorized, however, it is essential to explore the complex, underlying dynamics that tend to produce violence in both society and the state. States typologized as "failed" tend toward violence because they possess neither the hard nor the soft power necessary to guarantee a voluntary submission to order. It is worth noting that, historically, violence has not only constituted and legitimated the Dominican National Police but has also been a resource invoked by elites who demand an "iron fist" against criminals and more diffusely by the general population, who ask that the Dominican military back up the police in fighting crime.

The Economic Context

In situations of extreme economic insecurity, outbreaks of violence can be a consequence or may constitute an expression of the struggle for economic opportunity.
—Sebastiao Nacimiento, on Haiti, 2006

The recent surge in criminal violence in the Dominican Republic is associated with various factors, including globalization and neoliberalism. In societies such as the Dominican Republic, the diminished administrative capacities of the neoliberal state created vacuums that have been gradually filled by nonstate actors and autonomous bureaucratic elements able to capitalize on these conditions. Over the past three decades, during the transition from authoritarian to democratic regimes, Dominican society has indeed witnessed a disjunction between popular expectations and the capacity of the state to satisfy these demands. This phenomenon has been conceptualized by John Rapley as the emergence of the "new medievalism," meaning a process that empowers illicit actors who benefit from the new opportunities presented by the internationalization of these peripheral economies (2006). The unforeseen effects of political and economic liberalization have promoted a ferocious competition among bureaucratic units, as well as the perverse decentralization of security forces and their autonomization from state control (Davis 2006c).

In this context of institutional weakness, the actual increase of criminal activity, as well as a perception of insecurity by middle- and upper-class sectors, have allowed security forces to exercise excessive and extralegal power, diminishing the rule of law and the possibility of reinforcing democratic institutions. In other words, the institutional violence employed by the police and the military to address criminality has won approval from fearful segments of the population that see themselves as potential victims, building a consensus that reaffirms antidemocratic characteristics at both the institutional level and societal levels.

When the last Dominican caudillo, Joaquín Balaguer, relinquished the presidency in 1996, the government of the Partido de la Liberación Dominicana (PLD) came to power with a neoliberal economic agenda.[15] In the mid- to late 1990s, the Dominican economy proved to be among the most dynamic in Latin America, growing at an annual rate of 8 percent. Yet this growth did not last. The first years of the new millennium proved difficult ones for the Caribbean republic. Under the government of the Partido Revolucionario Dominicano (PRD), a social democratic party that won the presidency in 2000, the economy grew minimally in 2001 and 2002 and then actually contracted 1 percent in 2003, in part because of the collapse of a major bank. A series of corruption scandals further marred the image of the PRD. Popular discontent spilled into the streets as *apagones*, or power blackouts, plunged much of the nation into darkness for days at a time. When Fernández and the PLD returned to power in 2004, the economy began to recover slowly. Yet in 2005 some 47 percent of the population still lived below the poverty level, and over 24 percent lived in extreme poverty, a slight improvement from the previous years (CEPAL 2006).

More significant than baseline poverty are indicators of inequality. In 2003 the World Bank reported that the poorest quintile received only 3.9 percent of total income, while the richest quintile monopolized a full 56.8 percent. The extreme concentration of wealth is confirmed by the fact that the richest 10 percent received 46.8 percent of national income while the poorest decile claimed only 1.4 percent (USAID 2006). The same source suggests that economic fluctuations over time have not affected structural inequality: the percentage of the population unable to satisfy its basic needs has varied only slightly over the past three decades. As another measure of inequality, the difference between medical care available to the rich and that available to the poor is among the greatest in the Caribbean; not surprisingly, the nation has one of the most privatized medical systems in Latin America (USAID 2006). Thus, despite a gradual increase in the GNP by 2005, the country has maintained very high levels of inequality. The Gini index for 2003–5 was 0.5269. In 2002 the country had a Human Development Index of 0.738, in comparison to 0.777 for Latin America overall, and occupied the 98th position among 175 countries.[16] Despite solid GNP growth in 2002 the country's Human Development Index (HDI) showed little improvement (PNUD 2005). In 2005 the HDI improved to 0.779, locating the country in the 79th position among 175 countries. The level of improvement for the majority was, however, almost negligible.[17] In a sweeping critique of government policy since the fall of the Trujillo dictatorship, the United Nations Development Programme (UNDP) notes that while the Dominican Republic has had better economic growth than any other nation in the Caribbean and Latin America over the past 50 years, it has the region's second-worst record of using that growth to improve human development (UNDP 2007).

Stark economic inequality expresses itself in class discrimination, as many of those, especially young people, interviewed noted, stating that employers refused to hire them because they lived in notoriously poor and crime-ridden neighborhoods. Moreover, young people and adults commented that the lack of employment, recreation, education, and other resources contributed to the prevalence of crime in the poorest neighborhoods.

The literature on the relation between poverty and crime remains inconclusive. One study does positively correlate income inequality with homicide rates (Krahn, Hartnagel, and Gartrell 1986). Other works find that economic inequality and discrimination can trigger violence (Blau and Schwartz 1984; Blau and Blau 1982; Blau 1977). Blau and Blau find that a confluence of factors creating social inequality—ethnicity, gender, and religion—combine with differentials in wealth, income, and prestige to generate interpersonal violence. The social exclusion that results from these patterns of differentiation provokes irreconcilable antagonisms expressed in intergroup hostility, generalized violence, and outright conflict. Drawing on Peter Blau and Joseph Schwartz, Steven Messner (1989) has conceptualized economic discrimination as a causal factor and predictor of criminal violence, as "a form of consolidated inequality, where the access to economic resources ascribed social characteristics" (Messner 1989:599). For Messner, economic discrimination means "the denial of access to economic resources on the basis of largely ascribed social characteristics such as race, religion, and ethnicity" (599). Two indicators are most important in raising homicide rates: the percentage of the population subject to discrimination and the intensity of that discrimination (i.e., the question of how limited economic opportunities for the excluded groups are).

In the Dominican Republic economic discrimination based on social (and spatial) exclusion, marginalization, and stigmatization underlies a diffused violence, as Messner and Blau suggest (Messner 1989; Blau 1977). Marginalized populations from "pariah" barrios are the perpetrators, and the victims, of most of the nation's violence, including that directed at the poor by the police and armed forces.

Crime Challenges the State

Organized violence and new criminal networks have had an impact on the social fabric of the Dominican Republic in ways that escape the understanding of the apparatuses of control, fragmenting social space, fostering fear, and creating distrust in institutions. Those who suffer violence and crime tend to be the same population that has already been scarred by the cumulative effects of patterns of exclusion, with high rates of poverty and social marginalization, urban overcrowding, precarious social networks, and informal work patterns.[18] This exclusion has inhibited the development of initiatives sustained by inclusive, democratic processes and participation (Koonings and Kruijt 2007).[19] Also contributing to this scenario is the persistent absence of comprehensive, consistent, and focused social policies to reduce inequality and provide a minimum of social welfare and security, while respecting the civil rights that define a democratic society. Indeed, until recently the country lacked a specific crime-prevention policy that defined the roles and responsibilities of institutional actors and citizens within a scheme of public security.

With respect to its levels of violence and criminality, the Dominican Republic has ceased to be an exception in the Caribbean. In recent years the country has experienced the emergence of new criminal practices and organizations that involve unprecedented levels of violence and sophistication (kid-

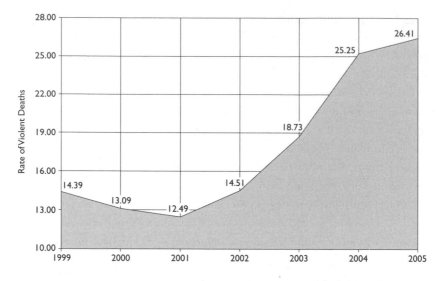

Figure 1. Number of violent deaths per one hundred thousand inhabitants in the Dominican Republic, 1999–2005. Source: Office of the Attorney General, Santo Domingo, Dominican Republic, 2005

napping, armed robbery, cyber crime), which has modified the pattern of "traditional" crime that in the past was largely characterized by nonviolent robbery, property crimes, and domestic violence. The abrupt rise and complexity of crime today is observed in the growth of the country's homicide rate, which was under 6 per one hundred thousand inhabitants in the 1980s and roughly 14 per one hundred thousand inhabitants in the 1990s. For 2005 the rate was 26.41 murders per one hundred thousand inhabitants (Procuraduría General de la República, Ministerio Público 2005). In about twenty years the country's murder rate thus more than quadrupled (see figure 1).

This sharp rise in homicide leveled off and began to decline in 2006, with the implementation of the government's Plan for Democratic Security (PSD). At the end of 2006, the murder rate descended to 23.56 per one hundred thousand inhabitants, representing a 10.78 percent reduction from the previous year (Procuraduría General de la República, Ministerio Público 2006).

Lethal violence is concentrated in the most urbanized areas of the three main provinces of Santo Domingo, Distrito Nacional (the province surrounding the capital), and Santiago. Official statistics indicate that from a total of 2,403 murders that occurred in 2005, 395 murders took place in the area of the Dominican capital, 26 of them in just one impoverished neighborhood. For

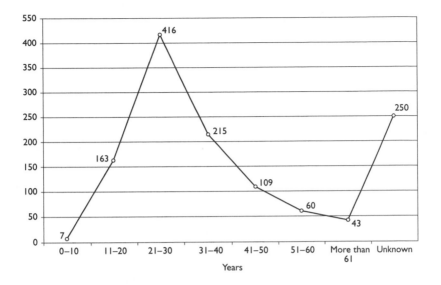

Figure 2. Homicides by age of victim (January-June 2005). Source: National Police Statistics, Dominican Republic, 2005

the same period there were 659 violent deaths in the province of Santo Domingo and 260 in Santiago, the second largest city (Procuraduría General de la República, Ministerio Público 2005). That same period registered an increase in acts of delinquency and feminicide and a growing presence of criminal gangs, particularly in low-income neighborhoods, with a corresponding increase in armed confrontations among gangs for territorial control and between gangs and the police.[20] Parallel to this increase, the number of persons killed by the police, in incidents euphemistically called "exchanges of fire," also rose. In 1997 there were 78 such extrajudicial killings, while 2004 saw over 200. In the latter year, one out of every five homicides resulted from police violence.

These developments have left ordinary Dominican citizens with the impression that the country is experiencing an unprecedented wave of violence from the beginning of 2000. In a study issued in 2004, 71 percent of the inhabitants of the twenty-two provinces surveyed stated that they felt insecure and unprotected from a wave of holdups. The same study determined that 43.6 percent of the interviewees had recently been victims of some kind of criminal act.[21]

Victims of the most serious crime, homicide, are largely young men between the ages of twenty and forty, as indicated by data collected by the attorney general for the first half of 2005. As figure 2 shows, a significant percentage of homicide victims are much younger, between eleven and twenty years old.

According to official sources, violent deaths occurred under the following circumstances in 2005: 656 people died in fights and disputes (including clashes between gangs), 383 died in robberies and holdups, and 437 were killed by the police, a number that represents 18 percent of total homicides. An increased civilian perception of insecurity is therefore unsurprising. Violent crime primarily related to drugs is now considered among the most serious problems that the country faces, along with the lack of electricity, unemployment, and the increase of the cost of living. The civilian perception of the problem is intensified by the fact that 43.2 percent of citizens surveyed believe that the National Police do not control delinquency appropriately (Fundación Justicia y Transparencia and Estudios Sociales y de Mercado 2004).

Factors Influencing the Rise of Organized Violence

According to Dominican citizens, the explosion of violence has multiple causes: (1) growing microlevel drug trafficking that fosters criminal behavior on the streets and is associated with the prevalence of gangs that recruit the youngest and most vulnerable; (2) a rise in indiscriminate armed violence in confrontations among gangs and between gangs and the police; (3) a lack of coordination among security state institutions; (4) police incapacity due to a lack of resources and a lack of legitimacy, since the police are perceived as corrupt; (5) inconsistent police work connected to arbitrary raids and inertia in the face of delinquency; (6) a crisis of public services (such as daily blackouts that leave streets dark and impassable roads that make patrolling difficult) that creates conditions that lead to higher crime rates (focus group, North part of Santo Domingo, March 2005).

Among the most significant crime-generating factors are inequality and the social and spatial exclusion that accompany it, undermining minimum standards of welfare for the population. In the past three decades, structural economic reforms have forced the informal and precarious employment of wide sectors of the population that migrated from rural areas to the capital and its environs. Of the sixty-six neighborhoods in the National District (Santo Domingo), fourteen neighborhoods alone concentrate a plurality (33 percent) of the impoverished homes in the city. The unemployment rate in these areas is higher than the level in the district overall (11.45 percent). Hit hardest are youths between eighteen and twenty-nine, the sector that represents most of the inhabitants of these areas, with an unemployment rate of 16.13 percent (Secretariado Técnico de la Presidencia, Oficina Nacional de Estadísticas 2002).

In one of the neighborhoods studied, unemployment and a lack of opportunity were listed as the most serious problems the community faces, followed by drug addiction and trafficking, as well as police corruption.

Frequently the adult population links the lack of opportunity for young people to their alleged proclivity to crime (focus groups, North part of Santo Domingo, January 2006). Criminality was also associated with the discrimination that youths face at potential workplaces and from the police, who often act on stereotypes of low-income youths, as occurs in other parts of Latin America (Savenije and Andrade-Eekhoff 2003:41; Ayres 1998; Leeds 1996). In the same way, studies carried out in other countries (Moser and McIlwaine 2004; Santacruz Giralt, Concha-Eastman, and Cruz 2001) confirm that juvenile groups are stigmatized, making it difficult to distinguish criminal gangs from other groupings that, despite resorting to violence at times, are primarily structured around social solidarity. I will discuss that distinction in more detail below.

Time and again the most socially underprivileged sectors perceive insecurity as associated with shortfalls in social investment, overcrowding, and in the case of youth, with the precariousness of public space, leisure, and education in their neighborhoods (Rubio 2006).[22] The failure to provide services and strengthen citizenship encourages young people to join gangs since they do not feel part of society, but rather part of a *parasociety* that consists of the marginalized or stigmatized residents of the poorest neighborhoods. Many of these residents told me that they do not admit to outsiders that they reside in notoriously dangerous barrios like Capotillo or La Cienega. As one resident said, "If an employer sees on your resume that you live in Capotillo, they just throw it away." They also feel that both the government and the media see only the problems of these neighborhoods and none of their efforts to make life better (Bobea, focus group, Capotillo, 2005; Santacruz Giralt, Concha-Eastman, and Cruz 2001).

On the scale of critical factors adding to perceptions of insecurity, the arming of the population figures as another important component. National Police sources indicate that there are more weapons in the hands of civilians than there are in those of the armed forces and the police together.[23] Illegal weapons, which are more likely to be used in crimes, are estimated to number over 1 million in a country of fewer than 10 million people. Carrying weapons is an ingrained cultural phenomenon in the country, and as long as the perception of civil insecurity continues to increase, it will be reflected in the arming of the population. Despite the professed goal of the Secretariat of the Interior and Police to reduce the number of firearms in private hands, between 2003 and the first half of 2005 the government issued 178,193 licenses to carry a weapon, mostly for private-use handguns.[24]

Security and Vulnerability from the Victims' Viewpoint

Given this national context, citizens often define the concept of security in terms of its shortcomings. For an important sector of the public, security means no more than "going about their business normally, without fear of being attacked, with the freedom to get home at any hour," and that their sons and daughters "can walk the neighborhood's streets undisturbed, knowing that there is an institution that can act in people's defense when they have been victims of aggression." In the words of one neighborhood leader, "For me, security is being at home with no worries . . . you can't even make it to the corner, you can't have your children in the streets" (community leader from Gualey, interview by the author, May 2005).

In the neighborhoods where we conducted our research, insecurity is linked to (1) varying levels in the organization of violence (different types of gangs and organized crime, low-level drug trafficking, and police actions); (2) the quality of the institutions of protection, especially the police and the justice system; and (3) specific local conditions such as areas of high risk and access to services and resources. Lacking basic guarantees, communities learn how to live with problems and somehow find mechanisms of survival despite conditions of risk and helplessness. In the pragmatic words of one resident concerning drug dealers in the neighborhood, "if you don't mess with them, they don't mess with you" (Manuel, community leader; focus group, Guachupita, 2005).

Settings, Dynamics, and Actors in Violence and Crime

There is nothing simple about the patterns of violence in the barrios, which weave a complex web that connects actors, social relations, institutions, employment, temporality, and discourses. Violence gives rise to hybrid dynamics such as the simultaneous rejection of police violence in the barrios and the demand that the police physically eliminate criminals. Violence traces a continuum between private and public domains, dislocating old associations and creating new ones.

Families as well as the state may routinely resort to violence, as Dominican health officials noted recently. According to their report, a majority of Dominican homes are undemocratic in the sense that physical and verbal abuse are "normal" punishments and in that parents exhibit a contradictory pattern of authoritarian rule and the neglect of their children (Pantaleón 2007). This pattern of violence at home presumably contributes to tolerance toward coercive and violent practices in other spheres. As the introduction to this volume notes, violence is "plural and dialectical—it stems from multiple sources . . . and configures daily life and the workings of governance in various ways" (Arias and Goldstein this volume).

Despite the large volume of literature that addresses the multiplicity of forms assumed by interpersonal, institutional, organized, and informal violence, few studies have explored the articulation *among* these different types of violence. The work of Caroline Moser and Cathy McIlwaine (2004, 2007) has pioneered the exploration of the relation between domestic violence and social and economic violence.[25] Their work explores the ontology of violence, examining how violence is manifested and negotiated among diverse actors, both victims and perpetrators, to such a degree that it permeates the social fabric and becomes routine. Other studies have focused on the codes underlying interpersonal relations in both private and public spheres, identifying a subculture of violence that is tolerated, for example, in the case of violent masculinity (Zaluar 2004). In the same way, Teresa Caldeira (2000) has used individual narratives to reconstruct forms of violence that connect domestic with community violence.

In the Dominican case that I have examined through surveys and focus groups, the connection between interpersonal violence and corporate violence in the community and its institutions emerges at times as continuous with and at other times as rupturing established patterns, sometimes transferring a pattern from one sphere to another. For example, it is difficult to push aside the connection between the violent socialization of young people in their homes and its transference to the street through the substitute families provided by *naciones* (nations), hierarchical criminal groups to which members swear allegiance, and gangs. As I indicate in the section dealing with this topic, the same holds true of the authoritarian and repressive practices and discourses that characterize these groups, even though they are adopted as supposed alternatives to dysfunctional families. For girls and young women in particular, the culture of the gangs has much in common with the domestic violence that many of them have experienced, with verbal and physical abuse and sometimes rape at home having their parallels in the gangs—in both spheres they suffer as the most vulnerable members. Thus their exposure to violence at home preconditions young women to victimization in the streets.

Along the same lines, one study conducted in 2002 with a sample of 104 youths in five Santo Domingo barrios with a significant gang presence asked whether or not the young people experienced physical violence at home—42 percent answered in the affirmative. In the same study 22 percent stated that they had been thrown out of their homes, while 9 percent reported having been punished by being locked inside their home. Another 59 percent said they had been the objects of verbal aggression. Not surprisingly, more than half of those interviewed said they did not feel comfortable at home, while 43 percent said that they felt rejected, above all by their siblings.

Another way that domestic and community violence reinforces institutional violence is through the shared tolerance of violent behavior. As the surveys conducted for this study indicate, the two most widely denounced forms of violence in the barrios are fights between neighbors and physical aggression against women and children. This data is supported by statistics from the attorney general's office, which show 177 feminicides among a total of 2,144 violent deaths from January to December 2006. Eighty-one of these women were killed by husbands, boyfriends, or other intimate acquaintances (Procuraduría General de la República, Ministerio Público 2005, 2006). The same source indicates that there were six hundred fights among residents in the barrios. In 2005 there were 190 feminicides among a total of 2,403 homicides reported at the national level, 98 of which were deemed so-called crimes of passion. In the face of this reality, both the community and the police display inertia and toleration; all seem to agree that intrafamiliar violence is a private matter that only concerns those involved. Similar institutional indifference is displayed toward the police killing of suspects. In 2005 there were 437 killings by the police. Although the numbers declined in 2006 and 2007, in 2008 they surged to 455, meaning that nearly 20 percent of all violent deaths in the country were killings by police action.[26] The high percentage of police homicides reflects a ready resort to lethal violence without fear of reprimand or investigation.

The connection between interpersonal and institutional violence is not necessarily evident to those who perpetrate it or to those who suffer it. Consequently, if we approach the problem through the perception of the people in poor neighborhoods, it is not surprising that they frequently describe the violence in their midst as something that comes from outside their communities. This point of view obviates the possibility of seeing the violence as something born in the private sphere of their homes and growing in the semipublic space of their neighborhoods. Thus residents' testimonies emphasize the "otherness" of the criminals they fear and the externality of the violence they produce, despite the victimization of parents by children and vice versa, residents by police, and so on. In various focus groups there was palpable tension when participants suggested that a son, father, or brother of a neighbor was involved in criminal activity. Interestingly, the young people partaking in the sessions often recognized that those most likely to be recruited by gangs were their peers from dysfunctional families in which parents had no control over their children or, worse still, in which parents encouraged crime. Young people understood that violent socialization by the family was a precursor to criminal involvement.

A generalized culture of repression and institutional authoritarianism goes far back in Dominican history and finds expression today in the relations between the state and its coercive apparatus and residents of the barrios, for example, in response to protests in those neighborhoods. But violence is also evident in intracommunity relations within the barrios, and not only among gang members. Violent discipline in schools, for example, makes these institutions models of repression more than centers for socialization and identity building. Likewise, the country's prison has a majority of young inmates (1.7 percent are minors, while 49 percent are between eighteen and twenty-nine years old); most of them either left school or were expelled from it. According to government statistics, 69.6 percent of the prison population did not go beyond the eighth grade. As several studies point out (see Rubio 2006), a correlation exists between dropouts and gang membership.

One important result of the perception of insecurity and fear is that residents lose control of space and time. This is expressed in the fragmentation of public spaces, which affects the capacity for socialization and for social cohesion.[27] In the local geography, high-risk drug sale points define borders inside the neighborhood, while police raids define the neighborhood against the areas around it, isolating the poorest and most crime-ridden zones. This has produced changes in behavior and habits among residents who avoid passing through or meeting in spaces that used to be public, for fear of being mugged or caught in the crossfire of a gang confrontation. This situation limits mobility and imposes a virtual curfew that usually starts at sundown and tends to be exacerbated during frequent power outages.

Paradoxically, instead of prompting organization and socialization, fear contributes to their disintegration. As one resident put it, "We are so afraid of everyone that we can't fight the criminals. Since the police don't help us, we are obliged to make friends with the criminals, I mean, be friendly with them, because if we tried to turn them in, they would kill us, and the police wouldn't do a thing about it" (focus group; Cristo Rey, 2006). During focus groups and interviews, I heard about crucial shortcomings in the social and spatial integration of neighborhoods. Deterioration is observed in intrafamily bonds, but also in intracommunity bonds. Neighborhood organization tends to be more precarious than in the past, although the needs and challenges of building a community are even greater.

Each scenario of conflictual coexistence in the barrios generates new levels of tolerance toward violent dynamics, and this helps recreate a cultural subsystem that makes violence even more common and permissible, legitimating it and establishing its own codes and modes of perpetration (Moser and Mcllwine 2004). On the one hand, people in the barrios of Santo Domingo associate violence with the presence of drugs, gangs, and a corrupt police force. On the other hand, they also speak of the verbal and physical violence that parents direct at their children, violence in classrooms inflicted by teachers and students, and conflicts that erupt between neighbors because of overcrowding, noise, and garbage thrown in scarce public spaces.

Violence has both an expansive and a fragmentary power in terms of the spaces in which it takes place and the subjects of victimization. It is practiced at home but also has an impact on public areas. In both scenarios women are victims of domestic abuse and petty crimes. Men are most often murdered by criminals or gangs, while children and teenagers experience violence at home or at school, as well as at the hands of criminals and the police. Relatively often they are both victims and perpetrators, closing the perverse circle around them.

To speak of "environments of violence" implies drawing connections between the home and the neighborhood. Different actors collaborate there, such as aggressors and victims that are members of the same nuclear family or residents of the same neighborhood. Violence as a way of life spreads from private to public spaces and vice versa. In this migration of behaviors, children learn violent conduct at home and transfer the lessons to other environments as part of a process of violent socialization. In studies of gangs in Central America, for example, the same sexist patterns that predominate in male-female relationships in the home are reproduced in the gang environment. In testimonies female gang members often recount how they are subjected to much greater violence because of their gender. They are victimized at their recruitment and during initiation; in most cases, rituals of initiation include being raped by gang members (Santacruz Giralt, Concha-Eastman, and Cruz 2001).

Despite the multiple origins of violent behavior, more than 70 percent of residents interviewed in five barrios blamed the "new" violence on an eruption of retail drug trafficking and consumption (Newlink Political 2005a). In seven barrios, more than 82 percent of the population interviewed declared street delinquency as the main problem in their communities, something associated in their view with the consumption of marijuana and cocaine, drugs under whose influence delinquents committed a large number of crimes (Newlink Political 2005a). A second study shows that 90 percent of people surveyed in twelve neighborhoods considered gangs a serious problem, while only 30 to 40 percent saw robbery as a major problem (Newlink Political 2006a). In the barrios where we did our research the disconnect between the people and the police speaks volumes: the police demand that residents report drug dealers and the location of sales points, while residents refuse to inform because they believe that gathering intelligence is the exclusive responsibility of the police. Given the organized nature of crime, inhabitants also feel vulnerable since any accusation could bring repercussions.

The sale of drugs is undoubtedly a growth industry at the national level, in the poorest barrios as well as in the wealthier areas of the National District.[28] Yet violence tends to concentrate in the former. Here the trade and consumption of drugs form a subculture of survival and tense coexistence among delinquents, the community, and law-enforcement agents. Consumption also involves a clientele from outside the neighborhoods, enhancing the consolidation of organized crime networks across and beyond the barrios. In these neighborhoods, street-level trafficking operates under a managerial and competitive logic that gradually incorporates individuals and legitimate businesses in the neighborhood to the point that, as one resident put it, "drugs are a form of part-time employment here" (Statement by local leader in focus group that took place in the northern part of Santo Domingo, 2005). The drug microeconomy trickles down far beyond dealers and their points of sale, since the circuits often draw in students, housewives, and the elderly who receive minimal payments (sometimes only the equivalent of a dollar or two) to deliver a small quantity of drugs to a dealer. Survival strategies involving illegal activities bring with them a kind of moral neutralization, evident in drug dealing. In these lower-income neighborhoods, over a third of the inhabitants surveyed stated that they knew someone involved in drug dealing.

Retail drug trafficking, especially the sale of cocaine, marijuana, and crack, is the domain of bands or gangs led by adult leaders who in turn recruit young people from a very early age. The "walkers" or "mules" are usually between the ages of nine and thirteen. Many reach adulthood with enough experience to create their own points of sale, and they follow the same modus operandi of recruiting minors. Gangs control the territories of the barrios and the inhabitants' hours of circulation, "making the day shorter" as one distressed neighbor acknowledged (men's focus group, Cristo Rey, 2006). When gangs engage in armed confrontations for the control of drug sale points, as they often do, residents are frequently caught in the crossfire. There have been reports of bullets piercing the walls and roofs of houses.[29]

Neighborhood residents do not see the police as offering appropriate responses to these challenging patterns of violence. First, they consider the police too ill-informed, ill-trained, and ill-equipped to face neighborhood crime. Second, police officers are often perceived as having partnered with criminals, thus the fear that information may leak out keeps people from filing formal accusations with the police. Third, "decent folk," as neighborhood residents characterize themselves, complain about violence coming from the police force itself in the form of arbitrary raids, abuse, and extrajudicial executions, which has distanced the police from the people. Because of residents' perceptions of police incapacity, and taking into account the authoritarianism that still permeates Dominican society, many residents unsurprisingly prefer that police officers be reassigned and that the military take their place.

The Resources and Capabilities of the Communities

It is essential to recognize that nearly all of these poor neighborhoods have a long tradition of self-organization in protest movements, formal groups, and less-formal organizations. These organizations fought against government attempts to expel residents from these marginal neighborhoods that had often been established on land seized from the state. Much of this organizational infrastructure survives in the 1,377 groups registered with the city government as recently as 2006. These groups include block associations, religious and church groups, parental and school-support groups, social, athletic, and youth clubs, and committees to defend neighborhood rights (Ayuntamiento del Distrito Nacional/UNDP, 2005). There are also coordinators who work to connect associations with similar interests in different barrios. At least two of these coordinators, who work with national and international NGOs, focus on violence and the promotion of peace. In the neighborhoods of northern Santo Domingo where I conducted interviews, residents had led marches against violence and launched educational programs related to the issue. Working with NGOs like the Centro Juan Montalvo, residents created plans for social work in their neighborhoods (*agendas sociales*). In other words, the poor and crime-ridden neighborhoods have significant social capital and, as Enrique Arias points out for Brazil, these networks "can change existing policies or discipline negligent officials," and can also "allow groups with different and often contradictory strategies to work together to achieve similar objectives" (2004:7). Over time, however, many of the organizations that began in opposition to government policy were co-opted by one or another political party, succumbing to the benefits provided by a clientelistic system, and thus lost some of their power to represent broader interests. Moreover, as organized crime and related violence increased in the neighborhoods, many of the community organizations felt disempowered and have even been silenced.

Symbiotic Relations: Citizens and Criminals

The *tigueres* know me, but the police don't.—focus group, La Joya, 2005

The context of deprivation, social exclusion, institutional indifference, and police repression is aggravated by the damage to community solidarity caused by turf wars among drug gangs, an influx of criminal outsiders, and new criminal patterns. As a result, traditional mechanisms of conflict resolution by community organizations that restrained antisocial behavior in the past have been lost. Without social controls and established codes of behavior, a new kind of violent socialization emerges. While communities may tolerate low-level drug dealing, and even see in it a form of subsistence, they strongly condemn the violence generated by drugs including robberies to support drug habits, armed conflict between gangs, and police violence against gangs which at times is indistinguishable from score-settling by the drug dealers themselves and has thus been referred to by Alba Zaluar as "perverse integration" (Zaluar, 2004). As barrio residents note themselves, "before they sold drugs and used them here, but there wasn't so much violence" (focus group, in Gualey, 2006).

Some segments of the population establish symbiotic and functional relations with gangs as a way to negotiate their disempowerment. The neighborhood "belongs" to the delinquents in the sense that they provide protection and help: "The crooks live on my street, they owe us favors, and we owe them favors. . . . If they need food we give them food. They are harmful, but they can also be helpful. They have known us their whole lives and they protect us—if somebody from another neighborhood robs us, they help us get our stuff back since the police don't" (Flor, a young woman in a focus group in Capotillo, 2005).

The legitimacy enjoyed by criminals is most pronounced among young people, even among those who have no ties to criminal activity. The young tend to express a more sympathic view of those who live outside the law: "Although they do bad things, they don't necessarily want others to become criminals, because they are not really bad deep down. There are those who became criminals because there was nothing else for them to do" (young people's focus group, Gualey, 2005). Moreover, residents understand that the criminals are not totally indifferent to their relations with the community, thus empowering local residents: "If you make even a little effort to be friendly, they get to know you. They know that having some kind of contact with a person *de buen vivir* [with a good reputation] in the barrio, paying us some respect, means that they will be more protected" (young people's focus group, Gualey, 2005).

In certain areas strong neighborhood loyalties still offer some protection for the residents. As one resident said about the "homeboys" in his barrio, "I feel safe and I can go out at any hour because they know me—but that doesn't mean that the barrio is safe or that everyone is safe" (men's focus group, La Joya, 2005). A resident of another barrio recalled, "Sometimes when I go out late I hear them say, 'he lives around here,' and they leave me alone" (focus group, La Outra Banda, 2005).

The strong sense of neighborhood identity also leads residents to make a clear distinction between criminals from the neighborhood and those from outside, leading to the notion of local criminals as hybrids who are in some ways alien yet who simultaneously belong to the neighborhood because they were born and raised there. Residents avoid conflict with them not just out of fear but because of a certain level of solidarity. "They are the same guys we grew up with and went to school with," one resident said, "so even if they didn't take the same path as us . . . we have to continue living among them anyway. We can't stop speaking to them, because if anything happens to us in the neighborhood, they come help us" (young people's focus group, Gualey, 2005). As noted, some members of the community believe that local criminals protect them from outsiders more effectively than the police. Thus the incapacity of the police is supplemented by the private dynamic of local criminals.

The same dynamic underlies the unwillingness of local residents to report criminals that the police regularly complain about. Even barrio residents who do not see the delinquents as positive alternatives to the police expressed reluctance to report drug dealers—partly out of a fear of reprisal, but also because of a grudging sense of community. "If I see somebody cutting drugs or stealing, I look the other way because that is not our job as leaders: that's the police's job" (leader's focus group, Capotillo, 2005). Under the circumstances, silence constitutes a resource that residents can deploy to mediate between the police and criminal elements in their neighborhoods. This resource provides residents with a kind of soft power that, even though it may be the fruit of fear, can nevertheless help them enter into a process of negotiation.

From time to time criminals can also co-opt the police's "hard power." Since reliable intelligence is one of the most serious deficits facing the police, they rely heavily on delinquents as informers. This blurs the line between police and criminals, since informers can become accomplices of corrupt agents, thus further delegitimizing the police in the eyes of the community.

Violent Actors

In the barrios, citizens do not speak of being victims of sporadic and anonymous violent acts, but rather of violence promoted by three distinct groups: gangs (*pandillas*), the so-called *naciones*, and individuals identified generically as *tigueres*, a term that can be used for police officers as well.[30]

In the Dominican Republic the *tiguere* is a cultural reference point. The *tiguere* flourishes in the adverse conditions of the barrio, usually using skills and strategies that take him outside the law. The term can be pejorative or admiring, in general serving to denote a person who embodies the nexus of legal and illicit, of the socially acceptable and the morally repugnant. *Tiguere* as a term identifies an individual attitude, perhaps closest to the English term *hustler*, and it does not necessarily imply involvement in organized crime. In the same way, in the barrios the term *tigueraje* (acting like a *tiguere*) identifies numerous economic activities that are illicit or at best semilicit but that may involve persons not necessarily seen as professional criminals. Among these "mixed" businesses range the fencing of stolen merchandise (cell phones, jewelry, electronics), the position of intermediary in drug transactions, buying and melting down of stolen copper wire, operating chop shops for stolen cars, and running protection rackets, which often involves active police officers.

Gangs, on the other hand, refer to more structured groups than *tigueres*. Youth gangs and youth violence in the Dominican Republic are not new phenomena. Diverse studies have confirmed the existence of *pandillas* in the 1970s and earlier (Abreu 2003, Alcántara 1995, Castillo 1983, González et al. 1981). Indeed, their origins can be located around such quintessential Dominican cultural products as caciques, the chiefs so preponderant in militant political parties (Vargas 2006). Nevertheless, a baseline survey applied in eight barrios showed that more than 75 percent of those interviewed believed that gangs had increased considerably in recent years.

Today's youth violence also exhibits new traits. In the barrios we studied, these traits include, for one, the integration of gangs into the daily life of the barrios, in contrast to earlier periods during which gangs remained isolated and operated largely outside their home neighborhoods. Yet despite their stronger local projection, the gangs are now simultaneously translocal and even transnational, coordinating criminal activities across barrios and across national borders. Gangs now also incorporate new segments of the population, especially the very young and those with fewer ties to schools, homes, churches, and community organizations. Finally, gangs are far more involved in the illegal drug trade and the sale of illegal firearms now and thus have become much more sophisticated. The Dominican press and the public often focus on the gangs' transnational links, especially on the role of *los deportados* (the Dominicans convicted of crimes in the United States and repatriated by the U.S. government), as major factors in the increase of crime in the country.

In every community we studied, over 90 percent of the residents considered the involvement of youths in gangs a serious matter. But although they frequently incorporate the young, criminal gangs are not exclusively juvenile. Nor are they confined exclusively to poor neighborhoods. They also appear in middle- and upper-class neighborhoods, although they do tend to concentrate in the most impoverished areas.

In recent years other youth groups have emerged to challenge Dominican cultural norms. The most important, which have taken shape only in the past decade, are the self-described *naciones*, or nations. The *naciones* offer an axis of intragenerational solidarity; in a context of absolute vulnerability, they recruit young people that have been multiply excluded.[31] *Naciones* have a hierarchical and centralized structure strictly regulated by a set of rules accepted unconditionally by their members.[32] Members of *naciones* explicitly swear allegiance to a criminal entity rather than to the sovereign state from which they feel thoroughly disenfranchised. The *naciones* reassimilate marginalized young people as citizens of a new organism that is translocal, violent, youthful, and freighted with symbolism.

Some members describe the *nación* as an alternative project of nationhood. "I was almost 100 percent proud to belong," one said, "because most of the norms, rules, and ideals of that *nación* were about putting an end to political corruption and discrimination" (Elvis, member of the *nación* Amor Dorado, Santo Domingo, October 2006). The rules of one *nación*, the Latin Kings, include a section titled "How Laws Are Made," specifying that "any member of the nación has the right to make a proposal" and explaining in detail how such proposals will be evaluated ("El Manifiesto" n.d.). *Naciones* can be seen as the grassroots verdict of the traditional state's failure.

At the level of sybolism *naciones* can be seen as a rejection of established norms, but they are also a resource of negotiation for issues that otherwise might be resolved through violent conflict, whether with other *naciones* or the authorities. They also serve to empower their members, giving them a status that they have otherwise been denied. *Naciones* work as integrated systems of loyalties and providers of necessary services, especially security, to their members. They share elements of the conventional culture that they overtly reject, not only in terms of a socialization to violence but also in terms of the authoritarianism, homophobia, sexism, and patriarchy evident in their hierarchies, which locate the "Inca" or "Supreme One" at the top, commanding loyalties and demanding favors from underlings. Their elaborate structures make *naciones* less flexible than criminal gangs, with which they may or may not be connected.

Naciones are guided by rules, statutes, and laws that uphold their commitment to loyalty and unconditional belonging. In consequence, although ritual initiation is not difficult, quitting or attempting to leave the group is. According to the rules of one *nación*, "once you have been baptized within this nación, you cannot leave or betray it, or you will be severely punished" ("El Manifiesto" n.d.). Disobeying the "bylaws" of the order or being disloyal can lead to a member's death, according to a recent survey (Universidad Autonoma de Santo Domingo, 2008). Tellingly, this feature parallels the values of another violent Dominican institution, the National Police, whose members prize loyalty to the institution and obedience to superiors above all else, according to a recent survey.

In contrast to the so-called *maras*, forms of gangs that prevail in Central America, Dominican *naciones* are a more recent phenomenon. They started in Dominican cities but have rapidly become more transnational and transterritorial, mainly due to the migration of young people to the United States and Europe and growing access to the Internet, which has become a medium of communication and propaganda through which the *naciones* project their identity globally. This is the case with the Ñetas Dominicanas, Dominicans Don't Play, and the Latin Kings, all of which have put down roots in Spain, nourished by first-generation children of Dominican immigrants. At least two hundred members of these groups are reported to be under surveillance by the

Spanish police. Another group active in Spain, Los Trinitarios, has over one hundred active "soldiers" in several parts of Madrid, most of them "deserters" from other *naciones* (Cornelio 2008).

Other groups active in Spain since 2004 originally came from barrios in Santo Domingo but draw on resources both in the home country and the United States. As a result, their "constituency" has grown more complex as they incorporate other nationalities. The Spanish branch of the Ñetas is made up primarily of Dominicans but includes Puerto Ricans and Ecuadorians as well. This diversity contributes to a more heterogeneous vision and doctrine among the different chapters of the group. For that reason, although each *nación* differentiates itself from others through symbolism and group solidarity, chapters of the same *nación* may also differ in terms of values and ethics, for example, concerning the use of violence and intimidation. Official sources claim that in Spain the *naciones* are in retreat as a result of police pressure. The same sources indicate about 1,300 members of the different *naciones* in Spain, of which only 287 are considered to be active.

In the United States, the rival *naciones* Dominicans Don't Play, Los Trinitarios, and Los Blood are considered the fastest-growing gangs in New York City. The same *naciones* have a presence in New Jersey, Massachusetts, Pennsylvania, Ohio, Georgia, and Florida, where they have gained a reputation for their violent methods, including murder (Messing 2008). But not all Dominican youth gangs have developed a transnational character. Some, such as Los Morenitos, Amor y Paz, and Amor Dorado, remain local groups rooted in Dominican territory (ERIC/IDIES/IDESO/IUDOP 2004a, 2004b).

As highly structured secret societies with their own brutal codes of *omertá* (conspiracy of silence), *naciones* are attractive as vehicles for organized crime. As noted, not all *naciones* use violence as a defining element. Nevertheless, as has been the case in Spain, all *naciones* have been targets of police investigations. In the context of the Dominican Republic, this police activity often turns lethal for the gang members.

The norms and ideologies of *naciones*, however, operate in contradiction with the wider use of *naciones* by organized crime. When a *nación* engages in criminal activity it betrays the spirit of the *nación* and reflects instead the idiosyncrasy of the members. "It's not the *nación*, it's the members, because the *nación* doesn't allow robbery," one member explained. "There are rules against it, I'm telling you, they don't let us steal if you're representing the *nación*, that is, wearing certain clothes, a ring, a bracelet, whatever identifies the *nación* you belong to" (Mateo, a former *nación* member, focus group, Capotillo, 2005).

Paradoxically, while some residents assert that young people do not follow rules or obey authority, their allegiance to *naciones* belies that perception (Ceballos 2004). *Naciones* operate in one respect as families and in another as quasi-military organizations, due to their levels of hierarchy, symbolism, regulation, and esprit de corps. Initiation rituals confirm their aspirations to create a miniature homeland that demands greater loyalty than the *patria* writ large ("El Manifiesto" n.d.).

Combating Uniformed Violence

That larger *patria* has struggled for decades to guarantee its people democracy, security, and well-being. The long transition to Dominican democracy that began in 1961 with the fall of the Trujillo dictatorship has been characterized by weak institutions. Over the years, initiatives for public-sector reform revealed security forces, essentially the National Police and the armed forces, that were sluggish and resistant to change.

Since the late 1990s a public debate has occurred on the reform of the National Police, a centralized body with ingrained military characteristics. Facing questions about its structure, mission, and functions, the police force lacked a guiding legal framework consistent with the democratic regime that would keep its actions under democratic control and focused on defending civil security. Nor was there a national policy that would rationalize the roles of the diverse institutional actors in the field of security. Even less functional was the hierarchical, personalist structure that facilitated a patronage system to the detriment of professionalization. Special police tribunals were the most evident sign that the forces of order were themselves above the law.

The first attempt to reform the police in the late 1990s succumbed to unified internal resistance, as well as to external pressure from military officers who had run the police force in the past. Seven years later the institution once again came under national scrutiny when, in the context of a reform of the penal code in 2004, the congress abolished the exclusive jurisdiction of police tribunals and obliged police officers to protect the rights of suspects in the event of arrest, search, and use of force.[33]

Although these changes modified the approach to civilian security for the first time in the Dominican Republic's history as a democracy, the resistance to change is still palpable among sectors of the police force, as members of the force themselves recognize. "The police were created during the Trujillo dictatorship seventy years ago, when their mission was to persecute ideas [i.e., political subversives]," one official noted. "Never before have we found ourselves immersed in a reform like the one we are moving toward today. We have always remained behind—we are backward" (Police Focus Group, October 2006).

As mentioned earlier, the passage of the new penal code has not halted extrajudicial executions. Killing suspects in "exchanges of fire" still constitutes a de facto tactic to fight delinquency in poor neighborhoods, in which police operations are concentrated. As statistics for these killings amply demonstrate, the police use force as a means of social cleansing. The indiscriminate use of force is evident in the responses given by police officers themselves in an internal survey, in which 22.2 percent of the lower-ranking officers admitted that they fired their guns frequently on the job.[34] More striking is that in 81 percent of the cases in which officials admitted using their weapons, the institution had made no attempt to investigate the circumstances. That fact in itself reinforces a culture of impunity already firmly rooted in Dominican society. Nevertheless, an important change in this pattern occurred after the implementation of the Plan for Democratic Security (PSD), in the second half of 2005, when the number of those killed in exchanges of fire was reduced considerably (figure 3). The office of the attorney general registered a 32.49 percent reduction in people killed by the police between 2005 and 2006, which represents a decline in the rate of exchanges of fire from 4.8 to 3.24 per one hundred thousand inhabitants (Procuraduría General de la República, Ministerio Público 2006).

It is in low-income neighborhoods that police forces traditionally have also carried out *redadas*, or raids, in which citizens, usually youths, are arrested indiscriminately and then booked, giving them a police record that is hard to expunge. In one operation alone 3,816 people were detained, of whom less than 10 percent were prosecuted (Estadísticas Policia Nacional 2004). The raids have had little impact, if any, on reducing violence and crime, and they are very unpopular in the barrios, since the many innocent and few guilty are carted away together. The new penal code promulgated in 2004, however, took aim at these indiscriminate raids.

The authoritarian practices of the police toward the public are less surprising given the abuses that plague the institution itself. During our research, police officials often insisted that the police force must be democratized before officers can be expected to behave democratically toward the public. In different focus groups low- and middle-rank officers complained regularly about abuses and excesses they suffered at the hands of their superiors, including arbitrary imprisonment without charges and without salary or transfers away

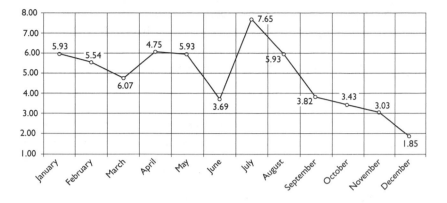

Figure 3. Rates of fatalities resulting from police shootings per one hundred thousand inhabitants, 2005. Source: Office of the Attorney General and Police Office, Santo Domingo, Dominican Republic, 2005

from their families as punishment. Rank-and-file officers complained about miserably low pay—the equivalent of US$140 a month—and poor working conditions as violations of their rights.

Given the low salaries of the police, corruption permeates the institution from top to bottom. As one officer noted, "a man who earns 3,000 or 4,000 pesos a month [$90 to $140] can't survive. Many police officers come from poor neighborhoods, they join the police looking for opportunities, they come from familias where their fathers beat their mothers. Then they confront the reality of their low salary. . . . Some police officers are honest, but others are not" (Police Focus Group, 2006).

Toward Democratic Security

Since the fall of Rafael Trujillo in 1961, the security strategies of both the authoritarian regimes (of Joaquín Balaguer, president six times from the 1960s through the 1990s) and the more democratically minded ones (those of the PLD and the PRD) have consistently focused on keeping violence and protests confined to poor neighborhoods through a strategy of quarantine. One technique, as already noted, has been the indiscriminate roundup of young men in working-class barrios. Another tactic has been to allow criminal gangs to exterminate each other in turf wars. But the violence is not only internal—it also comes to the barrios from outside. "At night one sees around here a parade of SUVs—the *riquitos* [rich] who come to buy drugs in the barrio," one resident commented (focus group, La Zurza, 2006). The rich can travel unmolested to poor neighborhoods, but if violence spills from the barrios into middle-class zones, the media carry stories of a crime wave and a crisis of security, and politicians clamor for the application of an iron fist to criminals.

Although the media have largely ignored the complexity of the phenomena, including the violence of social exclusion and police action, the residents of barrios understand the heterogeneous sources of violence. Conflict comes from multiple public and private actors. The situation was summed up by one barrio resident who wondered "if the bullet that killed my neighbor as she sat in front of her house came from *pandilleros* (gangbangers) or the police who were firing at them" (focus group, Guachupita, 2005). It was in this context of inaction and absence on the part of the authorities that the PSD was implemented.

The Plan for Democratic Security

In mid-2005 the recently elected president Fernández announced the country's first public policy strategy for civil security. Earlier in his term the judicial system had been reformed with the promulgation of a new penal procedure code championed by human rights organizations and other sectors of the country's civil society. This reform challenged the deep-rooted authoritarian and punitive culture by which a police officer was almost completely in charge of a case. Under the new model, the district attorney undertakes the investigation, obliging the police to submit the proof necessary to sustain an accusation. In this manner, the reform sought to end a system that rested on preventive detention.[35] Since coming into effect, the new code has faced criticism from diverse sectors of the public, who view the system as being too easy on criminals. The investigative police did not have the training or resources to gather evidence, nor had the police traditionally worked closely with prosecutors. Even as the new code was implemented the police themselves knew and understood little about it. Nevertheless, a reaction against the new code by the police and the public led to an attempt at counter-reform, which failed. Some of the problems mentioned have been alleviated through training and education.

To the Fernández government the controversy over the penal code evidenced the need for a comprehensive crime and civilian-security policy. In February 2005 the executive introduced the PSD to the public. From the start, the plan employed an integral, preventive concept of security based on strengthening institutional capacity to promote the democratic administration of security, the defense of human rights, and the preservation of the rule of law and of due process (Newlink Political 2004). The plan grew out of a series of studies of actual conditions in the barrios, including about perceptions of crime and of the police. Through community-based workshops, a dialogue was launched in the barrios that had the highest rates of violence. Gang members took part in some of the workshops, so that victims and perpetrators came together to discuss crime. Other gatherings included police, who heard firsthand the perception of barrio residents about their role in promoting or curbing violence.

Through these public discussions, genuine civilian security was understood to include improving social services and providing civilians with protection and the ability to move about freely, while ending the pattern of human rights abuses that had long characterized police intervention in poor neighborhoods. The PSD proposed the reform of justice and security agencies and the improvement of social well-being. Institutional reform would strengthen and professionalize the police and improve police-citizen relations by promoting community policing. Professionalization implies, among other things, demilitarizing and training the force; developing norms, codes of behavior, and procedures; establishing criteria for assessment, promotions, and sanctions; and improving pay and working conditions. The plan strengthened the role of the secretary of the interior and police as the official ultimately responsible for police anticrime strategies, for the cooperation of the National Police with other branches of government, and for the nation's overall internal security planning (Newlink Political 2005a).

As daunting as these changes are, implementing the PSD also implies broader institutional and contextual challenges, above all rooting out corruption at all institutional levels and ending the traditional culture of repression. To achieve those goals, police officers must be reeducated and exposed to an institutional environment less monolithic than the one that has evolved over seventy years. As one officer put it, "to implement the plan you need a different kind of police, in effect new police officers who understand that criminality is a social problem. The police need a culture of participation and need to be better integrated into the larger society, and that means that even old guys like me will need to be retrained" (police focus group, Santiago, 2006).The police themselves understand that "we have personnel who are a little backward, especially the rank and file, those below the level of sergeant, that need to have their consciousness raised, because they have a way of working that goes back many years and doesn't correspond to the requirements of the plan" (police focus group, Santiago, 2006).

The implementation of the plan has also demanded the territorial restruc-

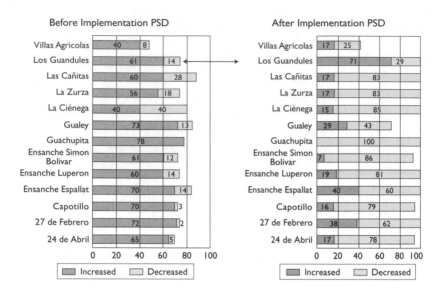

Figure 4. Perceptions of police violence by neighborhood before and after the implementation of the Plan for Democratic Security. Source: Baseline Plan de Seguridad Democratica and Barrio Seguro, Santo Domingo, Dominican Republic, Ministry of the Interior and Police, 2006

turing of the police force, with a new orientation toward the local by assigning supervisors and officers using a community-based approach. To implement a preventive approach to crime, supervisors meet with community members, local leaders, and groups of young people who have had conflicts with the law.

Since the PSD was launched in 2005, gradual changes have been observed. The number of violent deaths fell 6.3 percent in 2006 as compared to the previous year, especially in neighborhoods that reported the highest rates of victimization. Areas where the plan was put into action have also registered changes in the perception of police work and of police-citizen relations (figures 4 and 5) (Newlink Political 2006b).

This change is connected to an explicit effort to eradicate some atrocious police practices and to appoint trustworthy and legitimate police leaders in neighborhood commands.[36] However, the repressive and abusive culture of the police force and the illegal practices of many of its members continue to be one of the most serious challenges the PSD faces.[37] Accountability and respect for the rule of law are essential. Therefore, since the government is accountable and must protect the rights of citizens, the instruments of protection also must

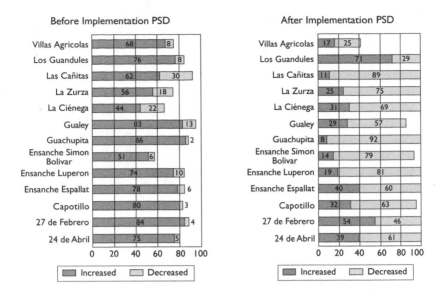

Figure 5. Perceptions of police corruption by neighborhood before and after the implementation of the Plan for Democratic Security. Source: Baseline Plan de Seguridad Democratica and Barrio Seguro, Santo Domingo, Dominican Republic, Ministry of the Interior and Police, 2006

be accountable to citizens. This medium- and long-term process requires support at the highest levels of state power.

Survey results also show a change in people's perceptions regarding police behavior and efficiency. This change parallels the drop in the perception of insecurity, with an increase from 44 percent to 53 percent in the number who felt more secure in three barrios after the implementation of the plan (Newlink Political 2006a).

While these advances are encouraging, the impact of the PSD must of course be measured over the long term. In the short term the plan still faces significant obstacles. One crucial advance will come when neither the armed forces nor the police see themselves as being responsible for public order but instead as instruments of the people. The laws passed by the legislature should provide mechanisms for cooperation, communication, and accountability between the citizenry and the forces of law and order, which include the judiciary. Another enormous challenge that the PSD has just begun to address consists of incorporating communities as equal partners empowered to defend citizen security. Initiatives to create or broaden the space of community unification in matters of security (such as networks, volunteer committees, and round tables) should come from the local levels to guarantee the sustainability of the community action for its own security.

A third challenge the PSD has faced from the beginning is that of achieving synergy between police action and public and private social investment. Critical services are still lacking in many poor neighborhoods. Unless social capital is developed locally and nationally, government efforts will tend to be excessively focused on control rather than on the prevention of violence and crime. Finally, alongside short-term goals and actions, an inclusive vision for constructing a safe nation should be defined and made public, which would imply investment, reform, and participation processes of a broad scope, as well as preventive and corrective approaches to problems. In this vein it is decisive to have a committed and accountable political leadership to address corruption and that is able to develop institutionality at all levels of government to guarantee the continuity of the reforms. Ultimately, it implies narrowing the gap between the willingness to carry out reforms and the realization of policies beyond partisan interests, so that reforms are, to paraphrase Mark Ungar, progressively less elusive (Ungar 2002).

Conclusions

As the title of this essay indicates, in their confrontation with the disorganized states of the Caribbean, criminals organize not only themselves but the social spaces that the state has failed to occupy. This violent restructuring of society happens on many planes: at the interpersonal level, between violent actors and the residents of the communities in which they live; at the level of "institutions" among the various organized, violent groups, including *pandillas*, *naciones*, and the police themselves; and even at the ideological level, as young Dominicans join *naciones* that offer laws and sovereignty that the republic has failed to uphold.

The reorganization of the social space of communities tends to be a violent process as gangs battle each other and the police for control of key areas at key times, trapping residents in the crossfire. Yet the process of respatialization is not always violent. It also happens when violent actors co-opt the police and community residents, or when they legitimize themselves in the eyes of residents, either as criminals who win tacit support from the community or as police who "earn" the right to exterminate suspects. The barrios have thus developed a contradictory dynamic among residents, criminals, and police that blends zero tolerance with a modus vivendi, solidarity with betrayal, and protection with victimization. These perverse dynamics develop primarily in the poorest and most marginal neighborhoods, in contrast to the simpler narrative in middle- and upper-class neighborhoods, which basically calls for the iron fist to be applied against the poor.

The hypothesis that unifies the essays in this volume is that violence has been a constant in the societies of the region, making it constitutive of Latin American democracies rather than an aberration. Future studies of individual countries over time will help clarify these trends, but they are beyond the purpose of this essay. In the more limited study presented here, I recognize the violent nature of the democratic transition in the Dominican Republic and attempt to explain it. My findings suggest that within systems of violent pluralism there are fluctuations—that is, moments of greater and lesser violence by the state and by its citizens—and that governments should pursue the goal of reducing both uniformed and criminal violence. The rhythm of violence in the Dominican Republic bears comparison with the cycles of homicide that Eric Monkkonen describes in his classic study *Murder in New York City*, which suggests that a variety of factors—including the economy, demography, access to guns and alcohol, the formation of gangs, anticrime policies, and ideological constructs of masculinity that demanded lethal violence in certain circumstances—all contributed to the increasing of homicide rates in New York (Monkkonen 2001).

That study suggests that societies can accomplish a reduction in levels of violence, and this is the theme that underlies the second part of my essay, which analyzes the impact of the Plan for Democratic Security introduced in the Dominican Republic in mid-2005. Although the plan is too incipient to permit any definitive conclusions, there is evidence that the Dominican government is for perhaps the first time confronting organized crime and violence in a systematic way that seeks to understand the origins of criminal violence, the complex dynamic in the barrios that produce most victims and perpetrators, and the need for a coordinated response that goes beyond repression to include the reform of the state security apparatus and the improvement of social services in the barrios most afflicted by crime. The fact that the plan began with a series of dialogues among victims, criminals, and police is a promising sign of its inclusive nature. While recent history cautions us to be pessimistic about the possibility of reform, contact with the long-suffering residents of the poorest barrios of the Dominican Republic can only make us hope that "violent democracy" describes a historical phase, one that will continue to evolve rather than being itself a permanent condition.

Notes

I thank Cyrus Veeser for his help in revising this essay. I also warmly thank Eduardo Gamarra of Newlink for giving me the opportunity to coordinate and conduct the research in the Dominican barrios. Some of the research for this essay was collaboratively conducted with Newlink Political, a consultancy based in Miami that conducted a study for the Plan de Seguridad Democratica.

1. For some scholars, these phenomena are associated with the implementation of neoliberal "structural adjustment" policies in the 1970s and 1980s. Those policies of fiscal austerity and belt-tightening increased income inequality and social polarization. Moreover, these emerging democracies lost popular support due to rampant corruption, pervasive clientelism, and a general absence of civil liberties. Other experts contend that the loss of legitimacy by democratic institutions in the region has more to do with their penetration by illicit economic actors, above all drug traffickers. See Espinal 2006; Gamarra 2004; and Chevigny 2003.

2. According to a report issued by the Caribbean Drug Control Coordination Mechanism, drug corruption provides Caribbean bureaucrats with an annual income of about US$320 million. As an example, in 2003 the Dominican Republic was the scenario of a major scandal related to drug trafficking and money laundering. The case, known as "Pepegate," involved a high-level officer, Major General Pedro Julio Goico Guerrero (Pepe Goico), at the time head of the presidential guard of President Hipolito Mejia. Goico and more than sixty other minor officials were responsible for a fraud of US$2.2 billion. This represents between 20 and 50 percent of GDP, or the equivalent of 80 percent of the country's annual budget. The fraud provoked the breakdown of a major bank (Baninter) and a destabilizing of the national economy. During Goico's prosecution the tremendous, mafia-type empire that he commanded while in office came to light: it was based on illicit activities that included the sale and transport of drugs in the Caribbean. In subsequent years new scandals involving public officials have continued to take place. In 2005 the Dominican president Fernández declared that "national and international drug traffickers have penetrated sectors of the armed forces and the police" and that "that fact constitutes one of the main causes of the recent crime wave" ("Presidente Leonel Fernández" 2005).

3. These diagnoses were commissioned by the consulting firm Newlink Political, which has assisted the Dominican authorities in the design and implementation of the Plan for Democratic Security.

4. According to Leo Morales, an agent of the Bureau of Immigration and Customs Enforcement (BICE), "Both huge and modest shipments of drugs are trafficked through here; undocumented aliens; weapons; counterfeit money or proceeds from illegal transactions en route to being laundered; Colombian emeralds and other jewels and precious stones; exotic birds and endangered species; pornogra-

phy; coffee; Cuban cigars; automobiles and other illicit, stolen merchandise" (*Diario Libre*, 23 June 2003).

5. In this regard president René Préval of Haiti has expressed his concern about how the penetration of the illicit drug business is putting at a real risk the already precarious governance of his country. On the other hand, a growing controversy about U.S. interdiction and certification policies is taking place among several high-level officials and heads of government in the Caribbean.

6. According to the National Directorate of Narcotics Control (DNCD), in 1988 a total of 437 people were arrested for drug dealing and consumption. By 1993 the number had grown to 3,370, and by 2003 to 4,372. Between 2004 and 2005, 3,950 illegal drug arrests were made and 1,475 suspects were prosecuted in court.

7. One of the most publicized cases has been the as yet unresolved assassination of Senator Darío Gómez while he was working on a bill on illegal trafficking in late 2001. More recently, Captain Quirino E. Paulino Castillo was arrested and extradited to the United States after a 1,387 kg shipment of cocaine was found in his possession.

8. Between 2006 and 2007, the director of the DNCD, a military official, expelled 5,000 of his force (also members of the military), most for their involvement in contraband, robbery, kidnapping, drug dealing, human trafficking, and forgery. See *Hoy Digital* 2008.

9. The term refers to the concomitance of international and domestic phenomena.

10. As data collected in PAHO 2003 shows, Latin America and the Caribbean possess the second-highest murder rates in the world, after sub-Saharan Africa. Most of these violent deaths are connected to clashes of interests and fighting in the drug trade. Anthony Harriott defines the criminogenic nature in the following terms: "Crime is becoming less a direct response to the crisis of the formal economy and the processes of social disorganization associated with it, than the direct outcome of the dynamics of doing business in a large and growing underground economy that is becoming more clearly articulated and progressively integrated with the national economy. It is more associated with a process of social reorganization than with social disorganization" (Harriott 2000:24).

11. In my research, community leaders stated that a great part of their ability to influence events in the barrios—which was based on the respect they commanded because of their long residence there and on personal ties to residents, including criminals and their families—has been lost due to the breakup of bonds of solidarity in the neighborhood and the appearance of new criminal elements from outside the immediate community. At the same time, residents of the barrios often see the police in the double role of protector and perpetrator whose aggressive actions and extortions generate mistrust and inhibit good relations with the community.

12. Many believe that organized crime and narcotics trafficking contribute to, or reflect, state weakness. The phrase "illicit drug trade" has also been employed by Harriott in several of his works. In evaluating the case of Jamaica, Harriott de-

scribes it as a well-integrated underground economy: crime incrementally becomes inserted in institutional relations and occupational roles; perverse criminality disrespects the law across all social classes; crime acquires resources that easily translate into social power; and crime is inserted in the judicial system and structures of authority (Harriott 2000:24–25). For a more detailed study of crime in the Caribbean, see CARICOM Regional Task Force 2002. Data refers mostly to the English-speaking Caribbean, however.

13. The same occurs with the pattern of social violence in which some social movements engage. As the recent cases of Mexico, Bolivia, and Venezuela show, popular unrest that is consolidating in suburban areas has driven a social movement that confronts local and national power on their inability to respond to social demands and to handle conflicts with their constituencies in nonauthoritarian ways.

14. In nearly every country in the region, this has resulted in the responses being militarized: the war on drugs, propelled by the United States since the 1980s; the war on *maras* and gangs, promoted by the Southern Command in 2005; the desperate actions of the people, including lynchings and defending the iron-fist approach, as in the case of Movement against Delinquency in Mexico.

15. With the ascent to power of the PLD, the economic reforms in the Dominican Republic were invigorated. At that moment, the administration prioritized the promotion of a more favorable insertion of the country in the international arena, as well as the correction of macroeconomic imbalances through new programs and initiatives. As indicated by the Economic Commission of Latin American Countries (ECLAC), the tourist sector increased its service capacity from five thousand rooms in the 1980s to forty-five thousand rooms in 1998. During a ten-year period, exports from the Dominican free zones skyrocketed from less than US$1 million in 1970 to US$117 million in 1980. They continued growing to US$859 million in 1990 and to US$4,300 million in 1999 (www.eclac.org). The free zones experienced a fast growth going from two to three hundred enterprises between 1970 and 1990, generating an increase of people employed from 126 to more than 130,000. According to ECLAC, by the end of the 1990s there were five hundred enterprises that employed 190,000 workers. All that stimulated the construction sector, projecting an increase of 8 percent between 1970 and 1990, and in telecommunication and transport sectors an increase on the order of 5.5 percent.

16. The Gini coefficient measures the concentration of income. The parameters oscillate between zero and one, zero being the stage of perfect equality at which all individuals have equal income, while one reflects perfect inequality (www.eclac.cl).

17. UNDP has established a classification of countries according to the HDI: On the one hand there are countries with a high human development index equal to or larger than 0.80; on the other hand, there are those with a medium HDI between 0.5 and 0.8. Finally there are those with a low HDI under 0.5. The 2006 report places sixty-three countries in the first group, eighty-three in the second, and thirty-one in the third group (www.undp.org).

18. According to the National Census on Population and Housing of 2002, the proportion of homes with high poverty rates in the National District is over 33 percent and unemployment is around 11.45 percent, concentrated specifically in the eighteen to twenty-nine age group.

19. Koonings and Kruijt 2007 also refers to this phenomenon.

20. In his study, Mauricio Rubio found Dominican gangs most frequently to engage in the following activities: consuming drugs and alcohol in public places (76 percent), fights among gangs (69 percent), petty theft (59 percent), armed robbery (50 percent), and assault (42 percent). According to Rubio, the frequency of these activities and gangsterism were reported to be greater in lower-class neighborhoods than in middle- and upper-class neighborhoods (Rubio 2006:34–35).

21. This was a study carried out by the Justice and Transparency Foundation in twenty-two of the country's provinces, on a sample of fourteen hundred people (Fundación Justicia y Transparencia and Estudios Sociales y de Mercado 2004).

22. Rubio's study again establishes a close connection between young people's dissociation from the school system and their joining gangs, as well as the possible effect that the quality of their neighborhood's infrastructure has on their sense of safety. Of the youths participating in this study, 18 percent hailed from neighborhoods in which they said that "the conditions of street maintenance, public spaces, and nighttime illumination of terrible quality" made them feel unsafe.

23. Stated by General Juan Tomás Taveras Rodríguez of the National Police (Molina 2004).

24. Despite that, there has been an effort from the Secretariat of the Interior and the Police to curb the tendency of escalating demand from private users.

25. Others look at this intersection from a normative perspective; see Felson 2000; and Miles-Doan 1998.

26. Statistics on the Procuraduría General de la República, Ministerio Público Web site. *Informe sobre muertes violentas, homicidios e intercambios de disparos*, www.pro curaduria.gov.do, accessed 25 June 2009.

27. In a survey taken in the barrios, only 21 percent of those interviewed declared not to be afraid to circulate in any part of the neighborhood. People mentioned public places that they considered too dangerous to visit, among them parks, markets, and particular streets. They also mentioned that everybody stayed indoors after dusk and during the night because those were the main hours of shootings among gangs, robberies, and violence. See Newlink Political 2005a.

28. According to the National Office for Drug Control, by September of 2005, 12,458.2 grams of cocaine were seized in low-income neighborhoods. On the other hand, 777,930.3 grams of cocaine were seized in middle-class and wealthy residential neighborhoods. In popular neighborhoods marijuana is the most-consumed drug, while the consumption of cocaine and ecstasy predominates in upper-class neighborhoods (qtd. in Campos 2008).

29. Between January and July 2005, 2,977 people suffered wounds caused by bullets

(cited in Brea de Cabral and Cabral Ramirez 2006). A related phenomenon, stray bullets, has introduced a new risk factor in the complex setting of urban violence. Between January and November of 2005, stray bullets wounded 25 people, most of them (21) children (Sánchez 2005).

30. *Tiguere* is a popular Dominican expression that refers to a person who is fearless and who can overcome any difficult situation.

31. Fabio Abreu determined that 60 percent of the young people he interviewed who belonged to *naciones* were under twenty-one (Abreu 2003:350).

32. In the words of a young former nation member, "A gang is a group of fifteen to twenty members that don't have control; they all do whatever they want, they are all superior, they're all the boss, they're all bullies, which means they have no direction" (Mateo, Focus Group, Capotillo, 2005).

33. The same structure exists in Brazil. See Zaverucha 1994.

34. Thirty-two percent of those that used their guns frequently admitted that they used them more than twelve times and 45 percent that they used them between one and three times in the previous year (Newlink Political 2006c).

35. In the first years of the new millennium, approximately 70 percent of all prisoners in Dominican jails and penitentiaries were classified as "preventive," meaning they had not been convicted of a crime in a court of law. (Ayuntamiento del Distrito Nacional/UNDP 2005:46). With the new penal code, the quantity of "preventive" detentions decreased to 49 percent by 2005 (Fundacion Institucionalidad y Justicia et al. 2006:18).

36. A recent survey of the National Police conducted by Newlink revealed that 97 percent of personnel across ranks agreed that the PSD had improved relations between the police and the community (Newlink Political 2006c).

37. Throughout 2007, the Secretariat of the Interior and the Police has focused on strengthening mechanisms of inner control and on recruiting new personnel.

Toward Uncivil Society
Causes and Consequences
of Violence in Rio de Janeiro

ROBERT GAY

Much has already been written—and said—about the failure of Latin American democracies to deliver (e.g., see O'Donnell 1996:34–35). Throughout the region military dictatorships that ruled by intimidation and fear have been replaced by democratically elected civilian regimes. In most cases, however, democracy exists as a shell institution, recognizable by its external form but devoid of any real meaning or significance. One of the main reasons for this is the widespread and dramatic increase in violence. Indeed, it could be argued that violence, and more to the point, the fear of violence, is *the* defining feature of contemporary Latin American democracy.

Brazil is no exception to this rule. On the face of it, Brazil is a strong and consolidated democracy. Since the Brazilian military relinquished power in the mid-1980s, the country has enjoyed a period of competitive, inclusive, and uninterrupted elections. Furthermore, Brazil is one of a handful of countries in the world in which voting is compulsory, and it is a source of much admired and imitated democratic social practices such as participatory budgeting, to name but one example. Yet Brazilian democracy is also becoming increasingly violent. Between 1980 and 2003 the number of homicides increased from 13,910 to 50,980 and the homicide rate almost tripled from 11.4 to 29.1 per one thousand people (*O Globo* 10 November 2004; 1 June 2005).[1] In addition, Brazil now ranks second in the world—behind Venezuela—in terms of death rates by firearms and the Instituto Brasileiro de Geografia e Estatística (IBGE) estimates that violence has reduced life expectancy in the country by two or three years despite spectacular gains in other areas of public health such as infant mortality (*O Globo* 1 December 2004).

The increase in violence in Brazil has transformed the way people go about their lives. It has forced them to avoid city streets, public parks, and other such deliberative spaces. It has prompted those with resources to sell up and relocate to increasingly distant and fortified neighborhoods. And it has severely compromised, if not undermined, the foundations of a civil society that was beginning to emerge toward the end of military rule. Finally, and perhaps most significantly, the increase in violence in Brazil has created a climate of intolerance and indifference. Instead of protesting the violation of the human rights of others, individuals, groups, and communities increasingly demand ever more heavy-handed, extreme measures by the state.

There is little doubt that the increase in violence in Brazil is linked to broader changes associated with neoliberalism and, in particular, the failure of neoliberal policies to generate economic growth (e.g., see Portes and Hoffman 2003). The situation has spawned violence not only on behalf of disenchanted and unruly segments of the proletariat but also on behalf of the state that has brought to bear the full weight of the national security apparatus that was established by the military regime; a condition that some have characterized as "neoliberal penality" (Wacquant 2003; Godoy 2005:161–62). The relationship between economic conditions and violence is by no means simple nor direct, however.[2] And in fact, compared to many other countries in Latin America, neoliberal reforms were introduced relatively late in Brazil, in the mid-1990s, and did not result in the large-scale dismantling of social protection programs that occurred elsewhere. If anything, such programs have indeed been enhanced and expanded over the past decade as a response to low levels of economic growth, and they have resulted in considerable progress in terms of reducing levels of inequality and poverty. So then the question becomes, what else is it about the past twenty years that explains such a sudden and dramatic increase in violence? I will argue that, in the case of Rio de Janeiro, it is the increase in global drug trafficking, and that it is only when drug trafficking is taken into account that the relationship between economic conditions and violence, and the abject failure of so many recent attempts at reform, can be understood.

Since the mid-1990s many attempts have been made to reduce the level of violence in Rio de Janeiro by attempting to shut down the drug trade, by going after drug gangs and prison-based criminal organizations, and by cracking down on police violence and corruption. As I discuss below, these attempts at reform have proven largely ineffective because they have been resisted by criminal elements and, far more important, by a police force that has resolutely defended its right to extort and kill with impunity. As a consequence, public authorities in Rio are generally perceived as both complicit with crime and ineffective at providing public security. This means that members of the public look increasingly to nonstate actors for conflict resolution and protection. Unfortunately, the more the public looks to other, largely unregulated, agents the worse the situation becomes, both in terms of the level of and the possibilities for violence and in terms of further undermining public authority, civil rights, the rule of law, and, ultimately, the institution of democracy.

Finally, while this essay focuses primarily on the causes and consequences of violence in Rio de Janeiro, it would be a mistake to assume that the discussion has no relevance for developments elsewhere in Brazil, or in Latin America as a whole, for that matter. While the particular configuration of conditions in Rio de Janeiro may well be unique to that city, the combination of poverty, inequality, drug trafficking, organized crime, institutional violence, and corruption is increasingly widespread, as evidenced by the widespread assault on public authorities in May 2006 by the Primeiro Comando da Capital in the neighboring state of São Paulo, and by the ongoing war between drug cartels and the police in Mexico.

Poverty, Inequality, and Informality

Brazil is *the* poster child for growth without equity. Over the course of the past four decades or so, Brazil has developed from a country dependent on a few primary product commodities to one of the world's largest and most sophisticated industrial economies. Despite consistently high rates of growth throughout the so-called miracle years of the late 1960s and early 1970s, however, the economy failed to absorb an expanding labor force created by agricultural decline and restructuring, massive internal migration from the impoverished northeast to the cities of the south, and high fertility rates.[3] The outcome was a country of extreme wealth and poverty, a situation exacerbated by the almost constant recessions and financial crises of the 1980s and early 1990s.[4]

Brazil competes with a handful of much poorer nations for the dubious distinction of being the most unequal place on earth. In terms of per capita income, Brazil is in the same league as countries such as Costa Rica, Malaysia, Bulgaria, and Chile. In terms of poverty rates, however, Brazil is much more like Panama, Botswana, Mauritania, and Guinea. In 2002 the Instituto de

Pesquisa Econômico Aplicada (IPEA) estimated that 53.9 million Brazilians, or fully 31.7 percent of the population, could be considered "poor," in that their household income totaled less than half a minimum salary per month.[5] The institute also calculated that in the same year 21.9 million Brazilians, or 12.9 percent of the population, could be considered "indigent," in that their household income totaled less than a quarter of a minimum salary per month, meaning that they could not afford a minimum diet of two thousand calories per day (*O Globo* 1 June 2005).

Considerable progress has been made in recent years in terms of moving the incomes of Brazil's poorest families toward the poverty line and reducing levels of inequality.[6] The most important program in this regard is Bolsa Família, which pays poor families a stipend of up to 95 reais per month to keep their children in school and ensure that they receive regular medical checkups. Bolsa Família was providing cash assistance to an estimated 11 million families in Brazil by November 2006 and has been widely praised, and imitated, as an effective and efficient antipoverty and antihunger program.[7] For all its advantages and successes, however, it should be kept in mind that the Bolsa Família program distributes extremely small amounts of money and that, as a cash assistance program, it fails to address the root cause of hunger, poverty, and inequality in Brazil, which is the absence of formal-sector jobs with decent pay.

It is often argued that social rights in Brazil—such as the minimum wage, the extra month's salary (known as the thirteenth), paid holidays, sick leave, unemployment benefits, and maternity leave—were established well in advance of political and civil rights.[8] Social rights in Brazil have always been restricted, however, to formal-sector workers, initially in urban areas and then, later on, in the countryside. The problem today is that 60 percent of the workforce in contemporary Brazil is employed informally.[9] This means that informal-sector workers in Brazil not only generally receive low wages but also that they lack the legal protections, guarantees, and potential benefits associated with a signed work card, or *carteira assinada*.[10] More important, it also means that they have been largely unaffected by recent increases in social spending, which have been absorbed by programs such as pensions and social security that benefit primarily workers in the formal sector (*O Globo* 3 May 2005).

In terms of Brazil in general, Rio de Janeiro remains one of the wealthiest and most developed states. The recessions and financial crises of the 1980s and 1990s hit Rio particularly hard, however, and accelerated what has been a long process of decline from its former position as the country's commercial and political capital.[11] In fact, over the course of the past twenty years or so, Rio de

Janeiro's economic performance has been worse than that of any other state in Brazil, despite the lucrative presence of the oil industry, and has resulted in a sharp decline in the state's contribution to the national economy and in real wages.[12] The situation has also been exacerbated by the fact that the state of Rio de Janeiro invests less than half the average for Brazil in public services and infrastructure, and less than any other state except Maranhão, the state with the lowest Human Development Index (HDI) in the federation (*O Globo* 6 August 2006).

The deteriorating economy and continued migration from other parts of the country have also meant an increase in the state's housing deficit and the further growth of Rio's favelas. Between 1991 and 2000 the population of the city of Rio's favelas increased by an estimated 24 percent, from 882,483 to 1,092,783.[13] This figure represents 18.6 percent of the city's total population, a percentage that is much higher than that for any other municipality in Brazil.[14] Coincidentally, the past decade or so has seen more money invested in favela improvement programs than at any time in the past, including massive financial assistance from international institutions such as the Inter-American Development Bank. While these programs have undoubtedly improved general conditions in the favelas, they have failed in their stated aim to integrate such neighborhoods into mainstream city life and to stem the steady stream of disaffected and marginalized youth that continue to be recruited by the drug trade and organized crime.

Drug Trafficking and Organized Crime

Brazil is not (yet) a major producer of illegal drugs, although marijuana is grown extensively in the interior of the northeast and the country has become an important exporter of precursor chemicals such as acetone and ether for illegal drug manufacture.[15] Yet over the past three decades Brazil has become an important transshipment point for cocaine, which is cultivated and processed in the neighboring countries of Bolivia, Peru, and Colombia and exported to North America and, increasingly, to expanding drug markets in southern Europe and the states of the former Soviet Union.[16] More significantly, a high percentage of the cocaine that finds its way into Brazil is sold locally (NEPAD and CLAVES 2000). In fact, it is now estimated that Brazil is the second largest consumer of cocaine in the world, behind the United States.[17]

In Rio, the distribution and selling points for cocaine—and, for that matter, for marijuana—have until recently been located in the city's favelas. Since the early to mid-1980s the favelas have been dominated and controlled not by public authorities but by heavily armed drug gangs. These drug gangs purchase cocaine from intermediaries that bring it in from neighboring countries and states.[18] The gangs then cut, mix, package, and resell the cocaine to wealthy clients in surrounding neighborhoods and, increasingly, to users and addicts in their own communities. The drug gangs in Rio are, in turn, loosely organized into networks or factions that compete militarily for territorial control of the trade in Rio. It is this competition for market share and for the millions of dollars in drug-related spoils that, more than anything, have transformed not just a select few neighborhoods but an entire city into a war zone.[19]

Drug gangs and drug-gang factions in Rio's favelas can be traced to criminal organizations that emerged from inside the walls of the state's penitentiaries. Between 1969 and 1975 the military government decided to place political prisoners engaged in armed struggle together with common criminals in a prison on the island of Ilha Grande, to the south and west of the city of Rio.[20] The political prisoners impressed on a small group of fellow, common criminal detainees the importance of organization, loyalty, and discipline and instructed them in the art of urban guerilla warfare. The product of this unlikely encounter was the Comando Vermelho.[21]

Initially, the Comando Vermelho sought to impose its control over Ilha Grande and other prisons in the system. It took out members of rival factions, introduced strict codes of prisoner conduct, and negotiated for improved conditions with suddenly besieged prison officials. Eventually, however, the reach of the Comando Vermelho extended beyond the prison system's walls to well-organized and clandestine cells that conducted bank robberies and, later on, kidnappings to finance the purchase of weapons and the oftentimes spectacular escapes of their incarcerated colleagues.[22] Then, around 1982, the decision was made to finance the Comando Vermelho's activities by means of what was becoming an increasingly widespread and lucrative drug trade (Amorim 1993:142).

The Comando Vermelho's decision to move in on the drug trade led to a period of intense and bloody civil war for control of Rio's favelas. By the end of the 1980s the Comando Vermelho profited from the sale of marijuana and cocaine from an estimated 70 percent of all the selling points, or *bocas de fumo*, in the city. Many of the leaders and rank-and-file members of the Comando Vermelho were originally from the favelas, so the connection between these areas and drug trafficking naturally followed. Furthermore, the haphazard and impenetrable nature of most favela neighborhoods provided the perfect terrain for drug-gang operations. Favela leaders who resisted the Comando Vermelho were forced out, kidnapped, or killed.[23] Alternatively, they turned for help and protection to one or the other of the Comando Vermelho's rival factions, the Terceiro Comando or the Amigos dos Amigos.

The ability of the Comando Vermelho, and of its rival factions, to operate the drug trade depended fundamentally on the relationship between each drug gang and the community in which it was embedded. Drug gangs rely on the local population as a source of new recruits for various roles and positions and, more generally, to provide cover for their activities and protect them from the police. It therefore became increasingly common for drug gangs to provide social services such as free transportation and medical treatment and to finance public works such as day-care centers and recreational facilities.[24] It also became increasingly common for drug gangs to take advantage of the absence and widespread mistrust of public authorities to punish those who disobeyed orders or who caused trouble. Thus while the emergence of heavily armed gangs in Rio's favelas was met with a degree of fear and trepidation, it also meant that, for perhaps the first time, residents of such areas had a means to resolve disputes and guarantee a measure of personal security.[25]

A second consequence of this transformation was a further decline in public authority in the favelas and, more significantly, in the prestige and capacity of neighborhood associations. In the waning years of the dictatorship favela neighborhood associations, in conjunction with progressive elements of the Catholic Church, had played a critical role in organizing and mobilizing low-income communities in Rio to break free of the grip of clientelist politicians and associated political machines, and in bringing pressure to bear on newly elected state and municipal administrations to provide resources for public works programs. When drug gangs first emerged in the early 1980s, they coexisted fairly peacefully with neighborhood associations, which continued to play a central and independent role in the orchestration of favela life. By the end of the decade, however, the vast majority of neighborhood associations and other social and political actors in the favelas were either directly controlled by or under the influence of drug gangs and drug-gang factions, which commanded armies of an estimated one hundred thousand men.

Effectively this meant that the democratic window of opportunity that had been opened by the military's withdrawal in the mid-1980s was now closed. This did not mean that politics and electoral procedures failed to operate in such areas; far from it. What it meant, however, was that democracy began to serve a very different set of interests that had nothing to do with transparency, accountability, or freedom of choice (see Arias 2006a; Aleixo de Souza 2002).

Police Violence

The emergence of rival drug gangs and drug-gang factions in Rio constitutes by far the most significant factor in the recent increase in violence, not only because drug-gang factions exist in an almost constant state of war but also because of the violent nature of the response that their presence and operations have elicited from the police. The police in Brazil are organized and operate at the state level. There is a small federal force that monitors interstate and international drug trafficking along Brazil's porous and remote nine-thousand–mile border. Yet the majority of the five hundred thousand or so police officers serve in the civil and military police forces that answer to each state governor. The civil and military police in Brazil are split along functional lines. The military police essentially constitute reserve units of the army that patrol the streets, maintain the peace, and respond to and investigate crimes in progress. The civil police, on the other hand, investigate crimes that have already been committed and oversee the operation of the various police precincts or *delegacias*.

Under military rule the police in Brazil acted with impunity when hunting down, torturing and, in some cases, executing political dissidents. In postauthoritarian Brazil the police operate in much the same way, but with a different and much larger population in mind.[26] In the past few years the police in Rio de Janeiro have been killing on average one thousand civilians each year. Most police victims have no criminal record or involvement whatsoever with crime. They are simply the wrong kind of people—in other words, poor, young, male, uneducated, and dark-skinned—caught at the wrong place at the wrong time. Occasionally, as in the case of the Candelària Cathedral and the Vigàrio Geral massacres, both in Rio in 1993, international outrage over police brutality forces state authorities to intervene. The effect of such intervention is always temporary, however, and before long the number of civilian deaths at the hands of the police begins to rise again.

A number of factors make the prevention of police homicides difficult. For one, the initial investigation of the crime scene lies in the hands of the police. In other words, the first people to arrive on the scene are often the perpetrators themselves. Second, the police always claim to be acting in self-defense, or in defense of others, and that extrajudicial killings are, in fact, the outcome of shootouts with dangerous and well-armed criminals.[27] The third factor has to do with the widespread use of unregistered and unauthorized guns. It is common practice for police in Brazil to plant guns on their already deceased victims to corroborate claims of a shootout. Finally, bodies are often removed to local hospitals to create the impression that the police tried to assist their victims and to compromise investigations of the crime scene.

There are also institutional factors that make the investigation and prevention of police homicides difficult. Until recently the military police in Brazil were encouraged by their superiors to eliminate, rather than detain, criminal suspects. In the mid- to late 1990s the military police in Rio de Janeiro were given pay raises and promotions for acts of "special merit" and "bravery," which, in essence, meant killing urban youth (HRW 1997:13). Also until recently military police tribunals were responsible for investigating crimes committed by the military police and could be counted on to determine that civilians were killed in acts of self-defense (see Zaverucha 1999).

In 1996 the situation appeared to change somewhat with the implementation of Brazil's first National Human Rights Plan, which transferred the oversight and jurisdiction of police homicides to civilian authorities. Even so it remains up to the police to determine what does and what does not constitute a homicide, and the military police retain the right to oversee such cases. Furthermore, civilian witnesses of police brutality are routinely threatened and discouraged from testifying, and few prosecutors have the time, resources, or political will to conduct their own investigations.[28] For many the execution of criminal suspects by the police is simply not a priority. And because the judicial system in Brazil is so overburdened and inefficient, changes in the oversight and processing of police crimes have had little, if any, effect.[29]

Finally, and perhaps most significant, there is also widespread support for extrajudicial police action among the general population (see Pandolfi 1999). Death squads comprising off-duty and retired police officers are often hired by local merchants to clear the streets of "undesirables" and are responsible for killing a large number of Brazilian youths each year (see HRW 1994; and Huggins 1998). There is even support for extrajudicial police action among those elements of the population most likely to be affected. It is not uncommon, for example, to hear relatives of innocent victims of police violence call for even more heavy-handed and extreme measures. This should in no way be seen as an endorsement of the police; far from it. Few Brazilians trust or make use of the police, a force perceived, quite rightly, as untrustworthy and violent (e.g., see Mesquita Neto 1999). It is, however, an indication of how far the situation has deteriorated and of the insecurity and fear of violence experienced by the residents of Brazil's major cities.[30]

The problem is that in recent years, violence—in particular, drug-related violence—has spilled beyond the low-income neighborhoods, the public housing projects, and the favelas into all areas of city life. There is now no safe haven in Rio. Government offices, supermarkets, and hotels have been targeted with gunfire, bombs, and grenades. Drug gangs have ordered banks, businesses, and schools to close their doors in protest of state policy or, more commonly, in honor of fallen comrades.[31] Buses are routinely held up at gunpoint and burnt to the ground.[32] Cars and trucks on Rio's major roads and highways are pulled over and shaken down by armed men who are often dressed as police. There have even been instances of heavily armed gangs invading public hospitals, police stations, and prisons to "liberate" their colleagues. It is within this context of generalized violence and fear and of the breakdown of public law and order that calls for the extension of human rights to police victims have fallen on deaf ears (see also Caldeira and Holston 1999).

Part of the problem has to do with the widespread availability of guns. There are an estimated 17.3 million firearms in Brazil. The authorities, including the armed forces, possess 1.7 million. The remaining 15.6 million are in the hands of civilians. Fewer than half of these guns are registered (and therefore legal) and an estimated 4 million are wielded by criminals (*O Globo* 18 March 2005). The vast majority of these guns are manufactured in Brazil and bought, or stolen, from private citizens, the military, or the police.[33] Others are sold legally to dealers in other countries and then smuggled back in. In July 2001 the state government in Rio destroyed more than one hundred thousand guns in a public appeal for peace. Unfortunately, the destruction of large quantities of guns has not made much of a difference. The drug gangs in Rio continue to be well armed and financed, in many cases even better armed and financed than the police.[34]

Part of the problem also has to do with the police. First, the police in Brazil are very poorly trained and ill equipped. Few police receive instruction in the basics of criminal investigation and, as a consequence, the few cases that are solved are solved because the perpetrator is caught in the act, a witness agrees to testify, or a confession is literally beaten out of a suspect.[35] Second, few police receive instruction in the use of firearms. It is small wonder, therefore, that so many people—including the police—are caught in the line of fire.[36] Third, the police are also extremely badly paid. Many of the seventy-five thousand or so military and civil police in Rio supplement their incomes by working second shifts, more often than not as private security guards.[37] Thus while a career in the police provides certain elements of the population with opportunities for advancement, it generally makes for an unattractive and hazardous proposition.[38] Finally, the police are subject to widespread mistrust and hatred. Police who live in drug gang–dominated neighborhoods, for example, are often forced to disguise what they do for a living; otherwise they are likely to be expelled or executed (e.g., see *Jornal do Brasil* 23 March 2003). Drug gangs have also been known to place bounties of as much as 15,000 reais on a police officer's head, and in recent years the police have been attacked and executed for their guns and ammunition while sitting in their patrol cars (e.g., see *O Globo* 16 October 2004; *Jornal do Brasil* 20 January 2005).

Institutional Corruption

A lot of police violence in Rio is fueled by corruption. The newspapers are full of reports of police involvement in all sorts of illegal activities, but particularly in the drug trade.[39] When the police go into a favela, for example, they more often than not seek a share of the spoils than individual members of a drug gang. And when they do manage to apprehend someone, they often have no intention of making a formal arrest; they are simply out to make money by holding a particular drug-gang member hostage. In fact, there have even been reports in the local press that military police recruits are *trained* in the art of extortion, or what's known locally as *mineiração* (*Jornal do Brasil* 13 March 2002).

When the drug trade is going well, there is enough money to go around. In fact, drug gangs often budget for the amount of money they need, each week, to pay off the police. The system breaks down, however, when things are not going well and the police go after what they perceive as their fair share.[40] It is also very common for drug gangs to pay the police to provide them with information and protection. As a consequence, police operations that target particular drug gangs or drug-gang leaders often come up empty because the individual or individuals involved have been warned well in advance. One of the most notorious instances of this occurred following the brutal murder of the *O Globo* reporter Tim Lopes in June 2002. Lopes was kidnapped, tortured, and killed because of an article he published on open-air drug fairs and research he was conducting on public sex acts in the favelas involving teenagers. It took months for the police to capture Lopes's killer, Elias Maluco, although they had a good idea of his whereabouts. The authorities attributed the delay to the fact that there was evidence that Maluco was paying the police (*Folha de São Paulo* 26 August 2002).

Occasionally, as in the case of police violence, steps are taken to reform and clean up the police force. In recent years the establishment of an anonymous hotline and the appointment of an independent police ombudsman have meant that police operations are subject to much closer public scrutiny (*Jornal do Brasil* 25 September 2004). The phone line, Disque-Denuncia, which was originally created to combat kidnappings, receives on average ten thousand calls per month, of which 30–35 percent have to do with information about drug trafficking. The phone line is supposed to be secure and anonymous. Many people refuse to use it, however, for fear of being overheard or turned in to the police or to drug traffickers.[41] Furthermore, very few of the thousands of complaints that have been lodged against the police have resulted in punishment, dismissal, or prosecution. And the overwhelming majority of those who have been punished have not been officers but low-level recruits (*Jornal do Brasil* 26 November 2002). Even more disturbing, perhaps, is the fact that specially trained antinarcotics units that are occasionally sent in to occupy violence-plagued areas of the city are themselves not immune to corruption. In fact, drug-gang members claim that they prefer a permanent police presence to a series of rotating shifts precisely because the former are more easily approached and compromised.[42]

Corruption also plagues the state prison system and has, until recently, undermined any attempt to break the power of prison-based criminal organizations. In 1988 a new maximum-security facility was opened in the neighborhood of Bangu in Rio's Zona Oeste to house and isolate the leaders of the Comando Vermelho, of Terceiro Comando, and, more recently, of the Amigos dos Amigos. All three organizations continue to function and thrive, however, as orders for drug and weapons transactions, the invasion of enemy territory, the torture and execution of debtors and informants, and threats and attempts to extort money from innocent civilians continue to be made from the inside.[43]

Orders from the inside are delivered in a number of different ways. Sometimes they are passed along by friends and family, sometimes by inmates' lawyers.[44] Most of the time, however, they are made directly by cell phone.[45] Until now the prison authorities have been unable to cut off either the supply of cell phones or cell phone transmissions, despite the enormous amount of money invested in cell phone–blocking technology.[46] Many of the cell phones, weapons, explosives, drugs, and other materials are smuggled in by visitors.[47]

The majority, however, are sold to inmates by prison workers and guards. Prison workers and guards have also been known to accept money to facilitate escapes and even the murder of prisoners from rival gang factions.[48] It is indeed often difficult, and dangerous, for prison guards and workers to do otherwise (e.g., see *Jornal do Brasil* 20 March 2003). In September 2000, for example, the director of the Bangu prison complex in Rio was executed on her doorstep by what were rumored to be either drug-gang faction members or the police. The director had been attempting to clamp down on the use of cell phones in Bangu and on a system of bribes and kickbacks that totaled an estimated 1 million reais per month.[49]

Recent Attempts at Reform (and Their Consequences)

On 11 September 2002 a *traficante* by the name of Fernandinho Beira-Mar led a rebellion of inmates associated with the Comando Vermelho in one of the prisons in the massive Bangu complex. With the obvious assistance of someone on the inside, Beira-Mar and his associates overcame two guards, passed through three steel doors, crossed a corridor, opened three other doors, and executed four drug-gang members from a rival faction. Beira-Mar's men had guns and keys to all the doors in the prison, even though a thorough search had been conducted only twenty-four hours earlier. Apparently a prison guard had been paid 400,000 reais to smuggle in the guns and make copies of the keys.

Incidents such as these prompted the state government in Rio to make a renewed and concerted effort to break the power of prison-based criminal organizations by placing their leaders in strict isolation, cutting back on visitation rights and other privileges, and redoubling their efforts to prevent messages from getting in and orders from reaching the outside.[50] While these measures mostly failed to rid the system of warring gangs and factions, they did make it more difficult for inmates to manage the drug trade.[51] As a consequence, the measures met with fierce resistance in the form of widespread prison riots, waves of coordinated attacks on public buses, government buildings, and the police, and the assassination of prison officials and employees.[52] More significant, the crackdown on prison-based criminal organizations broke long-standing and effective chains of command between gang leaders on the inside and their lieutenants and foot soldiers on the outside and sparked a new round of territorial disputes for control of Rio's favelas. It also led to the emergence of a new generation of drug-gang members who are younger, less disciplined, less accountable, and far more violent and cruel, both in their dealings with the police and with members of the communities in which they happen to be stationed.[53]

The most obvious manifestation of this new reality was the invasion of the favela of Rocinha, the largest in Rio, by a heavily armed convoy of sixty men on 9 April 2004. The attack marked an attempt by the Comando Vermelho to regain control of the favela on behalf of its former head, or *dono*. The *dono* had been serving time for nine years for homicide and drug trafficking. On 12 January, however, a judge granted him permission to spend his daytime hours with family. So, five days later, on the first day he was eligible, he walked out of the prison and never returned. According to tradition, *donos* who are released or escape from prison are entitled to reassume control of their communities. In this particular case, however, the *dono* who had taken his place in Rocinha refused to comply. Everyone knew that an attack was imminent.[54] The authorities were powerless to do anything about it, however, demonstrating, once again, that they had effectively lost control of large parts of the city.[55]

The attack on Rocinha, launched in broad daylight, and the general state of open warfare between rival gangs in Rio prompted the local authorities to react by calling in the military and special-operation police units, redoubling their efforts to hunt down local gang members and attempting to suffocate and shut down the drug trade by surrounding and occasionally occupying particularly strategic or problematic favelas. In 2003, for example, the Brazilian military deployed three thousand troops in twenty-five different locations in Rio to keep the city "safe" for tourists during carnival, a practice continued using local police forces ever since.[56] In February 2006 the first contingent of a newly constituted Força Nacional touched down in Rio. The Força Nacional is a ten thousand–strong police force made up of military police and firefighters with perfect disciplinary records from states across the country that has been deployed in Rio to provide protection for events such as the Pan American Games (*Jornal do Brasil* 10 August 2004).

The policy of attempting to suffocate the drug trade has been supported at the federal level by efforts to expand and strengthen police presence at the country's borders and international airports and by discouraging the trans-shipment of drugs via Brazilian airspace. On 16 July 2004, President Luiz Inácio Lula da Silva signed Decree 5144, which grants the Brazilian air force permission to shoot down unregistered planes from outside the country that refuse to respond to orders to land. The Brazilian government estimates that this change in policy alone has resulted in a 60 percent decline in unauthorized flights over the country between 2003 and 2004, although there is a strong suspicion that drug traffickers are finding other ways to make their way into the country. There is evidence, for example, that Colombian cocaine is now being transported by FARC (Revolutionary Armed Forces of Colombia) intermediaries through Bolivia to Paraguay, where it is delivered into the hands of Brazilian traffickers in exchange for dollars and munitions (*O Globo* 10 April 2005).[57]

There is little doubt that measures to restrict the movement of drugs have squeezed favela-based gangs in Rio. That does not mean, however, that their power has been undermined or diminished. Indeed, evidence suggests that in the absence of money to be made from drugs, gangs are moving to control and profit from other activities and enterprises. It is estimated, for example, that in 20 percent of Rio's favelas gangs charge a markup of up to 8 reais for a tank of cooking gas, bringing in as much as 20,000 reais per month, and that they siphon off a portion of neighborhood association dues and charges for the provision of water (*O Globo* 20 February 2005). In many favelas gangs also charge residents to park on the street and impose a surcharge on van and motor taxi services that ferry residents around internally. In some favelas gangs have even been known to impose curfews and to fine residents for coming home late (*Jornal do Brasil* 3 September 2004). Finally, it is very likely that the crackdown on drug sales explains the rapid increase in other crimes such as assaults on buses and pedestrians and false police blitzes on roads and highways.[58]

It should also be kept in mind that the effectiveness of all these state policies toward the drug trade continues to be compromised by corruption. In May 2003 the former governor and presidential hopeful Antonio Garotinho assumed the position of state secretary for public security in Rio and—in a bold but ultimately failed attempt to further his political career—pledged to reduce violent crime in a city that, in his own words, had gotten "out of control" (*Jornal do Brasil* 8 May 2003). A few months later, however, he was forced to admit publicly that his efforts were being undermined by widespread police corruption and the force's involvement in crimes.[59]

The police in Rio have been discovered charging motorists fees to liberate cars with improper paperwork during blitzes, laundering drug money, robbing apartments, stealing cars, kidnapping civilians, apprehending high-profile drug dealers and then extorting money for their release, drug trafficking and dealing, prostitution, and leaking and selling information about police activities in favelas.[60] Indeed, the situation has reached a point where the police authorities in Rio often do not tell their own officers where and when they are going until the very last moment (*O Globo* 11 April 2005). And they have even been known to rely on handpicked teams of evangelical police officers in particularly sensitive situations (*Jornal do Brasil* 28 November 2004).

The most embarrassing incident in recent years, however, involved the federal police. In September 2005, after two years of careful investigation, the federal police in Rio broke up a drug-trafficking ring that flew cocaine from Colombia to the state of Mato Grosso and then transported it by truck via Paraná to Rio, where it was hidden inside frozen meat to be shipped to Spain and Portugal. The police seized two tons of cocaine, the largest haul ever made in the state, and 2.1 million reais worth of currency. Within three days the money had disappeared from a safe inside the federal police headquarters in Rio. Furthermore, a subsequent investigation revealed that ninety kilos of cocaine that had been seized the year before had been replaced by look-alike substances and sold to drug gangs in Rio's favelas. This discovery prompted an investigation of all drug seizures made by the federal police in Brazil, which in turn revealed that 136 kilos of cocaine had been stolen and replaced in São Paulo (*O Globo* 16, 19, and 21 September; 8, 22, and 29 October 2005). It is clear, therefore, that one of the consequences of the war on drugs is the continued valorization of illegal narcotics as commodities.

Unfortunately, despite innumerous crackdowns on illegal police behavior and the large number of legal proceedings brought against the police, it is still proving extremely difficult to purge criminal and corrupt elements from the force.[61] A recent analysis of cases brought against the police since the existence of the office of police ombudsman in Rio, for example, revealed that of the 8,330 military and civil police men and women turned in on the basis of their participation in one type of crime or another, only 16 have been expelled from the force (*O Globo* 3 February 2006). Police involvement in crime and the unwillingness or inability of the authorities to punish those who are apprehended of course reinforces the already widespread impression that the police act with impunity, that they are a law unto themselves, and that, in a sense, they are not all that different from the criminal factions that dominate and tyrannize Rio's poor neighborhoods, public housing projects, and favelas.[62]

Indeed, one of the most disturbing developments in Rio in recent years has been the increase in the number of low-income neighborhoods controlled and governed by militias consisting of retired or off-duty police officers, known as *polícia mineira*. The militias in these neighborhoods, which at present appear to be concentrated in Rio's Zona Oeste (West Zone), act much like the gangs they have driven out in that they promote parties and cultural events and provide legal and medical services via each community's neighborhood association. They also charge a fee for protection and expel and confiscate the property of anyone suspected of being associated with drug trafficking. And while many of the residents of these areas are relieved to be out from under the control of drug gangs, they are aware that they have traded one authoritarian and unaccountable force for another. As one policeman who offered such services said, "We are a necessary evil. The residents oftentimes don't want us here, but they end up agreeing because they need to free themselves of violence" (qtd. in *O Globo* 21 March 2005).

The emergence of private militias, known to be linked to death squads, is part and parcel of the broader process of the privatization of public security in Rio, something that is in itself an indication of the general lack of faith in the capacity of public authorities. Ironically, however, a large proportion of those working in the private security sector *are* or *were* members of the police. According to the Sindicato dos Vigilantes do Rio, there are currently 130,000 people working as private security guards in Rio, only 30,000 of which are registered (*O Globo* 5 August 2004). One reason as many as 60,000 police officers and firefighters work clandestinely in this sector is because the law prohibits them from working a second shift, or *bico*. Furthermore, an estimated 80 percent of the illegal private security firms in Rio are actually controlled if not owned by police (*O Globo* 29 May 2005).

The question is, if the uniformed and on-duty police can get away with killing, on average, one thousand civilians each year, what possibility or mechanism is there for controlling and overseeing what is becoming the extralegal arm of an already deadly public security force?[63] As in other countries of Latin America, there is the strong suspicion that militias operate with the implicit approval, if not the support, of public authorities and that what we are witnessing here is a military-inspired campaign strategy to retake and hold, by whatever means necessary, territories that have been lost to the state.

Conclusion

When we think of the possible causes of the recent surge in violence in Latin America, drug trafficking is often mentioned as a contributing factor. Rarely, however, does drug trafficking take center stage. Similarly, when we think of drugs and drug-related violence in Latin America, we tend quite naturally to think of producer countries like Peru, Bolivia, and Colombia, in particular, or countries like Mexico, which are entry points to the world's largest drug market in the United States (e.g., see Youngers and Rosin 2005). In this essay I have argued that the dramatic increase in violence in Rio de Janeiro over the past two decades can be attributed to the globalization of the illegal drug trade and, in particular, to the establishment of transshipment routes through Brazil for Andean-produced cocaine. More than anything, I would argue, it was the arrival of cocaine and its ensuing habits and addictions that provided criminalized elements with the means to support their operations. And it was the immense profits to be made from the drug trade that generated intense and bloody rivalries for increased market share between increasingly well-armed and violent factions and the police.

Unfortunately, as drug-related violence has spilled beyond the confines of low-income neighborhoods, public housing projects, and favelas and has begun to terrorize the population of Rio de Janeiro in general, calls for more severe and more violent measures to eliminate so-called criminal elements have increased.[64] Few people seem to care that the violation of one person's human rights puts everyone else's at risk, and as a consequence, few people care about the thousands of young men who die each year unless it involves a high-profile massacre, or *chacina*, which galvanizes the human rights community and, momentarily at least, grabs the attention of the international press.[65]

The contradictions associated with the situation in Rio are perhaps best illustrated by an event that occurred on 12 June 2000 and has since been dramatized by the acclaimed docudrama *Bus 174*. In mid-afternoon, Sandro de Nascimento, twenty-one, held up a bus at gunpoint in a relatively wealthy neighborhood of the city. For the next four and a half hours, Nascimento negotiated with the police that had surrounded the bus for the release of the eleven passengers he had taken hostage. When he gave himself up, however, a police marksman opened fire and, in the confusion, killed the woman Nascimento was using as cover. Nascimento never made it to the police station alive; he was strangled to death in the back of a police van. As implausible as it may seem, Nascimento was one of the survivors of the massacre of eight street children by military policemen outside Candelària Cathedral in 1993. A few of my friends expressed sympathy for the victim. The vast majority, however, said that the police should have done the job right the first time. The public apparently agreed, since a jury subsequently acquitted the police involved in Nascimento's murder.[66]

Unfortunately, as I have demonstrated, efforts to resolve the situation in Rio have largely failed or have made matters worse. As we have seen only recently in the case of São Paulo, attempts to break the power of prison-based criminal organizations can have disastrous and unintended consequences, not the least of which is the spate of revenge killings committed by a suddenly besieged and overwhelmed police. Is it any wonder, then, that Brazilians are increasingly turning to other actors, such as private security guards, militias, and even the armed forces, to provide them with a measure of security?[67]

The loser in all this has been democracy. The early to mid-1980s at least held out the possibility that the various elements of the popular movement would reach across class and sectoral boundaries and consolidate a power base that could influence, if not determine, the nature and scope of public policy. Sadly, this is no longer the case. The question now is how to prevent a small but significant number of poor youths from signing up with the gangs that dominate their neighborhoods. And how to clean up and reform the police without driving disgruntled and criminal elements into the hands of the militias. And, finally, how to disarm both the gangs and the militias that outman and outgun the public security force.

Part of the problem, of course, has to do with the abyss that continues to exist between rich and poor in Brazil and, particularly in Rio, between citizens who enjoy rights and privileges guaranteed by law and the vast majority of sub- or quasi citizens who are in many ways left unprotected and forced to fend for themselves. In this context neoliberal programs and policies can be squarely blamed for failing to produce growth. For while the vast majority of gang members in Rio are teenagers, they are under no illusion as to where the sources of economic and social status lie. Part of the problem also has to do with the widespread corruption that appears to have infected and compromised every level of the political and institutional system. A significant part of this corruption can be directly attributed to the amount of money to be made from the trafficking of drugs. The most serious problem by far, however, is now the widespread availability of guns. The geographical distribution of homicides in Brazil is identical to the geographical distribution of deaths by firearms. Unfortunately, the growing sense of public insecurity in Brazil has made the issue of arms control a difficult sell.

In October 2005 Brazilians went en masse to the polls to vote on a referendum on arms control. If the referendum had passed, the sale of firearms and ammunition would have been restricted to the police, the military, certain security guards, gun collectors, and sports club participants. And, it would have reinforced and complemented a 2003 disarmament law that restricts who can purchase guns and carry them on the street and a successful disarmament campaign prior to the referendum that resulted in 464,000 guns being turned in—no questions asked—for cash.[68] The referendum was defeated by a wide margin, however, in no small part because of a total lack of confidence in the police and, more important, in the federal government's underfunded and failed security policy.[69]

Notes

1. For comparative statistics for Latin America, see Concha-Eastman 2002.
2. In recent years violence in Brazil has in fact spread—along with economic development—to the interior (Waiselfisz 2008). See also Adorno 2002.
3. Fertility rates were high in Brazil until the late 1980s. They are now at a level equivalent to those in the United States, and the population is expected to stabilize at about 230 million by the year 2030. Having said this, births to women of twenty years or younger have been on the increase since 1991 (*Jornal do Brasil* 18 December 2003).
4. Between 1960 and 1970 the Gini coefficient for Brazil increased at a rate of 0.8 per year. For trends in poverty and inequality in Latin America in general in the 1980s and 1990s, see Korzeniewicz and Smith 2000.
5. In 2002 the minimum wage in Brazil was equivalent to US$84.
6. The Gini coefficient for Brazil, for example, has declined from 0.593 in 2001 to 0.566 in 2005 (*O Globo* 18 October 2006).
7. It has been adopted in one form or another in countries as different as Mexico and the United States.
8. In the reverse order of the sequence suggested by T. H. Marshall in his seminal essay "Citizenship and Social Class"; see Marshall 1950.
9. According to the Instituto de Pesquisa Econômica Aplicada (IPEA), the percentage of formal-sector workers in Brazil increased from 37.5 percent in 1993 to 38.4 percent in 2002 but declined in urban areas over the same period from 55.5 percent to 49.7 percent. Furthermore, between 1993 and 2002 the percentage of poor workers with formal-sector jobs in Brazil declined from 22.2 percent to 20.7 percent (IPEA 2006:105). See also Power and Roberts 2000.
10. A *carteira assinada* is a signed work card that defines an employee's function and guarantees his or her rights. When an employer signs a work card he or she has to pay approximately 8 percent of the employee's salary into the federal social security system. It also costs the employee a portion of his or her salary.
11. Two events in particular accelerated this process. The first was the establishment of the port of Santos, which provided a coastal outlet for the emerging economy of the city of São Paulo. The second was the transfer of the nation's capital from Rio to the purpose-built city of Brasília in the interior in 1960.
12. The GDP per capita in metropolitan Rio de Janeiro shrank 20 percent between 1996 and 2002, and income per capita by 5.3 percent (*O Globo* 29 July 2006).

13. I say "estimated," because there is very little reliable information as to the population of such areas.
14. Fortaleza is second with 16.6 percent. São Paulo is a distant eighth with 8.8 percent (*O Globo* 12 September 2004; 6 August 2006).
15. Having said that, in recent years the police in Rio have discovered and shut down small laboratories that produce LSD and refine coca paste obtained in exchange for stolen cars in Paraguay (*Jornal do Brasil* 24 August 2004).
16. According to some estimates, the so-called Atlantic route through Brazil, Venezuela, and Guyana now accounts for half of the cocaine leaving Colombia (*Financial Times* 31 October 2003). For the origins of the drug trade in Brazil, see Geffray 2002.
17. Drug culture in Brazil is by no means confined to marijuana and cocaine, however. According to the fifth Levantamento Nacional sobre Consumo de Drogas entre Estudantes, which polled forty-eight thousand people, Brazilian students between thirteen and fifteen consume more solvents, among other things, than their peers in any other country in the world (*Jornal do Brasil* 1 June 2005).
18. It is often claimed that the drug problem in Brazil is confined to what is referred to as the "White Republic" of Rio. There is evidence, however, that in terms of sheer volume São Paulo is the far larger market. In the past there have been significant differences between the two. The market in Rio has been dominated by cocaine, as opposed to crack cocaine, and has been far more organized and violent. Recent events suggest, however, that the situation in both cities is changing. For the case of São Paulo, see Mingardi and Goulart 2002.
19. By way of illustration, the police in Rio recently estimated that the drug gangs that dominate the four Zona Sul favelas of Rocinha, Vidigal, Pavão-Pavãozinho, and Cantagalo take in about 4.5 million reais, or US$2 million, each week. A study of police inquiries and court cases in Rio de Janeiro dating to 1991 revealed that 57 percent of all the homicides in the city that year were linked in some way or another to drug trafficking.
20. For a visual tour of the now derelict prison, visit http://www.f8.com/FP/DC/index2.htm. For an account of prison conditions through the eyes of a foreign ethnographer, see Donna Goldstein 2003:137–42.
21. For an account of this process, see Amorim 1993:61–102. For an alternative perspective, see Misse 1999.
22. The most famous of these was the escape by "Escadinha" from the Ilha Grande prison by helicopter on New Year's Eve in 1985.
23. According to recent estimates, 400 neighborhood association leaders were executed and 450 more expelled between 1992 and 2002 (*Jornal do Brasil* 16 June 2002; 27 March 2005).
24. For the relationship between drug gangs and the surrounding community, see Alvito 2001:152; Leeds 1996; Ventura 1994:103–4; and Zaluar 1994.
25. There is, however, a tendency to exaggerate the degree to which local residents

support rather than fear drug gangs. Marcos Alvito makes what I think is a useful distinction between drug-gang leaders in the past, who were cruel but fair, and a new generation who are not respected because they torture and kill for the sake of it (Alvito 2001:152).

26. In 1992 the police in São Paulo killed 1,428 civilians, more than three times the number of people killed or disappeared during fifteen years of military rule.

27. It is clear that claims of self-defense cover for police executions. A study of police killings between 1993 and 1996 found that half the victims had four or more bullet wounds and that more than half had at least one gunshot wound from behind or to the head (Cano 1998).

28. About 40 percent of those enrolled in witness protection programs in Rio are being protected *from* the police. Another 40 percent are involved in drug-related crimes, including protection from death squads, which also involve the police (*Jornal do Brasil* 2 July 2004).

29. For problems associated with the Brazilian judiciary, see Pinheiro 2000; and Brinks 2003.

30. Jorge Balán argues that in cities of Latin America "fear is now as much a threat to democracy as violence itself, since it may justify repression, emergency policies that circumvent the constitutional rule, and, more broadly, alienation from the democratic political process" (Balán 2002:5).

31. In September 2002 and February 2003 whole areas of the city were closed for days by order of drug gangs. See *Jornal do Brasil* 12 September 2002; 3 March 2003.

32. According to the Federação das Empresas de Transportes de Pasageiros do Estado do Rio de Janeiro (Fetranspor) 639 buses were burned or laid to waste in Rio between 1999 and 2004 at a cost of 50 million reais (*Jornal do Brasil* 18 July 2004).

33. In 2001 the police apprehended 16,796 firearms in Rio; only 1,149 were manufactured abroad. Between 1998 and 2001 there were eighty-one reported incidences of firearms gone missing from military establishments in Brazil (*Jornal do Brasil* 26 April 2004; see also Dowdney 2003:100).

34. Press reports have claimed that drug gangs in Rio possess an arsenal of fifteen hundred rifles and machine guns, and in one favela in August 2004 the police discovered a stockpile of mines, grenades, and gun cartridges worth an estimated 500,000 reais (*O Globo* 16 June 2002; 19 August 2004; 10 May 2007).

35. Despite a 1997 antitorture law, a recent report by the United Nations states that "police routinely beat and torture criminal suspects to extract information, confessions or money," and that "the problem of police brutality, at the time of arrest or during interrogation, was reportedly endemic" (ONU 2001).

36. An estimated 30 percent of the police who are admitted to the military police hospital in Rio are injured by their own weapons (*Jornal do Brasil* 29 November 2000).

37. This figure also involves firefighters.

38. The police force has provided rare and significant opportunities for Afro-Brazilians.

39. For police involvement with the drug trade, see Leeds 1996; for police corruption in general, see Blat and Saraiva 2000.

40. For a discussion of the different kinds of relationship between drug gangs and the police, see Alvito 2001:105; and Ventura 1994:67.

41. Traffickers tell people that the telephones are bugged to discourage informants. They have also been responsible for destroying a lot of public telephones from where—obviously—these calls are made (*O Globo* 22 August 2004).

42. For a while, in the 1990s, community policing was seen as the answer to the problem of drug-related violence based on models imported from the United States.

43. It is common for drug-gang leaders in prison to accompany torture sessions and executions by phone. See, for example, *Jornal do Brasil* 6 September 2002.

44. In 2000 the Department for State Prisons (Desipe) sent the Brazilian Lawyers Association a list of 130 lawyers suspected of being involved with drug trafficking. It turned out that only 15 of them were actual lawyers; the other 115 had all obtained false documents (*Jornal do Brasil* 16 April 2001). For an interview with the attorney of the drug trafficker Fernandinho Beira-Mar, see *Jornal do Brasil* 28 March 2003.

45. The police have discovered digital and satellite-operated phone banks that can transfer calls to and from prison without revealing the identity of the caller and software that can clone privately owned cell phones and change their numbers up to twenty times per day. The equipment for this type of operation is extremely sophisticated and expensive, costing up to US$40,000, and is similar to technology used by guerilla fighters in Colombia (*Jornal do Brasil* 9 August 2002).

46. On 5 August 2002, for example, the prison authorities confiscated 114 cell phones and 135 cell-phone chargers in the Bangu prison complex in Rio (*Jornal do Brasil* 6 August 2002).

47. Most prisons in Brazil have generous visitation policies, including conjugal visits for male inmates. Visitation rights are often used as a disciplinary tool, however, and the visitors themselves have to stand in line for hours and are subjected to humiliating and intrusive searches by prison guards.

48. In 1998 a drug-gang member known as Celso de Vintém paid 90,000 reais to escape through the front door of a prison hospital. Inmates also on a regular basis escape through tunnels dug by inmates on the inside or, alternatively, by teams of paid workmen on the outside.

49. The Ministry of Justice calculates that 25 percent of every 1 million dollars generated by the drug trade is invested in the corruption of the authorities (*Veja* 18 September 2002).

50. Law 7.120, signed by President Lula, altered the Lei de Execução Penal and introduced the Regime Disciplinar Diferenciado, which states that inmates who threaten the social order from within prisons can be held in individual cells with limited access to visits and the open air for up to a year. The law has been criticized by the

Conselho Nacional de Política Criminal e Penitenciária as inhumane (*Jornal do Brasil* 20 August 2004). For a description of the new prison regulations, see *Jornal do Brasil* 19 November 2003.

51. In May 2004 thirty inmates were killed in a prison rebellion in Rio, some of them decapitated and burnt, because of an attempt by the authorities to "mix" gang members. A subsequent investigation revealed that prisoners are routinely asked to sign forms releasing the prison authorities from any responsibility for their safety (*Jornal do Brasil* 1 June 2004; 3 June 2005).

52. Since 2001 sixty-seven prison workers have been assassinated in Rio. Some of these individuals were executed because they were responsible for imposing harsh measures. Others were executed because they refused to take bribes or because they backed out of agreements to facilitate escapes. See, for example, *Jornal do Brasil* 5, 9, and 10 March 2004; 19 December 2005.

53. This refers to the fact that increasingly drug-gang members do not come from the communities in which they operate, which is also a function of this period of increased rivalry and conflict.

54. I was told, before it happened, that all the *donos* associated with the Comando Vermelho in Rio had signed a document approving the attack.

55. The attack on Rocinha prompted calls to build a wall around the favela.

56. This policy has met with limited success. In October 2004 a bus full of German tourists was held up on its way from the international airport to the Zona Sul by carloads of *traficantes* who then boarded the vehicle. The Germans, apparently, were so nonplussed that they thought it was some sort of pageant put on for their benefit (*O Globo* 26 October 2004).

57. There is also evidence that other drugs, such as heroin, are becoming increasingly common. The federal police seized 27.4 kilos of heroin in 2001, 56.6 kilos in 2002, and 66.2 kilos in 2003. The shift toward heroin production in Latin America is attributed to the fact that it is easy to cultivate and can be grown at high altitudes and on scattered plots that are more difficult to detect and eradicate than lowland crops such as cocaine (*Jornal do Brasil* 15 January 2003; and 18 January 2004; see also *New York Times* 8 June 2003).

58. Attacks on buses in Rio increased by 151 percent and on pedestrians by 55 percent between 2003 and 2004 (*O Globo* 8 December 2004; 16 July 2005).

59. There have even been instances of police involvement with schemes to exchange stolen cars for drugs and to service and maintain firearms on behalf of drug gangs (*Jornal do Brasil* 17 October, 25 and 30 November 2003).

60. They are also suspected of training criminal factions in the art of urban warfare. For example, the last time the favela of Rocinha was invaded by rival gang members in February 2006, the forty or so armed men possessed sophisticated maps and detailed instructions, were divided into four coordinated assault units, and wore black uniforms similar to those of the elite units of the Rio police.

61. The latest crackdown, named operation Navalha na Carne, began in February

2005. For more on this issue, see Lembruger, Musemeci, and Cano 2003; and Amar 2003.

62. In this respect it is also highly probable that any successful attempt to clean house would drive police expelled from the force into the ranks of criminal organizations. For evidence on this matter from elsewhere, see Davis 2006a; and Call 2003.

63. On a somewhat more positive note, following the latest massacre of thirty civilians by elements of the military police in the Baixada Fluminense on 31 March 2005, the chief of the civil police in Rio, Álvaro Lins, announced that in the future all cases of civilian deaths at the hands of the police will be investigated to determine whether or not the victims were executed (*Jornal do Brasil* 12 April 2005).

64. In recent months there has been a campaign to lower the age at which criminals can be tried as adults from eighteen to sixteen.

65. In a similar vein, Anthony Pereira argues that the "assumption that citizens will protest the abuse of others' rights for fear they might be victimized themselves has not held in Brazil" (Pereira 2000:233).

66. This story is not just about the situation in Rio. In February 2006 São Paulo's state Supreme Court annulled Colonel Ubiratan Guimarões's conviction for the 1992 Carandiru prison massacre. The court ruled that he had acted "in the lines of his duty." Tim Cahill, Amnesty International's researcher on Brazil, commented: "In light of this ruling nobody has been held responsible for the 111 deaths in the Carandiru prison 13 years ago. This is an affront to the victims and their relatives and sends the message that excessive use of force is acceptable in policing operations" (AI press release, AI Index, AMR 19/006/2006, 16 February 2006).

67. In March 2006 ten rifles and a handgun were stolen from a military barracks in downtown Rio de Janeiro. In response, the Brazilian military dispatched armored vehicles and hundreds of troops into sixteen different favelas until the weapons were found, twelve days later, in Rocinha. The military's intervention was widely perceived as a very public demonstration by the federal government that the local authorities could no longer be counted on to maintain law and order.

68. The disarmament campaign ran for sixteen months prior to the referendum and, according to the federal government, saved over three thousand lives (*O Globo* 25 October 2005).

69. The Fundo Nacional de Segurança Pública was created in 2001 to finance anti-crime policies in states and municipalities. In April 2005, however, 58 percent of its 412.9 million reais budget was cut (*O Globo* 5 April 2005). For a critical evaluation of the criminal justice system in Brazil, including recent changes introduced by President Lula and the Partido dos Trabalhadores (PT), see Jahangir 2003; see also AI 2005.

Violence, Democracy, and Human Rights in Latin America

TODD LANDMAN

Violence and democracy are endemic to the political history of Latin America. Through the periods of independence, state formation, and modern politics, violence has been a constant feature of social transformations and political processes in the region, including the initial violence of European colonization, struggles for liberation, and territorial and border disputes; the subordination of indigenous groups and suppression of popular unrest; protest, rebellion, civil war, and revolution; and prolonged periods of military authoritarianism. Moreover, despite the pendular movement between authoritarian and democratic forms of rule since independence, the region has had a general value orientation and cultural identification with civic republican models of governance, including the limited oligarchic democracies of the late nineteenth and twentieth centuries, the populist democracies of the early to middle twentieth century, and the so-called pacted democracies of the late twentieth century and the early twenty-first. Indeed, for over two centuries countries in the region have struggled in continuous yet uneven fashion to "consolidate representative regimes, accept the legitimacy of the opposition, expand citizenship, and affirm the rule of law" (Hartlyn and Valenzuela 1994:99). Even though periods of relative democratic stability have been interrupted by both short-term and long-term military authoritarianism, the militaries themselves were motivated by the need to restore law and order with the view to returning power to civilians.[1] And with the exception of a slight dip at the beginning of the twentieth century, there has been an overall positive trend in the growth of what many have called procedural democracy across the region (Smith 2005:33–43).

By the turn of the new millennium Latin America had thus truly joined the "democratic universe" (see Foweraker, Landman, and Harvey 2003:34–55), with Cuba remaining the only nondemocratic country in the region. But despite the development of democratic political institutions, many rights protections remain precarious, while commentators have observed that organized crime and everyday violence have not diminished and have actually *increased* in countries such as Brazil, Mexico, Peru, and Colombia (see, e.g., Pereira and Davis 2000; Caldeira and Holston 1999; Pereira and Davis 2000). In contrast to the expectations raised, the return to democracy has not brought with it a corresponding state capacity for countries to uphold their various legal obligations to respect, protect, and fulfill individual and collective rights, whether such obligations are found in national constitutions or international and regional human rights instruments. There is thus a significant and in some cases expanding gap between the de jure protection and the de facto realization of human rights across the region (see Landman 2006a; 2006c; 2005),[2] where states continue to be unable to guarantee the protection of citizens from rights violations committed by state and nonstate actors through various forms of organized and sporadic violence.

There is now an emerging set of studies that examine in systematic fashion the theoretical and empirical linkages between violence and democracy using the tools of comparative political science (Neumayer 2003; Krahn, Hartnagel, and Gartrell 1986; Messner 1982; Braithwaite and Braithwaite 1980), and Latin America has received significant attention here (Neumayer 2003:635; Frühling and Tulchin with Golding 2003; Bailey and Godson 2000; Neapolitan 1997, 1994). This essay makes a contribution to the extant work by engaging with the main arguments put forth in the introduction to this volume. First, it agrees with Enrique Arias and Daniel Goldstein that Latin America faces *plural* forms of violence, but it takes the argument one step further by seeking to clarify what is meant by violence by defining it and developing a typology that takes into account various forms of violence (legal and illegal) and the agents that principally engage in it (state and nonstate actors). Second, in agreement with the idea that the study of democracy in the region is not helped through assigning more and more adjectives (Collier and Levitsky 1997), it develops a framework that draws on Jack Donnelly's (1999a) notion of "rights-protective regimes" and concentrates on the various institutional and rights dimensions that feature across all forms of governance. Third, it uses the typology of violence and the regime framework to discuss the theoretical and empirical linkages between violence and democracy that inform the current problem of violence confronting the region. Finally, it discusses the policy implications for Latin America in confronting violent pluralism.

Violence

Violence comes in many forms, and historically the understanding of violence —how it is constructed and how it constructs—has changed dramatically. Acts once thought socially acceptable are now seen as unacceptable, and numerous practices and outcomes are now considered to be within the general ambit of violence, including microlevel person-to-person violence and the macroviolence of particular economic structures. John Keane (2004:34–35) argues that the meaning of violence has become democratized, such that its scope of application has been broadened, its meaning has become dependent on context, and its understanding varies over time and space. The World Health Organization (who) has developed a typology of violence that includes self-directed violence (suicide and self-abuse), interpersonal violence (in family and community), and collective violence (social, political, and economic), all of which can be physical, sexual, psychological, or constitute a form of deprivation and/or neglect (Krug, Dahlberg, and Mercy 2002:7). A political science of violence that attempts to link it to democracy is necessarily concerned with public forms of interpersonal and collective violence, and the field of comparative politics has accumulated a catalog of studies on insurrectionary violence, revolutionary violence, state violence, and structural violence. Keane (2004:35) provides the following useful definition of violence that excludes structural violence and that includes both interpersonal and collective forms of violence: "More or less intended, direct but unwanted physical interference by groups and/or individuals with the bodies of others, who are consequently made to suffer a series of effects ranging from shock, speechlessness, mental torment, nightmares, bruises, scratches, swellings, or headaches through to broken bones, heart attacks, loss of body parts, or death." This definition implies an agent or perpetrator of the violence as well as a victim, and it emphasizes violence as causing harm to bodies or living beings (see Ross 2004:3). This understanding of violence fits well with one of the main models adopted by many of the postconflict truth commissions for the analysis of large-scale human rights violations, in particular those of El Salvador (1992–93), Haiti (1995–96), Guatemala (1997–99), and Peru (2001–3) (see Landman 2006a:107–25; Ball et al. 2003; Ball, Spirer, and Spirer 2000). While this definition narrows down the object of inquiry to exclude systemic and long-term conditions that make violence possible, it does allow for a greater specification of concrete policy solutions designed to address the more immediate and salient forms of violence.

Keeping the focus on violence as a result of individual agency, the typology developed here includes two ideal-typical perpetrators (state and nonstate) and two forms of violence (legal and illegal). Table 1 shows the four types of violence that result from the logical combination of the perpetrators and forms that are the subject of this essay: legal state violence, illegal state violence, legal nonstate violence, and illegal nonstate violence. *Legal state violence* includes all those forms of the proportionate use of force needed to maintain peace, security, and order within the remit of national laws. Such an understanding is consistent with Max Weber's definition of the state as "a human community that (successfully) claims the monopoly of the legitimate use of physical force within a given territory" (1991:78). The history of state formation is one in which human communities abdicate some autonomy over their affairs in return for the protection of the state and its institutions (Bendix 1978, 1964; see also Bates 2001). This history is evident in the political sociology of modern citizenship, where the struggle for inclusion by subordinate groups and the expansive need for surplus by the state have led to a dialectical relationship between social mobilization and the gradual extension of the civil, political, and economic rights of citizenship (see Barbalet 1988; Marshall 1964). Similar patterns of contestation, social mobilization, and the piecemeal advance of rights protections have been evident in the initial periods of democratization in Latin America (Rueschemeyer, Stephens, and Stephens 1992), as well as in the liberalizing authoritarian regimes of Brazil (1964–85), Chile (1973–89), and Mexico (1968–90) (see Foweraker and Landman 1999, 1997).

While historically the understanding of *legal* violence has varied according to state form and regime type (see below), the development of international human rights and humanitarian law has provided a set of standards that delineates what constitutes proportionate use of force and violence in the domestic context.[3] Rather than see this development of human rights standards as some form of outward imposition, we must acknowledge the history of human rights as grounded in a variety of historical experiences. It has been described as the result of significant "social construction" (Donnelly 1999b), and in the context of the Inter-American system for the promotion and protection of human rights, precedents have been set that have had applicability within the region and beyond in human rights jurisprudence (Harris and

Table 1. A Typology of Violence

| Perpetrator(s) of violence | FORMS OF VIOLENCE | |
	Legal	Illegal
State actors	Proportionate use of force to keep peace, security, and law and order	Disproportionate use of force to suppress opposition, create a state of fear, and exercise state terror
Nonstate actors	Self-defense against crime Resistance to state repression (?)	Arbitrary and/or sustained use of force by uncivil movements, vigilantes, paramilitaries, guerillas, organized gangs, and individual criminals

Livingstone 1998).[4] *Illegal state violence* includes all those forms of the disproportionate use of force applied to suppress opposition, create a state of fear, and exercise state terror. The notion of "state terror" has found expression in extant measures of human rights protection (Landman 2005, 2004; Gibney and Dalton 1996; Poe and Tate 1994), and the term has been used to describe the practices carried out under the military authoritarian regimes such as those in Argentina (1966–73; 1976–82), Brazil (1964–85), Uruguay (1973–84), and Chile (1973–89).

Legal nonstate violence includes the common-law understanding of self-defense against criminal acts such as a burglary or another violent intrusion into one's private property. The legality of such a defensive use of violence comes from proper adjudication in the relevant court. Some have also argued, more controversially, that violence in the form of resistance to state oppression is also permitted. Some would say that it may be legitimate but nonetheless illegal. This form of violence has been the subject of much debate and has featured in the history of emancipation, liberation, anticolonial struggles, and revolution, among other forms of violence meant to overcome oppression (see, e.g., Keane 2004:30–41; Pereira and Davis 2000; Honderich 1973). As part of the process of democratic transition in South Africa, the truth and reconciliation commission there considered arguments that violent resistance by the African National Congress (ANC) to apartheid was legitimate, though it was never considered legal per se. *Illegal nonstate violence* includes the arbitrary and/or sustained use of force by "uncivil" movements, vigilantes, paramilitaries, guerillas, organized gangs, and individual criminals (Payne 2000). Leigh Payne (2000) is keen to stress that the uncivil movements she considers do not inhabit civil society in the same way that nonviolent social movement organizations do since they are consciously antidemocratic in orientation, use violence to further their ends, and perpetrate human rights violations.

But despite Payne's (2000) contribution and clarity, the line of distinction between different forms of nonstate violence has not been clear, and there ought to be more normative reflection on the use of such violence in suggesting possible policy solutions to the endemic problem of violence pluralism. On the one hand, Anthony Pereira and Diane Davis (2000:6) note that in the context of Latin America, both the defeat of insurrectionary movements and the experience of violence on a mass scale under authoritarian rule have shifted attitudes toward a greater rejection of violence as means to an end.[5] Violence to overthrow the state has been rejected as much as the violence employed to maintain the state during periods of military authoritarian rule. On the other hand, however, anthropological and ethnographic research on violence in Latin America reveals that many citizens living under conditions in which failing state institutions cannot provide adequate protections do not necessarily consider the use of violence as a means to an end illegitimate (e.g., Goldstein 2004; Huggins 1991).

Thus it appears that despite the need to delineate clearly between different forms of violence, it is precisely the point where such boundaries should be drawn that becomes contested, particularly in a region with such a long history of violence. But it seems paramount that some form of normative reasoning be applied to these acts of violence in the same way that it has been applied over the centuries to the various acts of violence employed by the state. Indeed, the development of democracy and institutions that provide vertical and horizontal forms of accountability are meant to curb the worst forms of predatory state behavior. While the differentiation between legal and illegal forms of state violence has become more transparent through the application of international, regional, and national laws on human rights, the jurisprudence remains underdeveloped for the violent practices of nonstate actors (see Clapham 2005).

Political Regimes: Institutions and Rights

The rapid spread and pace of democratization over the past thirty years has brought an equally rapid spread of terminology to describe democracy in its many forms as it has become the preferred form of government for a majority of countries in the world. As more and more countries meet the minimum set of criteria for democracy (e.g., see Dahl 1971; and more recently, Przeworski et al. 2000), more and more commentators have had to find new vocabulary to describe and classify the general phenomenon of an observable gap between the political institutions of electoral democracy and the precariousness of various rights protections. The "new" democracies were first celebrated for their successful transitions from authoritarian forms of rule (of both the right and the left) and then quickly criticized for falling far short of global expectations for their performance. Thus beyond the more traditional labels of *political*, *liberal*, and *social*, these new democracies variously became described as "pacted" (Higley and Gunther 1992), "delegative" (O'Donnell 1994), "pseudo" (Diamond 1999a), "disjunctive" (Caldeira and Holston 1999), and "illiberal" (Zakaria 2003; see also Smith 2005), to name a few of the more notable adjectives adopted.

What is really being described, however, is the degree to which democratic political institutions have developed and the degree to which states have the capacity to respect, protect, and fulfill rights obligations typically associated with democracy. A focus on state capacity and the degree to which a regime is "rights-protective" (Donnelly 1999b) shifts attention away from the hunt for more adjectives to put in front of the term *democracy* and provides an analytical framework that can be applied to all countries. Table 2 thus represents a preliminary typology of regimes based on how personnel fill the key institutions of government (elected or nonelected), the relative independence of the judiciary, and the degree to which different categories of rights are protected. Because the lines of distinction are drawn across fairly crude categories of analysis, great variation remains within each type depicted. Columns 1 and 2 contain regime types in which the executive and the legislature are not elected, and in which the judiciary is subordinate and/or nonexistent. Column 1 regimes have no rights protections in place (e.g., Burma), while those in Column 2 have protections in place for social and economic rights only (e.g., Cuba and North Korea).

The regimes in columns 3, 4, and 5 all have elected executives and legislatures (and therefore meet the minimal criteria for procedural democracy), but they have varying degrees of judicial independence and rights protection. The United States, for example, shows significant problems in the protection of economic and social rights, and since 9/11 has sought to curb the protection of civil rights (see, e.g., Brysk and Shafir 2007; Wilson 2005). The United Kingdom has fewer problems with the protection of social and economic rights

Table 2. A Typology of Political Regimes: Institutions and Rights

	Regime dimensions	REGIME TYPES				
		I	II	III	IV	V
Institutions	Executive	Not elected	Not elected	Elected	Elected	Elected
	Legislature	Not elected	Not elected	Elected	Elected	Elected
	Judiciary	Subordinate	Subordinate	Subordinate	Independent	Independent
Rights	Civil	Not protected	Not protected	Not protected	Protected	Protected
	Political	Not protected	Not protected	Protected	Protected	Protected
	Economic	Not protected	Protected	Not protected	Not protected	Protected
	Social	Not protected	Protected	Not protected	Not protected	Protected
Contemporary examples		Burma	Cuba	Brazil	USA	Denmark
			North Korea	Peru	UK (?)	Sweden
			Turkmenistan	Colombia		Finland
				Mexico		Germany
						Netherlands

(although see Weir 2006), and has also sought to limit the protection of civil rights in its fight against terror (see Landman 2007). Most of the Latin American democracies in the current era elect their executive and legislative branches and subordinate the judiciary; political rights are protected, but as Goldstein and Arias note in the introduction, their civil, social, and economic rights are not well protected (column 4).

These different combinations of institutions and rights protections provide for a great variety of political forms and regimes. They also offer a way of thinking about the conditions under which citizens live, the relation between the state and its citizens, and the circumstances under which contested understandings about violence may arise. In a regime with functioning political parties, regular elections, an independent judiciary, and reasonably secured civil and political rights, but with precarious protections for social and economic rights, certain citizens may well remain socially excluded and unable to fully exercise their rights. Social marginalization through low levels of educational attainment and poor health can limit the degree to which citizens participate in the public sphere. Moreover, social exclusion, alienation, and anomie can breed individual and collective frustration that may well be related to the use of violence in the ways that Ted Gurr (1970) originally posited. Citizens living under regimes in which civil, social, and economic rights are precarious face a situation in which the basic means for sustenance and survival are limited and where there are no guarantees protecting them from arbitrary incursions of the state into their lives. Thus in addition to general levels of social exclusion, they face an ever-present threat of illegal forms of state and nonstate violence. Moreover, in the absence of accountability mechanisms, few avenues of redress remain while agents of violence operate with impunity.

The Link between Violence and Democracy

Comparative historical analysis on the genesis of democracy and large-N statistical analysis on the effects of democratization have examined both the association of violence with the birth of democracy and the relationship between democratic transition and violence. In *The Social Origins of Dictatorship and Democracy*, Barrington Moore (1966) shows that in the cases of England, France, and the United States, bourgeois democracy was founded on a violent overthrow of the past. The English civil war (Puritan Revolution) in the seventeenth century, the French Revolution in the eighteenth century, and the American Civil War in the nineteenth century made democracy possible in these three countries through the violent destruction of feudal forms of governance. Subsequent analysis that adds further cases beyond Moore's original sample shows that violence is not necessarily a prerequisite for the establishment of democracy (Rueschemeyer, Stephens, and Stephens 1992), while others have shown that long and inconclusive social struggle (which in many cases turns violent) is a key factor in the process of democratization (Rustow 1970). In applying a political-economy approach and in echoing Max Weber, Robert Bates (2001) argues that locating the use of violence in the state frees local communities and businesses from having to defend themselves against violent attacks from competitors in a given territory and thus provides them with an increased opportunity for generating the kind of economic surplus that is essential for successful economic modernization, which in turn may well lead to democracy.

In addition to these comparative historical studies, large-N cross-national quantitative studies suggest a complex relationship between democracy and violence. The vast literature on the democratic peace shows not only that democratic pairs of states rarely, if ever, engage in warfare (see, e.g., Levy 2002) but also that the level of democracy itself in pairs of states significantly reduces the probability of any kind of militarized dispute (see, e.g., Russett and O'Neal

2001). Beyond the presence or level of democracy, other studies have shown that democratizing countries may well experience more interstate violence (Ward and Gleditsch 1998) in the short term, while in the long term, once democracy has become established, such patterns of violence subside. The work in human rights shows that on balance democracies have lower levels of "personal integrity rights" violations (see Landman 2005; Poe, Tate, and Keith 1999; Poe and Tate 1994). Such violations tend to decrease significantly after the first year of a democratic transition (Zanger 2000). In addition, in his analysis of nonstate violence, Eric Neumayer (2003) finds a similar short-term effect for homicide rates, where countries undergoing processes of democratic transition experience higher homicide rates until democratic institutions have become consolidated. These empirical patterns suggest that violence is no stranger to democracy, either before its establishment or during the democratic transition itself.

Such a set of findings does not suggest that levels of violence are decidedly higher in democracies than in nondemocracies, but nor should we expect the establishment of democracy to be a panacea for violence. Since democracy is merely another regime type and must govern its citizens, it will at times experience moments of nonstate violence to which it must respond, and in many cases such a response may well require state violence. Thus, at a normative level, liberal theory acknowledges the use of violence but seeks to establish principles for its use and conditions under which it can be limited through democratic institutions. For J. S. McClelland (1996:447) the use of violence must be linked to the state and the rule of law: "Liberals were therefore keen to limit and control violence, in so far as that was possible, by giving the state a monopoly on violence, as if it were like salt or tobacco. In the ideal liberal society, the only legitimate form of violence would be violence used by the state, under forms of law, for the detention and punishment of malefactors." The use of violence by a democratic state needs to be defended on the "assertion of just ends," where violent means have been "relative to and justified on the grounds of democratic ends, even when democracy perpetrated deadly violence" (Ross 2004:1). In similar fashion, Keane (2004:2) argues that violence and democracy have a much more ambiguous relationship, where "it might even be said that a distinctive quality of democratic institutions is their subtle efforts to draw a veil over their own use of violence." The key insight, therefore, is that the use of violence is subject to the control of democratic institutions, mechanisms for horizontal and vertical accountability, and the rule of law. The presence of such mechanisms rests on a certain breadth of state presence and a depth of state capacity to provide the necessary kinds of protections to citizens, where the reach of the state ought to cover the entire territory (which is not the case in contemporary Colombia) and should have functioning institutions at the subnational level. The legitimacy of the state is in turn a function of the degree to which citizens have equal access to decision-making processes at these different levels of governance. Before discussing possible solutions to the problems that have been identified, it is helpful to briefly consider patterns of different forms of violence observed in the region during the new democratic era.

While this democratic era began with the Peruvian democratic transition in 1980, it is safe to say that by the 1990s all the regimes in the region with the exception of Cuba, and Peru during Alberto Fujimori's post-coup presidency (1992–2000), had met the minimal and procedural criteria for democracy.[6] But a variety of indicators on state and nonstate violence for the period 1990–2004 shows that the region has been characterized by the persistence of human rights violations, an increase in homicide rates and in levels of intentional injury, and domestic conflict. Average scores for the "political terror scale" (see Poe and Tate 1994), which ranges from 1 (high protection of human rights) to 5 (low protection of human rights), for 1990–2004 suggest there remain significant problems with the persistence of state violence despite the advance of procedural democracy, particularly in the cases of Colombia, Guatemala, Brazil, and El Salvador. In addition, the use of torture remains particularly high in Brazil, Mexico, and Peru. While the patterns of torture have been high for Peru during its conflict primarily with the Sendero Luminoso (Shining Path),[7] the high levels of torture in Brazil and Mexico are not explained by the presence of an ongoing civil war. Events-based data on abuse carried out against human rights defenders (HRDs) suggest that the largest number of attacks have taken place in Colombia, Guatemala, and Mexico. The data on abuse against HRDs includes state and nonstate acts, where the largest number of perpetrators remains "unknown," followed by paramilitary groups and the military and/or armed forces (see Landman 2006a).

Mortality rates due to homicide and "intentional injury" rates collected by the WHO appear to be highest in Brazil, Colombia, and El Salvador, followed by Ecuador, Mexico, and Venezuela. As in the case of the comparative figures for torture, the high mortality rate is somewhat understandable in the case of Colombia, but it is not so obvious in the other countries. Finally, the International Country Risk Group (ICRG) produces an annual score for domestic political violence that includes state and nonstate forms of violence then aggregated into a twelve-point scale. The original score has components that include the threat of civil war or military coup, terrorism and political violence, and civil disorder. The scores for each of these components are given equal weighting and then aggregated, where those countries in which no armed or civil opposition to the government exists and in which the government does not indulge in indirect or direct arbitrary violence against its own people receive the highest score. The lowest rating is given to a country embroiled in an ongoing civil war.[8] These data suggest that state and nonstate political violence has declined in the region, where the severe cases in the Andean region and in Central America have seen decreases in conflict. Only Peru, Colombia, and Venezuela show increased levels of domestic violence.

Together, these data in some sense capture at an aggregate level the kind of state and nonstate violence described in much greater detail in the other essays in this volume. It thus seems clear from the evidence that the advance of democracy in the region has brought with it some decline in aggregate levels of violence but has not by far eliminated it yet. The transition from authoritarian rule has been accompanied by a decrease in state violence toward citizens in terms of gross violations of human rights, but there has been an increase in nonstate violence in the form of more extensive criminal activity. And it is this criminal activity that has brought renewed incidents of state violence in the form of arbitrary detention, torture, and extrajudicial killings. Such heavy-handed responses from the state are particularly harsh in the cases of Mexico and Brazil. The significant outlier in the region remains Colombia, which many commentators continue to classify as an "old" democracy (alongside Costa Rica and Venezuela) for having regular and competitive elections, yet it continues to be plagued with extreme political violence that has claimed thousands of lives and threatens the integrity of the Colombian state itself.

Policy Implications

One helpful way to examine these forms of violence is through the lens provided by a human rights perspective. These forms of violence fall within the notion of a state's obligation to *respect* and *protect* the human rights of its citizens. The obligation to *respect* human rights requires the state and all its organs and agents to abstain from carrying out, sponsoring, or tolerating any practice, policy, or legal measure that violates the integrity of individuals or impinges on their freedom to access resources to satisfy their needs. The obligation to *protect* human rights requires the state to prevent the violation of rights by other individuals or nonstate actors. Where violations do occur, the state must guarantee access to legal remedies. In both instances it appears from the consideration of evidence presented in this essay and others in the current volume that state organs in Latin America are directly responsible for violating human rights *and* at present lack much of the capacity to protect human rights adequately, although the countries in the region have ratified most of the international and regional human rights instruments (see Landman 2006a, 2005:60–71; Foweraker, Landman, and Harvey 2003:83–91).

States have not sufficiently addressed this failure to protect rights in the new democratic era, where improvements in rights protection have lagged far behind the more procedural dimensions of democracy. Furthermore, it is not a mistake to use the language of failure to develop a series of policy responses to the problem of unchecked violence. There are a number of possible explanations for the continued levels of violence of the kind illustrated here and in the other essays. In the case of illegal state violence, a number of institutional and cultural reasons exist for the continuation of human rights violations. First, most of the legal jurisdictions in the region require a confession to proceed to the prosecution stage. There is thus heavy pressure on the police to extract a confession from a suspect to have a successful prosecution, and such pressure leads to the use of torture and other coercive means of extracting information (Rodley 1999). While the use of torture to obtain information was the hallmark of the military authoritarian regimes that populated the region throughout the 1970s and 1980s, the return to democracy did not necessarily mean that such practices would end. Rather, the institutions and the culture that surrounds them have persisted throughout the current democratic period. Second, the military regimes created parallel police forces, and the return to democracy did not see the dismantling of the *policía militar*, for which there are weak mechanisms of oversight and accountability. The institutional and hierarchical integrity of the armed forces has remained to a large extent intact, thereby creating a realm of protection for those within these institutions that may be responsible for rights violations. Third, public opinion in Latin America very much favors the harsh treatment of criminal suspects, where quick convictions and rapid "justice" drive a logic of state response to crime that inevitably leads to human rights violations, particularly against the lower sectors in society (Pinheiro 1999).

As for nonstate violence, the continued existence of private security organizations, vigilante groups, and so-called uncivil movements has plagued Latin American societies as state institutions have lacked the capacity to curb their worst forms of violent activity. Many of the personnel of these groups are either former agents of the state or maintain positions in state security forces, but they are employed as off-duty members of these groups. In other instances, corruption, paybacks, and impunity hamper attempts at providing any sense of a rule of law. In this way the state has failed to maintain its monopoly over the use of force. In the absence of a state monopoly over the use of force, criminal elements become more courageous in their attempts to control sub-units of territory, while their rivalries with competing groups can lead to a spiral of violence that the state may well meet with increased violence. In Colombia, 40 percent of the national territory is controlled by groups other than the state, suggesting that this country has become a so-called failed state, where various forms of violence remain unchecked and the perpetrators continue to carry out their deeds with impunity. The nonstate violence carried out by everyday criminals as seen in the favelas of Rio de Janeiro and São Paulo, for example, has provoked a harsh and in many cases deadly violence from state organs during which whole communities face raids, shootings, and crossfire incidents that kill many innocent citizens.

But what are the possible solutions to such a wide-ranging set of problems? An irony of the human rights tradition is that states are both the *target for advocacy and reform* as well as the *primary agent in our present political system for protecting human rights*. This irony and tension permeates the literature on citizenship rights, normative political theory, comparative politics, and international relations. The history of state formation, democracy, and the proliferation of human rights norms has been one of both *empowering* and *taming* states. States have been empowered through the transfer of authority from the governed to the governors, and they have accumulated large surpluses of material and moral wealth along the way. These accumulated resources have given states a unique position to create the institutional environment in which the rule of law and respect for rights is made possible. But state institutions are populated by individuals, who, as the political-economy literature has shown, have many incentives to engage in rent-seeking behavior. Such rent seeking means that judicial, legal, and administrative state units may not function in ways conducive to establishing and maintaining a rights-protective regime.

Conclusion

This essay has argued that violence is not a stranger to democracy considered in a global comparative and historical perspective, and its patterns prove particularly compelling for the Latin American region. Violence has had a prominent role in the political history of the region, and it appears that the current period of democratic consolidation has not been accompanied by a dramatic decrease in violence. My essay agrees with the general claim advanced by the editors of this volume that violence in Latin America comes in many forms, but it tries to move the debate forward by suggesting that these different forms can be further differentiated by identifying the main agent that perpetrates the violence and the ends to which the violence is employed. It adopts the uneasy yet realistic position that there are forms of state violence that may well be necessary, though they should be exercised only under democratic mechanisms of vertical and horizontal accountability. The history of authoritarianism has meant that state agents who continue to occupy similar positions within the security apparatus as before will act in ways that undermine the legal exercise of state authority. In turn, the inability of the state to guarantee legal protections for citizens creates the conditions under which the distinction between legal and nonlegal forms of nonstate violence becomes increasingly contested. Finally, I argued that it is precisely this line of distinction that international, regional, and domestic human rights standards have sought to establish.

Notes

I thank Paola Cesarini, Dan Goldstein, Enrique Arias, Edzia Carvalho, Jaime Baeza Freer, Ricardo Luna Corral, Anna Mackin, and Marco Larizza.

1. For example, despite its repressive ferocity, the military junta that took power in Argentina in 1976 announced its Act of National Reorganization Process, which aimed to improve the economy, eliminate subversion, and create a new institutional framework (Manzetti 1993:50–53). In similar fashion, the military leaders who carried out the 1964 military coup in Brazil saw themselves as leading a revolution that would forestall a communist revolution and "re-establish order *so that legal reforms [could] be carried out*" (military manifesto sent out by the army chief of staff Castelo Branco, qtd. in Skidmore 1988:18; my emphasis). These two examples fit Alain Rouquie's (1994:238–39) notion of "new armies" in the region, which combined the professional training of their personnel and a "consciousness of competence," creating a greater disposition toward intervention and an identification with civic and national responsibilities. Such justifications have also been used by regimes in South Asia and Southeast Asia.

2. It is interesting to note that new democracies tend to ratify more international human rights treaties with fewer substantive reservations but are less able to protect civil and political rights (see Landman 2005). In comparison with other regions in the world, nearly all Latin American countries have ratified the main

international human rights instruments, as well as the instruments comprising the inter-American system for human rights (see Foweraker, Landman, and Harvey 2003:87–88).

3. In advanced liberal democracies during the current war on terror, the vertical accountability of international human rights law has to some degree limited the ability of states to use force against their own citizens and noncitizens. Certainly, in the United Kingdom, which is party to the European Convention on Human Rights (ECHR), key features of antiterror legislation such as the detention of foreigners without charge, the use of so-called control orders, and the use of evidence obtained through torture have been found to be incompatible with the ECHR, and the government has had to alter its legislation accordingly (see Landman 2007). Such vertical accountability has not been as effective for the United States, since it is not part of such a strong regional human rights system.

4. The history of human rights is in part one of particular struggles for rights by subordinated groups against the state, which in turn, has granted such rights. J. M. Barbalet (1988) shows, for example, that in the European case, grounded struggles for civil, political, and social rights took place across the eighteenth, nineteenth, and twentieth centuries. Edward Clearly (2007) argues that Latin America has its own rights tradition that parallels those of Europe and the United States, and that the region has forged its own system for the promotion and protection of human rights in the period after the 1948 Universal Declaration.

5. In other contexts the issue of the legitimacy of nonstate violence has been addressed by truth commissions and those working on transitional justice. For example, the South African Truth and Reconciliation Commission had to address issues of violence and human rights violations perpetrated by members of the African National Congress (ANC) that were committed during its struggle against apartheid (see, e.g., Villa-Vicencio and Verwoerd 2000).

6. A procedural definition or threshold condition for democracy typically includes a system in which the executive is elected, the legislature is elected, and there is a reasonable chance that the opposition can successfully challenge incumbents (see Przeworski et al. 2000).

7. This is not to say that the use of torture is in any way justified, but the findings of the truth commission show that the use of torture was widespread during the conflict, while the number of political killings and/or disappearances were estimated to be between 61,007 and 77,552 people (see Ball et al. 2003:7).

8. See International Country Risk Guide, http://www.icrgonline.com.

Conclusion

Understanding Violent Pluralism

ENRIQUE DESMOND ARIAS

In mid-2007 I traveled to a shantytown on the outskirts of Rio de Janeiro dominated by a *milícia*, a police-aligned vigilante group that typically imposes a localized authoritarian regime to prevent violations of neighborhood norms. Over the previous six months the growing *milícia* activities in Rio had attracted substantial press attention, as the groups waged a fight to drive drug gangs out of many shantytowns. After having spent a decade working in favelas dominated by drug traffickers, I was surprised by this community for several reasons, not the least of which was the local residents' association (AM). Whereas in most communities in which I had worked this building was usually quite small and humble, in this community it had the size of a football field and contained not just AM offices but a technical school, a large space for parties, and an extension campus of a university. The source of some of the money for all this was of course the local *milícia*, who instead of dealing drugs to support its operations taxed residents for the use of local services such as pirate cable television, gas, and water, and maintained robust contacts with the government through one of its leaders who also served as member of Rio's city council.

Several weeks later I visited a working-class *comuna* (group of contiguous neighborhoods) in the northeastern section of Medellín, Colombia. Here I spoke with a number of residents and observed a meeting of the neighborhood *presupuesto participativo*, an adaptation of the innovative Brazilian *orçamento participativo* (participatory budgeting) program. While scholars have widely viewed this effort as an important component in deepening democracy in Brazilian cities (Baiocchi 2005; Avritzer and Navarro 2002; Nylen 2002), in Medellín it constituted the site of tense conflict between demobilized paramilitaries who dominate official local representative groups and NGO workers and other activists from the community. The meetings were so tense that NGO leaders could not even attend many committee meetings. Where they could, there was a fear of violence. This was all part of a wider political effort by paramilitary groups around the city. Higher-level paramilitary leaders in Medellín are committed to using the new participatory budgeting program to more effectively deliver resources to their constituency.

For the past generation Latin America has had elective systems of rule in which the population chooses local, regional, and national leadership. These systems remain in place but, as the essays in this book have shown, violent organized nonstate groups drive much of the politics of the region. These two observations reflect the different ways in which armed groups operate in urban Latin America and their direct impact on political life. The spreading violence in the region represents not so much a failure of democratic institutions as, in many cases, the basis on which those institutions function. Similarly, as I will suggest in this conclusion, the phenomenon reflects not so much a deficit of citizenship rights as the proliferation of multiple sets of violent orders that impose different notions of political subjectivity on the population. These notions entail different sets of expectations for different parts of the population, which are often at odds but also sometimes in dialogue with the concept of democratic citizenship.

Democracy was expected to improve the conditions of human and civil rights in the region by taking power away from unelected officials and putting it into the hands of the people. The transition, however, did not go quite as expected and the new regimes, operating within states weakened by political choices made during the shift to democracy and by international financial pressures, did not hold onto the power to maintain order in national territory. On one level, police forces faced substantial tensions in the transition from authoritarian to more democratic security practices, with the leadership of these institutions often becoming torn between substantial segments that clung to systematically repressive tendencies and a minority with a more progressive orientation. To compound these problems underpaid police forces also often turned to corrupt practices to supplement meager wages. As a result, police forces fractured, in many countries leading to a complex environment that tolerated numerous abusive and corrupt practices while coexisting with some policing elements honestly attempting to enforce the law. More often than not the best and most effective police units have been reserved for portions of the national territory important to businesses and other better-off groups, leaving much of the population to their own devices. As violence increases, a range of citizens at times encourages more repressive policing by demanding so-called *mano dura* (iron fist) policies that can unleash substantial police repression on certain segments of the population. Indeed, as much as violence may appear repressive and authoritarian, there is clearly a "democratic" component to a substantial portion of state violence in the region. In response to the inevitable failings of *mano dura* and the overall fracturing of the police, nonstate armed groups have over time emerged to resolve disputes, maintain local order, and deliver "justice." These groups operate in legal and illegal markets and compete for social and political power. Their presence dramatically changes the nature of political practice and subjectivity in the region and puts it at variance with many of the assumptions of scholarship on democratic institutions. The anecdotes that begin this essay reflect similar processes in two very different cities, where armed groups operate within poor communities to achieve desired political outcomes. These observations illustrate in a small way the wider discussion in this book, which shows that diffuse and plural violence drives many political processes in Latin America. This conclusion will seek to summarize and synthesize the volume's essays by examining the impact of violence on politics in the region and discussing its importance for ongoing research.

What Are the Origins of Violent Pluralism?

Until now academic writing on democratization has suggested that conflict and disorder in Latin America stem from the failure of the state and the disorder that emerges from ineffective policing.[1] The essays in this book, however, suggest otherwise. In the introduction to this volume, Daniel Goldstein and I make clear that as a result of various social, economic, and political factors, power has diffused out of centralized political institutions into the hands of various segments of society. This does not mean that state institutions are not functioning; rather, there now exist new structures through which social and political actors deploy violence. This, of course, does not mean that violence is in some way new to the region; violence has long served as a political and social tool for different groups in Latin America. Instead, we suggest that violence is now practiced in some new ways, even as certain old practices continue or are revived from earlier periods. Understanding politics in the region necessitates understanding this new dynamic at least as well as we understand electoral behavior and political institutions. The misunderstanding of these challenges within the policymaking communities focused on Latin America is made quite clear in Lilian Bobea's essay, in which she examines the furor created in the Dominican Republic when *Foreign Policy* magazine labeled that country a failed state. Bobea notes that the editor of the journal, a respected observer of Latin American politics, tautologically suggests that the label "failed state" reflected places where governments "have lost the capacity to govern" (Bobea this volume). This, of course, ignited a substantial debate among Dominicans in which some argued that the country had had a regular rule of law and transfers of power for more than forty years.

Both of these sides miss the point. The violence affecting Latin America does not reflect state failure, nor does the existence of long-standing democratic institutions mean that there is no violence or that violence is not a serious national or regional problem. What this volume suggests is that systems of governance exist in Latin America today that tolerate the activities of multiple armed groups and high levels of crime. While this may involve certain particular institutional failures, it in no way reflects a broad failure of the state as discussed in *Foreign Policy*. Indeed, appearing unable to enforce a discreet rule of law may support the political projects of a number of state actors in Latin America. In these political regimes the government plays a substantially more limited role in enforcing order than is generally expected in the Western state system. The existence of violence in these countries does not mean that Latin America's states have failed, *nor* is ideal-type democracy the most cogent lens through which to understand regional politics. Rather, understanding politics in the region means understanding the multiple violent actors who persistently operate in many countries and how they affect political outcomes and lived social experience. The rule of law has not failed so much as multiple forms of order have developed, some more violent than others. Understanding why this has happened and in which direction it will take the region is essential for comprehending political life throughout the Western Hemisphere. More important, viewing politics through the limited lens of democratic institutions or the failure of the state reifies broader claims that the principal violent actor in Latin America is the central state and that, if institutions were improved, state power would be restored. The analyses in this volume, however, indicate that Latin American states have a much more symbiotic relationship with state and nonstate violent actors. State actors and armed groups accommodate one another and help each other accomplish their goals. Many both inside and outside the state have an interest in maintaining this situation, and further empowering the state may only serve to enhance already existing violence or to create new forms of conflict.

This book has further suggested that the problems facing Latin American states stem from a combination of wider structural factors and from the nature of the political pacts through which those systems were formed. Robert Gay cogently argues here that much of the issue facing Rio de Janeiro is the substantial problem of income inequality in that city, which causes large segments of the population to have difficulty accessing state services and which also forces many into the informal economy and into housing markets in which they depend on extraofficial social actors for protection (see also Harriott 2000). In her analysis of the trajectory of Mexican politics over the past century in the current volume, Diane Davis suggests that the economic dislocations and shifting trade patterns associated with the passage of NAFTA have contributed to insecurity and fear of violence in Mexico. Latin America has the highest levels of income inequality in the world, and in parts of the region these rates are growing. The pervasive conditions of inequality are likely a significant contributing factor to the problems of violence in the region as many individuals are formally excluded from state services and are forced to seek protection informally (Andreas 1999). Expanding trade with the United States and Europe and a declining presence of the state in the market have created conditions in which the poor seek economic security in the informal sector. This has led to an expansion of the drug and arms trades as well as the trade in human beings in the region. On the other hand, it has also alleviated the burden of trying to extend the law to all sectors of the population.

One important component of these broader structural trends is the growing cocaine trade that has benefited from more liberalized trade regulations and has contributed substantially to violence in much of the region. In light of this fact some may argue that the challenges described in this volume are historically specific and linked directly to the transitory influences of the cocaine economy. As in the Prohibition Era in the United States, these critics may argue, organized crime and violence have increased because of efforts to control the commodity. Some form of legalization may thus well resolve a substantial portion of the conflict in Latin America, as did the repeal of the Eighteenth Amendment in the United States. While we agree that the drug trade and its consequences are historically specific, so, too, is the current period of democratic governance. Indeed, as suggested in the previous paragraph and in the discussion of neoliberalism in the introduction to this volume, some of the same liberalizing forces that have supported the transition to democracy in the region have also supported the trade liberalization and the degree of informal social tolerance that have compounded drug sales over the past forty years. To take this argument further, the international prohibition on narcotics reflects a much broader and longer historical trend than prohibition in the United States, which lasted only thirteen years and was specific to the laws only of the United States, rather than reflecting a broader international consensus. Indeed, even if the prohibition of the cocaine trade is historically specific, it is unlikely to change in the foreseeable future, stems from some of the same factors that support elective governance, and could well outlast many of the current political regimes in the region.

But the argument made in the book goes well beyond this. While cocaine has clearly contributed to violence in the region, it is not its only source. The violence that exists in Colombia today long predates the commercialization of cocaine. Evidence from Jamaica shows that, up to the 1980s, much of the conflict facing that country emerged from political tensions. In the 1980s and 1990s the transshipment of cocaine contributed substantially to violence in Jamaica. Since then, though, cocaine has begun to bypass the island; still, conflict between gangs formerly associated with the drug trade, today involved in the informal security business, drives bloodshed. Even in Brazil, where spikes in violence in the southeast were closely tied to the expanding international drug trade in the 1980s, violence appears to have moved well beyond the regional trade and become part of a dynamic of political competition, the operation of death squads, local survival strategies, and neighborhood security efforts. Throughout the region much of the growing violence has also emerged from the ready availability of light combat weapons on domestic markets and the movements of people and goods across increasingly uncontrolled international borders. Those large-scale variables are then embedded in national and local conditions affected by transnational processes that include but are not limited to the cocaine trade. In the end, cocaine's impact on Latin America is likely to be more similar to that of opium in Asia, or of diamonds in West Africa, than that of liquor in the United States in that it constitutes a consistent fuel worsening conflicts but not the sole trigger that can be eliminated by the stroke of a presidential pen. Latin America will have to contend with the drug's impact on political, social, and economic life for a long time to come.

A second element of violent pluralism, as suggested in Todd Landman's essay, is the specific nature of the transition from authoritarian rule in Latin America. The pacted end of dictatorship emerged from a two-sided agreement. On the one hand, and much has been written about this, the left agreed not to bring the previous regimes' leadership to justice or to try to alter the national economic structure (O'Donnell and Schmitter 1986). These preconditions, with a special emphasis on the second, led to a neoliberal economic transition that accompanied the political transition in many countries but that only served to reinforce substantial economic inequalities at the very moment at which citizens were supposed to receive extensive guarantees of basic rights. Unfortunately, the poor and other marginalized groups usually did not have the resources to demand these rights through their representatives or the courts. These conditions of inequality contribute to what Teresa Caldeira and James Holston call "disjunctive democracy" (Caldeira and Holston 1999). The other side of this pact was the idea to shrink the state. By the 1980s the center and the left in much of Latin America had become upset with the systematic human rights abuses that characterized authoritarian regimes. At the same time, the center and the right, along with international financial institutions and other transnational advisors and lenders, wanted to shrink the state to minimize its role in the market and limit state spending and debt. The result of the transitions to democracy was not just an agreement to get the military out of politics and stop state human rights abuse in exchange for giving up efforts at wealth redistribution; it reflected the emergence of a political consensus about shrinking the state by reducing its ability to abuse citizen rights and by eliminating much of its capacity to lead the economy. The result has been freer markets and less spectacular state-based human rights abuses. On the other hand, the effective governance of much of Latin America has fallen by the wayside as states, with fewer resources, have restructured the way they manage some areas of territory and conceptualize their obligation in protecting individual rights. This is particularly striking in the case of Bolivia, where the government has diverted enormous resources to repressing drug growing even as the general citizenry had very different, and more pressing, public security concerns.

While in much of Latin America these pacts resulted from the ways in which dictatorships ended in the 1980s, broad regional patterns have led to similar outcomes throughout Latin America, even in cases where there was no transition to democracy or where the transition occurred in very different ways. Colombia, for example, has had democratic governance for over fifty years but suffers levels of violence much higher than most of its neighbors (Holmes, Guitirríez de Piñeres, and Curtin 2006:7–8; Sánchez and del Mar Palau 2006:2–3, 14–16; Moreno 2005:486–88). Jamaica experiences high levels of violence, but its democratization process coincided with decolonization rather than the end of a military dictatorship (Gunst 1998; Clarke 2006). Mexico recently democratized, but did so in a much more gradual way than did other countries in the region. Yet like many other countries, it continues to suffer from growing violence. All this suggests that the problems of violence are not just transitional and, in fact, form part of how contemporary politics functions in the Americas.[2] These differing patterns also indicate that countries can arrive at the current circumstances through a variety of routes (rather than through a simple linear trajectory toward "failure") and, as a close reading of these countries reveals, experience violence in different ways.

The concept of violent pluralism reflects this shifting organizational structure. States may formally guarantee rights but lack the organization, resources, or will to make those guarantees real. As a result, citizens must often secure those protections for themselves (see Goldstein 2004) or subject themselves to various forms of order created by armed actors. The essays by Mary Roldán, María Clemencia Ramírez, Bobea, and Gay reflect the ways in which multiple (armed) groups in the contemporary environment maintain autonomous forms of order by recreating law, politics, and political subjectivity at the local level. Davis's contribution emphasizes the ways in which changing relations within the state and an increasing reliance on private security have contributed to an altered public perception of the state and the notion of public good. Such a change restructures local-level political practice and provides a vision of political life at variance with standard institutional models.

Another result of these processes is the declining authority of the central state. While the government may possess titular sovereignty, many institutions, components of institutions, and actors within the state operate on their own as they work to secure resources for themselves and advance the agenda of their leaders. Of particular importance here are what Javier Auyero refers to as clandestine connections that informally link components of state and society in ways that transform the meaning of democratic rule. Thus we have police in Argentina allied with clientelist political leaders directing or allowing rioters to loot supermarkets (Auyero this volume). Alternatively, in Brazil and Colombia clandestine connections between drug traffickers and, in the latter case, paramilitaries, play an important role in determining localized political outcomes and forms of order (Arias 2006a:178–79).

These basic factors reflect complex new processes of building political order in Latin America, which intersect with democratic governance but which are at variance with basic assumptions about democratic rule. As Goldstein and I discuss in the introduction to this volume, most analyses of Latin America today reflect a focus on institutions and see violence as a failure of those institutions. Thus we get a breakdown of the rule of law and the emergence of low-intensity citizenship rather than a nuanced understanding of how order, political practice, and subjectivity have changed over the past generation in Central America, South America, Mexico, and the Caribbean. There may be elections and there may be competition for office, but political and social pluralism coexist with a pluralism of violence in which different groups maintain order over different levels of politics and society. Democracy and possible future instances of authoritarianism can only be understood in the wider context of the control of violence by private groups at the local and regional levels. Describing how this system works and its political effects are essential to understanding politics in Latin America. The writings in this book suggest several ways in which plural violence impacts political practice in the region.

The Operation of Violent Pluralism

At the most basic level, pervasive violence affects how people think of themselves within the wider political environment. While much of the academic debate about democracy focuses on how citizens operate within the wider political system, what rights they are guaranteed, and the extent to which they have access to those rights, the writings in this book suggest the importance of understanding localized systems of order and the extent to which individual rights are maintained within those systems. Bobea suggests the importance of *naciones* in the Dominican Republic in constituting localized identities and in promulgating laws in small communities. Gay discusses the role of drug traffickers in maintaining order in Rio's favelas and the growing role of vigilante groups in creating different types of order in some parts of that city. From a very different perspective, Roldán looks at the efforts of civic and political leaders in eastern Antioquia in working collectively to combat nonstate violence by building a new regional collective identity. Ruth Stanley shows that the perception of individual rights by police in Buenos Aires contributes to violence against the citizenry. These works reveal the important role that subnational and nonstate governance plays in shaping how people think about the political system and themselves as actors in it.

These processes, however, also have very practical effects. As group identities are constituted, new political forms of participation are created. In Rio, for example, drug gangs and religious affiliation (which, as Donna Goldstein has noted, is the critical factor that keeps some favela residents from involvement in violence) are central referents in choosing whom to vote for (Donna Goldstein 2003; Arias 2006a:78–80, 114–16, 159–60). In Buenos Aires clandestine clientele networks connect citizens to political actors and contribute to directing violence in that city. These same connections proved important in promoting the police inaction that facilitated looting and riots (Auyero this volume). Alternatively, as Stanley shows in the current volume, police treatment of the population has a substantial effect on broader perceptions of the political system. Critically, by focusing on police and state-police relations, Auyero and Stanley also show the extent to which even state violence has been pluralized. Understanding violence in the region means not seeing state violence as simply a failure of the state to order itself; rather, it is the active work of different coalitions with the state and its security agencies to use violence for particular ends. Violent pluralism, as these pieces show, resides not just in the relation between state and society but also in the internal relations of the state. The diffusion of violence into the hands of multiple actors thus concretely affects electoral and other politics in a variety of regions in Latin America. In Mexico, as Davis argues here, the broad scope of national fear regarding crime has impeded various efforts to control violence and, in fact, has become deeply aligned with growing partisan competition in rural areas (see also Villareal 2002). As a result, citizens have increasingly turned to private actors in a vain search for security.

The experience of plural violence also affects broader, national-level political ideologies. This is most notable in Colombia, where the concept of Democratic Security developed by the Uribe administration has played an important role in articulating an explicit relationship between the practice of nonstate violence and citizenship. In this formulation, as Ramírez observes in this volume, the position of the citizenry vis-à-vis different violent groups is critical to its position in the polity, with those who might see themselves as allied with the political goals of the left-wing guerilla factions cast as traitors and those who may see themselves as more allied with the interests of right-of-center paramilitary groups cast as defenders of the nation. The experience of Colombia, however, shows only one small part of the wider ways in which plural violence has affected political ideology in Latin America. As Susana Rotker accurately observes, fear of violence has become a pervasive component of life in Latin America and is critical in constituting the relationship between the government and the population (Rotker 2002a; also see Caldeira 2000). This growing fear, and the perception of the nation in the wider international sphere, clearly plays a role in the efforts of the Fernández government to deal with violence in the Dominican Republic, and in the state of civic life in Rio de Janeiro. In the end, as we observed in the introduction, what must emerge is a wider debate about what constitutes democracy and what kind of relationship exists between democracy and violence.

As the management of violence comes to more clearly drive regional and national political discourse, the shift in the control of violence away from the national state becomes apparent and governments move more to a position of managing multiple violent actors than of asserting comprehensive state control of violence in the national territory. The growing role of vigilante and paramilitary groups—often closely allied with the police, military, or private security firms—reflects the efforts of governments to manage nonstate violence, not with the reassertion of state power but through the deployment of multistranded relationships with violent nonstate actors (see Ramírez and Auyero this volume). This shift has critical repercussions both for the long-term stability of governments in Latin America and for the efforts of citizens to secure their rights. Residents of the region now increasingly look to nonstate actors (including themselves) rather than the state for protection. These new forms of protection, however, come with new ways of thinking about society and politics and reflect the ways in which a neoliberal logic of privatization and personal responsibility has been internalized by the population (Goldstein 2005).

The essays in this volume provide substantial evidence of the interaction between different scales of social and political life. For many years political scientists have worked under the Weberian assumption that the control of violence is allocated to national-level political institutions. As we have shown, however, the control of violence has shifted away from national-level actors as a result of both central political decisions and broader international pressures. As a result, the control of violence hovers within institutions that manage political life on different scales, with national governments and their component parts controlling official violence but with local-level security provision undertaken by very different actors. At the same time, transnational economic flows contribute to both national-level and local-level violent organizations, both by diffusing resources out of the state and by putting resources into the hands of local actors. Violent pluralism is characterized by new connections across different levels of politics and society. Scaler interactions contribute to the particular character of violent pluralism as it emerges in different countries.

Future Research Needs

The essays in this book emphasize a variety of areas that sorely need a stronger academic focus to deepen our understanding of political process in the region. This book also demonstrates the utility of interdisciplinary or cross-disciplinary theorizing and methodology for the study of violent democracies in Latin America. This section calls into focus a variety of places where cross-disciplinary study can provide essential insights into wider political and social processes in the region.

At the most basic level, understanding Latin America today involves developing a much more robust notion of the armed groups that operate there. Much contemporary political science scholarship on the region considers violence epiphenomenal to other processes. Political scientists and sociologists know a lot about elections and even occasionally about how violence affects elections (see Villareal 2002; Moreno 2005), but they know very little about the nature and internal workings of armed groups and the wider impact they have on the political system. Understanding nonstate violent groups in parts of the region not directly involved in civil wars—their structure, practices, ideology, and subjectivity—will allow a better comprehension of long-term trends. Political science and sociology need to develop analyses of the trajectories of these types of organizations, of the paths that they take from inception, and of the types of strategies and activities they impose on those living in the region. This volume has provided insights into these types of groups in the Dominican Republic, Colombia, and Brazil. The work of other scholars has provided some similar insights for Guatemala, Bolivia, and Jamaica, but much more analysis is needed in this area (Clarke 2006; Godoy 2005; Goldstein 2004; Gunst 1998).

The effort is important for two reasons. First, these groups operate within the political system, affecting electoral outcomes and providing public services that strengthen ties between them and much of the population. Indeed, in large parts of Latin America violent nonstate organizations play an important role in the citizenry's day-to-day life. Second, states invest a significant amount of resources in characterizing these groups in particular ways so as to justify policies, garner votes, and construct political relationships. Often these constructions are at odds with the relationships public officials actually maintain with these groups. Scholars need to understand these groups precisely to offer more complex and nuanced explanations of their workings. This work, however, cannot be done through the type of top-down analysis common in political science because this approach, in focusing its analysis so distinctly on the state, tends to see this data in an aggregated form as an effect of state failure rather than as a subtly varied independent phenomenon. As Guillermo O'Donnell has suggested, gathering and interpreting data on the phenomenon requires transdisciplinary skills discouraged in contemporary political science (O'Donnell 1999c:314–15, 333–34n). Without significant active scholarship in this area it will prove impossible to effectively respond to state characterizations of violent groups, comprehend the relationship of states to violent nonstate activity, and understand the role violent actors play in the political and social life of Latin Americans. As Goldstein and I write in the introduction, our project emerged from a collaboration between scholars from a number of disciplines, and it aims specifically to transcend divisions by bringing together the aggregate analyses common to political science and the more case-specific modes of study commonly seen in history and anthropology. I will discuss these contributions in more detail below.

Beyond analyzing particular groups, understanding violent pluralism also examines the relationships between state, civic, and violent nonstate actors, and ordinary citizens not directly engaged in violent activities. In the context of this volume this position has been developed most clearly by Auyero in showing how political contacts between police, politicians, and rioters in Argentina contributed to violence in that country. What Auyero's work, as well as that of Ramírez and Gay, points out is the importance of understanding the nature of occult contacts between legitimate political society and violent actors. This directly involves understanding how and by whom these contacts are mediated and what they are used for. At another level, however, it is important to look at how these contacts reconstitute both political institutions and political and social subjects. As Leigh Payne has pointed out, violent civic actors' long-term operation within the political system can undermine a democratic politics (Payne 2000). The work in this volume, however, goes well beyond this point. Contact between state actors and persistent violent actors compromises and changes state actors and their relation to the political system. As these types of contacts become more pervasive, the way in which people think about the political system and use its institutions can change substantially. Describing the ways in which these contacts alter the system marks the difference between democracy and violent pluralism.

This indicates the need for further research on the question of plural violence within the state. Much writing has focused on police impunity in Latin America and the ideologies and practices that give rise to it. In this volume the essays by Stanley, Gay, and Davis do an excellent job of addressing the question of police violence in Argentina, Brazil, and Mexico, respectively. Yet we need to know more about how different state actors engage in violence and why. Understanding more deeply the patterns of systemic violence within security forces and the relationships between violent state-security actors, legislators, politicians, and citizens is essential to understanding the broader processes of violence in Latin America. Why do certain patterns of violence emerge from different parts of the state? How do political leaders justify those patterns? How does violence construct the state and citizenship within it? How do contending social groups work to control state actions as a result of this violence? Finally, how do groups work to connect to the state to achieve political ends by controlling different elements of state violence?

Future research must also ask how plural violence affects the constitution of political subjects, a question central to contemporary anthropology. Work by Caldeira and by Daniel Goldstein has shown that the experience of violence and exclusion results in changing how Latin Americans think of themselves and others (Caldeira 2000:309–15, 339–45; Goldstein 2004). The experience of violence causes transformations of urban space and its inhabitants. Future studies need to examine this issue in more detail to understand how violence contributes to constituting political subjects in different parts of Latin America and, as the essays by Bobea, Roldán, and Ramírez do in this volume, how governments use notions of violence to reconstitute citizens and the relationship of political leaders to the country's residents. This constitutes a particular challenge for anthropologists whose field has developed effective and innovative ways of understanding political subjectivity but often does not connect nuanced analyses of subjectivity to aggregate political phenomena.

Another important question is how the diffusion of violence, and the implication of democratic practice in violence, affects political ideology and broader understandings of politics. While we know something about how the Colombian government has appropriated ideas relating security and democracy within a specific ideological framework into national discourse through the concept of Democratic Security (see Ramírez this volume), we know a great deal less about the very different and often implicit ways in which this happens in other places. Future studies need to develop understandings of how multiple forms of violence have affected Latin Americans' perceptions of state and society. The analysis of ideologies of violence has received little attention over the past generation in Latin America. Cross-disciplinary collaboration between political scientists, anthropologists, and sociologists could help make a major contribution to our understanding of this question in the coming years.

Finally, scholars need to develop more substantial analyses of the way in which plural violence affects polities in the aggregate. In the context of this volume we can see this most explicitly in the contributions by Davis and Landman. Future studies need to continue with some of these trends and move out of microlevel analyses of violence into examinations of how multiple sources of plural violence operate and affect the broader political system. This is particularly true for anthropology, where microlevel work is rarely used to comment on aggregate-level political phenomena. These studies need to look at the wider interactions of multiple violent groups and how they work together and compete with other elements of state and society. This involves, as Landman and Bobea have done in this volume, finding ways of categorizing different types of violent activities. It also involves building broader political and structural models of the conditions under which violent organizations evolve and of the likely impact they will have on the wider political system.

We must develop more systematic scholarship on violence in Latin America. To do so we have to move beyond understandings of contemporary Latin American democracy as somehow perfectible and appreciate the ways in which democracy in contemporary Latin America is, on some levels, built on violence. Scholars need to respond to the complex ways in which violence is embedded in existing Latin American political systems and becomes perpetuated by the successes of these regimes. Scholars need to develop better understandings of how institutions and actors contribute to both ongoing violence and the systems of order that exist in this violent context. For political scientists this means studying how armed actors participate in and influence elections and the complex relations between armed actors that dominate certain spaces and legitimate political authorities. For anthropologists and sociologists this means moving toward a critical analysis of how social relations build and perpetuate violence in the context of formally democratic social and political practices. For historians this means building effective narratives of the evolution of violence in different parts of the region and of the relationship between historic practices of violence and contemporary conflict. For scholars from a number of disciplines and practitioners working in NGOs and intergovernmental agencies this means moving beyond static and uncritical notions of citizenship that see simply a deficit of rights in the midst of uncontrolled violence, rather than the complex evolution of different systems of often authoritarian and abusive order that view social and political subjects quite removed from broader notions of citizenship.[3] By moving these questions and the broader question of the distribution of power in society to the center of scholarly analysis of Latin America, as the contributors to this volume have done, we will develop a robust and accurate picture of politics and society in this part of the world and see better what can be done to improve local conditions.

Iraq, Colombia, and Democratic Peace

This volume began with a discussion of the mistakes that some segments of the U.S. government and intellectual classes made in understanding the conflict in Iraq as an effort to build a peaceful democratic state.[4] For some time much of the academic establishment has viewed efforts to build democratic government as an essential component of building international peace and stopping war.[5] Much of the U.S. government's rhetoric surrounding the invasion of Iraq under George W. Bush was predicated on the notion that even violent efforts to establish democracy are justifiable because of the profoundly positive implications of electoral competition and open and popularly controlled institutions (Mansfield and Snyder 2005:1).

In the first half of 2007 it became increasingly clear that the U.S. position in Iraq had become deeply bound up in a differently violent vision of the future of that country. In early 2007 President Bush began to advocate a "surge" in U.S. forces to control Iraq's violence. Accompanying the increase in its troop strength, however, the United States began to support independent Sunni militias in their efforts to fight Shiite and Al-Qeada groups more antagonistic to the United States ("us Should Stop Arming Sunni Militias" 2002). The complex situation in Iraq is further compounded by a heavy reliance by coalition forces and the United States State Department on private military contractors for security and other services.

This support of militias and the use of private contractors in Iraq reflects an acknowledgment that U.S. interests are better served by abetting the strengthening of violent nonstate groups. In the current global political-economic environment, poor states, especially those dealing with serious ethnic and sectarian divisions, face often insurmountable difficulties in building central state power. In this context supporting violent nonstate groups whose interests may be congruent with one's own may seem the best short-term policy. The arming of Sunni militias may reflect a recognition by policymakers that conditions on the ground in Iraq simply do not lend themselves to the type of democracy envisioned in official U.S. rhetoric and in academic writing about democracy around the world. Technological, economic, and social conditions today lend themselves more easily to decentralized violence than to centralized state power. These are, in a sense, the type of conditions that also exist on the ground in Latin America. Even in the presence of democratic exchanges of power, nonstate actors will often control violence. Argentina, Brazil, Mexico, and Iraq are very different countries, but all experience problems with diffuse social and political violence.

The concept of violent pluralism and persistent low-level conflict bears heavily on U.S. policy and the academic debate concerning the democratic peace. If the regimes we have typically categorized as democracies really turn out to be something else, then this approach to policy is not terribly robust. If academics had been clearer about what the political regimes in Latin America actually are we might have had a more effective response to the Bush administration's claims about the effectiveness of democratizing Iraq. Indeed, if efforts to build democracy are equally successful in building functioning democracy and in simultaneously creating plural violence, then policy efforts in this direction will require some substantial rethinking since these efforts are likely to create conditions of future conflict. Only by developing a deeper understanding of violent pluralism and its differences from and interaction with democracy can we develop a stronger understanding of the effects of U.S. policy not just in Latin America but in many parts of the developing world. In the long run, understanding politics in Latin America depends on us recognizing the limitations of applying the concept of democracy to the region.

While the U.S. arming of militias in Iraq may make short-term sense for military policy, it is unlikely to have positive long-term results for the United States in the region or to create conditions in which social democracy will flourish. The strengthening of militias may very well deepen violence, normalize the activities of non-state violent actors in politics, and bring elements of state security services under the control of various social and political groups. The result could very well be a form of violent nonstate leadership specific to the social, political, and cultural conditions of the Middle East. While the U.S. government may argue that this is a democracy, life on the ground could reflect much more complex conditions.

Protecting Rights in a Plurally Violent Polity

Given the structural and technological conditions that support violent pluralism, there are no ready means available to more effectively protect the residents of Latin America against the predations of state and nonstate actors. Much of the literature on violence in Latin America is pessimistic for good reason. Violence is very much part of how politics in the region functions, and it is aided and abetted by international trends and local governments. In the context of the means available in the region, how can life conditions be improved for those who live there?

This conclusion contends that the only serious way to find an answer to Latin America's challenges in the area of public security is for scholars and policymakers to be honest with themselves about the complexity and depth of the problems in the region. O'Donnell is on the right path when he asks researchers to focus not on regime type but rather on the question of the rule of law (O'Donnell 2001). This means, on the one hand, investing heavily in analyses of how political institutions can be strengthened and restructured to, as Landman suggests in this volume, more effectively guarantee rights and the rule of law. The analysis of institutions, however, needs to evolve considerably. Political institutions do not exist in a vacuum. As Auyero so clearly shows here, they are complex entities deeply linked to both violent and nonviolent non-state actors. Understanding institutional reform requires us to look at these complex and competitive relationships. As state leaders try to assert order, criminal groups, uncivil movements, and paramilitaries will react and use their contacts with the state to try to shift reforms in ways that will benefit them. A reform of state institutions is critical to creating polities that more effectively protect those who live in their territory, but this reform process begins at a very different place than the one often suggested in the literature on violence in Latin America.[6] An effort to improve state institutions needs to begin from the notion that these institutions exist within a specific context and set of relations that often impede or undermine reform. Institutions in contemporary Latin American political systems are unlikely to simply become better and more effective over time because those institutions are a product of and depend on certain conditions of violence to succeed in their current political roles. Thus the police benefit from levels of disorganization because these provide them with operational freedom and the ability to take bribes; many political leaders benefit from current conditions because they are skilled at using patronage connections through violent groups to obtain votes; and some portions of the population will continue to tolerate these conditions because they fear other segments of the population or depend on the informal market for their livelihoods. Reform efforts must start here rather than beginning from the notion that violence is a result of failures in democratic institutions that can be improved with just the right policies that will enable Latin American political systems to more successfully echo the practices of political institutions in North America and Europe (see esp. Hinton 2006).

Landman's essay provides an important context through which to think about this challenge. In his conclusions he writes about the complex dynamics through which guarantees of rights emerge both by limiting and by empowering the state. Much of the last quarter century has been spent in efforts to publicly rein in the Latin American state. On the surface this meant that governments increasingly tolerated the existence of armed groups simply because they may not have had enough resources to deal with them. At a deeper level addressing these challenges meant creating conditions under which elements of the state in many parts of the region have actually empowered armed actors. Brazil is rife with stories of police and the military aiding in drug trafficking and participating in arms deals. In Mexico the privatization process in the 1990s was heavily corrupted in ways that empowered criminals and perverted but did not end the functioning of the state. As a result, the leadership of the drug-enforcement arm of the Mexican police arrested many drug dealers—just not so many from the cartel that was paying its commanding general. State power operates in collaboration with illegal groups not just to not enforce the law but also to enforce the law in ways that benefit those groups that can most successfully build ties to state institutions and its leadership. Indeed, as the famous Brazilian saying puts it: "For my friends everything, for everyone else the law."

Understanding how to protect the population means understanding the specific ways in which the state must be empowered to police itself and society but also to provide the necessary framework so that citizens can actively engage with state institutions to provide effective security and basic rights in their neighborhoods. More broadly, it also means working to build norms that do not tolerate social violence either as a means to survival or as a method of resolving conflicts.

However, reform efforts must go well beyond this. In this conclusion and in a variety of the essays, the contributors to this volume have emphasized the complex transnational and structural processes that have reconfigured the distribution of power in state and social institutions, creating conditions that build a type of order that both tolerates and depends on elevated levels of formal and informal state and social violence. An effective response to the experience of conflict in the region involves trying to build political relationships that attempt to minimize violence in the complex milieu of armed groups that has evolved in much of the region. This involves national and international political actors resolving to strengthen the Latin American state system by reconsidering the existing terms of trade, finding more effective and less violent ways to deal with drug trafficking, and limiting the small arms traffic in the region. This will require a very explicit rethinking of the relationship between Latin American governments, the United States, the European Union, and international financial organizations.

But this volume also suggests something further. Much of the debate on Latin America today focuses on the rule of law and its failure, on citizenship rights and the inability of citizens to actually receive support from the government. The problem, as so many of the essays here have demonstrated, is not that the rule of law has failed or that citizenship rights are not effectively extended to the population, but rather, because violence is now held plurally by both state and nonstate actors, that the rule of law and citizenship mean different things to different groups. Citizenship means one thing as laid out in the law, another as it is practiced in secure well-to-do neighborhoods, and yet another as it is practiced in poor neighborhoods dominated by armed groups. At the same time the practice of the law in the courts differs greatly from how the rule of law operates in a poor village caught in a land conflict or within areas controlled by guerilla groups in the Andean countryside. In many Latin American countries multiple forms of law and dispute resolution coexist at various levels of the political system. Similarly, citizenship is not the most meaningful concept for understanding political life in the region. Latin Americans live in spaces where there are different expectations of political participation and where they are subject to different forms of rights regimes, regimes that may vary according to the time of day or the week. The concepts of political subjectivity and the complex relationships of power reflected in this argument go well beyond the arguments outlined in the institutional analyses that dominate most political science analyses of the region. Only by understanding these variations, however, will we begin to understand how political life is lived in this part of the world today.

Politics in Latin American countries needs to be rethought to create more effective strategies for inclusion of the poor and other marginal groups. Indeed, political institutions play a critical role in the solution of a wide array of social problems. In this the editors do not disagree with the work of many institutionalist scholars. These links have to be built, however, with considerable thought to the role of the state in promoting violence and to the ways in which certain state institutions and operations empower violent actors and thus contribute to violent pluralism. In some parts of the region, for example, governments have developed innovative ways to extend resources and basic rights to larger segments of the population. Nonetheless, as I noted earlier, armed groups have sometimes appropriated resources associated with participatory budgeting, as, for example, in Medellín. Implementing such policies without a substantial reexamination in light of the observations in this volume will only contribute to the ability of armed actors to take control of inclusion efforts and to propagate violence. The question scholars, political leaders, and activists have to confront is how to properly orient the state in the links it builds with the population to support efforts to control violence rather than feed further into it by taking actions that consolidate the power of armed actors.

Landman's essay, in its discussion of different types of rights-protective regimes, provides a pathway for thinking about how to achieve this. In the context of the wealth inequality inherent in the political and economic systems of much of the region it is clear that simply securing basic political rights does relatively little to protect the civil rights of much of the populations. Indeed, as T. H. Marshall long ago observed, under conditions of poverty some degree of social protections may be necessary for the population to fully take advantage of its civil and political rights. Achieving the widespread protection of political rights involves finding ways to protect social and economic rights. The problem is that this often appears to be beyond the means of the state and that much of the violence affecting the region emerges specifically from groups trying to shore up their economic conditions and, as Elizabeth Leeds notes in her analysis of drug trafficking in Rio, to create a safety net in troubled times by working through the black market (Leeds 1996). Addressing the complex issue of social needs is essential to addressing wider questions of violence. Dealing with economic and social questions is one path through which multiple armed groups can be weakened. Doing this, though, means rethinking the role of the state in the region, the way the population relates to the state, and how states manage connections between particular localities and the transnational economy.

Another important insight in Landman's piece is the differentiation between the state's role in respecting rights and in protecting rights. Generally, we have relatively effective mechanisms today to force states to comply with international protocols and respect the rights of their citizens.[7] These same transnational mechanisms are not as effective at forcing states to actively protect the rights of citizens either against nonstate armed groups operating on their territory or against state officials acting outside of official orders. One critical undertaking in this regard is looking at how to promote state responsiveness to the broader question of rights protection. Achieving this type of behavior from states, however, goes well beyond the discourse of human rights and into the realm of effective governance. It means changing not just how the state acts but its capacity to act and the way it mediates its relations with the population. This type of shift requires a reconceptualization of the place of the state in Latin American life and, indeed, of its operations. These are not small institutional fixes but an extensive overhaul of states and the state system in the region.

The question of how to effectively deal with protecting rights links to another point in Landman's article: the contradictory tensions in taming state violence, on the one hand, and having an effective state that can control crime and not depend on armed actors for assistance, on the other. The question here is not one of controlling the state, but rather one of building it sufficiently while simultaneously creating controls around it that help effectively embed it in the social structure.

This set of concerns dovetails in a complex way with the question of popular support for *mano dura* policies noted in Stanley's essay. Violence, as we have discussed in this volume, is democratic, and much of the abuse that occurs in the region stems from popular tolerance for police violence and vigilantism. Particular ways in which the state is linked to the population promote violent outcomes on the part of the state. Efforts need to be taken at various levels, but especially in the realm of society, to change the discourse on state-controlled violence in the region. One strategy for doing this may be to promote engagement between multiple levels and segments of civil society to enable the emergence of dynamic new discourses about violence, and how state and society should interact as is made evident in Roldán's observations in eastern Antioquia. While *mano dura* policies will tend to fail for a variety of reasons, they will remain an opposing pole to more sophisticated efforts to control violence as long as they provide political benefit to certain elements of the state.

For state institutions to play a serious role in controlling violence in Latin America, state leaders and the mobilized public must address, but go well beyond, the question of police reform and the administration of criminal justice. As the contributors to this volume have shown, state engagement with society can only occur with the full awareness of the existence of systems of violent pluralism and of the way in which state actions can contribute to that plural violence. Conflict depends not just on the failures of the state. It also depends on active policy choices by some state officials and the structural and organizational factors beyond the state that support violent groups. For state actions to control violence state actors must empower groups in society that can effectively criticize state actions undermining democratic practice and contributing to the power of armed groups.

Thus, while inclusion is necessary to move forward, any efforts to address the challenges posed by violent pluralism must focus not just on extending links between the state and the citizenry but also on rethinking the nature of those links in the context of the way violence is controlled in the region. To achieve the types of basic rights that scholars hope to see and that many activists and politicians have vigorously worked toward for more than a generation, we need not just to extend rights but to change the types of relationships that exist between state and society.

Achieving this rethinking of politics involves promoting new types of engagement between various segments of the population and the state, understanding the role of international markets in promoting violence, and acknowledging the legitimate concerns of much of the population for real social inclusion and economic security. Until we begin to address these questions there will be no solution to the problems facing the region.

Notes

1. For a summary and discussion of this literature, see Arias and Goldstein, introduction to this volume.
2. For an argument that these problems are transitory, see Villareal 2002.
3. This does not mean that a variety of rights-abusing actors often actually use the language of rights and citizenship for their own ends.
4. For a further discussion of how Iraq has affected discussions of democratization among sectors in the United States, see Carothers 2002.
5. For an analysis and critique of this position, see Mansfield and Snyder 2005:12, 21–35.
6. For examples of this type of approach, see O'Donnell 2001; Dammert and Malone 2006.
7. On the role of the international system in promoting compliance with basic human rights, see Keck and Sikkink 1998.

REFERENCES

Abreu, Fabio. 2003. "Sujetos en riesgo: Un acercamiento al mundo de la juventud urbana marginada involucrada en problemas delictivos en Santo Domingo." *Entre el crimen y el castigo: Seguridad ciudadana y control democrático en América Latina y el Caribe*, ed. Lilian Bobea. Caracas: Nueva Sociedad. 345–68.

Adorno, Sérgio. 2002. "Exclusão socioeconômica e violência urbana." *Sociologias* 4 (8): 84–135.

Agamben, Giorgio. 2005. *State of Exception*. Trans. Kevin Attell. Chicago: University of Chicago Press.

Albro, Robert. 2006. "The Culture of Democracy and Bolivia's Indigenous Movements." *Critique of Anthropology* 26 (4): 387–410.

"Los alcaldes de la guerrilla." 1997. *Revista Semana* (Bogotá), 19 May, 26–31.

Alcantara, Hector. 1995. "Estudio criminologico de la Zona Oriental." Bachelor's thesis. Santo Domingo, Dominican Republic: Universidad Tecnologica de Santiago.

Alcantara, Manuel. 2005. "Politics and Society in Latin America at the Start of the New Millennium." *Social Forces* 83 (4): 1659–70.

Aleixo de Souza, Josinaldo. 2001. "Sociabilidades emergentes: Implicações da dominação de matadores na periferia e traficantes nas favelas." Master's diss. Universidade Federal do Rio de Janeiro.

Alsina, Griselda, and Andrea Catenazzi. 2002. *Diagnóstico preliminar ambiental de Moreno*. Buenos Aires: Universidad de General Sarmiento.

Alvito, Marcos. 2001. *As cores de acari: Uma favela carioca*. Rio de Janeiro: Getulio Vargas.

Amar, Paul E. 2003. "Reform in Rio: Reconsidering the Myths of Crime and Violence." *NACLA Report on the Americas* 37 (2): 37–42.

Amnesty International (AI). 2006. "Colombia: Reporting, Campaigning, and Serving without Fear: The Rights of Journalists, Election Candidates, and Elected Officials." 9 February, http://www.amnesty.org.

———. 2005. " 'They Come in Shooting': Policing Socially Excluded Communities." 2 December, http://www.amnesty.org.

———. 2003. "Honduras: No More Promises—Investigate Murders of Children and Youth." 25 February, http://www.amnesty.org.

Amorim, Carlos. 1993. *Comando vermelho: A história secreta do crime organizado.* Rio de Janeiro: Record.

Andreas, Peter. 1999. "When Policies Collide: Market Reform, Market Prohibition, and the Narcotization of the Mexican Economy." *The Illicit Global Economy and State Power*, ed. H. Richard Friman and Peter Andreas. Lanham, Md.: Rowman and Littlefield. 125–42.

———. 1998. "The Political Economy of Narco-Corruption in Mexico." *Current History* 618:160–70.

"Aplica la SPP plan de emergencia de control de 37 mil policía." 1999. *La Jornada* (Mexico City), 9 March.

Aranguren Molina, Mauricio. 2001. *Mi confesión: Carlos Castaño revela sus secretos.* Bogotá: Oveja Negra.

Arias, Enrique Desmond. 2006a. *Drugs and Democracy in Rio de Janeiro: Trafficking Social Networks and Public Security.* Chapel Hill: University of North Carolina Press.

———. 2006b. "The Dynamics of Criminal Governance: Networks and Social Order in Rio de Janeiro." *Journal of Latin American Studies* 38 (2): 293–325.

———. 2006c. "Trouble en Route: Drug Trafficking and Clientelism in Rio de Janeiro Shantytowns." *Qualitative Sociology* 29 (3): 427–45.

———. 2004. "Faith in Our Neighbors: Networks and Social Order in Three Brazilian Favelas." *Latin American Politics and Society* 46 (1): 1–38.

Arias, Enrique Desmond, and Corrine Davis Rodrigues. 2006. "The Myth of Personal Security: A Discursive Model of Local Level Legitimation in Rio's Favelas." *Latin American Politics and Society* 47 (4): 53–81.

Armony, Ariel, and Hector Schamis. 2005. "Babel in Democratization Studies." *Journal of Democracy* 16 (4): 113–28.

Armstrong, Gary. 1998. *Football Hooligans: Knowing the Score.* Oxford: Berg.

Aronskind, Ricardo. 2001. *¿Más cerca o más lejos del desarrollo? Tranformaciones económicas en los '90.* Buenos Aires: Centro Rojas.

Astorga, Luis. 2005. *El siglo de las drogas: El narcotráfico, del Porfiriato al nuevo milenio.* Mexico City: Plaza Janés.

———. 2000. "Organized Crime and the Organization of Crime." *Organized Crime and Democratic Governability: Mexico and the U.S.–Mexican Borderlands*, ed. John Bailey and Roy Godson. Pittsburgh: University of Pittsburgh Press. 58–82.

Auyero, Javier. 2007. *Routine Politics and Collective Violence in Argentina: The Gray Zone of State Power.* Cambridge: Cambridge University Press.

——. 2000. *Poor People's Politics: Peronist Survival Networks and the Legacy of Evita.* Durham, N.C.: Duke University Press.

Auyero, Javier, and Timothy Patrick Moran. 2004. "The Dynamics of Collective Violence: Dissecting Food Riots in Contemporary Argentina." Paper presented at the Janey Conference on Latin America, New School for Social Research, New York, 2 April.

Aveni, Adrian. 1977. "The Not-So-Lonely Crowd: Friendship Groups in Collective Behavior." *Sociometry* 40 (1): 96–99.

Avritzer, Leonardo, and Zanders Navarro, eds. 2002. *A inovação democrática no Brasil.* São Paulo: Cortez Editora.

Ayres, Robert L. 1998. *Crime and Violence as Development Issues in Latin America and the Caribbean.* Washington: World Bank.

Ayuntamiento del Distrito Nacional / United Nations Development Programme (UNDP). 2005. "Informe de diagnostico institucional y de la seguridad ciudadana en el distrito nacional." Santo Domingo: Ayuntamiento del Distrito Nacional / United Nations Development Programme.

Bailey, John. 2003. "Introduction: New Security Challenges in the South-North Dialog." Unpublished manuscript, Georgetown University.

Bailey, John, and Roy Godson, eds. 2000. *Organized Crime and Democratic Governability: Mexico and the U.S.–Mexican Borderlands.* Pittsburgh: University of Pittsburgh Press.

Baiocchi, Gianpaolo. 2005. *Militants and Citizens: The Politics of Participatory Democracy in Porto Alegre.* Stanford, Calif.: Stanford University Press.

Balán, Jorge. 2002. Introduction to *Citizens of Fear: Urban Violence in Latin America,* ed. Susana Rotker. New Brunswick: Rutgers University Press. 1–6.

Baldassare, Mark. 1994. *The Los Angeles Riots: Lessons for the Urban Future.* Boulder, Colo.: Westview.

Ball, Patrick, et al. 2003. "How Many Peruvians Have Died?" 28 August. American Association for the Advancement of Science (AAAS), http://shr.aaas.org.

Ball, Patrick, Louis Spirer, and Herbert F. Spirer, eds. 2000. *Making the Case: Investigating Large Scale Human Rights Violations Using Information Systems and Data Analysis.* Washington: American Association for the Advancement of Science.

Barbalet, J. M. 1988. *Citizenship: Rights, Struggle, and Class Inequality.* Minneapolis: University of Minnesota Press.

Baroni, Bruno. 2007. "Spatial Stratification of Street Vendors in Downtown Mexico City." Master's thesis, Massachusetts Institute of Technology.

"La batalla decisiva." 2000. *Revista Semana* (Bogota), 9 October, 56.

Bates, Robert H. 2001. *Prosperity and Violence: The Political Economy of Development.* New York: W. W. Norton.

Bendix, Reinhardt. 1978. *Kings or People? Power and the Mandate to Rule*. Berkeley: University of California Press.

———. 1964. *Nation-Building and Citizenship*. New York: J. Wiley.

Benitez Manaut, Raul. 2000. "Containing Armed Groups, Drug Trafficking, and Organized Crime in Mexico: The Role of the Military." *Organized Crime and Democratic Governability: Mexico and the U.S.–Mexican Borderlands*, ed. John Bailey and Roy Godson. Pittsburgh: University of Pittsburgh Press. 126–60.

Berger, Dina. 2006. *The Development of Mexico's Tourism Industry: Pyramids by Day, Martinis by Night*. New York: Palgrave Macmillan.

Bergesen, Albert, and Max Herman. 1998. "Immigration, Race, and Riot: The 1992 Los Angeles Uprising." *American Sociological Review* 63 (1): 39–54.

Bethell, Leslie, and Ian Roxborough, eds. 1993. *Latin America between the Second World War and the Cold War, 1944–1948*. Cambridge: Cambridge University Press.

Binder, Alberto. 2004. *Policías y ladrones: La inseguridad en cuestión*. Buenos Aires: Capital Intelectual.

Blat, José Carlos, and Sérgio Saraiva. 2000. *O caso da favela natal: Polícia contra o povo*. São Paulo: Editora Contexto.

Blau, Judith R., and Peter M. Blau. 1982. "The Cost of Inequality: Metropolitan Structure and Violent Crime." *American Sociological Review* 47 (1): 114–29.

Blau, Peter M. 1977. *Inequality and Heterogeneity: A Primitive Theory of Social Structure*. New York: Free Press.

Blau, Peter M., and Joseph E. Schwartz. 1984. *Crosscutting Social Circles*. Orlando: Academic.

Bliss, Katherine E. 2001. *Compromised Positions: Prostitution, Public Health, and Gender Politics in Revolutionary Mexico City*. University Park: Pennsylvania State University Press.

Blok, Anton. 2001. *Honor and Violence*. Cambridge: Polity.

Bobbio, Norberto. 1989. *Democracy and Dictatorship: The Nature and Limits of State Power*. Trans. Peter Kennealy. Cambridge: Polity.

Bodemaer, Klaus, Sabine Kurtenbach, and Klaus Meschkat. 2001. *Violencia y regulación en América Latina*. Caracas: Asociación Alemana de Investigación sobre América Latina–Adlaf.

Bohstedt, John. 1983. *Riots and Community Politics in England and Wales, 1790–1810*. Cambridge, Mass.: Harvard University Press.

Bonasso, Miguel. 2002. *El palacio y la calle*. Buenos Aires: Planeta.

Bonilla, María Elvira. 2000. "El general del Plan Colombia." *Revista de El Espectador*, 20 August, 14–22.

Bordenave, Serge, and Denise Davis. 2004. "Small Arms Demand and Violence in the Caribbean: Focus on Haiti." Paper presented at the "Regionalism, Regional Security, and Civil Society of the Greater Caribbean in the New Global Environment" seminar, Coordinadora Regional de Investigaciones Económicas y Sociales, Havana, 25–27 February.

Bourgois, Philippe. 2003. *In Search of Respect: Selling Crack in El Barrio*. Cambridge: Cambridge University Press.

——. 2001. "The Power of Violence in War and Peace." *Ethnography* 2 (1): 5–34.

Bouton, Cynthia. 1993. *The Flour War: Gender, Class, and Community in Late Ancien Régime French Society*. University Park: Pennsylvania State University Press.

Bowden, Mark. 2001. *Killing Pablo: The Hunt for the World's Greatest Outlaw*. London: Penguin.

Braithwaite, John, and Valerie Braithwaite. 1980. "The Effect of Income Inequality and Social Democracy on Homicide." *British Journal of Criminology* 20 (1): 45–53.

Brass, Paul R. 1997. *Theft of an Idol: Text and Context in the Representation of Violence*. Princeton, N.J.: Princeton University Press.

Braun, Herbert. 1980. *The Assassination of Gaitán: Public Life and Urban Violence in Colombia*. Madison: University of Wisconsin Press.

Brea de Cabral, Mayra, and Edylberto Cabral Ramirez. 2006. "Homicidios y Armas de Fuego en la Republica Dominicana." 6 May. *Revista Electronica Cientifica.com*, http://www.psicologiacientifica.com.

Brice, Arthur. 2009. "Drug Violence Spins Mexico Toward 'Civil War.'" 19 February. http://www.cnn.com/.

Brinks, Daniel. 2008. *The Judicial Response to Police Killings in Latin America: Inequality and the Rule of Law*. Cambridge: Cambridge University Press.

——. 2006. "The Rule of (Non)Law: Prosecuting Police Killings in Brazil and Argentina." *Informal Institutions and Democracy: Lessons from Latin America*, ed. Gretchen Helmke and Steven Levitsky. Baltimore, Md.: Johns Hopkins University Press. 201–26.

——. 2003. "Informal Institutions and the Rule of Law: The Judicial Response to State Killings in Buenos Aires and São Paulo in the 1990s." *Comparative Politics* 36 (1): 1–19.

——. 2002. "Informal Institutions and the Rule of Law: The Judicial Response to State Killings in Buenos Aires and São Paulo in the 1990s." Paper presented at the "Informal Institutions and Politics in the Developing World" conference, Harvard University, 6 December.

Brockett, Charles D. 2005. *Political Movements and Violence in Central America*. Cambridge: Cambridge University Press.

Brooks, David. 2004. "The Insurgency Buster." *New York Times*, 28 September.

Bryan, Anthony T. 2000. "Transnational Organized Crime: The Caribbean Context." October. Columbia International Affairs Online (CIAO), http://www.ciaonet.org.

Brysk, Alison, and Gershon Shafir, eds. 2007. *National Insecurity and Human Rights: Democracies Debate Counterterrorism*. Berkeley: University of California Press.

Bucheli, Marietta. 2006. *Curas, campesinos y laicos como gerentes del desarrollo: La construcción de un modelo de desarrollo emergente en Colombia*. San Gil, Columbia: EDISOCIAL.

Caldeira, Teresa. 2000. *City of Walls: Crime, Segregation, and Citizenship in São Paulo*. Berkeley: University of California Press.

Caldeira, Teresa, and James Holston. 1999. "Democracy and Violence in Brazil." *Comparative Studies in Society and History* 41 (4): 691–729.

Call, Charles T. 2003. "Democratization, War, and State-Building: Constructing the Rule of Law in El Salvador." *Journal of Latin American Studies* 35 (4): 827–62.

Camacho, Alvaro. 2003. "Narcotráfico y violencias en Colombia." Paper presented at the "Análisis histórico del narcotráfico en Colombia" conference, Museo Nacional, Bogotá, 30 October.

Camarasa, Jorge, with Patricia Veltri. 2002. *Días de furia: Historia oculta de la Argentina desde la caída de De la Rúa hasta la ascunción de Duhalde*. Buenos Aires: Sudamericana.

Campos, Niza. 2008. "Zonas exclusivas compiten con barrios en comercio de drogas." 7 November, *Diario Libre*. http://www.diariolibre.com.

Cano, Ignacio. 1998. *The Use of Lethal Force by Police in Rio de Janeiro*. Rio de Janeiro: ISER.

Caplan, Nathan. 1970. "The New Ghetto Man: A Review of Recent Empirical Studies." *Journal of Social Issues* 26 (1): 59–73.

Caplan, Nathan, and Jeffrey Paige. 1968. "Survey of Detroit and Newark Riot Participants." *Report of the National Advisor Commission on Civil Disorders*. New York: Bantam. 127–37.

CARICOM Regional Task Force. 2002. "Caribbean Community Report on Crime and Security." September.

Carothers, Thomas. 2002. "The End of the Transition Paradigm." *Journal of Democracy* 13 (1): 5–21.

Carpenter, Ted Galen. 2009. *Troubled Neighbor: Mexico's Drug Violence Poses a Threat to the United States*. 2 February, Cato Institute Policy Analysis Report 631, www.cato.org/.

Castillo, Hector. 1983. *Bandas: Violación de principios juridicos, consecuencias de las mismas, acciones para controlarlas*. Bachelor's thesis. Santo Domingo, Dominican Republic: Universidad Autonoma de Santo Domingo.

Ceballos, Ritam. 2004. " 'Las naciones': Violencia y juventud en la actualidad; Aportes para la reflexión." Paper presented at the Foro Juvenil Interbarrial (Santo Domingo), October 2003 and February 2004.

Centeno, Miguel Angel. 2002. *Blood and Debt: War and the Nation-State in Latin America*. University Park: Pennsylvania State University Press.

Centro de Estudios Legales y Sociales (CELS). 2008. *Derechos humanos en Argentina: Informe 2008*. Buenos Aires: Siglo XXI.

———. 1999. *Patti: Manual del buen torturador*. Buenos Aires: CELS.

Centro de Estudios Legales y Sociales (CELS) and Human Rights Watch (HRW). 1998. *La inseguridad policial: Violencia de las fuerzas de seguridad en la Argentina*. Buenos Aires: Eudeba.

Cerrutti, Marcela, and Alejandro Grimson. 2004. "Buenos Aires, neoliberalismo y después. Cambios socioeconómicos y respuestas populares." Princeton University, Center for Migration and Development, Working Paper 04–04d.

Chepusiuk, Ron. 2003. *The Bullet or the Bribe: Taking Down Colombia's Cali Drug Cartel*. Westport, Conn.: Praeger.

Chernick, Marc, and Michael Jimenez. 1990. "Popular Liberalism and Radical Democracy: The Development of the Colombian Left, 1974–1990." Working Paper No. 43, Columbia University / New York University Consortium.

Chevigny, Paul. 2003. "The Populism of Fear: Politics of Crime in the Americas." *Punishment and Society* 5 (1): 77–96.

Clapham, Andrew. 2005. *Human Rights Obligations of Non-State Actors*. Oxford: Oxford University Press.

Clarke, Colin. 2006. "Politics, Violence, and Drugs in Kingston, Jamaica," *Bulletin of Latin American Research* 25 (3): 420–40.

Collier, David, and Robert Adcock. 1999. "Democracy and Dichotomies: A Pragmatic Approach to Choices about Concepts." *Annual Review of Political Science* 2:537–65.

Collier, David, and Steven Levitsky. 1997. "Democracy with Adjectives: Conceptual Innovation in Comparative Research." *World Politics* 49 (3): 430–51.

Comisión Colombiana de Juristas. 2004. "En contravía de las recomendaciones internacionales: Seguridad democrática, derechos humanos y derecho humanitario en Colombia, agosto de 2002 a agosto de 2004." Bogotá: Embassies of Canada and Switzerland and the Consejería de Proyectos (CPS).

Comisión de Superación de La Violencia. 1992. *Pacificar la paz*. Bogotá: IEPRI, CINEP, Comisión Andina de Juristas, CECOIN.

Comisión Económica para América Latina (CEPAL). 2006. *Panorama social de América Latina*. Santiago: CEPAL.

———. 2005. *Anuario estadístico de América Latina y el Caribe*. http://www.eclac.cl (accessed 7 July 2006).

Comissão de Direitos Humanos da Organizaçao das Nações Unidas (ONU). 2001. *Relatório sobre a Tortura no Brasil*. ONU.

Concha-Eastman, Alberto. 2002. "Urban Violence in Latin America and the Caribbean: Dimensions, Explanations, Actions." *Citizens of Fear: Urban Violence in Latin America*, ed. Susana Rotker. New Brunswick, N.J.: Rutgers University Press. 37–54.

Consultoria para los Derechos Humanos y el Desplacamiento (CODHES). 2003. "La otra guerra: destierro y repoblamiento." 28 April. *Codhes Informa: Bolétin de la Consultoria para los Derechos Humanos y el Desplazamiento*, http://www .codhes.co.

Coordinadora contra la Represión Policial e Institucional (CORREPI). 2007. "Archivo de casos, 1983–2007." http://www.correpi.lahaine.org (accessed 24 March 2009).

Cornelio, Claudio. 2008. "Si faltas a otra reunión, te mato." 25 March. Sobre la Noticia, http://sobrelanoticia.wordpress.com.

Coronil, Fernando. 1997. *The Magical State: Nature, Money, and Modernity in Venezuela*. Chicago: University of Chicago Press.

Corporación Arco Iris. 2007. "Paramilitares y políticos." *Arcanos* 13 (March): 13.

Correa Sutil, Jorge. 1999. "Judicial Reforms in Latin America: Good News for the Underprivileged." *The (Un)Rule of Law and the Underprivileged in Latin America*, ed. Juan E. Méndez, Guillermo O'Donnell, and Paulo Sérgio Pinheiro. Notre Dame, Ind.: University of Notre Dame Press. 255–77.

Crandal, Russell. 2002. *Driven by Drugs: US Policy towards Colombia*. Boulder, Colo.: Lynne Rienner.

Cross, John. 1998. *Informal Politics: Street Vendors and the State in Mexico City*. Stanford, Calif.: Stanford University Press.

Dahl, Robert A. 1971. *Polyarchy: Participation and Opposition*. New Haven, Conn.: Yale University Press.

Dammert, Lucía, and Mary Fran T. Malone. 2006. "Does It Take a Village? Fear of Crime and Policing Strategies in Latin America." *Latin American Politics and Society* 48 (4): 27–51.

Danzger, M. H. 1975. "Validating Conflict Data." *American Sociological Review* 40:570–84.

Das, Veena, ed. 1990. *Mirrors of Violence: Communities, Riots, and Survivors in South Asia*. Oxford: Oxford University Press.

"DAS y convivir harán inteligencia conjunta." 1997. *El Tiempo* (Bogotá), 11 November.

Davenport, Christian, ed. 2000. *Paths to State Repression: Human Rights Violations and Contentious Politics*. Lanham, Md.: Rowman and Littlefield.

———. 1999. "Human Rights and the Democratic Proposition." *Journal of Conflict Resolution* 43 (1): 92–116.

Davenport, Christian, Hank Johnston, and Carol Mueller, eds. 2005. *Repression and Mobilization*. Minneapolis: University of Minnesota Press.

Dávila Ladrón de Guevara, Andrés. 1998. *El juego del poder: Historia, armas y votos*. Bogotá: Editorial Cerec and Uniandes.

Davis, Diane E. forthcoming. "Policing and Populism in the Cárdenas and Echeverría Administrations." *Men of the People: The Populist Presidencies of Lazaro Cárdenas and Luis Echeverria in Mexico*, ed. William Beezley. Tucson: University of Arizona Press.

———. 2009. "Who Polices the Police? The Challenges of Police Accountability in Newly Democratic Mexico." *Policing Developing Democracies*, ed. Mercedes S. Hinton and Timothy Newburn. London: Routledge. 188–212.

———. 2008. "Urban Violence, Quality of Life, and the Future of Latin American Cities: The Dismal Record So Far, and the Search for New Analytical Frameworks to Sustain a Bias towards Hope." *Approaches to Global Urban Poverty: Setting the Research Agenda*, ed. Allison Garland. Washington: Woodrow Wilson Center Press. 57–88.

———. 2006a. "Beyond the Quality of Democracy: Public Insecurity and the Collapse of Enlightenment Political Ideals in Contemporary Mexico." Paper presented at the Latin American Studies Association meeting, San Juan, Puerto Rico, 16–18 March.

———. 2006b. "Conflict, Cooperation, and Convergence: Globalization and the Politics of Downtown Development in Mexico City." *Research in Political Sociology* 15:143–78.

———. 2006c. "Undermining the Rule of Law: Democratization and the Dark Side of Police Reform in Mexico." *Latin American Politics and Society* 48 (1): 55–86.

———. 2004. *Discipline and Development: Middle Classes and Prosperity in East Asia and Latin America*. Cambridge: Cambridge University Press.

———. 1999. *Urban Leviathan: Mexico City in the Twentieth Century*. Philadelphia: Temple University Press.

———. 1998. "The Social Construction of Mexico City, 1930–1960." *Journal of Urban History* 24 (3): 364–413.

Davis, Diane E., and Arturo Alvarado. 1999. "Descent into Chaos? Liberalization, Public Insecurity, and Deteriorating Rule of Law in Mexico City." *Local Governance and Democracy* 99 (1): 95–197.

"Defienden calidad moral de jefes policiacos." 1999. *La Jornada* (Mexico City), 25 August.

"De frente, mar. . . ." 1999. *Revista Semana* (Bogotá), 20 September.

Delegación de la Comisión Europea para Colombia y Ecuador. 2004. "Presentación del II Laboratorio en el Oriente Antioqueño," Bogotá, 11 March.

Della Porta, Donatella. 1995. *Social Movements, Political Violence, and the State: A Comparative Analysis of Italy and Germany*. New York: Cambridge University Press.

Diamond, Larry. 2005a. "Lessons from Iraq." *Journal of Democracy* 16 (1): 9–23.

———. 2005b. *Squandered Victory: The American Occupation and the Bungled Effort to Bring Democracy to Iraq.* New York: Owl Books.

———. 1999a. *Developing Democracy: Toward Consolidation.* Baltimore: Johns Hopkins University Press.

———. 1999b. "Human Rights and the Democratic Proposition." *Journal of Conflict Resolution* 43 (1): 92–116.

———. 1996. "Is the Third Wave Over?" *Journal of Democracy* 7 (3): 20–37.

Diani, Mario, and Douglas McAdam, eds. 2003. *Social Movements and Networks: Relational Approaches to Collective Action.* New York: Oxford University Press.

Diaz, Juan Bolivar. 2005. "R.D. estado fallido o fallado?" 2 July. *Hoy Digital,* www.hoy.com.do.

Donnelly, Jack. 1999a. "Democracy, Development, and Human Rights." *Human Rights Quarterly* 21 (3): 608–32.

———. 1999b. "The Social Construction of International Human Rights." *Human Rights in Global Politics,* ed. Tim Dunn and Nicholas J. Wheeler. Cambridge: Cambridge University Press. 71–109.

Dowdney, Luke. 2008. "De aviãozinhos a soldados: O crescente envolvimento de crianças nas lutas de grupos armadas do tráfico de drogas no Rio de Janeiro." *Insegurança pública: Reflexões sobre a criminalidade e a violência urbana,* ed. Nilson Vieira Oliveira. São Paulo: Editora Nova Alexandria. 86–129.

———. 2003. *Children of the Drug Trade: A Case Study of Children in Organised Armed Violence in Rio de Janeiro.* Rio de Janeiro: 7Letras.

Doyle, Michael. 1986. "Liberalism and World Politics." *American Political Science Review* 80 (4): 1151–69.

DuBois, Lindsay. 2002. "The Looters Are Coming! The Looters Are Coming!: Moral Panic and the Argentine Crisis." Paper presented at the American Anthropological Association Annual Meeting, New Orleans, 20 November.

Earl, Jennifer, et al. 2004. "The Use of Newspaper Data in the Study of Collective Action." *Annual Review of Sociology* 30:65–80.

Earl, Jennifer, Sarah A. Soule, and John McCarthy. 2003. "Protest under Fire? Explaining the Policing of Protest." *American Journal of Sociology* 68:581–606.

Eley, Geoff. 2002. *Forging Democracy: The History of the Left in Europe, 1850–2000.* Oxford: Oxford University Press.

Elison, Graham, and Greg Martin. 2000. "Policing, Collective Action, and Social Movement Theory: The Case of the Northern Ireland Civil Rights Campaign." *British Journal of Sociology* 51 (4): 681–99.

Enders, W., and T. Sandler. 2006. *The Political Economy of Terrorism.* Cambridge: Cambridge University Press.

Equipo de Alternativa. 1997. "Convivir, embuchado de largo alcance." *Revista Alternativa* 8 (March 15–April 15).

Equipo de Reflexion, Investigacion y Comunicacion (ERIC), Instituto de Investigaciones Economicas y Sociales (IDIES), Instituto de Encuestas y Sondeos de Opinion (IDESO), Instituto Universitario de Opinion Publica (IUDOP), eds. 2004a. *Maras y pandillas en Centroamerica: Pandillas y capital social*. Vol. II. Managua: UCA, Publicaciones.

——. 2004b. *Maras y pandillas en Centroamerica: Politicas juveniles y rehabilitacion*. Vol III. Managua: UCA Publicaciones.

Escobar, Arturo, and Alvaro Pedrosa, eds. 1996. *Pacífico, desarrollo o diversidad? Estado, capital y movimientos sociales en el Pacífico colombiano*. Bogotá: Cerec.

Espinal, Flavio Dario. 2005. "El Embajador Espinal debate con Foreign Policy sobre condicion de 'estado fallido' a R.D." 8 September. *Clave Digital*, www.clavedigital.com.do.

Espinal, Rosário. 2006. *Democracia epiléptica en la sociedad del clic*. Santo Domingo, Dominican Republic: Editora Clave.

Estadísticas Policia Nacional. 2004. Santo Domingo, Dominican Republic.

"Estamos ganando." 2001. *Revista Semana* (Bogotá), 27 August, 30.

Evans, Michael, ed. 2002. *War in Colombia: Guerrillas, Drugs, and Human Rights in U.S. Colombia Policy, 1998–2002*. Washington: National Security Archive Electronic Briefing, 69, May 3.

Farah, Douglas. 1996. "Caribbean Key to U.S. Drug Trade: Islands Reemerging as Major Transit Zone for Cocaine, Heroin." *Washington Post*, 23 September.

FARC. 1998. "El poder local." *Revista Resistencia*, 17.

Farmer, Paul. 2003. *Pathologies of Power: Health, Human Rights, and the New War on the Poor*. Berkeley: University of California Press.

Feagin, Joe, and Harlan Hahn. 1973. *Ghetto Revolts: The Politics of Violence in American Cities*. New York: Macmillan.

Felson, Richard B. 2000. "The Normative Protection of Women from Violence." *Sociological Forum* 15 (1): 91–116.

Fichtl, Eric. 2004. "The Ambiguous Nature of 'Collaboration' in Colombia." 29 March. *Colombia Journal Online*, http://www.colombiajournal.org.

Foreign Policy. 2005. "The Failed State Index." July–August, http://www.asiaing.org.

Foweraker, Joe, and Todd Landman. 1999. "Individual Rights and Social Movements: A Comparative and Statistical Inquiry." *British Journal of Political Science* 29 (2): 291–322.

——. 1997. *Citizenship Rights and Social Movements: A Comparative and Statistical Analysis*. Oxford: Oxford University Press.

Foweraker, Joe, Todd Landman, and Neil Harvey. 2003. *Governing Latin America*. Cambridge: Polity Press.

Franzosi, Roberto. 1987. "The Press as a Source of Socio-historical Data: Issues in the Methodology of Data Collection from Newspapers." *Historical Methods* 20 (1): 5–16.

French, John. 1992. *The Brazilian Workers' ABC: Class Conflict and Alliances in Modern São Paolo*. Chapel Hill: University of North Carolina Press.

Friedman, Elisabeth Jay, and Kathryn Hochstetler. 2002. "Assessing the Third Transition in Latin American Democratization: Representational Regimes and Civil Society in Argentina and Brazil." *Comparative Politics* 35 (1): 21–42.

Frühling, Hugo, and Joseph S. Tulchin, with Heather A. Golding, eds. 2003. *Crime and Violence in Latin America: Citizen Security, Democracy, and the State*. Washington: Woodrow Wilson Center Press.

Fuentes, Claudio A. 2005. *Contesting the Iron Fist: Advocacy Networks and Police Violence in Democratic Argentina and Chile*. New York: Routledge.

Fundacion Institucionalidad y Justicia, Comisionado de Apoyo a la Reforma y Modernizacion de la Justicia, Oficina Nacional de Defensa Publica y Procuraduria General de la Republica. 2006. "Informe de resultados del primer censo nacional penitenciario." Santo Domingo, August.

Fundación Justicia y Transparencia and Estudios Sociales y de Mercado. 2004. "Encuesta de opinion sobre delincuencia y seguridad ciudadana en Republica Dominicana." Santo Domingo, Dominican Republic. September, www.justiciaytransparencia.org.

Fundación Mexicana para la Salud. 1997. *La violencia en la Ciudad de México: Análisis de la magnitud y su repercusión económica*. Mexico City: Fundación Mexicana para la Salud.

Gamarra, Eduardo. 2004. "Carlos Mesa's Challenges in Bolivia: Will He Succeed against Overwhelming Odds?" *LASA Forum* 35 (1): 4–5.

Gamson, William A. 1990 [1975]. *The Strategy of Social Protest*. Homewood, Ill.: Dorsey.

García Villegas, Mauricio. 2006. "Estado, derecho y crisis en Colombia." *Revista Estudios Políticos de the Universidad de Antioquia* 17:11–44.

García Villegas, Mauricio, and Rodrigo Uprimny. 2006. "El control judicial de los estados de excepción en Colombia." *¿Justicia para todos? Sistema judicial, derechos sociales y democracia en Colombia*, ed. Mauricio García Villegas, César A. Rodriguez Garavito, and Rodrigo Uprimny. Bogotá: Editorial Norma. 531–69.

Garro, Alejandro. 1998. "Access to Justice for the Poor in Latin America." *The (Un)Rule of Law and the Underprivileged in Latin America*, ed. Juan E. Méndez, Guillermo O'Donnell, and Paulo Sérgio Pinheiro. Notre Dame, Ind.: University of Notre Dame Press. 287–92.

Gay, Robert. 2005. *Lucia: Testimonies of a Brazilian Drug Dealer's Woman*. Philadelphia: Temple University Press.

Geffray, Christian. 2002. "Social, Economic, and Political Impacts of Drug Trafficking in the State of Rondônia, in the Brazilian Amazon." *Globalisation, Drugs, and Criminalisation*, ed. Christian Geffray, Guilhem Febre, and Michel Shiray. UNESCO / MOST. 33–47.

Gibney, M., and M. Dalton. 1996. "The Political Terror Scale." *Human Rights and Developing Countries*, ed. D. L. Cingranelli. Greenwich, Conn.: JAI Press. 73–84.

Girard, René. 1977. *Violence and the Sacred*. Trans. Patrick Gregory. Baltimore, Md.: Johns Hopkins University Press.

Gledhill, John. 2000. *Power and Its Disguises: Anthropological Perspectives on Politics*. Sterling, Va.: Pluto.

Godoy, Angelina Snodgrass. 2005. *Popular Injustice: Violence, Community, and Law in Latin America*. Stanford, Calif.: Stanford University Press.

——. 2002. "Lynchings and the Democratization of Terror in Postwar Guatemala: Implications for Human Rights." *Human Rights Quarterly* 24 (3): 640–61.

Goldberg, Jonathan. 2003. "Campaign Conscripts: How to Fill a Stadium with Argentina's Poor (and Other Ways to Win the Presidency)." *American Prospect*, online edition, April, http://www.prospect.org.

Goldstein, Daniel M. 2007. "Human Rights as Culprit, Human Rights as Victim: Rights and Security in the State of Exception." *The Practice of Human Rights: Tracking Law between the Global and the Local*, ed. Mark Goodale and Sally Engle Merry. Cambridge: Cambridge University Press. 49–77.

——. 2005. "Flexible Justice: Neoliberal Violence and 'Self-Help' Security in Bolivia." *Critique of Anthropology* 25 (4): 389–411.

——. 2004. *The Spectacular City: Violence and Performance in Urban Bolivia*. Durham, N.C.: Duke University Press.

——. 2003. "In Our Own Hands: Lynching, Justice and the Law in Bolivia." *American Ethnologist* 30 (1): 22–43.

Goldstein, Donna M. 2003. *Laughter Out of Place: Race, Class, Violence, and Sexuality in a Rio Shantytown*. Berkeley: University of California Press.

"Golpes de pecho." 1998. *Revista Semana* (Bogotá), 16 February, 30.

González, Fernán. 1999. "Colombia, una nación fragmentada." Bilbao: Bakeaz Working Paper, Centro de Documentación y Estudios para la Paz.

González, Fernando, et al. 1981. *Las pandillas juveniles: Un enfoque psicólogico*. Santo Domingo, Dominican Republic: Universidad Autonoma de Santo Domingo.

González Ruiz, Ernesto. 1998. *La política oficial de seguridad pública*. Mexico City: Ediciones Unión.

González Ruiz, Samuel, Ernesto López Portillo V., and José Arturo Yáñez. 1994. *Seguridad pública en México: Problemas, perspectivas, y propuestas*. Mexico City: Universidad Nacional Autónoma de México.

Grandin, Greg. 2004. *The Last Colonial Massacre. Latin America in the Cold War*. Chicago: University of Chicago Press.

Green, Linda. 1999. *Fear as a Way of Life: Maya Widows in Rural Guatemala*. New York: Columbia University Press.

Gregory, Joseph R. 1999. "Mexico: A Call to Fight Crime." *New York Times*, 27 February.

Grimson, Alejandro, et al. 2004. "La vida organizacional en zonas populares de Buenos Aires." Princeton University, Center for Migration and Development, Working Paper.

Grupo Oriente. 2004. Paper presented at the "III Encuentro por el Respeto de los Derechos Humanos y el DIH en el Oriente Antioqueño, en el Municipio de El Peñol" conference, 17 April.

Gunst, Laurie. 1996. *Born Fi' Dead: A Journey through the Jamaican Posse Underworld*. New York: Henry Holt.

Gurr, Ted R. 1986. "The Political Origins of State Violence and Terror: A Theoretical Analysis." *Government Violence and Repression: An Agenda for Research*, ed. Michael Stohl and George A. Lopez. Westport, Conn.: Greenwood. 45–72.

———. 1970. *Why Men Rebel*. Princeton, N.J.: Princeton University Press.

Gutierrez, Juan. 2004. "Humanization of Extremists." January. Beyond Intractability, http://www.beyondintractability.org/.

Gutmann, Matthew C. 2002. *The Romance of Democracy: Compliant Defiance in Contemporary Mexico*. Berkeley: University of California Press.

Hale, Charles R. 2002. "Does Multiculturalism Menace? Governance, Cultural Rights, and the Politics of Identity in Guatemala." *Journal of Latin American Studies* 34:485–524.

Harriott, Anthony. 2000. *Police and Crime Control in Jamaica: Problems of Reforming Ex-Colonial Constabularies*. Kingston: University of the West Indies Press.

Harris, David J., and Stephen Livingstone, eds. 1998. *The Inter-American System of Human Rights*. Oxford: Clarendon.

Hartlyn, J., and A. Valenzuela. 1994. "Democracy in Latin America since 1930." *Politics and Society*, vol. 6, pt. 2 of *The Cambridge History of Latin America*, Leslie Bethell. Cambridge: Cambridge University Press. 99–162.

Harvey, David. 2005. *A Brief History of Neoliberalism*. Oxford: Oxford University Press.

Hathaway, Oona A. 2002. "Do Human Rights Treaties Make a Difference?" *Yale Law Journal* 111 (8): 1870–2042.

Hibbs, Douglas A. 1973. *Mass Political Violence*. New York: John Wiley.

Higley, J., and Gunther, R., eds. 1992. *Elites and Democratic Consolidation in Latin America and Southern Europe*. Cambridge: Cambridge University Press.

Hinton, Mercedes. 2006. *The State on the Streets: Police and Politics in Argentina and Brazil*. Boulder, Colo.: Lynne Rienner.

———. 2005. "A Distant Reality: Democratic Policing in Argentina and Brazil." *Criminal Justice* 5 (1): 75–100.

Hirsch, Eric L. 1990. "Sacrifice for the Cause: Group Processes, Recruitment, and

Commitment in a Student Social Movement." *American Sociological Review* 55 (2): 243–54.

Holmes, Jennifer S., S. A. Guitirríez de Piñeres, and K. M. Curtin. 2006. "Drugs, Violence, and Development in Colombia: A Department Level Analysis." *Latin American Politics and Society* 48 (3): 157–84.

Holston, James. 1999. "Spaces of Insurgent Citizenship." *Cities and Citizenship*, ed. Holston. Durham, N.C.: Duke University Press. 155–76.

Honderich, T. 1973. "Democratic Violence." *Philosophy and Public Affairs* 2 (2): 190–214.

Hoy Digital. 2008. "DNCD ha despedido 5,000 por mala conducta." 24 July. http://www.hoy.com.do.

———. 2005. "Texto integro de la carta del embajador Flavio Dario Espinal." 8 September. www.clavedigital.com.do.

Huggins, Martha K. 1998. *Political Policing: The United States and Latin America.* Durham, N.C. Duke University Press.

———. 1991. "Vigilantism and the State: A Look South and North." *Vigilantism and the State in Modern Latin America: Essays on Extralegal Violence*, ed. Huggins. New York: Praeger. 1–18.

Huggins, Martha K., Mika Haritos-Fatouros, and Philip G. Zimbardo. 2002. *Violence Workers: Police Torturers and Murderers Reconstruct Brazilian Atrocities.* Berkeley: University of California Press.

Human Rights Watch (HRW). 2001. *The "Sixth Division": Military-Paramilitary Ties and U.S. Policy in Colombia.* Washington: Human Rights Watch.

———. 2000. *The Ties That Bind: Colombia and Military-Paramilitary Links.* Washington: Human Rights Watch.

———. 1997. *Police Brutality in Urban Brazil.* New York: Human Rights Watch.

———. 1994. *Final Justice: Police and Death Squad Homicides of Adolescents in Brazil.* New York: Human Rights Watch.

Huntington, Samuel. 1991. *The Third Wave: Democratization in the Late Twentieth Century.* Norman: University of Oklahoma Press.

Instituto de Pesquisa Econômica Aplicada (IPEA). 2006. *Condições de funcionamento e infra-estrutura das institui ções de longa permanência no Brasil.* Brasilia: Instituto de Pesquisa Econômica Aplicada.

Instituto Nacional de Estadísticas y Censos (INDEC-EPH). 2003. *Encuesta permanente de hogares.* Buenos Aires: INDEC.

International Crisis Group (ICG). 2005. "War and Drugs in Colombia." Washington: Latin American Report. January 27, 11:24.

"Iran OKS More Talks with U S about Iraqi Foreign Ministcı Says Tehran Ready for High-Level Meeting in 'Near Future.'" 2007. July 18. MSNBC online, http://www.msnbc.com.

Isla, Alejandro, and Daniel Miguez, eds. 2003. *Heridas urbanas. Violencia delictiva y transformaciones sociales en los noventa*. Buenos Aires: Editorial de las Ciencias.

Jahangir, Asma. 2003. "Report of the Special Rapporteur on Extrajudicial, Summary, or Arbitrary Executions." New York: United Nations Commission on Human Rights.

Jairo González, José. 1992. *El estigma de las repúblicas independientes 1955–1965*. Bogotá: CINEP.

Jaramillo, Ana Maria. N.d. "La fuerza de la razón sobre las armas: Resistencia civil no violenta y participación ciudadana en el Oriente Antioqueño, Colombia (2001–2004)." Report. Medellín: Corporación de Región.

Jelin, Elizabeth. 1996. "Citizenship Revisited: Solidarity, Responsibility, and Rights." *Constructing Democracy: Human Rights, Citizenship, and Society in Latin America*, ed. Elizabeth Jelin and Eric Hershberg. Boulder, Colo.: Westview. 101–19.

Jelin, Elizabeth, and Eric Hershberg. 1996. "Introduction: Human Rights and the Construction of Democracy." *Constructing Democracy: Human Rights, Citizenship, and Society in Latin America*, ed. Jelin and Hershberg. Boulder, Colo.: Westview.

Jimenez, Luis Emilio. 2006. "Posesion civil y tráfico de armas pequeñas y livianas en el Hemisferio Occidental." *Proyecto armas pequeñas y livinas: Una amenaza a la seguridad hemisférica*. San Juan, Costa Rica: FLACSO.

Kakar, Sudhir. 1996. *The Colors of Violence: Cultural Identities, Religion, and Conflict*. Chicago: University of Chicago Press.

Kaplan, Marcos. 1991. *El estado Latinoamericano y el narcotráfico*. Mexico City: Editorial.

Katz, Jack. 2002. "From How to Why: On Luminous Description and Causal Inference in Ethnography (Part II)." *Ethnography* 3 (1): 73–90.

———. 2001. "From How to Why: On Luminous Description and Causal Inference in Ethnography (Part I)." *Ethnography* 2 (4): 443–73.

Keane, John. 2004. *Violence and Democracy*. Cambridge: Cambridge University Press.

Keck, Margaret E., and Kathryn Sikkink. 1998. *Activists beyond Borders: Advocacy Networks in International Politics*. Ithaca, N.Y.: Cornell University Press.

Kirk, Robin. 2003. *More Terrible Than Death: Massacres, Drugs, and America's War in Colombia*. New York: Public Affairs.

Kirschke, Linda. 2000. "Informal Repression, Zero-Sum Politics, and Late Third Wave Transitions." *Journal of Modern African Studies* 38 (3): 383–403.

Klein, Axel, Marcus Day, and Anthony Harriot, eds. 2004. *Caribbean Drugs: From Criminalization to Harm Reduction*. New York: Zed Books.

Kline, Harvey F. 2003. "Colombia: Lawlessness, Drug Trafficking, and Carving Up the State." *State Failure and State Weakness in a Time of Terror*, ed. Robert I. Rotberg. Washington: Brookings Institution Press. 161–82.

———. 1990. "Colombia: The Struggle between Traditional 'Stability' and New Visions." *Latin American Politics and Development*, 3rd edition, ed. Howard J. Wiarda and Kline. Boulder, Colo.: Westview. 231–57.

Klipphan, Andres. 2004. *Asuntos internos: Las mafias policiales contadas desde dentro*. Buenos Aires: Aguilar.

Knight, Alan. 1986. *The Mexican Revolution*. 2 vols. Cambridge: Cambridge University Press.

Knight, Alan, and Will Pansters, eds. 2005. *Caciquismo in Twentieth-Century Mexico*. London: Institute for the Study of the Americas.

Kohl, Benjamin, and Linda Farthing. 2006. *Impasse in Bolivia: Neoliberal Hegemony and Popular Resistance*. London: Zed.

Koonings, Kees, and Dirk Kruijt, eds. 2007. *Fractured Cities: Social Exclusion, Urban Violence, and Contested Spaces in Latin America*. London: Zed.

———. 2004. *Armed Actors, Organised Violence, and State Failure in Latin America*. London: Zed.

Koopmans, Ruud, and Dieter Rucht. 2002. "Protest Event Analysis." *Methods of Social Movement Research*, ed. Bert Klandermans and Susan Staggenborg. Minneapolis: University of Minnesota Press. 231–59.

———. 1999. "Protest Event Analysis: Where to Now?" *Mobilization* 4 (2): 123–30.

Korzeniewicz, Roberto, and William Smith. 2000. "Poverty, Inequality, and Growth in Latin America: Searching for the High Road to Globalization." *Latin American Research Review* 35 (3): 7–54.

Krahn, H., T. Hartnagel, and J. Gartrell. 1986. "Income Inequality and Homicide Rates: Cross-National Data and Criminological Theories." *Criminology* 24 (2): 269–95.

Krug, E. G., L. Dahlberg, and J. A. Mercy, eds. 2002. *World Report on Violence and Health*. Geneva: World Health Organization.

"II Laboratorio de Paz—Resumen Proyecto."

Landman, Todd. 2007. "United Kingdom: The Continuity of Terror and Counter Terror." *National Insecurity and Human Rights: Democracies Debate Counterterrorism*, ed. Alison Brysk and Gershon Shafir. Berkeley: University of California Press. 75–91.

———. 2006a. "Development, Democracy, and Human Rights in Latin America, 1976–2000." *Human Rights and Capitalism: A Multidisciplinary Perspective on Globalisation*, ed. J. Dine and A. Fagan. Cheltenham: Edward Elgar. 330–57.

———. 2006b. "Holding the Line: Human Rights Defenders in the Age of Terror." *British Journal of Politics and International Relations* 8 (2): 123–47.

———. 2006c. *Studying Human Rights*. London: Routledge.

———. 2005. *Protecting Human Rights: A Comparative Study*. Washington: Georgetown University Press.

———. 2004. "Measuring Human Rights: Principle, Practice, and Policy." *Human Rights Quarterly* 26 (4): 906–31.

"Latin Kings: 'Nuestro objetivo es mantenernos unidos como hermanos.'" 2008. 21 January. Puyence, http://www.puyence.com.

Lear, John. 2001. *Workers, Neighbors, and Citizens: The Revolution in Mexico City.* Lincoln: University of Nebraska Press.

Leeds, Elizabeth. 1996. "Cocaine and Parallel Polities on the Brazilian Urban Periphery: Constraints on Local Level Democratization." *Latin American Research Review* 31 (3): 47–83.

Lembruger, Julita, Leonardo Musemeci, and Ignacio Cano. 2003. *Quem vigia os vigias? Um estudo sobre controle externo da polícia no Brasil.* Rio de Janeiro: Record.

"Leonel Fernández denuncia plan para intervenir a la Republica Dominicana. Rechazo por calificación de Estado Fallido." 2005. 14 July. *El Caribe,* www.elcaribecdn.com.

Levine, Felice, and Katherine Rosich. N.d. "Social Causes of Violence: Crafting a Science Agenda." American Sociological Association, http://www.asanet.org (accessed 30 January 2003).

Levitsky, Steven. 2003. *Transforming Labor-Based Parties in Latin America: Argentine Peronism in Comparative Perspective.* Cambridge: Cambridge University Press.

Levitsky, Steven, and Lucan Way. 2002. "The Rise of Competitive Authoritarianism." *Journal of Democracy* 13 (2): 51–65.

Levy, J. 2002. "War and Peace." *Handbook of International Relations,* ed. W. Carlsnaes, T. Risse, and B. Simmons. London: Sage. 350–68.

Lieberson, Stanley, and Arnold R. Silverman. 1965. "The Precipitants and Underlying Conditions of Race Riots." *American Sociological Review* 30:887–98.

"El llamado del Tío Sam." 2002. *Revista Cambio* (Bogotá), 18 November, 30.

Lofland, John. 1981. "Collective Behavior: The Elementary Forms." *Social Psychology: Sociological Perspectives,* ed. Morris Rosenberg and Ralph H. Turner. New York: Basic Books. 411–46.

López Maya, Margarita, ed. 1999. *Lucha popular, democracia, neoliberalismo: Protesta popular en América Latina en los años del ajuste.* Caracas: Nueva Sociedad.

López Montiel, Angel Gustavo. 2000. "The Military, Political Power, and Police Relations in Mexico City." *Latin American Perspectives* 27:79–94.

López Portillo Vargas, Ernesto. 2003. "La policía en Mexico: Función política y reforma." *Crimen transnacional y seguridad pública: Desafíos para México e Estado Unidos,* ed. John Bailey and Jorge Chabat. Mexico City: Plaza y Janes Editores. 187–216.

Lupsha, Peter A. 1996. "Transitional Organized Crime versus the Nation-State." *Transnational Organized Crime* 2 (1): 21–48.

MacFarquhar, Larissa. 2003. "The Strongman: Where Is Hindu-Nationalist Violence Leading?" *New Yorker*, 26 May.

"El Manifiesto de la Poderosa Nación de Reyes Latinos." N.d. Unpublished manuscript.

Mansfield, Edward D., and Jack Snyder. 2005. *Electing to Fight: Why Emerging Democracies Go to War*. Cambridge: MIT Press.

Manwaring, Max G. 2001. "U.S. Security Policy in the Western Hemisphere: Why Colombia, Why Now, and What Is to Be Done?" Carlisle: U.S. Army College, Strategic Studies Institute.

Manzetti, Luigi. 1993. *Institutions, Parties, and Coalitions in Argentine Politics*. Pittsburgh: University of Pittsburgh Press.

Marin, Wilder. 2004. "Antioquia sera un laboratorio de paz." 4 April. University of Antioquia, http://altair.udea.edu.co.

Markoff, John. 1996. *The Abolition of Feudalism: Peasants, Lords, and Legislators in the French Revolution*. University Park: Pennsylvania State University Press.

Marshall, T. H. 1964. *Class, Citizenship, and Social Development*. Garden City, N.Y.: Doubleday.

———. 1950. *Citizenship and Social Class and Other Essays*. Cambridge: Cambridge University Press.

McAdam, Douglas. 1988. *Freedom Summer*. New York: Oxford University Press.

———.1982. *Political Process and the Development of Black Insurgency, 1930–1970*. Chicago: University of Chicago Press.

McAdam, Douglas, and Dieter Ruch. 1993. "The Cross-National Diffusion of Movement Ideas." *Annals of the American Academy of Political and Social Science* 528:56–74.

McAdam, Douglas, Sidney Tarrow, and Charles Tilly. 2001. *Dynamics of Contention*. Cambridge, Mass: Cambridge University Press.

McClelland, J. S. 1996. *A History of Western Political Thought*. London: Routledge.

McIlwaine, Cathy, and Caroline O. N. Moser. 2007. "Living in Fear: How the Urban Poor Perceive Violence, Fear and Insecurity." *Fractured Cities: Social Exclusion, Urban Violence, and Contested Spaces in Latin America*, ed. Kees Koonings and Dirk Kruijt. London: Zed Books. 117–137.

McPhail, Clark. 1992. *Acting Together: The Organization of Crowds*. New York: Aldine de Gruyter.

———. 1991. *The Myth of the Madding Crowd*. New York: Aldine de Gruyter.

———. 1971. "Civil Disorder Participation: A Critical Examination of Recent Research." *American Sociological Review* 36:1058–73.

McPhail, Clark, and John McCarthy. 2005. "Protest Mobilization, Protest Repression, and Their Interaction." *Repression and Mobilization*, ed. Christian Davenport, Hank Johnston, and Carol Mueller. Minneapolis: University of Minnesota Press. 3–32.

McPhail, Clark, and Ronald Wohlstein. 1983. "Individual and Collective Behaviors within Gatherings, Demonstrations, and Riots." *Annual Review of Sociology* 9:579–600.

Meade, Teresa A. 1997. *"Civilizing" Rio: Reform and Resistance in a Brazilian City, 1889–1930*. University Park: Pennsylvania State University Press.

Medina Gallego, Carlos, and Mireya Téllez-Ardila. 1994. *La violencia parainstitucional, paramilitar y parapolicial*. Bogotá: Rodríguez Quito Editores.

Méndez, Juan E., Guillermo O'Donnell, and Paulo Sérgio Pinheiro, eds. 1999. *The (Un)Rule of Law and the Underprivileged in Latin America*. Notre Dame, Ind.: University of Notre Dame Press.

Merry, Sally. 1981. *Urban Danger: Life in a Neighborhood of Strangers*. Philadelphia: Temple University Press.

Mesquita Neto, Paulo. 1999. "Violência policial no Brasil: Abordagens teóricas e práticas de controle." *Cidadania, justiça e violência*, ed. Dulce Pandolfi et al. Rio de Janeiro: Getulio Vargas. 130–48.

Messing, Philip. 2008. "School's Gangs Scourge, Bloody Turf War Hits HS Campuses." *New York Post*, 14 January.

Messner, Steven F. 1989. "Economic Discrimination and Societal Homicide Rates: Further Evidence on the Cost of Inequality." *American Sociological Review* 54:597–611.

——. 1982. "Societal Development, Social Equality, and Homicide: A Cross-National Test of a Durkheimian Model." *Social Forces* 61 (1): 225–40.

"Mexico Says Drug Cartel Had Spy in President's Office." 2005. *New York Times*, 7 February.

Meyer, Carrie. 1998. "The Shifting Balance among States, Markets, and NGOs." Paper presented at the meeting of the Latin American Studies Association, Chicago, 24–26 September.

Miles-Doan, Rebecca. 1998. "Violence between Spouses and Intimates: Does Neighborhood Context Matter?" *Social Forces* 77 (2): 623–45.

Mingardi, Guaracy, and Sandra Goulart. 2002. "Drug Trafficking in an Urban Area: The Case of São Paulo." *Globalisation, Drugs, and Criminalisation*, ed. Christian Geffray, Guilhem Febre, and Michel Shiray. UNESCO / MOST. 65–84.

Misse, Michel. 1999. "Malandros, marginais e vagabundos: A acumulação social da Violência no Rio de Janeiro." PhD dissertation, Instituto Universitário de Pesquisas do Rio de Janeiro.

Moinat, Sheryl, et al. 1972. "Black Ghetto Residents as Rioters." *Journal of Social Issues* 28 (4): 45–62.

Molina, Ubaldo Guzman. 2004. "Mayoria de armas legales estan en manos de civiles." 29 August. *Hoy Digital*. http://www.hoy.com.do.

Monkkonen, Eric H. 2001. *Murder in New York City*. Berkeley: University of California Press.

Moore, Barrington. 1966. *Social Origins of Dictatorship and Democracy: Lord and Peasant in the Making of the Modern World*. Harmondsworth, UK: Penguin.

Moreno, Erika. 2005. "Whither the Colombian Two-Party System: An Assessment of Political Reforms and Their Limits." *Electoral Studies* 24 (3): 485–509.

Moser, Caroline O. N. 2004. "Urban Violence and Insecurity: An Introductory Roadmap." *Environment and Urbanization* 16 (2): 3–16.

Moser, Caroline O. N., and Cathy McIlwaine. 2004. *Encounters with Violence in Latin America: Urban Poor Perceptions from Colombia and Guatemala*. New York: Routledge.

Mueller, Carol. 1997. "International Press Coverage of Eastern German Protest Events." *American Sociological Review* 62:820–32.

Muggah, Robert. 2005. "Securing Haiti's Transition: Reviewing Human Insecurity and the Prospects for Disarmament, Demobilization, and Reintegration." Occasional Paper No. 14, Small Arms Survey, Graduate Institute of International Studies, Geneva.

Myers, Daniel. 1997. "Racial Rioting in the 1960s." *American Sociological Review* 62:94–112.

Myers, Daniel, and Beth Schaefer Caniglia. 2004. "All the Rioting That's Fit to Print: Selection Effects in National Newspaper Coverage of Civil Disorders, 1968–1969." *American Sociological Review* 69:519–43.

Nash, June. 2001. *Maya Visions: The Quest for Autonomy in an Age of Globalization*. New York: Routledge.

Neapolitan, Jerome L. 1997. "Homicides in Developing Nations: Results of Research Using a Large and Representative Sample." *International Journal of Offender Therapy and Comparative Criminology* 41(4): 358–74.

———. 1994. "Cross-National Variation in Homicides: The Case of Latin America." *International Criminal Justice Review* 4 (1): 4–22.

Nelson, Diane. 1999. *A Finger in the Wound: Body Politics in Quincentennial Guatemala*. Berkeley: University of California Press.

NEPAD and CLAVES. 2000. *Estudo global sobre o mercado ilegal de drogas no Rio de Janeiro (Relatório de Pesquisa)*. Rio de Janeiro: NEPAD/UERJ; CLAVES/FIOCRUZ.

Neufeld, María Rosa, and María Cristina Cravino. 2003. "Entre la hiperinflación y la devaluación: 'Saqueos' y ollas populares en la memoria y trama organizativa de los sectores populares del Gran Buenos Aires (1989–2001)." Unpublished manuscript, Universidad Nacional de General Sarmiento.

Neumayer, Eric. 2003. "Good Policy Can Lower Violent Crime: Evidence from a Cross-National Panel of Homicide Rates, 1980–1997." *Journal of Peace Research* 40 (6): 619–40.

Newlink Political. 2006a. "Baseline Survey for the Plan de Seguridad Democratica, 2006." March, http://www.newlinkpolitical.com.

———. 2006b. "Democratic Security Plan Mid-Term Evaluation." August, http://www.newlinkpolitical.com.

———. 2006c. "Encuesta interna a la policia nacional, Republica Dominicana." October, http://www.newlinkpolitical.com.

———. 2005a. "Plan de seguridad democratica para la República Dominicana." Unpublished Concept Paper. Miami and Santo Domingo, February.

———. 2005b. "Survey on Security Neighborhoods, National District." November, http://www.newlinkpolitical.com.

Nordstrom, Carolyn, and Antonius C. G. M. Robben, eds. 1995. *Fieldwork under Fire: Contemporary Studies of Violence and Survival*. Berkeley: University of California Press.

"El nuevo enemigo." 2004. *Revista Semana* (Bogotá), 23 May.

Nugent, David L. 1999. "Democracy, Modernity, and the Public Sphere: Latin American Perspectives on North American Models." Paper presented at the Visions and Voices Conference, University of Manchester, Manchester, 27–31 October.

Nylen, William R. 2002. "Testing the Empowerment Thesis: The Participatory Budget in Belo Horizonte and Betim, Brazil." *Comparative Politics* 34 (2): 127–46.

O'Donnell, Guillermo. 2004. "Why the Rule of Law Matters." *Journal of Democracy* 15 (4): 32–46.

———. 2002. "In Partial Defense of an Evanescent Paradigm." *Journal of Democracy* 13 (3): 6–12.

———. 2001. "Democracy, Law, and Comparative Politics." *Studies in Comparative International Development* 36 (1): 7–36.

———. 1999a. "And Why Should I Give a Shit? Notes on Sociability and Politics in Argentina and Brazil." *Counterpoints: Selected Essays on Authoritarianism and Democratization*. Notre Dame, Ind.: University of Notre Dame Press. 81–105.

———. 1999b. "Horizontal Accountability in New Democracies." *The Self-Restraining State: Power and Accountability in New Democracies*, ed. Andreas Schedler, Larry Diamond, and Marc F. Plattner. Boulder, Colo.: Lynne Rienner. 29–51.

———. 1999c. "Polyarchies and the (Un)Rule of Law in Latin America: A Partial Conclusion." *The (Un)Rule of Law and the Underprivileged in Latin America*, ed. Juan E. Méndez, Guillermo O'Donnell, and Paulo Sérgio Pinheiro. Notre Dame, Ind.: University of Notre Dame Press. 303–38.

———. 1996. "Illusions about Consolidation." *Journal of Democracy* 7 (2): 34–51.

———. 1994. "Delegative Democracy." *Journal of Democracy* 5 (1): 55–69.

———. 1993. "On the State, Democratization, and Some Conceptual Problems: A Latin American View with Glances at some Post-communist Countries." *World Development* 21 (8): 1355–69.

O'Donnell, Guillermo, J. Vargas Cullell, and O. M. Iazzetta, eds. 2004. *The Quality of Democracy: Theory and Aplications.* Notre Dame, Ind.: University of Notre Dame Press.

O'Donnell, Guillermo, and Phillipe Schmitter. 1986. *Transitions from Authoritarian Rule: Tentative Conclusions about Uncertain Democracies.* Baltimore, Md.: Johns Hopkins University Press.

Oliveira, A., and S. Tiscornia. 1998. "Estructura y práctica de las policías en la Argentina: Las redes de la illegalidad." *Control democrático en el mantenimiento de la seguridad interior,* ed. Hugo Frühling. Santiago de Chile: Centro de Estudios del Desarrollo. 157–74.

Olzak, S. 1989. "Analysis of Events in Studies of Collective Action." *Annual Review of Sociology* 15:119–41.

Ong, Aihwa. 1999. *Flexible Citizenship: The Cultural Logics of Transnationality.* Durham, N.C.: Duke University Press.

Ortega, Alicia. 2005. "Interview: Moisés Naim." 8 September. *Clave Digital,* www .clavedigital.com.do.

Oszlak, Oscar. 1981. "The Historical Formation of the State in Latin America: Some Theoretical and Methodological Guidelines for Its Study." *Latin American Research Review* 16 (2): 3–32.

Oxhorn, Philip D., and Graciela Ducatenzeiler, eds. 1998. *What Kind of Democracy? What Kind of Market? Latin America in the Age of Neoliberalism.* University Park: Pennsylvania State University Press.

"País en conmoción interior." 2002. *El Tiempo* (Bogotá), 12 August.

Palacios, Marco, and Frank Safford. 2001. *Colombia: Fragmented Land, Divided Society.* Oxford: Oxford University Press.

Paley, Julia. 2004. "Accountable Democracy: Citizens' Impact on Public Decision Making in Postdictatorship Chile." *American Ethnologist* 31 (4): 495–513.

———. 2002. "Toward an Anthropology of Democracy." *Annual Review of Anthropology* 31:469–96.

———. 2001. *Marketing Democracy: Power and Social Movements in Post-dictatorship Chile.* Berkeley: University of California Press.

Pan-American Health Organization (PAHO). 2003. *Statistics on Homicides, Suicides, Accidents, Injuries, and Attitudes towards Violence.* Washington: PAHO.

Pandolfi, Dulce. 1999. "Percepção dos direitos e participação social." *Cidadania, justiça e violência,* ed. Pandolfi et al. Rio de Janeiro: Getulio Vargas. 45–58.

Pantaleon, Doris. 2007. "Maltrato físico y verbal predominan en el hogar." 21 January. *Listín Diario,* http://www.listin.com.do.

" 'Paras'-bandas, alianza mortal." 1998. *El Tiempo* (Bogotá), 21 May.

Patterson, Orlando. 2007. "The Other Losing War." *New York Times,* 13 January.

Payne, Leigh. 2000. *Uncivil Movements: The Armed Right Wing and Democracy in Latin America.* Baltimore, Md.: Johns Hopkins University Press.

Pécaut, Daniel. 2001. *Guerra contra la sociedad.* Bogotá: Planeta Colombiana.

Pereira, Anthony W. 2005. *Political (In)Justice: Authoritarianism and the Rule of Law in Brazil, Chile, and Argentina.* Pittsburgh: University of Pittsburgh Press.

———. 2000. "An Ugly Democracy? State Violence and the Rule of Law in Postauthoritarian Brazil." *Democratic Brazil: Actors, Institutions, and Processes,* ed. Peter R. Kingstone and Timothy J. Powers. Pittsburgh: University of Pittsburgh Press. 217–35.

Pereira, Anthony W., and Diane E. Davis. 2000. "New Patterns of Militarized Violence and Coercion in the Americas." *Latin American Perspectives* 27 (2): 3–17.

Piccato, Pablo. 2004. "A Historical Perspective on Crime in Twentieth Century Mexico City." Paper presented at the Janey Conference on Security and Democracy in the Americas, New School for Social Research, Graduate Faculty, 2 April.

———. 2001. *City of Suspects: Crime in Mexico City, 1900–1931.* Durham, N.C.: Duke University Press.

Pimentel, Stanley A. 2000. "The Nexus of Organized Crime and Politics in Mexico." *Organized Crime and Democratic Governability: Mexico and the U.S.–Mexican Borderlands,* eds. John Bailey and Roy Godson. Pittsburgh: University of Pittsburgh Press. 33–57.

Piñeyro, José Luis. 2004. "Fuerzas Armadas y combate a las drogas en México: ayer y hoy." *Sociología* 19 (54): 157–81.

Pinheiro, Paulo Sérgio. 2000. "Democratic Governance, Violence, and the (Un)-Rule of Law." *Daedalus* 129 (2): 119–44.

———. 1999. "Torture and Conditions of Detention in Latin America." *The (Un)Rule of Law and the Underprivileged in Latin America,* ed. Juan E. Méndez, Guillermo O'Donnell, and Paulo Sérgio Pinheiro. Notre Dame, Ind.: University of Notre Dame Press. 1–18.

———. 1997. "Popular Responses to State Sponsored Violence in Brazil." *The New Politics of Inequality in Latin America: Rethinking Participation and Representation,* ed. Douglas A. Chalmers et al. Oxford: Oxford University Press. 261–80.

Pita, M. V. 2005. "Mundos morales divergentes: Los sentidos de la categoría de familiar en las demandas de justicia ante casos de violencia policial." *Derechos humanos, tribunales y policías en Argentina y Brasil: Estudios de antropología juridical,* ed. Sofia Tiscornia and M.V. Pita. Buenos Aires: Antropofagia. 205–35.

———. 2004. "Violencia policial y demandas de justicia: Acerca de las formas de intervención de los familiares de víctimas en el espacio público." *Burocracias y violencia: Estudios de antropología jurídica,* ed. Sofia Tiscornia. Buenos Aires: Antropofagia. 435–62.

Piven, Frances Fox, and Richard A. Cloward. 1979. *Poor People's Movements: Why They Succeed, How They Fail.* New York: Vintage.

Pizarro Leongómez, Eduardo. 2004. *Una democracia asediada: Balance y perspectivas del conflicto armado en Colombia*. Bogotá: Grupo Editorial Norma.

———. 1991. *Las FARC (1949–1966): De la autodefensa a la combinación de todas las formas de lucha, 1949–1966*. Bogotá: Tercer Mundo Editores and Instituto de Estudios Políticos y Relaciones Internacionales de la Universidad Nacional de Colombia.

Plattner, Marc. 2005. Introduction to *Journal of Democracy* 16 (1): 5–8.

Poe, Steven, and C. Ned Tate. 1994. "Repression of Human Rights to Personal Integrity in the 1980s: A Global Analysis." *American Political Science Review* 88 (4): 853–72.

Poe, Steven C., C. Ned Tate, and Linda Camp Keith. 1999. "Repression of the Human Right to Personal Integrity Revisited: A Global Cross-National Study Covering the Years 1976–1993." *International Studies Quarterly* 43 (2): 291–313.

Portes, Alexandro, and Kelley Hoffman. 2003. "Latin American Class Structures: Their Composition and Change during the Neoliberal Era." *Latin American Research Review* 38 (1): 41–82.

Posada-Carbó, Eduardo. 2004. "What Failed State? Colombia's Resilient Democracy." *Current Affairs* 103 (670): 68–73.

Postero, Nancy Grey. 2007. *Now We Are Citizens: Indigenous Politics in Postmulticultural Bolivia*. Stanford, Calif.: Stanford University Press.

———. 1999. "Bolivia's *Indígena* Citizen: Multiculturalism in a Neoliberal Age." Paper presented at the American Anthropological Association Annual Meeting, Chicago, 17–21 November.

Postero, Nancy Grey, and Leon Zamosc, eds. 2004. *The Struggle for Indigenous Rights in Latin America*. Eastbourne, UK: Sussex Academic Press.

Power, Timothy J., and J. Timmons Roberts. 2000. "A New Brazil? The Changing Sociodemographic Context of Brazilian Democracy." *Democratic Brazil: Actors, Institutions, and Processes*, ed. Peter R. Kingstone and Timothy J. Power. Pittsburgh: University of Pittsburgh Press. 236–62.

Presidencia de la República, Departamento Nacional de Planeación (DNP). 2003. *Hacia un estado comunitario: Primeros resultados del Plan Nacional de Desarrollo; Seguridad democrática*. Bogotá: División Nacional de Planeación.

———. 2002. *Bases del Plan Nacional de Desarrollo, 2002–2006: Hacia un estado comunitario*. Bogotá: División Nacional de Planeación.

"Presidente Leonel Fernández anuncia proceso de profesionalización FF.AA y policía." 2005. 28 June. Partido de la Liberación Dominicana, http://www.pld.org.do.

Procuración General de la Nación, Comisión Investigadora de Procedimientos Fraguados (PNG). 2003. "Relevamiento y sistematización de casos detectados ordenados por dependencia policial interviniente." 1 May. Ministerio Público Fiscal de Argentina.

Procuraduría General de la República, Ministerio Público. 2005. *Reporte estadístico de homicidios.* Santo Domingo, Dominican Republic, www.procuraduria .gov.do.

———. 2006. *Reporte estadístico de homicidios.* Santo Domingo, Dominican Republic, www.procuraduria.gov.do

Programa de las Naciones Unidas Para el Desarollo (PNUD). 2005. *Informe nacional de desarrollo humano, Republica Domincana.* Santo Domingo, Dominican Republic: Editorial Corripio.

Przeworski, Adam, et al. 2000. *Democracy and Development: Political Institutions and Well-Being in the World, 1950–1990.* Cambridge: Cambridge University Press.

———. 1996. "What Makes Democracies Endure." *Journal of Democracy* 7 (1): 39–55.

Puex, Nathalie. 2003. "Las formas de la violencia en tiempos de crisis: Una villa miseria del conurbano bonaerense." *Heridas urbanas: Violencia delictiva y transformaciones sociales en los noventa,* ed. Alejandro Isla and Daniel Miguez. Buenos Aires: Editorial de las Ciencias. 33–60.

Quarantelli, E. L., and Russell Dynes. 1977. "Response to Social Crisis and Disaster." *Annual Review of Sociology* 3:23–49.

———. 1970. "Property Norms and Looting: Their Patterns in Community Crises." *Phylon* 31 (2): 168–82.

"¿Quién manda aquí?" 2006. *Revista Semana* (Bogotá), 21 August. 48–50.

Radu, Michael. 2005. "The End of Bolivia? Foreign Policy Research Institute." E-Notes, 21 December, http://www.fpri.org/.

Rafecas, D. 2002. "Los procedimientos policiales fraguados y su difusión en los medios de prensa." Unpublished manuscript, Buenos Aires.

Ramírez, María Clemencia. 2001. *Entre el estado y la guerrilla: Identidad y ciudadanía en el movimiento de los campesinos cocaleros en el Putumayo.* Bogotá: Instituto Colombiano de Antropología e Historia-Colciencias.

Ramírez Tobón, William. 2005. "Autodefensas y poder local." *El poder paramilitar,* ed. Alfredo Rangel. Bogotá: Fundación Seguridad y Democracia. 137–204.

Rangel, Alfredo. 1998. *Colombia: Guerra en el fin de siglo.* Bogotá: Tercer Mundo Editores, Universidad de los Andes, Facultad de Ciencias Sociales.

Rapley, John. 2006. "The New Middle Ages." *Foreign Affairs* 85 (3): 95–103.

Rappaport, Joanne. 2005. *Intercultural Utopias, Public Intellectuals, Cultural Experimentation, and Ethnic Pluralism in Colombia.* Durham, N.C.: Duke University Press.

Ravelo, Carlos. 1968. Editorial. *Excelsior,* 31 October.

"Recetan a policía del DF: Proponen fusionar a preventivas y judiciales para garantiza la prevención e indagación del delito." 2003. *Reforma* (Mexico City), 18 January.

Rivera, Fernando Valencia. 2005. "IV Encuentro Regional por los Derechos Humanos y el DIH en el Oriente Antioqueño." 25 June.

Riveros Serrato, Hector. 2001. "Ni tanto que queme al santo." *Revista Semana* (Bogotá), 1 August, 917.

Rodley, N. 1999. "Torture and Conditions of Detention in Latin America." *The (Un)Rule of Law and the Underprivileged in Latin America*, ed. Juan E. Méndez, Guillermo O'Donnell, and Paulo Sérgio Pinheiro. Notre Dame, Ind.: University of Notre Dame Press. 25–41.

Rodríguez Beruff, Jorge, and Gerardo Cordero. 2005. "The Caribbean: The 'Third Border' and the War on Drugs." *Drugs and Democracy in Latin America: The Impact of U.S. Policy*, ed. Coletta A. Youngers and Eileen Rosin. Boulder, Colo.: Lynne Rienner. 303–37.

Roig-Franzia, Manuel. 2008. "Mexico's Police Chief is Killed in Brazen Attack by Gunmen." *Washington Post*, 9 May.

Roldán, Mary. 2002. *Blood and Fire: La Violencia in Antioquia, Colombia, 1946–1953*. Durham, N.C.: Duke University Press.

"Romería a la Machaca." 1999. *Revista Cambio* (Bogotá), 31 May.

Rose, Harold M. 1971. *The Black Ghetto: A Spatial Behavioral Perspective*. New York: McGraw-Hill.

Rosenfeld, Michael. 1997. "Celebration, Politics, Selective Looting, and Riots: A Micro Level Study of the Bulls Riot of 1992 in Chicago." *Social Problems* 44 (4): 483–502.

Rosnow, Ralph. 1988. "Rumor as Communication: A Contextualist Approach." *Journal of Communication* 38 (1): 12–28.

Ross, Daniel. 2004. *Violent Democracy*. Cambridge: Cambridge University Press.

Rother, Larry. 2003. "Argentine Moves against Police Corruption." *New York Times*, 16 November.

Rotker, Susana. 2002a. "Cities Written by Violence: An Introduction." *Citizens of Fear: Urban Violence in Latin America*, ed. Rotker. New Brunswick, N.J.: Rutgers University Press. 7–22.

——, ed. 2002b. *Citizens of Fear: Urban Violence in Latin America*. New Brunswick, N.J.: Rutgers University Press.

Rouquie, Alain. 1994. "The Military in Latin America since 1930." *Politics and Society*, vol. 6, pt. 2 of *The Cambridge History of Latin America*, Leslie Bethell. Cambridge: Cambridge University Press. 233–306.

Roy, Beth. 1994. *Some Trouble with Cows: Making Sense of Social Conflict*. Berkeley: California University Press.

Rubio, Mauricio. 2006. "Del narcosendero a la Pandilla: Violencia juvenil en la Republica Dominicana." Final Consulting Report, Inter-American Development Bank, February.

Rudé, George. 1964. *The Crowd in History*. New York: John Wiley.

Rueschemeyer, D., E. H. Stephens, and J. Stephens. 1992. *Capitalist Development and Democracy*. Cambridge: Polity.

Ruiz, Carlos. N.d. *Un pueblo en lucha: El Oriente Antioqueño; Historia del primer y segundo paro cívico regional y acuerdos firmados el 15 de octubre de 1982.* Unpublished pamphlet.

Rule, James. 1988. *Theories of Civil Violence.* Berkeley: University of California Press.

Rummel, R. J. 1997. *Power Kills: Democracy as a Method of Non-violence.* New Brunswick, N.J.: Transaction.

——. 1995. "Democracy, Power, Genocide, and Mass Murder." *Journal of Conflict Resolution* 39 (1): 3–26.

——. 1985. "Libertarian Propositions on Violence within and between Nations: A Test against Published Results." *Journal of Conflict Resolution* 29 (3): 419–55.

Russett, B., and J. O'Neal. 2001. *Triangulating Peace: Democracy, Interdependence, and International Organizations.* New York: W. W. Norton.

Rustow, Dankwart A. 1970. "Transitions to Democracy: Toward a Dynamic Model." *Comparative Politics* 2 (3): 337–63.

Sadler, Louis R. 2000. "The Historical Dynamics of Smuggling in the US–Mexican Border Region, 1550–1998: Reflections on Markets, Cultures, and Bureaucracies." *Organized Crime and Democratic Governability: Mexico and the U.S.–Mexican Borderlands*, eds. John Bailey and Roy Godson. Pittsburgh: University of Pittsburgh Press. 161–76.

Sain, Marcelo. 2004. *Política, policía y delito: La red bonaerense.* Buenos Aires: Capital Intelectual.

——. 2002. *Seguridad, democracia y reforma del sistema policial en la Argentina.* Buenos Aires: Fondo de Cultura Económica.

Salazar, Alonso. 2001. *La parábola de Pablo: Auge y caída de un gran capo del narcotráfico.* Bogotá: Editorial Planeta.

"Saldo fatal de menores." 2005. *El Caribe.* 20 November, http://www.elcaribecdn.com.

Salert, Barbara, and John Sprague. 1980. *The Dynamics of Riots.* Ann Arbor: Inter-University Consortium for Political and Social Research.

Sanabria, Harry. 2000. "Resistance and the Arts of Domination: Miners and the Bolivian State." *Latin American Perspectives* 27 (1): 56–81.

Sánchez, Fabio, and Maria del Mar Palau. 2006. "Conflict, Decentralization, and Local Governance in Colombia, 1974–1982." Working Paper, Centro Sobre Desarrollo Económico, Universidad de Los Andes (Bogotá).

Sánchez, Julio. 2005. "Paises que sufren por las balas perdidas." *Diario Horizonte*, 28 December, http://www.diariohorizonte.com.

Sanjuán, Ana María. 2002. "Democracy, Citizenship, and Violence in Venezuela." *Citizens of Fear: Urban Violence in Latin America*, ed. Susana Rotker. New Brunswick, N.J.: Rutgers University Press. 87–101.

Santacruz Giralt, María L., Alberto Concha-Eastman, and José Miguel Cruz. 2001. *Barrio adentro: La solidaridad violenta de las pandillas.* San Salvador: Instituto

Universitario de Opinión Pública, Universidad Centroamericana José Simeón Cañas.

Savenije, Wim, and Katharine Andrade-Eekhoff. 2003. *Conviviendo en la orilla: Violencia y exclusion social en el area metropolitana de San Salvador*. San Salvador: FLACSO.

Schedler, Andreas. 1998. "What Is Democratic Consolidation?" *Journal of Democracy* 9 (2): 91–107.

Scheper-Hughes, Nancy, and Philippe Bourgois. 2003. "Introduction: Making Sense of Violence." *Violence in War and Peace: An Anthology*, ed. Scheper-Hughes and Bourgois. London: Wiley-Blackwell. 1–32.

Schirmer, Jennifer. 1998. *The Guatemalan Military Project: A Violence Called Democracy*. Philadelphia: University of Pennsylvania Press.

Schmidt, Steffen W. 1974. "La Violencia Revisited: The Clientelist Bases of Political Violence in Colombia." *Journal of Latin American Studies* 6 (1): 97–111.

Secretariado Técnico de la Presidencia, Oficina Nacional de Estadísticas. *Censo de poblacion y vivienda 2002*, Vol. V. Santo Domingo, Dominican Republic. http://www.one.gob.do (accessed July 2007).

Serrano, Rosso José. 1999. *Jaque Mate: De como la policia le gano la partida a "El Ajedrecista" y a los carteles del narcotrafico*. Bogotá: Editorial Norma.

Serulnikov, Sergio. 1994. "When Looting Becomes a Right: Urban Poverty and Food Riots in Argentina." Latin American Perspectives (21) 3: 69–89.

Shaheed, Farida. 1990. "The Pathan-Muhajir Conflicts, 1985–86: A National Perspective." *Mirrors of Violence: Communities, Riots, and Survivors in South Asia*, ed. Veena Das. Delhi: Oxford University Press. 194–214.

Sives, Amanda. 2002. "Changing Patrons, from Politicians to Drug Don: Clientelism in Downtown Kingston, Jamaica." *Latin American Perspectives* 29 (5):66–89.

Skidmore, Thomas E. 1988. *The Politics of Military Rule in Brazil, 1964–1985*. New York: Oxford University Press.

Smith, Peter H. 2005. *Democracy in Latin America: Political Change in Comparative Perspective*. Oxford: Oxford University Press.

Smulovitz, Catalina. 2003. "Citizen Insecurity and Fear: Public and Private Responses in Argentina." *Crime and Violence in Latin America: Citizen Security, Democracy, and the State*, ed. Hugo Frühling and Joseph Tulchin. Washington: Woodrow Wilson Center Press. 125–51.

Snow, David, et al. 1998. "Disrupting the 'Quotidian': Reconceptualizing the Relationship between Breakdown and the Emergence of Collective Action." *Mobilization* 3 (1): 1–22.

Spilerman, Seymour. 1970. "The Causes of Racial Disturbance: A Comparison of Alternative Explanations." *American Sociological Review* 35:627–49.

Stanley, Ruth 2005. "Controlling the Police in Buenos Aires: A Case Study on

Horizontal and Social Accountability." *Bulletin of Latin American Research* 24 (1): 71–91.

Stark, Margaret Abudu, et al. 1974. "Some Empirical Patterns in a Riot Process." *American Sociological Review* 39:865–76.

Tarrow, Sidney. 2005. *The New Transnational Activism*. New York: Cambridge University Press.

———. 1998. *Power in Movement: Social Movements and Contentious Politics*. New York: Cambridge University Press.

Taylor, Julie. 1993. "The Outlaw State and the Lone Rangers." *Perilous States: Conversations on Culture, Politics, and Nation*, ed. George E. Marcus. Chicago: University of Chicago Press. 283–303.

Taylor, Lynne. 1996. "Food Riots Revisited." *Journal of Social History* 30 (2): 483–96.

Thompson, E. P. 1993. *Customs in Common*. New York: New Press.

Los Tiempos. 2006. "Vicepresidente: 'Nunca más Bolivia con indígenas al margen.' " 23 January. http://www.lostiempos.com.

Thoumi, Francisco. 2003. *Illegal Drugs, Economy, and Society in the Andes*. Washington: Woodrow Wilson Center Press.

Tierney, Kathleen. 1994. "Property Damage and Violence: A Collective Behavior Analysis." *The Los Angeles Riots: Lessons for the Urban Future*, ed. Mark Baldassare. Boulder, Colo.: Westview. 149–74.

Tilly, Charles. 2004. "Observations of Social Processes and Their Formal Representations." *Sociological Theory* 22 (4): 595–602.

———. 2003. *The Politics of Collective Violence*. Cambridge: Cambridge University Press.

———. 1986. *The Contentious French*. Cambridge, Mass.: Harvard University Press.

———. 1978. *From Mobilization to Revolution*. Reading, Mass.: Addison Wesley.

———. 1974. "Town and Country in Revolution." *Peasant Rebellion and Communist Revolution*, ed. John Wilson Lewis. Stanford, Calif.: Stanford University Press. 271–302.

Tilly, Charles, Louise Tilly, and Richard Tilly. 1975. *The Rebellious Century, 1830–1930*. Cambridge, Mass.: Harvard University Press.

Tiscornia, Sofia. 2008. *Activismo de los derechos humanos y burocracias estatales: El caso Walter Bulacio*. Buenos Aires: Editores del Puerto.

Torresi, Leonardo. 2005. "El coloso olvidado." 22 May. *Clarín Digital*, http://www.clarin.com.

Turner, Ralph, and Lewis Killian. 1987. *Collective Behavior*. Englewood Cliffs, N.J.: Prentice-Hall.

Ungar, Mark. 2002. *Elusive Reform: Democracy and the Rule of Law in Latin America*. Boulder, Colo.: Lynne Rienner.

United Nations Development Programme (UNDP). 2007. *Fighting Climate Change: Human Solidarity in a Divided World*. New York: Palgrave Macmillan.

———. 2005. *Democracy in Latin America: Towards a Citizens' Democracy*. Trans. Merril Stevenson et al. Buenos Aires: Auilar, Altea, Taurs, Alfaguara.

United Nations Office on Drugs and Crime. 2003. "Caribbean Drugs Trends 2000–2002." Bridgetown, Barbados, February.

United States Agency for International Development (USAID). 2006. *Latin America and the Caribbean: Selected Economic and Social Data, 2006*. Washington: Bureau for Latin America and the Caribbean.

United States State Department. 2001. "Fact Sheet on U.S. Policy toward the Andean Region." 17 May. http://www.ciponline.org/.

Universidad Autonoma de Santo Domingo. 2008. "Características de las bandas juveniles denominadas 'las naciones'; Estudio exploratorio." Mimeograph posted on *Sociologia Dominicana*, November, http://sociologiadominicana .blogspot.com.

Uprimny Yepes, Rodrigo, and Mauricio García Villegas. 2005. *El control judicial de los estados de excepción*. Bogotá: DeJusticia.

Uprimny Yepes, Rodrigo, and Alfredo Vargas Camacho. 1990. "La palabra y la sangre: Violencia, ilegalidad y guerra sucia en Colombia." *La irrupción del paraestado: Ensayos sobre la crisis colombiana*, ed. Germán Palacio. Bogotá: Instituto Latinoamericano de Servicios Legales Alternativos. 105–65.

Useem, Bert. 1998. "Breakdown Theories of Collective Action." *Annual Review of Sociology* 24:215–38.

———. 1985. "Disorganization and the New Mexico Prison Riot of 1980." *American Sociological Review* 50:677–88.

"US Should Stop Arming Sunni Militias: PM Maliki." 2002. 17 June. *Reuters*, www .reuters.com.

Van Cott, D. 2006. "Dispensing Justice at the Margins of Formality: The Informal Rule of Law in Latin America." *Informal Institutions and Democracy: Lessons from Latin America*, ed. Gretchen Helmke and Steven Levitsky. Baltimore, Md.: Johns Hopkins University Press. 249–73.

Vargas, Tahira. 2006. "Las bandas juveniles en la sociedad dominicana." *Clave Digital*, 22 August, http://www.clavedigital.com/.

"Los vecinos encubiertos." 2002. *El Tiempo* (Bogotá), 11 August.

Ventura, Zuenir. 1994. *Cidade partida*. São Paulo: Companhia das Letras.

Verdery, Katherine. 1996. *What Was Socialism, What Comes Next?* Princeton, N.J.: Princeton University Press.

Villamarín, Luis Alberto. 1996. *El cartel de las Farc*. Bogotá: Ediciones El Faraón.

Villareal, Andres. 2002. "Political Competition and Violence in Mexico: Hierarchical Social Control in Local Patronage Structures." *American Sociological Review* 67:477–98.

Villa-Vicencio, Charles, and Wilhelm Verwoerd, eds. 2000. *Looking Back, Reaching*

Forward: Reflections on the Truth and Reconciliation Commission of South Africa. Cape Town: University of Cape Town Press.

Volkov, Vadim. 2002. *Violent Entrepreneurs: The Use of Force in the Making of Russian Capitalism*. Ithaca, N.Y.: Cornell University Press.

Wacquant, Loïc. 2003. "Toward a Dictatorship of the Poor? Notes on the Penalization of Poverty in Brazil." *Punishment and Society* 5 (2): 197–205.

Waiselfisz, Julio Jacobo. 2008. *Mapa da Violência dos Municípios Brasileiros: 2008*. Brasília: Ministério de Justiça.

Wallace, Claire, and Rossalina Latcheva. 2006. "Economic Transformation outside the Law: Corruption, Trust in Public Institutions, and the Informal Economy in Transition Countries of Central and Eastern Europe." *Europe-Asia Studies* 58 (1): 81–102.

Wallman, Joel. 2000. "Common Sense about Violence: Why Research? Year 2000." Occasional Paper 8, Harry Frank Guggenheim Foundation.

Walton, John, and Charles Ragin. 1990. "Global and National Sources of Political Protest: Third World Responses to the Debt Crisis." *American Sociological Review* 55: 876–90.

Walton, John, and David Seddon. 1994. *Free Markets and Food Riots: The Politics of Global Adjustment*. Cambridge: Blackwell.

Walton, John, and Jon Shefner. 1994. "Latin America: Popular Protest and the State." *Free Markets and Food Riots: The Politics of Global Adjustment*, ed. John Walton and David Seddon. Cambridge: Blackwell. 97–134.

Ward, M., and K. Gleditsch. 1998. "Democratizing for Peace." *American Political Science Review* 92 (1): 51–61.

Warren, Kay B. 2002. "Voting against Indigenous Rights in Guatemala: Lessons from the 1999 Referendum." *Indigenous Movements, Self-Representation, and the State*, ed. Kay B. Warren and Jean E. Jackson. Austin: University of Texas Press. 149–80.

———. 2000. "Conclusion: Death Squads and Wider Complicities; Dilemmas for the Anthropology of Violence." *Death Squad: The Anthropology of State Terror*, ed. Jeffrey A. Sluka. Philadelphia: University of Pennsylvania Press. 226–47.

Weber, Max. 1991. "Politics as a Vocation." *From Max Weber: Essays in Sociology*, ed. Hans H. Gerth, C. Wright Mills, and Bryan S. Turner. London: Routledge.

Weir, Stuart. 2006. *Unequal Britain: Human Rights as a Route to Social Justice*. London: Politico's.

Whitaker, Bill. 2009. "Mexico Drug Cartel Violence Soaring." February 11. *CBS Evening News*, www.cbsnews.com.

Whitfield, Teresa. 2004. "Elections and Insurgents." *New York Times*, 2 October, http://www.nytimes.com.

Wilkinson, Steven. 2004. *Votes and Violence: Electoral Competition and Ethnic Riots in India*. Cambridge: Cambridge University Press.

Wilson, Richard Ashby, ed. 2005. *Human Rights in the "War on Terror."* Cambridge: Cambridge University Press.

Wilson, Scott. 2003. "Colombian Fighters' Drug Trade Is Detailed." *Washington Post*, 25 June.

Winn, Peter, ed. 2004. *Victims of the Chilean Miracle: Workers and Neoliberalism in the Pinochet Era, 1973–2002.* Durham, N.C.: Duke University Press.

Wohlenberg, Earnest H. 1982. "The 'Geography of Civility' Revisted: New York Blackout Looting, 1977." *Economic Geography* 58 (1):29–44.

Women's Association of Eastern Antioquia (AMOR). 2007. "I Will Never Be Silenced: Testimonies of Hope from Colombian Women." 29–30 July. American Friends Service Committee.

Women's Institute for Alternative Development. 2005. "A Human Security Concern: The Traffic, Use, and Misuse of Small Arms and Light Weapons in the Caribbean." Belmont, Trinidad and Tobago: Women's Institute for Alternative Development.

World Health Organization (WHO). 2002. *World Report on Violence and Health.* Geneva: World Health Organization.

Yashar, Deborah. 1999. "Democracy, Indigenous Movements, and the Postliberal Challenge in Latin America." *World Politics* 51 (1): 76–104.

Young, Gerardo, et al. 2002. "La trama política de los saqueos." 19 December. *Clarín Digital*, http://www.clarin.com/.

Youngers, Coletta, and Eileen Rosin, eds. 2005. *Drugs and Democracy in Latin America: The Impact of U.S. Policy.* Boulder, Colo.: Lynne Rienner.

Zakaria, F. 2003. *The Future of Freedom: Illiberal Democracy at Home and Abroad.* New York: W. W. Norton.

Zaluar, Alba. 2004. "Urban Violence and Drug Warfare in Brazil." *Armed Actors: Organised Violence and State Failure in Latin America*, ed. Kees Koonings and Dirk Kruijt. London: Zed. 139–54.

——. 1994. *Condomínio do diabo.* Rio de Janeiro: Revan.

Zanger, S. C. 2000. "A Global Analysis of the Effect of Regime Changes on Life Integrity Violations, 1977–1993." *Journal of Peace Research* 37 (2): 213–33.

Zapata Yepes, Rubén Darío. 2003. "Los campesinos del Oriente Antioqueño entre el miedo el encierro." *Prensa Rural*, 11 December, http://www.prensarural.org.

Zaverucha, Jorge. 1999. "Military Justice in the State of Pernambuco after the Brazilian Military Regime: An Authoritarian Legacy." *Latin American Research Review* 34 (2): 43–74.

——. 1994. *Rumor de sabres: Tutela militia ou controle civil.* São Paulo: Aica.

Zepeda Lecuona, Guillermo. 2004. *Crimen sin castigo: Procuración de justicia penal y ministerio público en México.* Mexico City: Fondo de Cultura Económica.

CONTRIBUTORS

ENRIQUE DESMOND ARIAS is an associate professor in the Department of Political Science at the John Jay College of Criminal Justice, CUNY, and in the Doctoral Program in Criminal Justice at the Graduate Center, CUNY. He is the author of *Drugs and Democracy in Rio de Janeiro: Trafficking, Social Networks, and Public Security* (2006).

JAVIER AUYERO is the Joe R. and Teresa Lozano Long Professor of Latin American Sociology at the University of Texas, Austin. He is the author of *Poor People's Politics: Peronist Networks and the Legacy of Evita* (2000); *Contentious Lives: Two Argentine Women, Two Protests, and the Quest for Recognition* (2003); *Routine Politics and Collective Violence in Argentina: The Gray Zone of State Power* (2007); and *Flammable: Environmental Suffering in an Argentine Shantytown* (2009). He is the current editor of *Qualitative Sociology*.

LILIAN BOBEA is a sociologist at the Latin American Social Science Faculty in Santa Domingo, Dominican Republic.

DIANE E. DAVIS is a professor of political sociology and the head of the International Development Group in the Department of Urban Studies and Planning at MIT.

ROBERT GAY is a professor of sociology and the director of the Toor Cummings Center for International Studies and the Liberal Arts at Connecticut College.

DANIEL M. GOLDSTEIN is an associate professor of anthropology and the director of the Center for Latin American Studies at Rutgers University, New Brunswick. He is the author of *The Spectacular City: Violence and Performance in Urban Bolivia* (2004).

TODD LANDMAN is a reader in the Department of Government and the director of the Centre for Democratic Governance at the University of Essex, United Kingdom. He has numerous publications in the areas of development, democracy, and human rights and has worked extensively on the politics of Latin America.

MARÍA CLEMENCIA RAMÍREZ is a research associate and the former director of the Colombian Institute of Anthropology and History in Bogotá.

MARY ROLDÁN is an associate professor of history at Cornell University. She is the author of *Blood and Fire: La Violencia in Antioquia, Colombia, 1946–1953* (2002).

RUTH STANLEY teaches in the Institute of Political Science at the Free University of Berlin.

INDEX

centralization: by Colombian government, 86; of decision making, 11; by Dominican *naciones*, 184; of Dominican National Police, 187; by Mexican government, 41, 43, 49; of political institutions, 39, 244

certification of collective action, 121–24

Chad, 106

Chávez, Hugo, 80, 129

Chiapas, Mexico, 24

children: in Brazil, 204, 218; as Dominican gang members (*naciones*), 185; as information source, 121; malnutrition in, 74; as soldiers, 66, 73; violence against, 72–73, 75, 138–40, 152, 174–77, 199n29, 218. *See also* youth

Chile, 26, 203, 229–30

church groups, 180. *See also* Catholic Church

citizenship: in Bolivia, 1–2; in Brazil, 219; criminals and, 181–83, 195; decentralized state and, 41; democracy and, 5, 12, 15, 19, 31, 51, 191–93; institutional protections for, 231–37; media role in, 150; mobilization of, 51–53, 60n12, 64–67, 70–71, 77–78; modification of, 3–4, 28–29, 34nn23–24, 35, 226, 261; Poverty and, 39, 137, 156; research on, 134, 136, 239; rule of law and, 37, 261; security concerns of, 36, 86, 97, 171–72, 174; sociology of, 229; state intrusion on, 40, 47–50; substantive citizenship, 25; violent pluralism and, 20, 23, 27, 30, 243–56; youth attitudes concerning, 173

civic engagement: in Argentina, 148, 240n1; in Brazil, 252; in Colombia, 65, 67–68, 71, 74, 77–80, 81n6, 82n22, 250; human rights and, 226–27; in Mexico, 58; 76; violent pluralism and, 254

civil disorder, 6–8, 12, 109, 237

civil rights: in Argentina, 148, 153, 155–56; in Brazil, 202–4; in Colombia, 80, 97–99; democratization and, 11, 64, 196, 243, 262; in Dominican Republic, 169, 190; institutional protections for, 229, 232–34; iron fist policies and, 22. *See also* human rights

civil society: in Argentina, 149–50; in Bolivia, 2, 33n1; in Brazil, 202; clandestine connections and, 131; in Colombia, 65, 67, 76, 79–80, 81n5, 97–100, 103, 105; democratization and, 17–18, 25, 28, 38–39; in Dominican Republic, 162, 164–67, 169, 180, 188, 191, 194–95; human rights and, 231, 235, 238; in Mexico, 38, 47, 49, 52, 55, 59; politics and, 43, 63, 254, 263; vigilantism and, 36; violent pluralism and, 2–5, 13–14, 20–25, 27, 30–31, 244, 249–52, 255–60, 263. *See also* citizenship; rule of law

civil war: absence in Dominican Republic of, 166; American Civil War, 234; in Colombia, 7, 67, 87; in El Salvador, 7; English Civil War, 234; in Latin America, 11, 38, 226; in Rio favelas, 206, 236, 237, 253

clandestine connections: in Argentina, 125–27; in Brazil, 206–7; democracy and, 128–29; horizontal and vertical ties in, 118; of legal and illegal political actors, 29; violence and, 56–57, 108–31, 249, 251

Clarín (newspaper), 114, 122, 127, 129

class: in Argentinian politics, 126, 248; in Bolivian politics, 1–2; in Brazil, 219; in Colombian politics, 65, 91, 242–43; in Dominican politics, 163, 167; drug trafficking and, 199n28, 242–43; economic inequality and, 13, 168; gang violence and, 184, 197n12, 199n20; Iraq war policies and, 257; in Mexican politics, 42, 46–47, 56; police targeting

cooperatives: agricultural, 65, 67, 72, 78

Coordinadora contra la Represión Policial e Institucional (CORREPI), 135–36, 149, 154–55, 159

Cordero, Gerardo, 163

Coronil, Fernando, 18

Corporación Nuevo Arco Iris, 107

corruption: in Bolivia, 1, 8; democracy and, 239; drug-related, 163–64, 196n2, 215–16, 223n49; Latin American increase in, 17; police corruption, 36–39, 42–54, 58, 60n12, 61n13, 123–24, 173, 189, 193, 202–3; political corruption, 66, 100, 104, 184–85, 194, 196n1, 219; prevention of, 166–67, 191; rates of, 44; violent pluralism and, 157. *See also* institutional corruption

Costa Rica, 26, 203, 237

Council on Hemispheric Affairs, 8

counterinsurgency, 86–87, 92, 93–96, 104, 106n11

Counterinsurgent Constitutional State, 18

counter-revolutionaries, 41–42

coup d'etat, 14, 18, 128–29, 166, 237, 240

crime and criminals, 215, 222; in Argentina, 122–24, 132n3, 134, 137, 139–42, 145–47, 149, 150, 156–58; arms traffic and, 210, 219; in Bolivia, 22; in Brazil, 202–3, 206–18; in Caribbean region, 162–65; citizen-criminal symbiosis and, 181–82; civil mobilization against, 37; clientelism and, 132n2; in Colombia, 63–64, 95; community resources and capabilities against, 180–81; control of, 20, 22, 25, 190–94, 225; democracy and, 10–11, 227, 238, 245, 251, 263; in Dominican Republic, 161–80, 187–95, 200n35; gang involvement in, 22, 49–50, 55, 175–80, 182–86, 224n60; human rights and, 20, 174, 239; inequality and, 172–74; in Iraq, 6, 9; in Latin

America, 7–8, 12, 17, 35–37; lynching of suspects, 2; media images of, 151, 216; in Mexico, 49–50, 52, 55–56, 62n16, 260; military and, 35, 42, 51; nonstate violence against, 230–31, 237; police involvement in, 35, 45, 51–52, 60n6, 62n21, 136–37, 143, 148–51, 157, 159n4, 208–9, 222n35, 225n62; poverty and, 150, 155–56, 172–74; prisons and, 202–3, 212–13; rates of, 201, 235–36; research on, 8, 11–12; state institutions vs., 162–63, 168–72, 197n12, 239, 259; street crime, 7, 161; victims' security and vulnerability and, 174; vigilantism and, 36; violent pluralism and, 3, 26–27, 30; youth and, 172–73. *See also* organized crime

Crónica (newspaper), 114, 126, 127

Cronica-Chubut (newspaper), 114

Cuba, 26–27, 164, 227, 232, 236

culture, 185; drugs and, 221, 136, 145, 154, 188; of repression, 177, 190–92, 238; of survival, 179; of violence, 175

customs, 45, 196

cybercrime, 170

da Silva, Luis Inácio ("Lula"), 214, 223, 225n69

Davis, Diane E., 28, 227, 230–31, 246, 249, 251, 254, 256

death penalty, 138, 152–53

death squads, 20–21, 209, 217, 222n28, 247

decentralization, 11, 41, 43, 67–68, 100, 167, 257

De La Rua, Fernando, 108

Delegacion de la Comision Europea, 66

D'Elia, Luis, 108, 130

delinquents, 123, 179–83. *See also* crime and criminals

democracy: in Colombia, 63–105, 257–58; disjunctive democracy, 3, 4, 167,

232, 248; in Dominican Republic, 165–66, 189–95; globalization and, 54–56; histories and discourses on, 13–19, 80, 187, 239; Iraq war and, 6–10; limits of, 10–13; Mexico and legacy of, 56–59; participatory democracy, 63–80; procedural democracy, 15, 226, 232, 236, 238, 241; state violence in Argentina and, 133–58; third wave of democratization, 6, 33; violence and, 128–29; violent pluralism and, 19–32, 233–40

Democracy in Latin America (UNDP Report), 11–12

democratic peace theory, 32, 234, 257–58

Democratic Republic of Congo, 106

Democratic Security Plans: Colombia, 81n3, 82n23, 87, 95–98, 104, 251, 255; Dominican Republic, 30, 162, 170, 188–94, 193n3

demonstrations, 148–49, 225. *See also* lootings; riots

deportation, 8, 184. *See also* immigration

development: in Caribbean region, 163, 168; clandestine connections and, 56; in Colombia, 65, 70–72, 76, 78, 81n6, 82n21, 86, 96, 102; democratic socialism and, 14; globalization and, 54–55; industrialization and, 40; in Latin America, 37–40; in Mexico, 42, 45, 50, 57–59, 60n8; polyarchy and, 12; rule of law and, 23; violence and, 28; violent pluralism and, 7, 9–11, 31, 258

Diamond, Larry Jay, 8–9, 23, 33

Diaz Ordaz, Gustavo, 42

dictatorship(s): in Argentina, 156, 159; in Bolivia, 2; in Brazilian favelas, 207; in Colombia, 63, 85, 91, 104, 105n1; in Dominican Republic, 168, 187; in Guatemala, 18; in Iraq, 6; in Latin America, 14, 201, 247–49; in Mexico, 42. *See also* authoritarianism

Dirección Federal de Seguridad, 61

dirty war, 85–88, 91, 104

disappearances, 36, 80, 91, 157, 222, 241n7

discourse: on cold war, 104; on democracy, 13–19; on human rights, 149–50; on iron fist, 174; on Mexican democracy, 59; nonviolence in Colombia and, 69; on security, 87, 94–96; on social movements, 76; on terrorism, 64; violence against women and, 252; violent pluralism and, 27, 252, 255, 262–63

displaced persons, 65, 67, 73–74, 76, 78

Disque-Denuncia phone line (Brazil), 212

dissident movements, 61, 110, 208

Distrito Federal. *See* Mexico City

Distrito Nacional. *See* Santo Domingo

domestic abuse, 3, 8, 17, 174, 178, 252–53

Dominican National Police, 166, 185, 187–88

Dominican Republic, 245, 250, 252–53, 255; and authoritarianism, 167, 177, 180, 187, 189; armed groups in, 183–87, 200n34; citizen-criminal symbiosis in, 181–83; community resources and capabilities in, 180–81, 197n11; culture of violence in, 174–80, 183–87, 200; democratic security initiatives, 189–94; deportation and, 184; drug-related crime in, 163, 179–80, 196n2, 196n4, 196nn6–7, 196n10, 199n28; economic conditions in, 166–69, 198nn15–16; failed state vs. challenged democracy, 165–66; family violence in, 174–80; organized crime and violence in, 161–62, 172–73, 194–95, 199n20, 199n22, 200n32; police presence in, 187–89, 191–94, 200nn36–37; poverty and violence in, 30, 161, 195, 199n18; prisons in, 190–91, 200n35; regional perspective on, 162–65; state weakness against organized crime, 169–72, 197n12, 245; uniformed violence in,

Dominican Republic (*continued*)
187–89, 197n8; victim security and vulnerability in, 161–62, 173, 199n27, 199n29. See also *naciones donos*, 214, 224n54

drugs and drug trafficking: addiction and, 149, 173; in Argentina, 122–23, 137; in Bolivia, 248; in Brazil, 30, 158n3, 202–3, 205–20, 221nn17–18, 223n44, 224n53, 242, 247, 250, 260; in Caribbean region, 162–65, 196n2, 197n10, 197n12, 247; cartels, 55–58; clandestine connections and, 113, 122–23, 249–50; clientelism and, 22; in Colombia, 63–64, 87, 89, 92–96, 102–5, 106n11; consumption of, 163, 179, 197, 199; culture and role of, 221; dealers and, 158, 174, 179, 181–82, 215, 260; in Dominican Republic, 161–62, 172–74, 177–80, 182, 189, 196n1, 196n4, 197n6, 199n20, 199n28; gang involvement in, 161–62, 178–84; guerrilla and paramilitary alliances and, 92–96, 102, 104; in Haiti, 197n5; in Latin America, 20–21, 197n10, 260–62; marketing and competition in, 162, 179, 206; in Mexico, 52, 55–58, 62n23; military involvement in, 49, 51, 197n8; organized crime and, 36; police involvement in, 51–52, 122–23, 137; production of, 94, 248; seizure of, 216; trade policies effect on, 17, 31, 246–47; violence and, 161–64, 178–79, 189, 210, 217, 223; violent pluralism and, 26, 250; war on drugs rhetoric, 1, 16, 92–94, 102, 198n14. See also specific drugs

dry submarine (torture practice), 159n12
DuBois, Lindsay, 126–27
Duhalde, Eduardo, 156
duopoly, 85–86

Ecclesial Base Communities, 65
Echandía, Camilo, 89

Economic Commission on Latin American and the Caribbean (ECLAC), 198
economic conditions: in Argentina, 118–19, 124, 129, 147, 155–56; in Brazil, 202–5, 220n9, 220nn11–12; in Colombia, 66–73, 77, 86, 93, 100, 104; democratization and, 3–4; in developing world, 8–9, 14; in Dominican Republic, 162–63, 166–69, 172, 175, 179, 183, 195, 196n1, 197n10, 197n12, 198n15; drugs and, 179–80, 246–47; inequality and, 16–17, 262; in Latin America, 35–40, 252; in Mexico, 42–46, 50, 54–59, 59n4, 62n21, 246; neoliberalism and, 14–16, 24, 248; politics and, 234, 246, 248, 257, 264; polyarchy and, 25; rioting and, 110–11; violence and, 228–34, 240n1; violent pluralism and, 1–2, 15, 17–19, 27–32, 244–45. See also development; globalization; industrialization

Ecuador, 2, 66, 186, 236
Ejército Liberación Nacional (ELN, National Liberation Army, Colombia), 65, 72, 74
Ejército Popular de Liberación (ELP, Popular Liberation Army, Colombia), 106
El Cruce (Argentina), 115, 119–22, 124–25
elections: in Argentina, 119, 148, 158; in Bolivia, 1–3, 8; in Brazil, 201–2, 207; clandestine connections and, 109–10; in Colombia, 63–68, 84–85, 100, 104, 132n2, 257; conditional authoritarianism and, 34n25; democracy defined by, 241n6; human rights and, 232–34; in Iraq, 6–7, 33n1, 257; in Latin America, 10–11, 18–20, 28, 32, 35–36, 243; in Mexico, 49–51, 56–57, 62n16; polyarchy paradigm and, 134; violence and, 237; violent pluralism and, 22, 245, 247, 250–51, 253, 256

Eley, Geoff, 15
elites: in Argentina, 29–30, 158; in Carib-

First National Guerrilla Conference, 88

focus groups, 161, 175, 177–78, 188

Força Nacional, 214

Foreign Policy Research Institute, 2

France, 234

fraud, 9, 66, 196

Freire, Paulo, 72

French Revolution, 234

frontier, 271. *See also* borders

Fuentes, Claudio, 148

Fuerzas Armdas Revolucionarias de Colombia (FARC), 65, 72–74, 86–96, 100–
101, 103, 106, 215. *See also* guerillas

Fund for Peace, 165

Fundo Nacional de Segurança Pública
(Brazil), 225n69

Gallego, Leonardo, 92

gangs: in Argentina, 137; arms trafficking
and, 219–20, 224nn59–60, 225n67; in
Brazil, 20, 22, 202, 206–8, 210–19,
222n31, 242, 250; in Caribbean region,
161–65; in Central America, 178; clientelism and, 22; community symbiosis
with, 180–83, 191–92, 221n25; in Dominican Republic, 171–84, 191–92,
194–95, 199n20; drug trafficking and,
202, 206–8, 210–11, 213–16, 224n53,
247, 250; financing systems of, 210–11,
215, 221n19, 223n49; in Honduras, 22;
in Jamaica, 20, 113, 247; in Mexico, 45,
49–50, 52, 55; military response to,
198n14; organized violence by, 172–74;
police and, 60n6, 137, 210–12; prisons
and, 213, 223n48, 224n51; religious affiliation and, 250; in Spain, 186; structure of, 183–87, 200; as substitute
families, 175–77; territorial domination by, 234, 242; terrorism and, 22;
transnational gangs, 8; in the United
States, 186, 195; violence among,
199n27, 214, 223n43, 230–31; violent

pluralism and, 26, 242; youth gangs,
172–73, 175–77, 179, 184, 199n22,
200n32, 219. *See also specific gangs*

García Liñera, Alvaro, 1–2

García Villegas, Mauricio, 84, 91

Garotinho, Anthony, 215

Garré, Nilda, 148

Gas War, 2, 16

Gay, Robert J., 30, 201, 246, 249, 250, 254

gays and lesbians, 64

gendarmería, 156, 160. *See also* police

gender, 168

geography, 72–75, 85–91

Girard, René, 21

girls: violence against, 175. *See also*
women

globalization, 15–16, 37–38, 54–58, 162,
166, 218, 257

Goico Guerrero, Pedro (Pepe) Julia, 196

Goldstein, Daniel, 22, 63, 87, 91, 97–98,
110–11, 152, 221, 233, 244, 249–50, 255

Goldstein, Donna, 113, 250

Gómez, Dario, 197

Gomez, Mónica, 119, 145, 197

government and governance: in Argentina, 123, 128, 148, 156, 160n16; in
Bolivia, 1–2, 33n1, 248; in Brazil, 206,
210, 213–14, 225n68; in Caribbean, 8,
164–65, 197n5; in Central America, 8;
clandestine connections and, 108–9,
112–13, 249; in Colombia, 65–70, 74,
80–88, 92, 96–101, 104, 105n6, 106n11,
106n13; in criminal networks, 26; democracy and, 14–15; in Dominican
Republic, 162–64, 168, 170–74, 180–81,
190–92, 194–95; failed states and, 245;
in Haiti, 163, 197n5; human rights and,
226–27, 231–34, 236–37, 239, 241n3; international trade and, 31; in Iraq, 6–9,
33n5; in Latin America, 4, 6, 17–18, 35–
39, 63–64, 245–51; in Mexico, 42–45,
48, 50–56, 59n4, 62n16; nonstate actors

impunity (*continued*)
69; Dominican culture of, 188; in Latin America, 35–40, 234, 239; Mexican cycle of, 41–43, 45, 47–50, 53–56, 62n17; of police, 20, 30, 37, 62n21, 254

income distribution: alternative sources for underpaid police, 44, 50, 55, 123, 211; in Brazil, 203–4, 220n12, 246; drug trafficking motivated by, 92–93, 95, 162, 196n2; Gini coefficient of, 198n16; globalization and, 54–55; in Latin America, 7, 246; neoliberal policies and, 16, 196n1; police and, 44, 50, 55, 123, 211; poverty and, 167–68. *See also* gross domestic product; poverty

independence, 38–39, 226

India, 112

indigenous peoples, 1–3, 8, 13, 15, 24, 76, 82, 226

industrialization, 14, 28, 37–43, 45–46, 58. *See also* development

inequality: Brazilian reduction programs for, 202–4, 246; in Colombia, 81n6; crime linked to, 172; democracy and, 156; disjunctive democracy and, 248; Gini coefficient and, 198n16; indicators of, 167–69; institutional structures of, 155–56; in Latin America, 3–4, 7, 17, 36, 246, 248, 262; neoliberalism and structural adjustment policies and, 196n1

informal repression, 112

informal sector: in Brazil, 203–4, 246; clandestine connections and, 118–19, 249; in Dominican Republic, 169, 172; in Jamaica, 247; in Latin America, 259; in Mexico, 38, 40, 49–50, 54–57, 59

information technology (IT) sector, 55

insecurity. *See* security

Inspección General de Policía, 48

institutional corruption, 38–39, 43, 203,

211–13, 215, 219, 223n49. *See also* corruption; police: corruption of

institutional failure: in Dominican Republic, 167, 174, 187; human rights and, 231; in Latin America, 6, 8–11, 16, 19, 245, 250

institutionalization, 34, 37, 49, 161

Instituto Brasileiro de Geografia e Estatística, 201

Instituto de Pesquisa Econômico Aplicada (IPEA), 204, 220

insurgency, 6, 7, 33, 63–64, 90, 94, 109

Inter-American Court, 160

Inter-American Development Bank, 115, 126, 205

internal violence: in Argentina, 134–37; in Colombia, 65, 67, 87, 98–99; in Dominican Republic, 187, 189; history of, 7, 13; in Latin America, 251, 253; in Mexico, 41

International Country Risk Group, 236

International Country Risk Guide, 241

International Crisis Group, 96

international humanitarian law, 97–98, 229, 240–241, 262. *See also* human rights

international institutions, 75, 107, 205, 248, 261

international norms, 136, 160. *See also* norms

international trade, 16; arms trafficking and, 17, 31; drug trafficking and, 17, 31, 246–47

Iraq, 6–10, 32–33, 106, 257–58

iron fist policies. See *mano dura*

Ivory Coast, 106

Jamaica, 8, 20, 113, 162–63, 197n12, 247–48, 253

Jaramillo, Ana Maria, 68, 81

judicial police, 41–42, 47, 51–52, 59, 61, 98–99

judicial systems and the judiciary: in Argentina, 124, 134–35, 138, 145–49, 153–54, 157, 159, 160n19; in Brazil, 209, 214, 225n66; in Colombia, 63; in Dominican Republic, 174, 190, 193, 197n12; in Latin America, 17, 38; in Mexico, 41, 49–50, 52, 54; rights and independence of, 230, 232–33, 239

Juntas de Acción, Comunal, 65, 71

justice: barriers to, 4, 25, 134–35, 139, 141, 147, 149, 152–54, 156; in Latin America, 50, 238, 244; state institutions and, 15, 90, 190, 263; transnational justice, 241n5; vigilantism as, 16, 20, 36

Justice and Transparency Foundation, 199

Kakar, Sudhir, 112

Keane, John, 228, 230, 235

Kenya, 112

kidnapping: in Brazil, 206, 212, 215; clandestine connections and, 122; in Colombia, 72, 89, 105; in Dominican Republic, 197; in Mexico, 49; violent pluralism and, 6

killings. *See* homicides

King, Rodney, 110

Kirchner, Nestor, 156

Kline, Harvey F., 81

Krischke, Linda, 112

labor, 42–45, 47, 56, 71, 76, 203. *See also* workers

Labor Party (Mexico), 43

land conflict and land reform, 13, 20, 65, 71, 89, 261

Landman, Todd, 29, 31, 247, 256, 259–60, 262–63

land mines, 65, 74

language, 1, 7, 17, 24, 27, 67, 76, 78, 82, 238, 256, 286

Latin America: collective violence in, 128–29; corruption, 17, 41, 217; democracy and, 38; development in, 31, 37, 39–40; economy, 167–68, 198, 220; failed states in, 106, 165–66, 238–39, 245; histories and discourses on, 13–19, 34n24, 80, 187, 239; human rights in, 225–40, 240n2, 241nn3–5; inequality and, 246; institutional failure in, 6, 8–11, 16, 19, 250; international relations and, 13, 80, 82, 258, 261; neoliberalism in, 14, 17, 34, 202; participatory democracy in, 63–80; research issues in, 34, 239, 245, 255–62; violent pluralism in, 19–27, 30–31, 243–61

Latin Kings (gang), 184–85

La Violencia (Colombian civil war): clandestine connections during, 112–13; FARC and, 86–90; Oriente No Violence movement and, 65, 67, 69–70, 82n22; paramilitaries and, 98; violent crimes committed during, 105n5

legal pluralism, 22, 26

legitimacy: of Argentinian state, 133, 137; clandestine connections and, 125; of Colombian state, 70–71, 84, 86, 90, 94–95, 98, 100, 103–4; delegitimized states and, 38, 99, 183, 231; Dominican Republic, 164, 166, 172, 178–79, 182, 192, 194, 196n1; human rights violations and, 226–29, 229–30, 235–36, 241n3, 241n6; of Latin American states, 4, 7–8, 18–19; of Mexican state institutions, 50, 54, 57; of social movements, 24; of violence, 31; violent pluralism and, 152–53, 157, 254, 256

Lei de Execucão Penal, 223

lending agencies, 17, 112

Levantamento Nacional Sobre Consumo de Drogas entre Estudantes, 221n17

liberal democracy, 10, 222, 241n3

liberalism. *See* neoliberal policies

culture, 60; democracy in, 35, 37, 38, 49–50, 52, 132, 249, 258; drug trafficking in, 55, 57–58, 62, 203, 217, 260; economic conditions in, 54–57, 246, 260; Movement Against Delinquency in, 198n14; revolution in, 39–43; social movements in, 198n13; state violence in, 41–45, 48, 59, 61; torture in, 236; violent pluralism in, 2, 24, 28, 227, 250, 258, 260

Mexico City, 40–42, 45, 48–50, 52, 54–61

Middle East, 6, 258

Miguez, Daniel, 124

military(ies): anti-guerilla operations of, 87–94, 96, 102; in Argentina, 133, 152, 156, 240; in Brazil, 208–11, 214, 216, 218–19, 222n33, 222n36, 225n63, 225n67, 260; in Colombia, 63–64, 73–74, 79, 82n23, 84–85, 87–102, 105n6, 106n7; clandestine connections and, 110; criminal behavior of, 35–38, 197n8, 260; democracy and, 234–37, 248, 252; in the Dominican Republic, 164, 166–67, 180, 197n8; drug trafficking and, 49–53, 55, 73–74, 79, 87–90, 92, 197, 260; intelligence, 96, 101; in Mexico, 39–53, 55, 59, 60n2, 62n20; military contractors, 257; military technology, 17; police relations with, 39–53, 55, 59, 62n20, 208, 260; technological improvements in, 17; in United States, 93–94, 101, 257–58; violent pluralism and, 13, 17, 20–21, 28–29, 252

military police, 208–9, 211, 214, 216, 218, 222n33, 222n36, 225n63, 225n67, 238

military regimes and dictatorships: in Argentina, 152, 156, 240n1; in Brazil, 201–2, 206–8, 222n26, 240n1; in Colombia, 64, 69, 85, 105n1, 105n6, 106n7; democracy as legitimation of, 18; in Latin America, 15, 226–27, 230–31,

237–38, 240n1; torture practices during, 238; transition to civilian rule, 18

militias, 9, 20, 43, 216–19, 242, 257, 258

mineiração (Brazilian extortion), 211

M-19 Guerillas Group (Colombia), 89, 106

Molina, Mauricio Aranguren, 93

money laundering, 21, 196n415

Monkkonen, Eric, 195

Montalvo, Juan, 180

Moore, Barrington, 234

Morales, Evo, 1, 2, 16

Morales, Leo, 196n4

mordida (Mexican police rent seeking), 44

Moser, Caroline O. N, 175

Movement against Delinquency, 198n14

Movement Towards Socialism (MAS), 1

Movimiento 19 de Abril, 106n19

Muerte a los Seuqestradores (MAS), 1–2, 33, 89, 286

multiculturalism, 2, 24

municipalities: in Brazil, 205, 225n69; clandestine connection in, 120; in Colombia, 64–68, 71, 72, 74, 76–77, 81n6, 82n15, 83n24; 96, 100–102; in Mexico, 41, 43

murder. See homicides

naciones (Dominican gangs), 183–87, 194, 200n32, 250

Naim, Moíses, 165

narcoterrorism, 89, 92–94

narcotics: prohibition of, 247; trafficking of, 65 197. See also drugs and drug trafficking

Nariño (Colombia), 68, 81

de Nascimento, Sandro, 218

Nash, June, 24

National Census on Population (Dominican Republic), 199n18

National Development Plan, 96

National Directorate of Narcotics Control, 197
National Front (Colombia), 82, 85, 88, 106n7
National Indigenous Alliance, 64
National Liberation Army, 65
National Office for Drug Control (Dominican Republic), 197, 199n28
national police: clandestine connections with, 124; in Colombia, 92, 97, 106n10, 124; in Dominican Republic, 166, 172–73, 185, 187, 191
neighborhoods: in Argentina, 138, 140–41, 159n9; in Brazil (favelas), 202, 205–7, 210–11, 215–19; clandestine connections in, 108–9, 120, 126–27; in Colombia, 79, 103; in Dominican Republic (barrios), 162–64, 168, 170–74, 176–84, 190, 192, 197n11, 199n20, 199n27; in Iraq, 6; in Mexico and Mexico City, 51, 53, 56–57; police presence in, 79, 180, 188–89, 191–92, 218–19, 260; violent pluralism and, 242, 247, 261
neoliberal policies: in Brazil, 202; in Colombia, 97; democracy and, 34; in Dominican Republic, 166–67, 196n1; food lootings and, 130; violent pluralism and, 1, 5, 13–17, 22
Ñetas (Dominican Republic gangs), 185–86
networks: Argentinian victims' networks, 135; in Brazilian favelas, 206–7; clientelist networks, 65, 130, 132n2; Colombian coercion and terror networks, 90; criminal networks, 26–27, 134, 162–63, 169, 179; global networks, 57, 162; Mexican coercion and corruption networks, 45–47, 50–51; violent pluralism and, 32. *See also* clandestine connections; social networks
Neumayer, Eric, 227, 235
New York, 7, 113, 123, 186, 195

New York Times, 7, 123, 224
Nicaragua, 22
nongovernmental organizations (NGOs), 65, 71–72, 76, 81–82, 90, 180, 243, 256
nonstate actors: in Argentina, 134; in Brazil, 203; in Colombia, 80, 86–96, 99, 103–5; democracy and, 227, 229–31, 234–40, 241n5; in Dominican Republic, 166–67; human rights and, 237, 240; political insecurity and, 38, 250; violent pluralism and, 17, 19–22, 29, 31, 243–45, 250–54, 257–59, 261–62
nonviolence, 29, 49, 64, 259. *See also* Oriente No-Violence movement
norms: clandestine connections as, 131; of gang culture in Dominican Republic, 184–85, 191; of violence in Argentina, 136, 184–185, 191; violent pluralism and, 5, 23, 239, 242, 260
North America, 10, 12, 25, 27, 31, 205, 259
North American Free Trade Agreement (NAFTA), 55, 56, 246
North Korea, 106, 232
Nuñez, José Manuel, 47

Ochoa, Marta Nieves, 89
O'Donnell, Guillermo, 3, 11, 25, 33–34, 134, 155, 254, 259
O Globo (newspaper), 211
oil (petroleum), 69, 72, 102, 205
oligarchy, 88
omertá, 186
Operation Marquetalia, 88, 106n7
Operation Navalha na Carne, 224n61
opposition: clandestine connections with, 112; in Colombia, 80–81, 91; in democracies, 39; in Dominican Republic, 181; human rights of, 226, 230, 237, 241n4; in Mexican politics, 41, 43, 51; state violence against, 152, 160nn15–16; violent pluralism and, 15, 22, 263
Orçamento Participativo, 242

order: in Brazil, 210, 223n50; clandestine connections and, 109–10; in Colombia, 68, 81, 84–88, 95, 98–99, 102–5; democracy and establishment of, 35; in Dominican Republic, 165–66, 193; in Mexico, 40, 51; human rights and, 226, 229; nonstate imposition of, 237, 240, 243–45; violent pluralism and, 5, 9, 11, 26, 249–51, 256, 260–62

organized crime: in Brazil, 203, 205–8; Dominican Republic as center for, 162–65, 183–86, 195; drug trafficking and, 162, 178–91, 246; in Latin America, 227; police involvement in, 137–38; state disorganization in face of, 162–95, 197n12

Oriente (Colombia), 64–82

Oriente No-Violence Movement, 64, 66–72, 76–77, 80

pacted transitions to democracy, 226, 232, 248

Pact of San José, 153

Pakistan, 6

Paley, Julia, 18–19, 34

Panama, 26, 203

Pan American Games, 214

Pan-American Health Orgnaization (PAHO), 197

pandillas, 183, 190, 194

Paraguay, 141, 215, 221

paramilitaries: in Colombia, 63–66, 69–75, 85–86, 90–96, 98–104; emergence of, 8, 20–21, 29; human rights and, 230, 236; violent pluralism and, 243, 249, 251–52, 259. *See also* armed groups; *specific paramilitary organizations*

participatory budgeting, 201, 243, 262. *See* Orçamento Participativo

participatory democracy, 15, 63–80, 103; as Colombian anti-violence measure,

75–79; geography and resources and, 72–75; no-violence movements and, 67–72

Partido de Accion Nacional (PAN), 52

Partido de la Liberación Dominicana (PLD), 167, 189, 198n15

Partido de la Revolucion Mexicana (PRM), 48

Partido Revolucionario de los Trabajadores (PRT), 106n9

Partido Revolucionario Dominicando (PRD), 51–52, 167

Partido Revolucionario Institucional (PRI), 50–52, 62n16

party systems, 38, 63–88, 100, 103, 105, 106n9

Pastrana, Andres, 93, 96, 98, 100–101, 106n11

patriarchy, 185

Patriotic Union (Argentina), 106n9

patronage, 26, 50, 132, 187, 259. *See also* clientelism

Patti, Luis, 158

Paulino Castillo, Quirino E., 197n7

Pavão-Pavãozinho (Rio de Janeiro, Brazil), 221

Payne, Leigh, 22, 231, 254

Peace Communities (Colombia), 103, 107n17

peace initiatives: in Brazil, 208, 210; in Colombia, 77, 81–82, 90–91, 100–101, 106n9; in democratic ideal of, 3, 32; in Dominican Republic, 180; human rights and, 229; in Mexico, 58

Peace Laboratory, 68, 82

peasant producer cooperatives, 65, 72

peasants, 43, 45, 65, 67, 72–73, 91, 100. *See also* campesinos

Pedagogy of the Oppressed (Freire), 72

pehlwan, 112

pentito, 146, 160n13

Pereira, Anthony, 227, 230–31

Peronism and Peronist Party (Argentina), 108–9, 117, 119–21, 123–25, 128, 148

Peru, 7, 22, 205, 217, 227–28, 236–37

petroleum. *See* oil

Phillips, Peter, 162

physical security, 12

Piven, Frances Fox, 128, 131

Plan Colombia, 93, 94, 101, 106n11

Plan for Democratic Security: in Colombia, 79, 81–82, 87, 95–98, 104–5, 251, 255; in Dominican Republic, 30, 162, 165, 170, 188, 190–96.

Plan Patriota, 81, 101

pluralism. *See* violent pluralism

police: accountability of, 48–49, 123, 208; administration of, 8, 190; in Argentina, 133, 143–45, 157, 160n18; authoritarianism and, 187–88, 190, 208, 238, 243; in Brazil, 202–3, 207–19, 222nn26–28, 225nn62–63; in Buenos Aires, 160n16; clandestine connections with, 108–12, 114–18, 120–23, 125–28, 130; in Colombia, 73, 87, 90, 92–93, 95, 106n10; corruption of, 36–39, 42–54, 58, 60n12, 61n13, 173, 189, 193; criminal activities of, 35, 45, 51–52, 60n6, 62n21, 136–37, 143, 148–51, 157, 159n4, 208–9, 222n35, 225n62; democracy and role of, 39–42, 156, 159; in Dominican Republic, 180, 183, 187–88, 190–95, 200n36; framing of victims by, 151, 160n19; illegal detention by, 136–37, 141–42, 160n15, 243; impunity of, 20, 30, 37, 62n21, 254; involvement in drug trafficking, 51–52, 122–23, 137; media image of, 150–52, 158; in Mexico, 42–55, 58, 59nn1–2, 59n4, 60nn5–7, 60n12, 61nn13–15, 62nn16–21; private security and, 62nn20–21; reform of, 133, 148, 159–60, 263; secret police, 61n13; state violence and, 133, 160n15; training of,

41, 44, 154, 180, 190–91, 210–12; tribunals, 187, 209; violent pluralism and, 3, 8, 11, 16–17, 20–21, 30–31, 223–24, 242, 249, 251–52, 260

policia mineira, 216

political parties. *See specific parties*

political prisoners, 156, 206–7

political science, 5, 23, 27, 30, 228, 252–56

politics: in Argentina, 155–56, 167, 169; clandestine connections and, 108–21, 123–25, 128, 130–32; clientelism and, 65, 119, 132; in Colombia, 66–67, 81, 84–85, 87–88, 103, 150; culture and, 18, 85, 91, 98, 226, 233, 238, 258; democratization and, 34, 131, 207, 226; economics and, 3, 252; in Mexico, 56; military involvement in, 47, 207, 248; origins of violence and, 35–59; third-party movements, 71, 82, 128; violent pluralism and, 1–32, 244–45, 253, 255, 258, 261

politiquería, 71

Polo Democratico Alternativo (PDA), 64, 80

Polo Democratico Party, 81

polyarchy, 10–13, 19, 25, 31–32, 134

Popular Liberation Army. *See* Ejército Populato de Liberación

Populism, 45–46, 82, 106n8, 156, 165, 226

Portugal, 38, 216

post-authoritarian politics, 17, 28, 34, 131, 208

Postero, 24, 34

poverty: in Argentina, 136–37, 155; in Brazil, 199, 202–4, 208, 216, 219–20, 262; citizenship and, 39, 137, 156; clandestine connections and, 108–9, 111, 115–16, 118–20, 126; in Colombia, 70, 74, 81; crime and, 150, 155–56, 172–74; democracy and, 34; in Dominican Republic, 30, 161, 167–69, 172–73, 176–77, 179–81, 184, 188–91, 194–95, 199n18;

inequality and, 150, 155, 167–68, 179, 204; in Mexico, 56; in neighborhoods, 244, 261; violence and crime and, 134, 136, 150, 155–156; violent pluralism and, 1–9, 11, 22, 248, 261

power: abuse, of, 40, 49, 60; balance of, 67; brokers of, 28; clandestine connections and, 109, 112, 125, 128, 130–31; coercive power, 39, 155; corruption and, 9, 47, 162; democracy and, 38–40; economic, 58, 65–66, 79–80, 93; human rights and, 226, 239–40; soft power, 166, 183; violent pluralism and, 7, 9, 13–14, 18–19, 21–23, 30, 243–46, 248, 252, 257, 260–63

Poxiràn, 159n10

Prefectura Naval, 135, 156, 158, 160

Preval, Rene, 197

Preventive Police (Mexico), 41–43, 46–47, 51, 59

priests, 68, 78, 100

prisons: in Argentina, 135, 137, 144–45, 149, 153–54, 158; in Brazil, 202, 206, 212–14, 218, 221n20, 221n22, 223nn43–48, 223n50, 224nn51–52, 225n66; in Dominican Republic, 177

private policing, 46, 53, 62, 90, 102, 217, 219

private security: in Argentina, 135, 158; in Brazil, 211, 217, 219; clandestine connections and, 120; in Colombia, 90; democracy and emergence of, 36, 38, 249, 251–52; human rights and, 238; in Mexico, 46–47, 53, 62n20; violent pluralism and, 8, 16, 20, 22, 257; See also armed groups; police

privatization, 53, 55, 70, 129, 217, 252, 260

producer associations, 65, 67, 77, 82

promotoras de salud, 71

prosecutors, 101, 143, 141–47, 153, 159–60, 209

protests, 24, 129, 135, 149–51, 177, 189

public works, 207

Puerto Ricans, 186

Puex, Nathelie, 123

Pulque, 44

Putumayo, Colombia, 86–88, 90–91, 94, 98–105

Quilmes, 116, 123

Quintín Lame, 106

race, 2, 34, 110, 169

radio, 71, 54, 76, 122

Radu, Michael, 2

Ramírez, Luis Cueto, 62

Ramírez, Maria Clemencia, 29, 249, 251, 255

rape, 49, 105, 175, 178, 228

Rapley, John, 167

Rappaport, Joanne, 76

rebellion, 36, 39, 52, 213, 224, 226

reciprocities, 56

Rede de Comunidades, 158, 159

reform: in Argentina, 133, 148, 159–60, 162, 165; in Brazil, 203, 212–23, 219, 263; clandestine connections and, 112, 123–24, 131; in Colombia, 81, 91; democratization and, 34; in Dominican Republic, 187–88, 190–91, 194–95; economic, 17, 26, 172, 198, 202; human rights and, 239–40, 259–260; in Mexico, 41, 46–48, 51–54, 59n1, 60n2, 62nn16–17; violent pluralism and, 12–13, 16, 31, 259–60

refugees. See displaced persons

Regime Disciplinar Diferenciado, 223

regimes. See government and governance

regulations, 40, 44, 57, 59, 95, 187, 246

religion, 69, 112, 168–69, 180, 250

rent-seeking, 42, 44–45, 48, 50, 239

repression: in Argentina, 152, 156, 159; clandestine connections and, 110, 112;

tarianism and, 28, 36; in Brazil, 203, 210, 219; citizenship and, 12, 161, 187, 190–91, 193; in Colombia, 87, 94–95; corruption and, 122–23, 161, 163–64, 215; democratization and, 37–38, 189–95; in Dominican Republic, 161, 163–67, 172–74, 177, 189–95, 199n22; economics and, 35–38; human rights and, 238; in Mexico, 50–58, 62n20; mobilization of, 52–53, 150; private security, 120, 249, 251–52; research on, 259; in United States, 95; violent pluralism and, 3, 8, 10, 16–17, 22, 28–30, 243, 246–47, 257. *See also* private security

Security Law, 98, 138

self-defense groups, 84, 88, 89–90, 98, 105n6

Sendero Luminoso, 236

Serrano, Rosso José, 92, 93, 96

sexism, 34, 185

sexual violence. *See* rape

Shaheed, Farida, 112

shantytowns, 74, 113, 118, 123, 126, 155–56, 242. *See also* favelas

Shiv Sena, 112

shopkeepers, 124

Sierra Leone, 6, 106

signaling, 119–21

Sindicato dos Vigilantes do Rio de Janeiro, 217

social cleansing, 89, 188

social conflict, 7, 14

social control, 109, 156, 164, 181

social exclusion, 103, 168–69, 172, 181, 190, 233–34

socialism, 13, 16

social movements: in Argentina, 134, 150, 156, 160; in Brazil, 219; clandestine connections and, 107, 109, 114, 118, 121; in Colombia, 64–68, 71, 74, 76–77, 80, 85, 89, 91; in Dominican Republic, 180, 198; in Mexico, 62n16, 219; violent plu-

ralism and, 2–3, 13, 15–17, 22, 24–25, 29, 256. *See also specific social movements*

social networks: Argentinian victims' networks, 135, 159; in Brazilian favelas, 181, 204, 220; clandestine connections and, 130, 132; in Colombia, 65, 67, 97; organized violence as threat to, 169–71, 194; politics and, 48, 57; security and, 46

social order, 5, 20, 29, 40, 51, 87–88, 104, 223

society, 28, 30, 68, 128, 229, 253, 255–56. *See* civil society

soldiers, 16, 20, 44, 66, 73, 75, 84, 186, 213. *See also* children: as soldiers; military(ies); militias

Somalia, 106

South Africa, 230, 241

South America. *See* Latin America

South Asia, 240

Southeast Asia, 111, 240

Southern Command, 94, 198

Southern Cone, 11, 27, 39, 85

Southern Europe, 205

sovereignty, 37–38, 96, 106, 184, 194, 249

Soviet Union, 31, 205

Spain, 38, 185–86, 216

spatial exclusion, 169, 172

Special Public Order Zones, 98

Squandered Victory (Diamond), 9

Stanley, Ruth, 26, 29, 30, 250–51, 254, 263

statecraft, 18–19

state formation and state institutions: in Argentina, 133–48, 152–57, 161; authoritarianism and, 39; in Bolivia, 1, 16, 33n1; in Brazil, 202–6, 208, 211–15, 217; in Caribbean region, 162–65; clandestine connections and, 103–5, 111–13, 116, 121, 125; in Colombia, 64, 66–71, 73, 77–81, 83–88, 100–105; contested state formation, 38–40; corporatism

Ungar, Mark, 40, 194
Unidad Básica, 108, 121
Unified High Command, 88
uniformed violence, in Dominican Republic, 187–89
Union Patriótica, 106
United Kingdom, 232, 241
United Nations, 81, 162, 166, 222
United Nations Development Program, 11–12, 33–34, 168
United Self-defense Forces. See Autodefensas Unidas de Colombia
United States: arms trafficking and, 17; clandestine connections and, 109; Colombia and, 79–80, 83n25, 92–93, 95; community policing in, 223n42; democracy in, 3, 12; democratic peace theory of, 32; Dominican criminals repatriated from, 184, 197n7; Dominican migration to, 185–86; drug market in, 205, 217–18, 220n3, 246–47; drug trafficking and policies of, 55, 92, 198n14; human rights protection in, 232, 241nn3–4; Iraq War and, 6–10, 257–58; Latin America and, 246, 261; military coups and dictatorships backed by, 14; violence and democracy in, 234
Universal Declaration of Human Rights, 241
Uprimny, Rodrigo, 84, 91
urbanization: democratic violence and, 37–38; lootings and, 116; police power and, 40, violence in Dominican Republic and, 170
Uribe Vélez, Alvaro, 67, 70, 79–81, 84, 95–99, 101, 104, 106, 251
Uruguay, 26, 129, 230

Valencia, Guillermo León, 106, 108
Vales, Laura, 119
vendedores ambulantes, 44
Venezuela: cocaine traffic in, 221n16; domestic violence, 237; homicide rate in, 201, 236; Latin American influence of, 80; lootings in, 129; social movements in, 198n13; violent pluralism in, 2, 8, 14, 18
vertical clandestine connections, 118
victimization, 175, 177–78, 192, 195
vigilantism: democratization and, 36; human rights and, 238; in Mexico, 53; violent pluralism and, 4, 8, 16, 20, 22, 242, 250, 252, 263
Villamarín, Louis Alberto, 92
Villar, Samuel del, 51
violence: Argentinian state and, 133–58; arms and, 65; authoritarian violence, 36, 38–39, 45–49, 175; in Brazil, 201–20; in Caribbean region, 162–65; clandestine connections and collective violence, 108–31, 211–12; in Colombia, 72–79, 80; democratization and, 49–54, 56–59, 234–36; domestic violence, 3, 8, 17, 174, 178, 252–53; Dominican state and, 161–95; economic context for, 166–69; geography and resources and, 72–75; globalization and, 54–56; human rights and, 226–240; impunity and, 38–40; legacy of, 18, 28, 37–38; in Mexico, 41–49; narratives of, 175, 195, 256; participatory democracy as tool against, 75–79; policy implications of, 237–39; political and economic origins of, 35–38, poverty and, 11; Putumayo nonstate actors and, 88–91; social violence, 169, 197, 260; structural violence, 17, 21–22, 34, 156–57, 228; typology of, 228–31; uniformed violence in Dominican Republic, 187–89; women and, 177–78; youth and, 175–78, 183–85
violent pluralism: alternative paradigm for, 19–27; in Argentina, 152–58; clandestine connections and, 111,113; in

Library of Congress Cataloging-in-Publication Data

Violent democracies in Latin America / edited by

Enrique Desmond Arias and Daniel M. Goldstein.

p. cm. – (The cultures and practice of violence series)

Includes bibliographical references and index.

ISBN 978-0-8223-4624-1 (cloth : alk. paper)

ISBN 978-0-8223-4638-8 (pbk. : alk. paper)

1. Violence–Latin America. 2. Democracy–Latin

America. I. Arias, Enrique Desmond. II. Goldstein,

Daniel M., 1965– III. Series: Cultures and practice of

violence series.

HN110.5.Z9V584   2010

303.6098—dc22   2009041170